COUNTRIES, REGIONAL STUDIES, TRADING BLOCKS, UNIONS, WORLD ORGANIZATIONS

U.S. INVOLVEMENT IN POLITICAL, ECONOMIC AND SOCIAL CONDITIONS OF LATIN AMERICA

Countries, Regional Studies, Trading Blocks, Unions, World Organizations

Additional books in this series can be found on Nova's website under the Series tab.

Additional E-books in this series can be found on Nova's website under the E-books tab.

COUNTRIES, REGIONAL STUDIES, TRADING BLOCKS, UNIONS,
WORLD ORGANIZATIONS

U.S. INVOLVEMENT IN POLITICAL, ECONOMIC AND SOCIAL CONDITIONS OF LATIN AMERICA

ALLEN P. LOWELL
EDITOR

Nova Science Publishers, Inc.
New York

Library of Congress Cataloging-in-Publication Data

U.S. involvement in political, economic and social conditions of Latin America / editor, Allen P. Lowell.
p. cm.
Includes index.
ISBN 978-1-61209-781-7 (hardcover)
1. United States--Relations--Latin America. 2. Latin America--Relations--United States. I. Lowell, Allen P. II. Title: United States involvement in political, economic and social conditions of Latin America.
F1418.U24 2011
327.7308--dc23

2011039367

Published by Nova Science Publishers, Inc. † New York

CONTENTS

PREFACE*

This new book examines U.S. involvement in various political, economic and social issues of Latin America. Topics discussed include U.S. Free Trade Agreements with Colombia; Cuban migration to the United States; U.S. restrictions on travel and remittances in Cuba; political, economic and social conditions of El Salvador, including U.S. relations; Honduran-U.S. relations, Chile-U.S. relations and U.S.-Mexico economic relations.

Chapter 1 - The 111th Congress in coming months might take up free trade agreements (FTAs) signed by the Bush Administration with Colombia, Panama, and South Korea under trade promotion authority, or fast-track rules, designed to expedite congressional consideration of these agreements. Liberalizing trade in agricultural products, particularly the pace of expanding market access for the more sensitive agricultural commodities, was one of the more difficult areas that trade negotiators faced in concluding each of these FTAs. In each instance, issues dealing with food safety and animal/plant health matters (technically not part of the FTA negotiating agenda) were not resolved until later.

While U.S. negotiators sought to eliminate high tariffs and restrictive quotas to U.S. agricultural exports to these three country markets, they also faced pressures to protect U.S. producers of import-sensitive commodities (beef, dairy products, and sugar, among others). FTA partner country negotiators faced similar pressures. One Bush Administration policy objective was for FTAs to be comprehensive (i.e., cover all products). For the more import-sensitive agricultural commodities, negotiators agreed on long transition periods, temporary additional protection in the case of import surges, or indefinite protection of a few commodities. To illustrate the latter, because of political sensitivities for the United States or its partners, negotiators agreed to retain in perpetuity quantitative import limits and prohibitively high tariffs on some of the most import- sensitive commodities. In one exception, though, the United States agreed to Korea's insistence that rice be completely excluded from their FTA.

Of these three, the FTA with South Korea would be the most commercially significant one for U.S. agriculture since the North American Free Trade Agreement (NAFTA) took effect with Mexico in 1994. Because Colombia is a large market that imposes a high level of border protection on agricultural imports, the Colombia FTA has the potential to significantly

---

* Versions of these chapters were also published in *Current Politics and Economics of South and Central America*, Volume 3, Issues 1-4, edited by XX, published by Nova Science Publishers, Inc. They were submitted for appropriate modifications in an effort to encourage wider dissemination of research.

increase U.S. agricultural exports. Though Panama represents a relatively small market, U.S. exporters would have numerous opportunities for additional sales.

Conversely, each pending FTA partner would have additional access to the U.S. market for those agricultural commodities that are now protected by restrictive U.S. import quotas. Of these, the U.S. sugar sector would face competition from increased imports of sugar from Colombia and Panama. The small increase in additional imports from South Korea would likely be primarily ethnic foods. Also, because these three countries consume most of the beef and dairy products that they produce, any additional sales would likely be accommodated by the large U.S. market with little effect.

The Obama Administration has signaled its intent to address outstanding issues of concern to some Members of Congress in order to submit the Panama FTA to Congress for consideration, possibly later this year. With respect to the Colombia and South Korea FTAs, officials have stated their intent to work with Members of Congress to develop "benchmarks" to use to determine when these agreements might be sent to Capitol Hill for debate.

Chapter 2 - Cuba, which remains a hard-line communist state with a poor record on human rights, commemorated the 50th anniversary of its revolution on January 1, 2009. Cuba's political succession from the long-ruling Fidel Castro to his brother Raúl in 2006 was characterized by a remarkable degree of stability. Fidel stepped down from power temporarily in July 2006 because of health reasons, and Raúl assumed provisional control of the government until February 2008, when he officially became President. After Raúl Castro officially assumed the presidency, his government announced a series of economic changes that included lifting restrictions on the sale of some electronic consumer products and cell phones. A major reform effort has focused on the agriculture sector in an effort to boost food production. While additional economic changes are likely, there has been disappointment that further reforms have not been forthcoming. The economy was hard hit by storms in 2008 that resulted in $10 billion in damages, and the current global financial crisis is causing further strains. Few observers expect the government to ease its tight control over the political system, which is backed up by a strong security apparatus.

Since the early 1960s, U.S. policy toward Cuba has consisted largely of isolating the communist nation through economic sanctions. The Bush Administration tightened sanctions significantly in 2004 through increased restrictions on travel to Cuba, especially family travel. A second U.S. policy component over the years has consisted of support measures for the Cuban people, including private humanitarian donations, U.S.-sponsored radio and television broadcasting to Cuba (Radio and TV Marti), and support for human rights and democracy on the island. The Bush Administration significantly increased support for Cuba democracy funding in recent years.

As in past years, the main issue for U.S. policy toward Cuba in the 111th Congress is how best to support political and economic change in Cuba. In light of Fidel Castro's departure as head of government, many observers have called for a re-examination of policy. In this new context, two broad approaches have been advanced: a stay the course approach that would maintain the U.S. dual-track policy of isolating the Cuban government while providing support to the Cuban people; and an approach aimed at changing attitudes within the Cuban government and society through increased contact and engagement. President Barack Obama vowed during the electoral campaign to change policy by allowing unlimited family travel and remittances, although he also pledged to maintain the embargo as a source of leverage to bring about change in Cuba.

Over the past several years, various legislative initiatives have been introduced to ease U.S. economic sanctions on Cuba, but none of these have been enacted. In the 111th Congress, however, Congress approved three provisions in the FY2009 omnibus appropriations measure (P.L. 111-8) intended to ease sanctions on family travel, travel for the marketing of agricultural and medical goods, and payment terms for U.S. agricultural exports to Cuba. Other initiatives that would ease sanctions are H.R. 188 and H.R. 1530 (overall embargo), H.R. 874/S. 428 and H.R. 1528 (travel), H.R. 332 (educational travel), and H.R. 1531 (U.S. agricultural and medical exports and travel). Another initiative, H.R. 1103, would modify a provision of law restricting the registration or enforcement of certain Cuban trademarks.

Chapter 3 - Many of the issues surrounding Cuban migration are unique but not new. Normal immigration from Cuba has been elusive since Fidel Castro came to power. Over the past 50 years, the practice of Cubans fleeing by boat to the United States has become commonplace, and at some points reached the levels of a mass exodus. Since the last upsurge of "boat people" in the mid-1990s, the United States and Cuba worked toward establishing safe, legal immigration, which includes returning migrants interdicted by the U.S. Coast Guard. These migration policies, however, are not without critics.

The immigration of Cubans to the United States has increased since 1995, although the actual admission numbers have ebbed and flowed over this period. Cuba consistently ranks among the top 10 source countries for legal permanent residents (LPRs). Cuba ranked fifth as a top immigrant-sending country—after Mexico, China, India, and the Philippines—in FY2008. A total of 49,500 Cubans became LPRs in FY2008.

U.S. Coast Guard interdictions of Cubans have fluctuated since the mid-1990s, yet the general trend has moved upward. Cuban interdictions reached a 12-year high of 2,868 in FY2007. In FY2008, the U.S. Coast Guard reported 2,199 Cuban interdictions. Similarly, U.S. Border Patrol apprehensions of Cubans peaked at 4,295 in FY2007 and slipped to 3,351 in FY2008. Cubans who arrived at ports of entry without documents exhibited a comparable pattern, reaching a high of 13,019 in FY2007 and falling slightly to 11,278 in FY2008.

The change in leadership of both the United States and Cuba may provide openings for revisions in U.S. policy on Cuban migration. Fidel Castro's departure as head of government in July 2006 has prompted some observers to call for a reexamination of U.S. policy toward Cuba overall, and a potential opportunity to restart the migration talks that had occurred semi-annually for a decade after the 1994 U.S-Cuba Migration Accord. After serving temporarily, Raúl Castro, brother of Fidel Casto, officially assumed the Cuban presidency in February 2008. This transfer of power between the Castro brothers led some to question whether there would be much of an opening for renewed migration talks between the United States and Cuba.

During the 2008 U.S. presidential campaign, however, President Barack Obama stated he would seek to change U.S. policy by allowing unlimited family travel and remittances to Cuba, signaling to some the possibility of resuming the migration talks. In his opening speech at the Summit of the Americas on April 17, 2009, President Obama expressed the hope of "a new beginning with Cuba," specifically mentioning migration as an issue. A bipartisan group of congressional leaders are expressing support for a resumption of the migration talks with Cuba. On May 31, 2009, a U.S. State Department official reported that Cuban officials had indicated that they want to resume migration talks.

Chapter 4 - Restrictions on travel to Cuba have been a key and often contentious component in U.S. efforts to isolate Cuba's communist government for much of the past 40 years. Under the Bush Administration, restrictions on travel and on private remittances to Cuba were tightened. In March 2003, the Administration eliminated travel for people-to-people educational exchanges unrelated to academic coursework. In June 2004, the Bush Administration further restricted family and educational travel, eliminated the category of fully-hosted travel, and restricted remittances so that they could only be sent to the remitter's immediate family. Initially there was mixed reaction to the Bush Administration's June 2004 tightening of Cuba travel and remittance restrictions, but opposition to the policy grew, especially within the Cuban American community regarding the restrictions on family travel and remittances.

Dating back to 2000, there have been numerous legislative efforts to ease restrictions on travel to Cuba in various ways. From 2000-2004, one or both houses of Congress approved amendments to appropriations bills that would have eased restrictions on travel, but these provisions ultimately were stripped out of final enacted measures. The Bush Administration regularly threatened to veto legislation if it contained provisions weakening Cuba sanctions. In the 110th Congress, several House and Senate committee versions of appropriations bills (H.R. 2829, S. 1859, H.R. 7323, S. 3260, and S. 3289) had provisions that would have eased restrictions on travel to Cuba in various ways, but no final action was taken before the end of the Congress.

During the 2008 electoral campaign, President Obama pledged to lift restrictions on family travel to Cuba as well as restrictions on Cuban Americans sending remittances to Cuba. Senator Hillary Clinton reiterated President Obama's pledge during her confirmation hearing for Secretary of State on January 15, 2009, but indicated that the Administration did not yet have a timeline on the change. A number of observers expect that the Administration will fulfill President Obama's campaign pledge before the upcoming fifth Summit of the Americas in Trinidad and Tobago scheduled for April 17-19, 2009.

The 111th Congress, however, already has taken action to ease some restrictions on travel to Cuba by including two provisions in the FY2009 omnibus appropriations measure (P.L. 111-8), signed into law on March 11, 2009. The first provision eases restrictions on family travel, which the Treasury Department implemented by issuing a general license for such travel as it existed prior to the Bush Administration's tightening of family travel restrictions in June 2004. Family travel is now allowed once every 12 months for an unlimited length of stay to visit a close relative who is no more than three generations removed from the traveler. The second provision eases travel restrictions related to the marketing and sale of agricultural and medical goods to Cuba, and requires the Treasury Department to issue a general license for such travel. The Treasury Department maintained that it would issue regulations in the coming weeks.

Several additional initiatives have been introduced in the 111th Congress that would ease restrictions on travel to Cuba: H.R. 188 and H.R. 1530 would lift the embargo, including travel restrictions; H.R. 1531 would facilitate the export of U.S. agricultural products to Cuba and also prohibit restrictions on travel to Cuba; H.R. 874/S. 428 and H.R. 1528 would prohibit restrictions on travel to Cuba; and H.R. 332 would ease restrictions on educational travel.

Chapter 5 - Throughout the last few decades, the United States has had a strong interest in El Salvador. During the 1 980s, El Salvador was the largest recipient of U.S. aid in Latin

America as its government struggled against the Farabundo Marti National Liberation Front (FMLN) insurgency during a 12-year civil war. A 1992 negotiated peace accord brought the war to an end and formally assimilated the FMLN into the political process as a political party. After the peace accords were signed, U.S. involvement shifted towards helping the government rebuild democracy and implement market-friendly economic reforms.

Successive National Republican Alliance (ARENA) governments, including that of the current president, Tony Saca, have maintained close ties with the United States. The Saca Administration has cooperated in counter-narcotics operations, supported the U.S. coalition forces in Iraq, and implemented the Dominican Republic-Central America-United States Free Trade Agreement (CAFTA-DR). However, ARENA governments—including the Saca Administration—have struggled to reduce violence and poverty in El Salvador.

FMLN candidate Mauricio Funes won a close election for El Salvador's presidency in March 2009, marking the first FMLN presidential victory and the first transfer in political power between parties since the end of El Salvador's civil war. Funes' victory followed strong showings by the FMLN in the January 2009 municipal and legislative elections, in which the party won a plurality of the seats in National Assembly and the largest share of the municipal vote. Funes will take power in June 2009 and has pledged to govern in a moderate fashion. He will likely need to confront the high levels of violence and poverty in the country as well as deal with the effects of the global financial crisis.

Although some Members of Congress have expressed reservations about working with an FMLN administration, relations between El Salvador and the United States will likely remain friendly during the Obama Administration. President-elect Funes has pledged to remain in CAFTA-DR and expressed his willingness to work with the United States on immigration and counter- narcotics issues. Following his election, the Obama Administration congratulated President-elect Funes for his victory and pledged to work with him to build on the already strong ties between the United States and El Salvador.

Chapter 6 - The Central American nation of Honduras, one of the hemisphere's poorest countries, faces significant challenges in the areas of crime, human rights, and improving overall economic and living conditions. While traditional agricultural exports of coffee and bananas are still important for the economy, nontraditional sectors, especially the maquiladora, or export-processing industry, have grown significantly over the past decade. Among the country's development challenges are a poverty rate over 60%, high infant mortality, and a significant HIV/AIDS epidemic. Despite these challenges, increased public spending on health and education have reaped significant improvements in development indicators over the past decade.

Current President Manuel Zelaya of the Liberal Party won a four-year term in the November 2005 elections. The country has enjoyed 27 years of uninterrupted elected civilian democratic rule. The economy, which grew 6.3% in 2007 and is expected to have grown 4% in 2008, has benefitted from significant debt reduction by the international financial institutions that is freeing government resources to finance poverty-reduction programs. The U.S. recession and global financial crisis, however, are expected to slow Honduran economic growth sharply in 2009.

The United States has a close relationship with Honduras, characterized by an important trade partnership, a U.S. military presence in the country, and cooperation on a range of transnational issues. In addition to being a party to the Dominican Republic-Central America Free Trade Agreement (DR-CAFTA), Honduras has cooperated extensively with the United States on counternarcotics and port security. Some 78,000 Hondurans living in the United States have been provided temporary protected status (TPS) since the country was devastated by Hurricane Mitch in 1998.

U.S. foreign aid to Honduras amounted to $44 million in FY2008 and an estimated $47 million in FY2009. Honduras is also likely to receive a portion of the $105 million in assistance dedicated to Central America in 2009 under the Mérida Initiative, which was designed to boost the region's capabilities to interdict the smuggling of drugs, arms, and people and support a regional anti-gang strategy. For FY2010, the Obama Administration requested over $68 million in assistance for Honduras as well as an additional $100 million for the continuation of the Mérida Initiative in Central America. Beyond traditional foreign assistance, the Millennium Challenge Corporation approved a five-year $215 million compact with Honduras in 2005.

Chapter 7 - Haiti shares the island of Hispaniola with the Dominican Republic. Since the fall of the Duvalier dictatorship in 1986, Haiti has struggled to overcome its centuries-long legacy of authoritarianism, extreme poverty, and underdevelopment. While some progress has been made in developing democratic institutions, they remain weak. Economic and social stability have improved considerably. But poverty remains massive and deep, and economic disparity is wide.

In May 2006, René Préval began his second five-year term as President of Haiti. During his first two years in office, Préval began to establish internal political stability by attempting to strengthen democratic institutions and creating an environment that would attract private investment and spur job creation. Haiti's fragile stability has been repeatedly shaken, however, if not by political problems, then by climatic ones. In 2008, a worsening food crisis led to violent protests and the removal of Haiti' s Prime Minister. Parliament rejected Préval' s first two choices for a new prime minister, but finally confirmed Michele Pierre-Louis, a highly-regarded educator and economist, as Prime Minister in September 2008. In the summer of 2008, four major storms caused widespread devastation in Haiti.

Haiti remains the poorest country in the western hemisphere. Over half the population of 8.2 million people live in extreme poverty. Since Haiti's developmental needs and priorities are many, and deeply intertwined, the Haitian government and the international donor community are implementing an assistance strategy to address these many needs simultaneously. The Préval administration presented a revised strategy at a donors' conference on April 14. Haiti received aid commitments of $353 million. The United States pledged $68 million in new FY2009 assistance, including $20 million in targeted budget support. The United Nations Stabilization Mission in Haiti (MINUSTAH) has been in Haiti to help restore order since the collapse of former President Jean-Bertrand Aristide's government in 2004. MINUSTAH's current strength is 9,089 troops.

The main priorities for U.S. policy regarding Haiti are to strengthen fragile democratic processes, continue to improve security, and promote economic development. Other concerns include the cost and effectiveness of U.S. aid; protecting human rights; combating narcotics, arms, and human trafficking; addressing Haitian migration; and alleviating poverty. The FY2009 aid request for Haiti was $246 million. The Omnibus Appropriations Act of 2009 (P.L. 111-8) provided for an additional $41 million in bilateral economic and international security assistance for Haiti. The FY20 10 aid request for Haiti is $293 million.

The 111th Congress may consider the balance and scope of assistance to Haiti. Members have already requested that the Obama Administration grant Temporary Protected Status

(TPS) to Haitians living in the United States. Of immediate concern to Congress may be ensuring that second round elections scheduled for June 21 for 11 Haitian Senate seats are free, fair, and—in light of recent violent protests—peaceful. Prohibited from running on technicalities, former President Aristide's Lavalas party boycotted the first round vote; turnout nationwide averaged 11%. Congress may take up debt relief for Haiti again.

Current law related to Haiti includes P.L. 111-8, P.L. 110-161, P.L. 110-246, and P.L. 109-432. Pending legislation related to Haiti includes H.Con.Res. 17, H.R. 144, H.R. 264, H.R. 331, H.R. 416, H.R. 417, H.R. 1567, S. 730, and S. 1183; for details see sections on Legislation.

Chapter 8 - Following a violent coup against democratically elected Marxist President Salvador Allende in 1973, Chile experienced 17 years of military rule under General Augusto Pinochet before reestablishing its elected civilian democracy in 1990. A center-left coalition of parties known as the Concertación has governed Chile for the nearly two decades since the end of the dictatorship. The coalition has enacted a number of constitutional changes to strengthen civilian control of the military and to undertake the prosecution of those alleged to be responsible for human rights violations during the Pinochet-era. Chile has made significant economic progress under the Concertación's free market economic policies and moderate social programs, which have produced notable economic growth and considerable reductions in poverty.

Current President Michele Bachelet has faced a number of challenges since her 2006 election. Widespread demonstrations over education, increased militancy by indigenous groups, and opposition control of the legislature have hindered President Bachelet's ability to govern. The global financial crisis is President Bachelet's latest challenge, though the government's timely decision to save recent fiscal surpluses has allowed Chile to pursue counter-cyclical policies and minimize the effects of the economic downturn. The government will likely spend much of 2009 coping with the effects of the financial crisis while political parties prepare for the December presidential and legislative elections.

Chile has enjoyed close relations with the United States since its transition back to democracy. Both countries have emphasized similar priorities in the region, designed to strengthen democracy, improve human rights, and advance free trade. Chile and the United States have also maintained strong commercial ties, which have become more extensive since the bilateral free trade agreement between them entered into force in 2004. Additionally, U.S. officials have expressed appreciation for Chile's leadership and moderating influence in a region increasingly characterized by political unrest and anti-American populism.

Chapter 9 - Mexico has a population of about 110 million people making it the most populous Spanish- speaking country in the world and the third most populous country in the Western Hemisphere. Based on a gross domestic product (GDP) of $1.0 trillion in 2008 (about 7% of U.S. GDP), Mexico has a free market economy with a strong export sector. Economic conditions in Mexico are important to the United States because of the proximity of Mexico to the United States, the close trade and investment interactions, and other social and political issues that are affected by the economic relationship between the two countries.

The United States and Mexico have strong economic ties. An important feature of the relationship is the North American Free Trade Agreement (NAFTA), which has been in effect since 1994. In terms of total trade, Mexico is the United States' third largest trading partner, while the United States ranks first among Mexico's trading partners. In U.S. imports, Mexico ranks third among U.S. trading partners, after China and Canada, while in exports Mexico ranks second, after Canada. The United States is the largest source of foreign direct investment (FDI) in Mexico. These links are critical to many U.S. industries and border communities.

In 2008, about 11% of total U.S. merchandise exports were destined for Mexico and 10% of U.S. merchandise imports came from Mexico. In the same year U.S. exports to Mexico increased almost 10%, while imports from Mexico increased about 3%. For Mexico, the United States is a much more significant trading partner. About 82% of Mexico's exports go to the United States and 50% of Mexico's imports come from the United States. FDI forms another part of the economic relationship between the United States and Mexico. The United States is the largest source of FDI in Mexico. U.S. FDI in Mexico totaled $91.7 billion in 2007. The overall effect of NAFTA on the U.S. economy has been relatively small, primarily because two-way trade with Mexico amounts to less than three percent of U.S. GDP. Major trade issues between Mexico and the United States have involved the access of Mexican trucks to the United States; the access of Mexican sugar and tuna to the U.S. market; and the access of U.S. sweeteners to the Mexican market.

Over the last decade, the economic relationship between the United States and Mexico has strengthened significantly. The two countries continue to cooperate on issues of mutual concern. On March 23, 2005, the leaders of the United States, Canada, and Mexico met to discuss issues related to North American trade, immigration and defense. After the meeting, the three leaders announced the Security and Prosperity Partnership of North America (SPP), an initiative that is intended to increase cooperation and information sharing in an effort to increase and enhance prosperity in the United States, Canada, and Mexico. In April 2008, the North American leaders held a summit to discuss how they might further advance the goals of the SPP. The three leaders decided that their respective ministers should continue to renew and focus their work in the five SPP priority areas.

In: U.S. Involvement in Political, Economic and Social … ISBN: 978-1-61209-781-7
Editor: Allen P. Lowell

Chapter 1

AGRICULTURE IN PENDING U.S. FREE TRADE AGREEMENTS WITH COLOMBIA, PANAMA AND SOUTH KOREA

Remy Jurenas

ABSTRACT

The 111th Congress in coming months might take up free trade agreements (FTAs) signed by the Bush Administration with Colombia, Panama, and South Korea under trade promotion authority, or fast-track rules, designed to expedite congressional consideration of these agreements. Liberalizing trade in agricultural products, particularly the pace of expanding market access for the more sensitive agricultural commodities, was one of the more difficult areas that trade negotiators faced in concluding each of these FTAs. In each instance, issues dealing with food safety and animal/plant health matters (technically not part of the FTA negotiating agenda) were not resolved until later.

While U.S. negotiators sought to eliminate high tariffs and restrictive quotas to U.S. agricultural exports to these three country markets, they also faced pressures to protect U.S. producers of import-sensitive commodities (beef, dairy products, and sugar, among others). FTA partner country negotiators faced similar pressures. One Bush Administration policy objective was for FTAs to be comprehensive (i.e., cover all products). For the more import-sensitive agricultural commodities, negotiators agreed on long transition periods, temporary additional protection in the case of import surges, or indefinite protection of a few commodities. To illustrate the latter, because of political sensitivities for the United States or its partners, negotiators agreed to retain in perpetuity quantitative import limits and prohibitively high tariffs on some of the most import-sensitive commodities. In one exception, though, the United States agreed to Korea's insistence that rice be completely excluded from their FTA.

Of these three, the FTA with South Korea would be the most commercially significant one for U.S. agriculture since the North American Free Trade Agreement (NAFTA) took effect with Mexico in 1994. Because Colombia is a large market that imposes a high level of border protection on agricultural imports, the Colombia FTA has the potential to significantly increase U.S. agricultural exports. Though Panama represents a relatively small market, U.S. exporters would have numerous opportunities for additional sales.

Conversely, each pending FTA partner would have additional access to the U.S. market for those agricultural commodities that are now protected by restrictive U.S. import quotas. Of these, the U.S. sugar sector would face competition from increased imports of sugar from Colombia and Panama. The small increase in additional imports from South Korea would likely be primarily ethnic foods. Also, because these three countries consume most of the beef and dairy products that they produce, any additional sales would likely be accommodated by the large U.S. market with little effect.

The Obama Administration has signaled its intent to address outstanding issues of concern to some Members of Congress in order to submit the Panama FTA to Congress for consideration, possibly later this year. With respect to the Colombia and South Korea FTAs, officials have stated their intent to work with Members of Congress to develop "benchmarks" to use to determine when these agreements might be sent to Capitol Hill for debate.

BACKGROUND

The 111th Congress may take up free trade agreements (FTAs) with Colombia, Panama, and South Korea. The timing of when the White House submits each agreement reportedly depends on when Congress completes consideration of health care reform and other high-priority legislation, and on the resolution of outstanding issues (e.g., labor, tax, automobiles) with each country. While the terms of U.S. beef access to South Korea's market might receive attention from policymakers in the interim, the agricultural provisions in each FTA largely have been received positively by most U.S. agricultural organizations and food industry associations.

U.S. farmers and ranchers, agribusiness firms, and food manufacturers view efforts to expand commodity and food exports as vital to improving farm income and business profitability. For this reason, many U.S. policymakers since the mid-1980s have viewed negotiating trade agreements as a way of creating opportunities to increase agricultural sales overseas, primarily by seeking to lower and/or eliminate other countries' trade barriers (e.g., tariffs and quotas). To accomplish this, the United States has had to reciprocate by lowering similar forms of border protection on farm and food products imported from prospective trading partners. Because of the import sensitivity of some U.S. commodity sectors (e.g., beef, dairy, and sugar, among others) to the prospect of increased competition from foreign suppliers, the executive branch has had to take the concerns of producers of these commodities into account during negotiations, in order to secure congressional approval of concluded trade agreements.

The 1994 Uruguay Round Agreement on Agriculture negotiated under the structure of the multilateral institution that preceded the World Trade Organization (WTO) created substantial export opportunities for U.S. agriculture and agribusiness by partially lowering then-existing trade barriers worldwide. However, the U.S. FTAs that took effect with Canada in 1989 and with Mexico in 1994 (when both were combined into the North American Free Trade Agreement (NAFTA)) were more ambitious than the Uruguay Round in reducing barriers to bilateral agricultural trade. With these two trade agreements setting into motion a process that removed most forms of border protection by the end of 10- or 15-year transition periods, respectively, Canada and Mexico have become two of the fastest-growing markets for U.S. agricultural exports.

The United States has also entered into FTAs with 15 other, smaller trading partners. Most of these have only taken effect in the last five years [1] Three FTAs negotiated and signed by the Bush Administration with Colombia, Panama, and South Korea await congressional consideration. Under the trade promotion authority (TPA) that applies, President Obama has discretion on when to submit each to Congress for a vote. TPA details the process for submitting implementing legislation to Congress for these FTAs, and the expedited legislative procedures to be followed that limit debate, prohibit amendments, and require a simple up or down vote. Before an FTA can take effect, Congress must approve the implementing bill [2].

The timing of when each pending FTA might be submitted by the White House to Congress will depend on how issues of concern identified by the Obama Administration and Members of Congress are addressed in bilateral discussions to be held with each country in coming months. Accordingly, agriculture as covered in each pending trade agreement is examined in this report in the order that Congress likely will take up these agreements, based upon statements made to date by Obama Administration officials and Members of Congress.

KEY AGRICULTURAL ISSUES IN FTAS

FTAs negotiated by the United States are generally comprehensive in scope. In addition to addressing market access for agricultural and food products, they cover trade in all other goods (including textiles and apparel), improved market access commitments for services and government procurement, and protections for investment and intellectual property rights. They also include provisions on dispute settlement, labor, the environment, customs administration, among other matters.

FTAs establish a framework for liberalizing trade in agricultural commodities and food products between partners within an agreed-upon time period. The primary objective in negotiating an FTA is to achieve preferential access to each other's market, to secure a competitive edge over other countries that sell into either partner's market. Accomplishing this requires that negotiators work to reduce and eventually eliminate tariffs and quotas on most agricultural goods. Because the United States and each prospective FTA partner have some agricultural products that benefit from high levels of border protection, negotiators spend much of their time wrestling with how to reduce barriers for these import-sensitive products [3].

The United States also has sought to address other non-tariff barriers (particularly those dealing with food safety and animal/plant health—commonly referred to as sanitary and phytosanitary [SPS] measures) on a separate, but parallel, track. Although U.S. negotiators assert that resolution of outstanding bilateral SPS disputes is not on the formal FTA negotiating agenda, the negotiating process has witnessed U.S. and partner country negotiators seeking to resolve such disputes and using them as leverage to achieve other FTA negotiating objectives. Further, resolving these disputes is viewed as essential to ensure that FTA partners do not resort to using these barriers to undercut the openings created for U.S. exporters in market access talks.

PANAMA

On December 19, 2006, after almost a year's hiatus, U.S. and Panamanian negotiators reached agreement on a comprehensive FTA that includes market access provisions for exports of interest to U.S. agriculture. Though separate from this trade agreement, both governments on the next day also signed an agreement detailing how SPS measures and technical standards will be applied to bilateral agricultural trade. (See "Sanitary and Phytosanitary Agreement," below.) With these near-simultaneous developments, both sides resolved outstanding differences over Panama's earlier unwillingness to accept the equivalency of the U.S. meat inspection system [4] and achieved a balance in bilateral market access for sensitive agricultural products (sugar for the United States; rice, onions, and potatoes for Panama). Panama's legislature ratified the FTA on July 11, 2007. Action by the U.S. Congress depends on when the White House decides to submit implementing legislation, possibly later in 2009.

Overview of Agricultural Trade

The United States runs a strong positive agricultural trade balance with Panama (Figure 1). In 2008, Panama ranked 43rd as an overseas market for U.S. farm products, with U.S. agricultural exports totaling $430 million. Leading exports were corn, soybean meal, wheat, rice, and food preparations (Table 1). Agriculture's share of all U.S. merchandise exports to Panama stood at just over 9% in 2008, down from nearly 15% in 2001. U.S. sales accounted for 51% of Panama's nearly $1.0 billion agricultural import market in 2008. Other major country competitors were Costa Rica and Mexico. Imports from Panama were $55 million, placing it 64th as a supplier of agricultural commodities to the United States. Leading imports were raw cane sugar, coffee, pineapple, bananas, and bakery products (Table 1). Agricultural imports accounted for 15% of total U.S. merchandise imports from Panama in 2008.

Agricultural Provisions

Currently, less than 40% of U.S. agricultural exports have duty-free access to Panama's market. Other agricultural products face an average 15% tariff, but some key products are subject to much higher rates. Tariffs on meat can reach as high as 70%, and on grain up to 90%. U.S. chicken leg quarters face a 260% tariff. Under the Panama Trade Promotion Agreement (PTPA), almost two- thirds of present U.S. farm exports to Panama would receive immediate duty-free treatment, according to the U.S. Department of Agriculture (USDA) [5]. This would apply to sales of high quality beef, mechanically de-boned chicken, frozen whole turkeys and turkey breasts, pork variety meats, whey, soybeans and soybean meal, crude vegetable oils, cotton, wheat, barley, most fresh fruits (including apples, pears, and cherries), almonds, walnuts, many processed food products (including soups and chocolate confectionery), distilled spirits, wine, and pet food. Panama agreed to establish preferential tariff-rate quotas (TRQs) [6] for U.S. pork, chicken leg quarters, specified dairy products, corn, rice, refined corn oil, dried beans, frozen french fries, fresh potatoes, and tomato paste.

Quotas for these import-sensitive commodities would be phased out in 5 to 20 years. The longest transition period (20 years) would apply to rice, Panama's most sensitive agricultural commodity. However, Panama agreed to increase tariff-free access for U.S. rice if needed to cover a shortfall in domestic output. Border protection on U.S. chicken leg quarters would end in year 18. Quotas to be created for fresh onion and fresh potatoes would expand slowly in perpetuity; high tariffs would apply to imports that exceed quota amounts [7].

Almost all of Panama's agricultural exports to the United States already enter duty free under the Caribbean Basin Initiative trade preference program. Of U.S. commodities subject to quota protection, much attention focused on the additional market access granted to sugar from Panama. Additional sugar would be allowed entry into the U.S. market under preferential quotas that would be in addition to Panama's access for sugar under an existing U.S. multilateral trade commitment. For more than 25 years, Panama has had a minimum 2.7% share (30,540 metric tons [MT]) of the U.S. raw cane TRQ under U.S. WTO commitments. Under the PTPA, three new preferential quotas for sugar and sugar-containing products would in the aggregate represent a 23% increase over Panama's current access. The largest duty-free TRQ (for raw sugar) would be set initially at 6,000 MT. It would then increase each year by 60 MT (1%) for 10 years, and then be capped at 6,600 MT indefinitely. All sugar product over-quota tariffs would indefinitely remain at high levels (e.g., at an estimated tariff equivalent of 86% for raw cane sugar, using FY2008 data). In the aggregate, these quotas represent most of the sugar surplus that Panama recently has had available to export each year. To provide another tool to manage U.S. sugar supplies and meet sugar program objectives, negotiators also included a sugar compensation mechanism which the United States would be able to exercise at its sole discretion. If activated, the United States would commit to compensate Panama for sugar that its sugar industry would not be allowed to ship under these sugar TRQ provisions [8]. Other U.S. preferential TRQs would be established for cheeses, condensed and evaporated milk, and ice cream imported from Panama, to be phased out completely in 15 to 17 years.

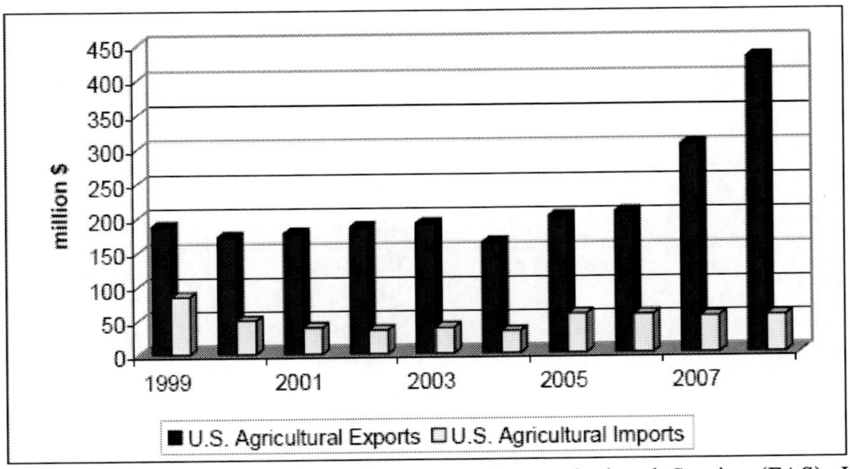

Source: U.S. Department of Agriculture (USDA), Foreign Agricultural Service (FAS), U.S. Trade Internet System database.

Figure 1. U.S. Agricultural Trade with Panama.

Potential Impact on U.S. Agricultural Exports

Because Panama is a small market for U.S. agriculture, gains from additional exports under the PTPA are projected to be small relative to those projected under the FTAs with Colombia and South Korea. Two studies analyzed what these gains might be compared to the no-trade agreement scenario—one issued by the U.S. International Trade Commission (USITC) and another prepared by the American Farm Bureau Federation (AFBF). The USITC estimated that U.S. exports of agricultural commodities and processed foods to Panama would be $46 million higher (or about 20% above the 2006 level) when the agreement is fully implemented, compared to exports under a no-agreement outlook. Exports of corn and rice would be $27 million higher; sales of processed foods—$10 million higher, and sales of meat—$7 million higher [9]. The AFBF study projects that U.S. agricultural exports at the end of the transition period (2027) would be $195 million (46%) higher under the PTPA than would be the case otherwise. Sales of corn and rice would be $66 million higher; sales of poultry, pork and beef—$43 million higher; sales of soybeans and products—$29 million higher [10].

Table 1. Composition of Agricultural Trade with Panama, 2008

Leading U.S. Exports			Leading U.S. Imports		
Product	Value Million $	Share Of Total	Product	Value Million $	Share of Total
Corn	90.8	21.1%	Raw Cane Sugar	15.9	29.1%
Soybean Meal	59.0	13.7%	Coffee a	15.3	27.9%
Wheat	42.3	9.8%	Fresh Pineapple	5.8	10.6%
Rice	23.7	5.5%	Fresh Bananas	3.4	6.2%
Food Preparations	19.2	4.5%	Bakery Products	2.3	4.2%
Chocolate & Cocoa-Containing Foods	16.7	3.9%	Fresh Pumpkins & Squash	2.1	3.9%
Vegetables, Prepared, & Preserved	12.8	3.0%	Cocoa Beans	1.6	2.9%
Frozen					
Cheese	12.7	3.0%	Fresh Papayas	1.1	2.1%
Poultry Meat	11.8	2.7%	Beverages, Nonalcoholic	0.8	1.4%
Fresh Fruit, Decidious b	9.6	2.2%	Fresh Yams & Dasheens	0.6	1.2%
Subtotal, Top 10	298.6	69.5%	Subtotal, Top 10	48.9	89.5%
All Other Agricultural Products	131.0	30.5%	All Other Agricultural Products	5.7	10.5%
Total	429.6	100.0%	Total	54.6	100.0%

Source: Derived by CRS from trade data available online at USDA's FAS U.S. Trade Internet System.

a. Primarily unroasted.

b. Primarily fresh grapes and fresh apples.

The wide disparity in estimates presented in these two analyses reflects the use of widely different methodologies and assumptions to estimate the projected change in future U.S. agricultural exports under this trade agreement [11]. Neither analysis looked at possible changes in agricultural imports under the PTPA.

Sanitary and Phytosanitary Agreement

In the separate SPS agreement, Panama agreed to accept the U.S. meat and poultry inspection system "as equivalent to its own." This means that all Panamanian facilities that USDA certifies as meeting U.S. food safety standards are eligible to export meat products to the U.S. market, without the need for further inspection by Panama. The SPS agreement also commits Panama to provide access for all U.S. beef, poultry, and related products, on the basis of accepted international standards. It also streamlines import documentation requirements for U.S. processed foods and affirms Panama's recognition of the U.S. beef grading system. USDA notes that this agreement eliminates "long-standing regulatory barriers faced by a variety of U.S. products" in Panama's market [12].

Outlook for Congressional Consideration

The Obama Administration has signaled its intent to resolve two outstanding issues with Panama before proceeding to a congressional vote on the PTPA, perhaps later in 2009. The first would involve changes to Panama's labor laws to address concerns raised by the International Labor Organization (such as the requirement that a minimum of 40 workers are needed to form a union). The second deals with negotiating a bilateral information exchange treaty to address allegations that Panama is a tax haven through which money can be easily laundered. Though the Administration earlier stated it would like to have Congress consider the PTPA before the current Panamanian President's term ends on July 1, statements made by a USTR official at a May 21 Senate Finance Committee hearing signaled a tactical shift—sending it to Capitol Hill once the Administration is assured that there is "broad support that would create forward momentum to pass more controversial trade deals" such as the FTA with Colombia. Though the chairman and ranking member of Senate Finance advocated moving the PTPA quickly, some House Members advocate renegotiating the agreement while other Members would prefer to see the labor and tax haven issues addressed before a vote is scheduled [13]

COLOMBIA

Although U.S.-Colombian negotiators announced on February 27, 2006, that they had concluded an FTA, remaining differences over two agricultural market access issues took another four months (until July 8, 2006) to resolve. Further, the signing ceremony for the U.S.-Colombia Free Trade Agreement (CFTA) was not scheduled until Colombia took steps to fulfill a separate commitment to allow, by no later than October 31, 2006, the entry of U.S. beef imports. (See "SPS Side Letter," below.) The CFTA was formally signed on November

22, 2006. Colombia's legislature completed the approval process for the CFTA on October 30, 2007. Action by the U.S. Congress depends on when the White House decides to submit implementing legislation, perhaps late this year or in early 2010.

Table 2. Composition of Agricultural Trade with Colombia, 2008

Leading U.S. Exports			Leading U.S. Imports		
Product	Value Million $	Share Of Total	Product	Value Million $	Share of Total
Corn	625.7	37.3%	Unroasted Coffee	805.0	45.5%
Wheat	330.0	19.7%	Fresh Roses	239.9	13.6%
Soybean Meal	98.9	5.9%	Fresh Bananas	162.7	9.2%
Soybeans	95.9	5.7%	Fresh Chrysanthemums	66.4	3.8%
Soybean Oil	71.1	4.2%	Fresh Carnations	61.7	3.5%
Cotton	66.8	4.0%	Fresh Plantains	45.4	2.6%
Corn Gluten Meal	55.4	3.3%	Raw Cane Sugar & Sugar Confectionery	30.7	1.7%
Food Preparations	31.4	1.9%	Bakery Products	20.7	1.2%
Animal Feed Preparations	23.2	1.4%	Palm Oil	16.8	0.9%
Inedible Tallow	17.1	1.0%	Glue Stock from Animal Hides/Skins	14.9	0.8%
Subtotal, Top 10	1,415.6	84.4%	Subtotal, Top 10	1,464.1	82.7%
Product	Value Million $	Share Of Total	Product	Value Million $	Share of Total
All Other Agricultural Products	261.2	15.6%	All Other Agricultural Products	305.2	17.3%
Total	1,676.8	100.0%	Total	1,769.4	100.0%

Source: Derived by CRS from trade data available online at USDA's FAS U.S. Trade Internet System.

Overview of Agricultural Trade

Colombia is the second largest market for U.S. farm products in Latin America after Mexico, and ranked as the 15th largest market for U.S. agriculture in 2008. As U.S. agricultural exports since 2006 have increased at about a 40% annual rate, U.S.-Colombian agricultural trade has nearly come into balance (Figure 2). In 2008, U.S. agricultural exports totaled almost $1.7 billion. Shipments of corn, wheat, soybean meal, soybeans, and soybean oil led the list (Table 2). Agriculture's share of all U.S. merchandise exports to Colombia stood at almost 16%, up from 13% in 2001.

In 2008, U.S. sales accounted for 44% of Colombia's $4.2 billion agricultural import market, compared to a 30% share earlier in this decade. Other major competitors in this market were Argentina, Brazil, Chile, and members of the Andean Common Market (Bolivia,

Ecuador, and Peru). U.S. agricultural imports from Colombia reached nearly $1.8 billion. Leading imports were coffee, roses, bananas, chrysanthemums, and plantains (Table 2). In 2008, agricultural imports accounted for almost 14% of total U.S. merchandise imports from Colombia, down from an almost 16% share in 2001.

Agricultural Provisions

Currently, no U.S. agricultural export has duty-free access to Colombia's market. Applied tariffs on agricultural imports range from 5% to 20%, but under WTO rules, Colombia could raise these to bound levels which range from 15% to 388% [14].

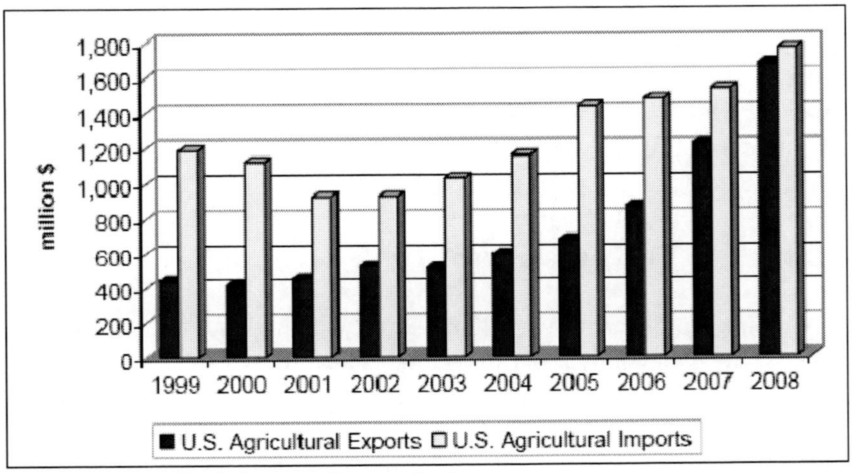

Source: USDA, FAS, U.S. Trade Internet System database.

Figure 2. U.S. Agricultural Trade with Colombia.

The CFTA would eliminate tariffs and quotas on all agricultural products traded bilaterally (except for sugar) and establish long transition periods for the more sensitive commodities. The United States would secure immediate duty-free access to Colombia for more than one-half of its current exports by value. This would apply to high-quality beef, bacon, cotton, wheat, soybeans, soybean meal; apples, pears, peaches, and cherries; and frozen french fries and cookies, among other food products. Also, Colombia agreed to immediately eliminate price bands for some 150 products—a mechanism that added fees onto existing tariffs which fluctuated depending upon world prices. This effectively had resulted in a higher level of border protection than would usually be the case [15]. Colombia's tariffs on most other farm and food products imported from the United States would be phased out in periods ranging from 3 to 15 years. For its most sensitive commodities (including those subject to price bands), Colombia would eliminate quotas and over-quota tariffs for corn and other feed grains in 12 years, for dairy products in 15 years, for chicken leg quarters in 18 years, and for rice in 19 years. Both countries would also commit to consult and review the implementation and operation of provisions on trade in chicken about midway through the long transition period [16].

Almost all of Colombia's agricultural exports to the United States would continue to benefit from current duty free access under the Andean Trade Preferences Act, [17] which the

CFTA would make permanent. Of those commodities subject to U.S. quota protection, much attention focused on the amount of additional sugar that would be allowed access to the U.S. market. Additional sugar would be allowed entry into the United States under a preferential quota that would be in addition to Colombia's current access for sugar under an existing U.S. multilateral trade commitment. Under the CFTA, the United States would triple Colombia's access to the U.S. sugar market— from its historic 2.3% share of the U.S. raw cane sugar TRQ (25,273 MT)—by an additional 50,000 MT of sugar and specified sugar products in the first year. This new quota would expand by 750 MT (1.5%) annually starting in year 2 in perpetuity, while the current high U.S. tariff on over-quota sugar entries would be applied indefinitely [18]. The CFTA also includes a sugar compensation provision designed to protect the operation of the U.S. sugar program. Crafted so that if the United States exercised its sole discretion to activate this mechanism, the U.S. Government would commit to compensate Colombia for sugar that its exporters would not be allowed to ship under the CFTA's preferential access provision. In addition, preferential TRQs would be established for imports from Colombia of beef, specified dairy products, and tobacco. These would expand slowly until phased out in 10, 11, or 15 years.

Potential Impact on U.S. Agricultural Trade

Because Colombia protects its agricultural sector with high tariffs and import quotas, two analyses project that their elimination over time under the CFTA would benefit the U.S. agricultural sector. The U.S. International Trade Commission (USITC) estimated that U.S. agricultural exports to Colombia would be $170 million, or 24% higher, with full implementation of these provisions, compared to a baseline scenario of no policy change. Gains for U.S. agriculture would accrue primarily to the corn, wheat, rice, and soybean sectors. The USITC also projects that sales of beef, pork, and processed foods would increase. Agricultural exports alone would account for 16% of the projected increase in all U.S. merchandise exports to Colombia under this FTA [19]. Separately, the American Farm Bureau Federation (AFBF) estimated that U.S. agricultural exports to Colombia would be $693 million higher in 2026 when the FTA is fully implemented than would occur otherwise. The AFBF study similarly expects that most of the additional exports would be of U.S. corn, wheat, and soybean products [20]. The wide disparity in estimates presented in these two analyses reflects the use of different methodologies and assumptions to estimate the projected change in future U.S. agricultural exports under this trade agreement [21].

Only the USITC study considered the CFTA's impact on U.S. agricultural imports. It estimated that such imports would be $223 million, or 11% higher, than under the no-agreement scenario. Additional imports of sugar would account for almost half of the estimated increase in farm product imports. The increased access for Colombian sugar and sugar-containing products to the U.S. market are likely to have only a minor effect on U.S. imports and production, according to the USITC's analysis. Cut flower imports from Colombia could increase if permanent duty-free access stimulates investment in the country's flower sector and diverts trade away from other flower-exporting countries in South America [22]. Agricultural imports from Colombia would account for 46% of the increase in total U.S. merchandise imports from Colombia under this FTA.

SPS Side Letter

Thought to have been resolved at the time negotiators concluded the CFTA, the separate SPS issue dealing with the terms of access under which U.S. beef and beef products would be allowed to enter Colombia was not resolved until later. The Colombian government in a second exchange of letters on August 21, 2006, committed to permit such imports of cattle over 30 months old, by no later than October 31, 2006 [23]. In turn, on August 24, President Bush notified Congress of his intent to enter into an FTA with Colombia. Once Colombia issued regulations to fulfill its beef import pledge on October 27, the White House agreed to set November 22, 2006, as a date for the FTA's formal signing.

Though an FTA normally is not used as the mechanism to address the substance of SPS issues, this timeline illustrates how U.S. negotiators exercised leverage to achieve a desired outcome for the domestic beef sector. This likely reflected the Bush Administration's recognition that such efforts were essential to gain support from an agricultural group that may be vital to secure the agreement's approval by Congress.

Outlook for Congressional Consideration

Though U.S. agriculture would gain from significant additional market access to Colombia under the CFTA, concerns expressed by some Democratic Members of Congress over the longstanding violence directed at labor union officials in that country has affected congressional consideration of this trade agreement. Reflecting these concerns, the House on April 10, 2008, voted 224-195 to suspend fast-track rules (H. Res. 1092) in response to President Bush's decision to submit the CFTA and implementing legislation (H.R. 5724/S. 2830) to Congress for consideration. At present, it is unclear when the 111th Congress might consider implementing legislation for the pending CFTA. The Obama Administration has signaled that it will work with Members of Congress to develop benchmarks for use to determine when the CFTA might be submitted to Congress. The USTR and other newly-appointed trade officials have begun to meet with Colombian officials to identify benchmarks and a possible timetable.

SOUTH KOREA

Expanding export opportunities for U.S. agriculture to the large South Korean market was the main goal pursued by U.S. agricultural officials in negotiating the U.S.-Korea Free Trade Agreement (KORUS FTA). Their objective reflected the interests of the U.S. agricultural sector, which eyes potential for further export gains in a major food importing country with a high level of border protection. U.S. exporters in particular see opportunities for increasing sales of higher- value food products to an expanding middle class. Compromises on the final package, reached in the final hours before the April 1, 2007 deadline, [24] would provide for much improved market access for all U.S. agricultural products (except for rice) to the Korean market. However, numerous Members of Congress then signaled that their support for the KORUS FTA depends on South Korea following through on its separate and subsequent commitment to fully reopen its market to U.S. beef.

(See "Korea's Rules for U.S. Beef Imports," below.) Parliamentary committees in Korea's National Assembly have approved the bill to ratify the agreement, but a final floor vote has not yet been scheduled. Action by the U.S. Congress depends on when the White House decides to submit implementing legislation. This is not expected until 2010 at the earliest.

Overview of Agricultural Trade

The United States runs a strong positive agricultural trade balance with South Korea (Figure 3). In 2008, South Korea was the 5th largest market for U.S. farm products in the world, as U.S. export sales totaled almost $5.6 billion. Leading exports were corn, wheat, beef, cattle hides, and pork (Table 3). Agricultural shipments accounted for almost 17% of all U.S. merchandise exports to South Korea, up from 12% in 2001.

In 2008, U.S. sales accounted for 34% of South Korea's $19 billion agricultural import market. Major competitors in South Korea's commodity and food import market over the last decade have been China, Australia, and Brazil.

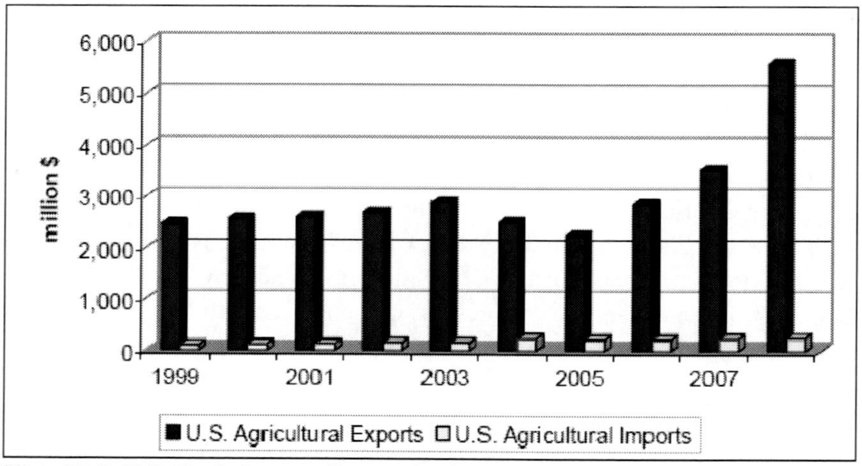

Source: USDA, FAS, U.S. Trade Internet System database.

Figure 3. U.S. Agricultural Trade with South Korea.

U.S. imports from South Korea were small—$249 million—consisting primarily of ethnic foods, and do not appear to compete directly with U.S. agricultural and manufactured-food products. Leading imports were pasta products (with ramen noodles likely accounting for a large portion), food preparations, nonalcoholic beverages, fresh pears, and various baked products (Table 3). In recent years, agricultural imports accounted for one-half of 1% of all U.S. merchandise imports from South Korea.

Also, Korea extensively uses TRQs with prohibitive over-quota tariffs to limit imports of oranges (50%), various dairy products (89% to 176%), potatoes (304%), onions (135%), non-malting barley (300% or 324%), corn starch (226%), and numerous other agricultural products [25].

Table 3. Composition of Agricultural Trade with South Korea, 2008

Leading U.S. Exports			Leading U.S. Imports		
Product	Value Million $	Share Of Total	Product	Value Million $	Share of Total
Corn	2,153.5	38.7%	Pasta Products [a]	37.5	15.1%
Wheat	526.1	9.4%	Food Preparations	30.8	12.4%
Beef & Veal, Fresh-Chilled-Frozen	285.0	5.1%	Nonalcoholic Beverages	27.9	11.2%
Cattle Hides	232.8	4.2%	Fresh Pears	21.6	8.7%
Pork, Fresh-Chilled-Frozen	229.3	4.1%	Baked Products & Pastries	19.4	7.8%
Soybeans	186.7	3.4%	Vegetables & Preparations	11.0	4.4%
Hay & Other Animal Forage Products	153.9	2.8%	Sauces & Condiments	10.7	4.3%
Cotton	124.8	2.2%	Returned Meat & Poultry	5.3	2.1%
Food Preparations	116.8	2.1%	Coffee Extract	3.7	1.5%
Fresh Oranges	90.2	1.6%	Bean Cake & Stick Miso	3.6	1.5%
Subtotal, Top 10	4,099.1	73.6%	Subtotal, Top 10	171.4	68.9%
All Other Agricultural Products	1,468.7	26.4%	All Other Agricultural Products	77.4	31.1%
Total	5,567.7	100.0%	Total	248.8	100.0%

Source: Derived by CRS from trade data available online at USDA's FAS U.S. Trade Internet System.

[a.] Large portion likely is ramen noodles.

Agricultural Provisions

In 2008, South Korea's average applied tariff on agricultural imports was almost 53%. Average tariffs are highest for vegetable products (over 100%). Tariffs on pistachios and shelled walnuts are 30%, on pork either 22.5% or 25%, on poultry and egg products from 18% to 27%, on beef 40%, on oranges 50%.

The KORUS FTA would eliminate tariffs and quotas on most agricultural products traded bilaterally. The United States would receive immediate duty-free access to Korea for almost two- thirds of current U.S. agricultural exports once it takes effect. This would apply, among other products, to wheat, corn, soybeans for crushing, whey for feed use, hides and skins, cotton, cherries, pistachios, almonds, orange juice, grape juice, and wine. Tariffs and import quotas on most other U.S. agricultural goods would be phased out within 10 years. However, longer transition periods would apply to Korea's more sensitive commodities. This means tariffs, quotas, and safeguards to protect against import surges would be phased out in various stages ranging up to 23 years. Tariffs on beef and potatoes for chipping would be removed in 15 years, [26]. on fresh grapes in 17 years, on ginseng products and fresh pears in 20 years, and on fresh apples in 23 years. Tariff-rate quotas (TRQs) with long phase-out periods (10 to 18 years) would apply to other sensitive products as cheeses, butter, dairy-based infant foods, barley, whey for food use, animal feed supplements and hay, corn starch, and ginseng. However, seven U.S. agricultural products (skim and whole milk powders, evaporated milk, in-season oranges, potatoes for table use, honey and identity-preserved soybeans for food use) would be subject to Korean TRQs that slowly expand in perpetuity. Shipments against these quotas would enter duty-free, but over- quota amounts would indefinitely face prohibitively-high tariffs. USDA notes that these TRQs ensure access for U.S. exporters that South Korea could have easily changed under its multilateral trade commitments. Also, because of the sensitivity of marketing during harvest, quotas and/or tariffs and phase-out schedules would vary, depending on the season of the year that U.S. oranges, table grapes, and potatoes for chipping enter Korea's market [27].

Unique to this FTA, South Korea secured the right to specify the state entities and trade associations that would administer each TRQ under either an auction or licensing system. Safeguards (e.g., in the form of special add-on tariffs applied in case of import surges) would be triggered if imports from the United States of some sensitive agricultural products exceed specified levels. Korea succeeded in excluding rice and rice products from the agreement—its main objective in negotiating agricultural issues. This outcome reflected the prevailing view that rice is vital to maintaining, and inseparable from, Korea's national identity, and the political reality that rice farming preserves the basis for economic activity in the countryside. However, the United States will continue to be able to sell rice under quotas created to meet South Korea's multilateral WTO commitments.

Because U.S. agricultural imports from South Korea are small and largely complementary, there was little controversy in negotiating Korean access to the U.S. market. The United States agreed to phase out tariffs and quotas on all agricultural imports from South Korea in stages ranging up to 15 years. This longest period would apply to imports from Korea of beef, some dairy products, rice, and malt extract.

Potential Impact on U.S. Agricultural Trade

With the immediate elimination and phase out over time of much of South Korea's relatively high agricultural trade barriers under the KORUS FTA, the U.S. agricultural and food processing sectors would noticeably benefit from additional exports. The U.S. International Trade Commission (USITC) estimated that the increase in U.S. exports of agricultural commodities and processed foods would account for up to one-third of the entire projected increase in total U.S. merchandise exports to South Korea's market once the KORUS FTA's provisions are fully implemented. U.S. sales of agricultural products would be from \$1.9 billion to \$3.8 billion (44% to 89%) higher than exports under a no-agreement scenario. Almost half of this export increase would accrue to the U.S. beef sector, based on the USITC's assumption that U.S. beef exports recover to the 2003 level before South Korea imposed for human health reasons its restrictions on U.S. beef imports. About 20% of the export increase would benefit U.S. producers and exporters of pork, poultry, and other meat products [28]. The American Farm Bureau Federation (AFBF) projected that U.S. agricultural exports by the end of the transition period (2027) would be more than $1.5 billion (45%) higher under the KORUS FTA than would be the case otherwise. Sales of beef, poultry, and pork would account for $644 million (or 42%) of this increase [29].

The wide disparity in projected U.S. agricultural export estimates under the KORUS FTA presented in these two analyses reflects the use of different methodologies and assumptions [30]. One major factor that accounts for the difference is that the AFBF projects that U.S. beef sales would be much lower than the USITC-estimated level.

Only the USITC looked at the impact of the KORUS FTA on U.S. agricultural imports. It projects that U.S. imports of primarily processed food products from South Korea would be from $52 million to $78 million (12% to 18%) higher than such imports under a no-agreement scenario [31].

Korea's Rules for U.S. Beef Imports

By the time that negotiators concluded the KORUS FTA on April 1, 2007, they had not reached a breakthrough on the separate but parallel issue of how to resolve differences on the terms of access for all U.S. beef in a way that would address Korea's human health concerns. In 2003, South Korea was the third-largest market for U.S. beef exports. However, in late December 2003, Korea's government imposed an import ban after the first U.S. cow infected with mad cow disease, or BSE (bovine spongiform encephalopathy), was discovered in the U.S. cattle herd. However, then-South Korean President Roh, in a national address the same day, stated he had personally promised President Bush that his government would "uphold the [yet to-be-released] recommendations" of the World Organization for Animal Health (OIE) on the BSE risk status of the United States and "open the Korean [beef] market at a reasonable level."As soon as the OIE formally found on May 22, 2007, that the United States is a "controlled risk" country for the spread of mad cow disease, USDA immediately requested that South Korea amend its import requirements for U.S. beef within a specified time frame to reflect this determination and to reopen its market to all U.S. cattle and beef products.

Talks to resolve this outstanding issue concluded just before newly-elected South Korean President Lee met with President Bush at Camp David. On April 18, 2008, U.S. and Korean negotiators reached agreement on the sanitary rules that Korea will apply to beef imports from the United States. It allows for imports of all cuts of U.S. boneless and bone-in beef and other beef products from cattle, irrespective of age, as long as specified risk materials known to transmit mad cow disease are removed and other conditions are met. However, candlelight vigils held by thousands protesting this agreement, calls by opposition parties that these terms be renegotiated, and President Lee's apologies for how his government mishandled this matter, prompted the Korean government to secure additional changes to allay public concerns about the safety of U.S. beef. Subsequent difficult negotiations led to the announcement of a "voluntary private sector arrangement" on June 21, 2008, that limits sales to U.S. beef only from cattle less than 30 months old. Both countries view this as a transitional step intended to improve Korean consumer confidence in U.S. beef.

By year-end 2008, exports of U.S. beef to South Korea had reached almost $300 million, slightly more than one-third of the record 2003 sales level. Though Australia is the main competitor in Korea's beef market, U.S. beef exporters did gain noticeable market share in the July to October 2008 period. Sensing a change in consumer sentiment, three large Korean discount department stores began selling U.S. beef in late November. In early April 2009, sales resumed at two major supermarket chains. However, exports, while variable, have fallen in recent months. Future sales will depend largely on two factors. These include the price competitiveness of U.S. beef compared to Australian beef; [32] and the impact that Korea's economic crisis continues to have on household meat consumption, particularly in restaurants—traditionally a major outlet for U.S. beef.

Outlook for Congressional Consideration

The Obama Administration has not indicated if and when it will send the draft implementing bill for the KORUS FTA to Congress. The Administration has stated that it is developing "benchmarks for progress" on resolving "concerns" it has with this trade agreement, particularly over the terms of access for U.S. automobiles in South Korea's market. While U.S. Trade Representative Ron Kirk during his confirmation hearings called attention to the economic opportunities that the KORUS FTA presents, he also said that if the Administration's concerns are not resolved, "we'll be prepared to step away ... " Meeting on the sidelines of the G-20 summit on April 2, 2009, Presidents Obama and Lee "committed to working together to chart a way forward" on the trade agreement. Afterward, an Administration official said that Obama told Lee he wants to "make progress," and that the two leaders agreed that the two countries' staffs should "discuss how to move the agreement forward."The next milestone for a possible indication of a decision on a timetable for U.S. consideration of the KORUS FTA may come when the two Presidents hold a scheduled meeting on June 16, in Washington.

The issue of full access for U.S. beef (i.e., securing access for beef from cattle older than 30 months) might be addressed in upcoming bilateral discussions on how to proceed with the pending agreement. U.S. Trade Representative Ron Kirk, in his confirmation hearings, stated that beef access will be an Administration priority as efforts resume to normalize beef trade with Korea and other Asian markets. Though some press accounts suggest that the beef issue may be addressed before the agreement's auto provisions, Kirk did acknowledge that "U.S. beef from cattle under 30 months of age is selling well in Korea." [33] Others have noted "diminished interest in pressing this issue because South Korea has given the U.S. more than 90 percent of its beef access by value" under the arrangement agreed to in June 2008 covering beef products from cattle younger than 30 months of age [34]

References

[1] These include, by date of entry, Israel (1985), Jordan (2001), Singapore (2004), Chile (2004), Australia (2005), Morocco (2006), El Salvador (2006), Honduras (2006), Nicaragua (2006), Guatemala (2006), Bahrain (2006), Dominican Republic (2007), Costa Rica (2009), Oman (2009), and Peru (2009). For more information on the agricultural provisions in these FTAs, see archived CRS Report RL34134, *Agriculture in U.S. Free Trade Agreements: Trade with Current and Prospective Partners, Impact, and Issues*, by Remy Jurenas.

[2] For background, see CRS Report RL33743, *Trade Promotion Authority (TPA): Issues, Options, and Prospects for Renewal*, by J. F. Hornbeck and William H. Cooper.

[3] A country's designation of certain agricultural commodities as "sensitive" usually reflects high levels of border protection (e.g., high tariffs, restrictive quotas, price bands) to preclude competition from lower-priced imports and/or the political strength of producers of these commodities that benefit financially from such border protection.

[4] The FTA talks collapsed in January 2006, when Panama's Agriculture Minister resigned, stating that the U.S. Trade Representative's request that the trade agreement include a side letter accepting the U.S. Department of Agriculture's safety certification would lower the country's food and health standards and increase the risk of introducing animal diseases. Subsequently, Panama's government changed its position, and agreed to sign this separate SPS agreement

[5] USDA, FAS, Fact Sheet summarizing the PTPA's agricultural provisions, April 2009, available at http://www.fas.usda.gov/info/factsheets/Panama/Panama1Pager07.pdf.

[6] A TRQ is a two-part tool used by countries to protect their more sensitive agricultural and food products, often while transitioning over time to free trade. The quota component provides for duty-free access of a specified quantity of a commodity, which in an FTA usually expands over time. Imports above this quota are subject to a prohibitive tariff that in an FTA frequently declines over time. At the end of a product's transition period to free trade under an FTA, both the quota and tariff no longer apply (unless an exception is agreed to), allowing for its unrestricted access to the partner's market.

[7] A detailed description of commodity-specific market access provisions (transition periods, TRQ amounts and growth rates, and safeguards) is found in the USDA fact sheet "U.S.-Panama Trade Promotion Agreement Benefits for Agriculture,"April 2009, available at http://www.fas.usda.gov/info/factsheets/Panama/Panamaoverall0707.pdfFact sheets on the PTPA's impacts for major agricultural commodities in 45 states are available at http://www.fas.usda.gov/info/ factsheets/Panama/us-PanamaTPAfactsheets.asp.

[8] It is similar to a provision found also in the Dominican Republic-Central America FTA, the Peru FTA, and the pending FTA with Colombia.

[9] Derived by CRS from Table 2.4 in USITC, *U.S.-Panama Trade Promotion Agreement: Potential Economy-wide and Selected Sectoral Effects*, September 2007, p. 2-7.

[10] AFBF, *Implications of a Panama Trade Promotion Agreement on U.S. Agriculture*, 2007, p. 17. The AFBF assumed the PTPA would have taken effect in 2007.

[11] For an explanation of these differences, see Appendix A in CRS Report RL34134, *Agriculture in U.S. Free Trade Agreements: Trade with Current and Prospective Partners, Impact, and Issues*, by Remy Jurenas.

[12] USDA, PTPA Fact Sheet, p. 1, available at http://www.fas.usda.gov/ info/factsheets/Panama/Panamaoverall0707.pdf.

[13] Bureau of National Affairs, International Trade Daily, "Levin, Doggett Seek Delay on Panama FTA Until Tax Haven Concerns Are Addressed," May 21, 2009, and "President Obama to Lay Out New Framework For Trade, Panel Told at Panama FTA Hearing," Mat 22, 2009; Inside U.S. Trade, "Administration Sees Panama FTA as Part of Wider Domestic Agenda," May 22, 2009, pp. 1, 2 1-22.

[14] A bound tariff represents the maximum tariff that a country can impose on imports of a particular product, and reflects the outcome of the last set of WTO multilateral negotiations concluded in 1993. Bound rates are incorporated as an integral component of each country's schedule of concessions or commitments to other WTO country members. However, a country can decide to impose a lower, or applied, tariff rate on imports of this particular agricultural commodity (i.e., because of changing supply or demand factors). Just as easily, though, it has the right to increase an applied tariff back up to the bound rate, which could adversely affect trade flows.

[15] Price bands serve to insulate producers and processors from trade competition when the world price for any commodity falls below a calculated reference price (e.g., a price target comparable to a commodity support level). The domestic sector is protected by a variable fee imposed on the imported commodity, which when added to the lower world price or a selected international reference price, raises the importer's cost to this adjusted import price. This fee can fluctuate, depending on changes in the reference price (adjusted for freight, insurance, and other factors) to equal this pre-determined minimum import price. Under the CFTA, Colombia would convert the level of border protection that their price bands provide into a relatively high over-quota tariff—frequently the product's bound rate—which would then be reduced to zero during a specified transition period.

[16] For a detailed description of the CFTA's agricultural provisions, see USDA, Foreign Agricultural Service (FAS), "U.S.- Colombia Trade Promotion Agreement Overall Agriculture Fact Sheet," August 2008, available at http://www.fas.usda.gov/info/factsheets/Colombia/Colombiadetailedfinal0308.pdf. Fact sheets on the CFTA's impacts for major agricultural commodities in 45 states are available at http://www.fas.usda.gov/info/factsheets/Colombia/usColombiaTPAfactsheets.asp.

[17] This trade preference program extends special duty treatment to certain U.S. imports that meet domestic content and other requirements from designated countries in the Andean region. Its purpose is to promote economic growth in the Andean region and to encourage a shift away from dependence on illegal drugs by supporting legitimate economic activities. For Colombia, P.L. 110-436 extended ATPA benefits through December 31, 2009. For additional information, see CRS Report RS22548, *ATPA Renewal: Background and Issues*, by M. Angeles Villarreal.

[18] Using raw cane sugar to illustrate, the tariff equivalent of protection (ad valorem) would be about 86% of the FY2008 import price.

[19] Derived by CRS from Table 2-4 in USITC, *U.S.-Colombia Trade Promotion Agreement: Potential Economy-wide and Selected Sectoral Effects*, Publication 3896, December 2006, p. 2-11.

[20] AFBF, *Implications of a Colombia Trade Promotion Agreement on U.S. Agriculture*, October 2006, p. 17. The AFBF assumed the CFTA would have taken effect in 2007.

[21] For an explanation, see Appendix A in CRS Report RL34134, *Agriculture in U.S. Free Trade Agreements: Trade with Current and Prospective Partners, Impact, and Issues*, by Remy Jurenas.

[22] USITC, U.S.-*Colombia Trade Promotion Agreement: Potential Economy-wide and Selected Sectoral Effects,* Publication 3896, December 2006, pp. 3-1 to 3-3.

[23] Colombia, among many other countries in late 2003, imposed a ban on the import of U.S. beef following the discovery of a cow with *bovine spongiform encephalopathy* (BSE) or mad cow disease in Washington state. To restore beef trade export flows, the U.S. government has pressed trading partners to recognize the U.S. measures taken to address the BSE measures as conforming with internationally recognized scientific guidelines governing meat trade.

[24] This was the last day that the Executive Branch could conclude a trade agreement under 2002-enacted trade promotion authority (TPA) and notify Congress of its intent to sign it.

[25] WTO, *Trade Policy Review – Report by the Secretariat – Republic of Korea*, September 3, 2008, p. 44; and USDA, FAS, "Fact Sheet – U.S.-Korea Free Trade Agreement – Benefits for Agriculture," October 2008, available at http://www.fas.usda.gov/info/factsheets/Korea/ KORUSFactSheet-Updated10-29-08.pdf.

[26] Though South Korea would completely phase out its 40% tariff on beef muscle meats in 15 years, a separate bilateral agreement on the terms of access for U.S. beef into Korea's market that addressed Korean food safety concerns was not concluded until June 2008 (see "Korea's Rules for U.S. Beef Imports").

[27] A summary of commodity-specific market access provisions (tariff reduction schedules, transition periods, TRQ amounts and growth rates, and safeguards) is found in the USDA fact sheet "U.S. - Korea Free Trade Agreement Benefits for Agriculture," October 2008, available at http://www.fas.usda.gov/info/factsheets/korea.asp. Detailed fact sheets on the agreement's commodity provisions and impacts for agriculture in selected states are available at http://www.fas.usda.gov/ info/factsheets/Korea/us-koreaftafactsheets.asp.

[28] Derived by CRS from Table 2.2 in USITC, *U.S.-Korea Free Trade Agreement: Potential Economy-wide and Selected Sectoral Effects*, pp. 2-8 and 2-9.

[29] Derived by CRS from American Farm Bureau Federation's (AFBF) *Implications of a South Korea-U.S. Free Trade Agreement on U.S. Agriculture*, July 2007, p. 17. To be consistent with the agricultural and food product categories used to derive the USITC's estimate, AFBF's exports of fish products are not included in the estimated increase in agricultural exports and agriculture's share stated above. The AFBF assumed the KORUS FTA would have taken effect in 2007 in developing its projections for 2027.

[30] For an explanation of these differences, see Appendix A in CRS Report RL34134, *Agriculture in U.S. Free Trade Agreements: Trade with Current and Prospective Partners, Impact, and Issues*, by Remy Jurenas.

[31] USITC report referenced in footnote 28, pp. 2-8 and 2-9.

[32] Between February 2008 and January 2009, the U.S. dollar strengthened by nearly 50% against the Korean won. As the dollar:won rate strengthened, U.S. beef became more expensive. At the same time, the Australian dollar has weakened against the U.S. dollar, giving Australian beef a price advantage in the Korean market.

[33] Yonhap English News, "Kirk pledges to address beef, auto issues before Korea FTA's ratification," March 13, 2009; "Finance Committee Questions for the Record," submitted by Ronald Kirk per his confirmation hearing held March 9, 2009, p. 9, available at http://www.finance.senate.gov/hearings/testimony/2009test/031

109QFRs%20for%20SubmissionRK.pdf; USTR, *2009 National Trade Estimate Report on Foreign Trade Barriers*, March 31, 2009, p. 308.

[34] *Inside U.S. Trade*, "U.S., Korea To Review FTA Ahead of June Visit; NSC Seeks Passage," p. 25.

In: U.S. Involvement in Political, Economic and Social ... ISBN: 978-1-61209-781-7
Editor: Allen P. Lowell

Chapter 2

CUBA: ISSUES FOR THE 111TH CONGRESS

***Mark P. Sullivan*[#]**

Cuba, which remains a hard-line communist state with a poor record on human rights, commemorated the 50th anniversary of its revolution on January 1, 2009. Cuba's political succession from the long-ruling Fidel Castro to his brother Raúl in 2006 was characterized by a remarkable degree of stability. Fidel stepped down from power temporarily in July 2006 because of health reasons, and Raúl assumed provisional control of the government until February 2008, when he officially became President. After Raúl Castro officially assumed the presidency, his government announced a series of economic changes that included lifting restrictions on the sale of some electronic consumer products and cell phones. A major reform effort has focused on the agriculture sector in an effort to boost food production. While additional economic changes are likely, there has been disappointment that further reforms have not been forthcoming. The economy was hard hit by storms in 2008 that resulted in $10 billion in damages, and the current global financial crisis is causing further strains. Few observers expect the government to ease its tight control over the political system, which is backed up by a strong security apparatus.

Since the early 1960s, U.S. policy toward Cuba has consisted largely of isolating the communist nation through economic sanctions. The Bush Administration tightened sanctions significantly in 2004 through increased restrictions on travel to Cuba, especially family travel. A second U.S. policy component over the years has consisted of support measures for the Cuban people, including private humanitarian donations, U.S.-sponsored radio and television broadcasting to Cuba (Radio and TV Marti), and support for human rights and democracy on the island. The Bush Administration significantly increased support for Cuba democracy funding in recent years.

As in past years, the main issue for U.S. policy toward Cuba in the 111th Congress is how best to support political and economic change in Cuba. In light of Fidel Castro's departure as head of government, many observers have called for a re-examination of policy. In this new context, two broad approaches have been advanced: a stay the course approach that would maintain the U.S. dual-track policy of isolating the Cuban government while providing

---

[#] E-mail: msullivan@crs.loc.gov

support to the Cuban people; and an approach aimed at changing attitudes within the Cuban government and society through increased contact and engagement. President Barack Obama vowed during the electoral campaign to change policy by allowing unlimited family travel and remittances, although he also pledged to maintain the embargo as a source of leverage to bring about change in Cuba.

Over the past several years, various legislative initiatives have been introduced to ease U.S. economic sanctions on Cuba, but none of these have been enacted. In the 111th Congress, however, Congress approved three provisions in the FY2009 omnibus appropriations measure (P.L. 111-8) intended to ease sanctions on family travel, travel for the marketing of agricultural and medical goods, and payment terms for U.S. agricultural exports to Cuba. Other initiatives that would ease sanctions are H.R. 188 and H.R. 1530 (overall embargo), H.R. 874/S. 428 and H.R. 1528 (travel), H.R. 332 (educational travel), and H.R. 1531 (U.S. agricultural and medical exports and travel). Another initiative, H.R. 1103, would modify a provision of law restricting the registration or enforcement of certain Cuban trademarks. This report tracks developments in U.S. policy toward Cuba and legislative initiatives in the 111th Congress.

Recent Developments

On March 11, 2009, President Obama signed into law the Omnibus Appropriations Act, 2009 (H.R. 1105, P.L. 111-8), which has three provisions intended to ease U.S. sanctions on Cuba for family travel (Section 621 of Division D), travel related to the marketing and sale of agricultural and medical exports (Section 620 of Division D), and payment terms for U.S. agricultural exports to Cuba (Section 622 of Division D). (For further background, see the legislative section in "Restrictions on Travel, Remittances, and Agricultural Exports" below.)

- As implemented by the Treasury Department's Office of Foreign Assets Control (OFAC), the provision easing family travel reinstates a general license as it existed prior to the Bush Administration's tightening of family travel restrictions in June 2004. Travel is now allowed once every 12 months to visit a close relative for an unlimited length of stay, and the limit for daily expenditure allowed by family travelers is the same as for other authorized travelers to Cuba (State Department maximum per diem rate for Havana, currently $179 day). The new general license also expands the definition of "close relative" to mean any individual related to the traveler by blood, marriage, or adoption, who is no more than three generations removed from that person.
- With regard to the provision related to the marketing and sale of agricultural and medical goods, OFAC maintained that it would issue regulations in the coming weeks, although a letter from Secretary of the Treasury Timothy Geithner published in the Congressional Record stated that the new regulations "would provide that the representatives of only a narrow class of businesses would be eligible, under a new general license, to travel to market and sell agricultural and medical goods." The Secretary also maintained that "any business using the general license would be required to provide both advance written notice outlining the purpose and scope of the planned travel and, upon return, a report outlining the activities conducted,

including the persons with whom they met, the expenses incurred, and business conducted in Cuba." (*Congressional Record*, March 10, 2009, p. S2933.)

- A third omnibus provision prohibits funds in the Act from being used to administer, implement, or enforce a February 25, 2005 amendment to the Cuban embargo regulations clarifying that the term "payment of cash in advance" means that payment is to be received prior to the shipment of the goods from the port at which they are loaded. The Trade Sanctions Reform and Export Enhancement Act of 2000 (TSRA) requires either the "payment of cash of advance" for such exports (or financing by third country financial institutions), but TSRA provides no definition of cash in advance. Prior to the February 2005 amendment to the Cuban embargo regulations, U.S. exporters could be paid for the goods before they were unloaded in Cuba. OFAC guidance on the implementation of the omnibus provision states that TSRA's statutory provisions remain in place that agricultural exports to Cuba be either paid for by "cash in advance" or financed using a third-country bank. In a letter published in the *Congressional Record*, however, Secretary of the Treasury Geithner provided additional guidance on the implementation of this provision, stating that "exporters will still be required to receive payment in advance of shipment." Given this interpretation, it appears that the omnibus provision will have little, if any, practical effect. (*Congressional Record*, March 10, 2009, p. S2933.)

On March 2, 2009, President Raúl Castro orchestrated a government shake-up ousting a dozen high-ranking officials, including Foreign Minister Felipe Pérez Roque and Cabinet Secretary Carlos Lage. (See "March 2009 Government Shake-Up" below.)

On February 27, 2009, the State Department issued its 2009 International Narcotics Control Strategy Report (INCSR), which maintained that U.S.-Cuban counter-narcotics cooperation continued in 2008. See the full INCSR report, available at: http://www.state. gov/p/inl/rls/nrcrpt/2009/index.htm.

On February 25, 2009, the State Department issued its 2008 human rights report on Cuba, which maintained that the Cuban government "continued to deny its citizens their basic human rights and committed numerous, serious abuses." See the report, available at: http://www.state.gov/g/drl/rls/hrrpt/2008/
wha/119155.htm.

On February 2, 2009, the independent Cuban Commission on Human Rights and National Reconciliation (CCDHRN) documented at least 205 political prisoners in Cuba, down from 234 in January 2008. The Commission maintains that the government has resorted to short-term arbitrary detentions to target suspected dissidents, with more than 1,500 such detentions in 2008. (See "Human Rights" below.)

On January 22, 2009, the Government Accountability Office (GAO) issued a report citing concerns with Radio and TV Martí's adherence to relevant laws and standards, and maintaining that its audience is small despite its broadcasts to Cuba through multiple methods. (U.S. GAO, "Broadcasting to Cuba, Action Are Needed to Improve Strategy and Operations, GAO-09-127. January 22, 2009, available at: http://www.gao.gov/products/GAO-09-127)

On January 22, 2009, Fidel Castro stated that he had reduced the number of his published essays ("Reflections of the Commander") so as not to interfere with the authority of party or government officials, and insisted that they should not feel bound by his occasional essays or even his state of health or death. Castro also maintained that he does not expect to be in such a position to meditate and write about events when Obama's first term has ended. ("Text of Fidel Castro's Online Essay," *Associated Press Newswires*, January 22, 2009)

On January 15, 2009, during her Senate Foreign Relations Committee confirmation hearing for Secretary of State, Senator Hillary Clinton reiterated President-elect Obama's pledge to lift restrictions on family travel and remittances as well as his position that it is not time to lift the embargo since it provides an important source of leverage for further change in Cuba. Clinton also responded to written questions for the record that the new Administration expected to undertake a review of U.S. policy toward Cuba. (See "Obama Administration Policy" below.)

On January 15, 2009, Cuba released Varela Project activist Reynaldo Labrada Peña from prison following the completion of his six-year sentence. Peña was one of the "group of 75" political prisoners who have been incarcerated since 2003. With Peña's release, 54 of the "group of 75" remain in prison. Overall, there are more than 200 political prisoners in Cuba. (See "Human Rights" below.)

On January 1, 2009, Cuba celebrated the 50th anniversary of the Cuban Revolution.

On December 17, 2008, Cuban President Raúl Castro offered to exchange some imprisoned Cuban political dissidents for five Cubans imprisoned in the United States since 2001 for espionage. The State Department rejected the offer, insisting that the jailed dissidents in Cuba should be released immediately without any conditions.

On December 10, 2008, the House Appropriations Committee reported its version of the FY2009 Financial Services and General Government Appropriations bill, H.R. 7323, with several provisions that would have eased restrictions on the sale of U.S. agricultural exports and family travel to Cuba. No final action was taken on the measure.

On November 26, 2008, Cuban President Raúl Castro stated in an interview that he would be willing to meet with President-elect Barack Obama, and suggested the U.S. Naval Base at Guantanamo Bay, Cuba, as a location.

On November 24, 2008, the Government Accountability Office (GAO) issued a second report examining USAID's Cuba democracy program. While GAO lauded the efforts taken by USAID to improve oversight and address problems with the program, it also maintained that USAID needed to hire more staff to implement monitoring activities, and that it needed to periodically assess the program's efforts regarding grantees' adherence to internal controls, procurement practices, and compliance with laws and regulations. (U.S. GAO, *Foreign Assistance: Continued Efforts Needed to Strengthen USAID's Oversight of U.S. Democracy Assistance for Cuba*, GAO09-165, November 2008.)

On November 8, 2008, Hurricane Paloma struck Cuba devastating the town of Santa Cruz del Sur. Raúl Castro stated that overall damages from the series of hurricanes and tropical storm since August amounted to some $10 billion.

Political Conditions

Raúl Castro officially became Cuba's President on February 24, 2008. On that day, Cuba's legislature selected him as President of the 31-member Council of State, a position that officially made him Cuba's head of government and state. Most observers expected this since he already had been heading the Cuban government on a provisional basis since July 2006 when his brother Fidel Castro, Cuba's long-ruling communist leader, stepped down as President because of poor health [1].

For many years, Raúl, as First Vice President of the Council of State and the Council of Ministers, had been the officially designated successor and was slated to become chief of state with Fidel's departure. Raúl also had served as Minister of the Revolutionary Armed Forces (FAR) since the beginning of the Cuban Revolution. When Fidel stepped down from power in late July 2006 because of poor health, he signed a proclamation that ceded political power to Raúl on a provisional basis, including the positions of First Secretary of the Cuban Communist Party (PCC), Commander in Chief of the Revolutionary Armed Forces (FAR), and President of the Council of State. Despite the change in government in February 2008, Fidel still holds the official title of First Secretary of the PCC.

While it was not a surprise to observers for Raúl to succeed his brother Fidel as head of government, the selection of José Ramón Machado Ventura as the Council of State's First Vice President was a surprise. A physician by training, Machado is 77 years old, and is part of the older generation of so-called *históricos* of the 1959 Cuban revolution. He has been described as a hard-line communist party ideologue, and reportedly has been a close friend and confident of Raul for many years [2] Machado's position is significant because it makes him the official successor to Raúl, according to the Cuban Constitution. Many observers had expected that Carlos Lage, one of five other Vice Presidents on the Council of State, would have been chosen as First Vice President. He was responsible for Cuba's economic reforms in the 1990s, and at 56 years of age, represents a younger generation of Cuban leaders. While not rising to First Vice President, Lage nevertheless retained his position as a Vice President on the Council of State, and will continue to serve as the Council's Secretary.

Several key military officers and confidants of Raúl also became members of the Council, increasing the role of the military in the government. General Julio Casas Regueiro, 72 years of age, who already was on the Council, became one of its five vice presidents. Most significantly, Casas, who had been first vice minister in the FAR, was selected by Raúl as the country's new Minister of the FAR, officially replacing Raúl in that position. Casas also is chairman of GAESA (Grupo de Administracion Empresarial, S.A.), the Cuban military's holding company for its extensive business operations. Two other military appointments to the Council were Gen. Alvaro López Miera, the army's chief of staff, and Gen. Leopoldo Cintra Frías, who commanded the Western army, one of Cuba's three military regions [3]

Since Fidel stepped down from power in 2006, Cuba's political succession from Fidel to Raúl Castro has been characterized by a remarkable degree of stability. Although initially there were not any significant economic changes under Raúl, there were signs that changes could be coming. In a July 2007 speech, Raúl maintained that structural changes were needed in the Cuban economy in order to increase efficiency and production. In his first speech as President in February 2008, Raúl promised to make the government smaller and more efficient, to review the potential revaluation of the Cuban peso, and to eliminate excessive bans and regulations that curb productivity [4] Since March 2008, the government has implemented a number of economic changes that from the outside might not seem significant, but are noteworthy policy changes for a government that has heretofore followed a centralized communist economic model. (See "Economic Changes Under Raúl" below.)

Source: Adapted by CRS from Magellan Geographix.

Figure 1. Map of Cuba.

While additional economic changes under Raúl Castro are likely, few expect there will be any change to the government's tight control over the political system, which is backed up by a strong security apparatus. Some observers point to the reduced number of political prisoners, from 283 at the end of 2006 to around 219 in mid-2008, as evidence of a lessening of repression, but dissidents maintain that the overall situation has not improved. Some observers contend that if the new government of Raúl Castro becomes more confident of ensuring social stability and does not feel threatened, it could move to soften its hard repression, but for now the government is continuing its harsh treatment of the opposition. The selection of José Ramón Machado as First Vice President also appears to be a clear indication that the Cuban government has no intention of easing tight control over the political system.

In early 2009, there were numerous press reports about a setback in Fidel Castro's health, but by late January 2009 new reports and photos of Castro with visiting Argentine President Cristina Fernández de Kirchner dispelled rumors that he was on his deathbed. Fidel did note in one of his published essays ("Reflections of the Commander") on January 22, 2009, that he had reduced the number of essays so as not to interfere with the authority of party or government officials, and insisted that they should not feel bound by his occasional writings or even his state of health or death. Castro also maintained that does not expect to be in such a position to meditate or write about events when Obama's first term has ended [5].

With the PCC's sixth congress, expected to be held at end of 2009 (the last was held in 1997), some analysts believe that additional policy changes will become evident, with a more invigorated role for the party. Some observers speculate that Fidel Castro could officially be replaced as the head of the party at that time, and it is likely that some of the PCC's 25-member Political Bureau (Politburo) will also be replaced.

Some analysts maintain that once Fidel is gone, hardliners in Cuba's political system will have a more difficult time holding back the advance of needed economic reforms [6] Some maintain that Raúl will be liberated to move more quickly to usher in needed economic reforms, although few observers believe that the Cuban leader will take any actions that could threaten the stability of the communist government. Some observers also do not expect Raúl Castro to serve another term as President, and believe that the government will pass to a younger generation after the next National Assembly election and selection of a new President in early 2013.

March 2009 Government Shake-up

In early March 2009, President Raúl Castro orchestrated a government shake-up that combined four ministries into two and ousted a dozen high-ranking officials, most notably including Foreign Minister Felipe Pérez Roque, Council of Ministers Secretary Carlos Lage, and Minister of Economy and Planning José Luis Rodriguez García. The streamlining combined the portfolios of food and fishing into one ministry and the foreign investment and trade portfolios into another ministry. Changes in the bureaucracy had been anticipated since February 2008 when Raúl Castro vowed to make the government smaller and more efficient, but the ouster of both Felipe Pérez Roque and Carlos Lage, who lost all their government and party positions, caught many observers by surprise. Pérez Roque was replaced by career diplomat Bruno Rodriguez Parrilla, who served for eight years (1995-2003) as Cuba's UN Ambassador and most recently served as vice foreign minister. Carlos Lage, who most significantly lost his position as a Vice President of the Council of State, was replaced by military General José Amado Guerra who had worked for Raúl Castro as secretary of the FAR.

What was unexpected about the simultaneous ouster of both Pérez Roque and Lage was that they represented different tendencies within Cuba's communist political system. Pérez Roque, a former private secretary to Fidel, was known as a hardliner, while Carlos Lage, who was responsible for Cuba's limited economic reforms in the 1990s, was viewed as a potential economic reformer. Some observers maintain that the ouster of both Pérez Roque and Lage was a move by Raúl to replace so-called Fidelistas with his own supporters. Fidel, however, wrote in one of his reflections in the Cuban press that both officials had been seduced by ambitions for power, and that a majority of the other officials who were replaced by Raúl had not originally been appointed by Fidel [7] Along these lines, a number of observers maintain that the ouster of Pérez Roque and Lage had more to do with removing potential contenders for power in a post-Castro Cuba. In a related ouster, former UN Ambassador and head of the Cuban Interests Section in Washington Fernando Remírez reportedly was ousted from his position as the head of the PCC's Foreign Relations Department. Well known in Washington, DC, Remírez was reported to be a close friend of Carlos Lage [8].

What appears clear from the recent government shake-up is that Raúl Castro has begun to put his mark on the Cuban government bureaucracy. Some observers contend that Raúl is moving forward with his pledge to make the government more efficient. According to this view, ideology did not play a role in the appointments, and several of those brought in as ministers were relatively unknown technocrats [9].

The new appointments also continued the trend toward bringing more military officials into the government. In addition to Gen. José Amado Guerra becoming Secretary of the Council of Ministers, another military official, General Salvador Pardo Cruz, became Minister of the Steelmaking Industry. Three other military officials already head the ministries of the FAR, Interior, and Agriculture.

Background to the Succession

Until Fidel stepped down in 2006, he had ruled the island nation since the 1959 Cuban Revolution, which ousted the corrupt government of Fulgencio Batista. In April 1961, Castro stated that the Cuban Revolution was socialist, and in December 1961, he proclaimed himself to be a Marxist-Leninist. From 1959 until 1976, Castro ruled by decree. A Constitution was enacted in 1976 setting forth the PCC as the leading force in state and society, with power centered in a Political Bureau headed by Fidel Castro. In October 1997, the Cuban Communist Party held its 5th Congress (the prior one was held in 1991) in which the party reaffirmed its commitment to a single party state and reelected Fidel and Raúl Castro as the party's first and second secretaries.

Cuba's Constitution also outlines national, provincial, and local governmental structures. Legislative authority is vested in a National Assembly of People's Power that meets twice annually for brief periods. When the Assembly is not in session, a Council of State, elected by the Assembly, acts on its behalf. According to Cuba's Constitution, the President of the Council of State is the country's head of state and government. Executive power in Cuba is vested in a Council of Ministers, also headed by the country's head of state and government, i.e. the President of the Council of State. From the promulgation of the 1976 Constitution until February 24, 2008, Fidel served as served as head of state and government through his position as President of the Council of State.

Although National Assembly members were directly elected for the first time in February 1993, only a single slate of candidates was offered. Direct elections for the National Assembly were again held in January 1998 and January 2003, but voters again were not offered a choice of candidates. In contrast, municipal elections at the local level are competitive, with from two to eight candidates. To be elected, the candidate must receive more than half of the votes cast. As a result, runoff elections between the two top candidates are common.

National Assembly elections were held on January 20, 2008 (along with elections for 1,201 delegates to 14 provincial assemblies), and Fidel Castro was once again among the candidates elected to the now 614-member legislative body. As in the past, voters were only offered a single slate of candidates.

On February 24, 2008, the new Assembly was scheduled to select from among its ranks the members of the Council of State and its President. Many observers speculated that because of his poor health, Fidel would choose not be re-elected as President of the Council of State, which would officially confirm his departure from heading the Cuban government. Statements from Castro himself in December 2007 hinted at his potential retirement. That proved true on February 19, 2008, when Fidel announced that he would not accept the position as President of the Council of State, essentially confirming his departure as titular head of the Cuban government.

Before Fidel stepped down from power in July 2006 for health reasons, observers discerned several potential scenarios for Cuba's future after Fidel. These fit into three broad categories: the continuation of a communist government; a military government; or some type of democratic government, whether it be a democratic transition or fully democratic government. According to most observers, the most likely scenario, at least in the short term, was the continuation of the regime under the leadership of Raúl. This was likely for a variety of reasons, but especially because of Raúl's designation by Fidel as successor in the party and his position as leader of the FAR. The FAR has been in control of the government's security apparatus since 1989 and has played an increasing role in Cuba's economy through the ownership of numerous business enterprises. The scenario of a military-led government was viewed by some observers as a possibility only if a successor communist government failed because of divisiveness among leaders or political instability. For many observers, the least likely scenario upon Fidel's death or departure was a democratic transition government. With a strong totalitarian security apparatus, the Castro government successfully impeded the development of independent civil society, with only a small and tightly regulated private sector, no independent labor movement, and no unified political opposition [10].

Human Rights

Overview

Cuba has a poor record on human rights, with the government sharply restricting freedoms of expression, association, assembly, movement, and other basic rights. It has cracked down on dissent, arrested human rights activists and independent journalists, and staged demonstrations against critics. Although some anticipated a relaxation of the government's oppressive tactics in the aftermath of the January 1998 visit of Pope John Paul II, government attacks against human rights activists and other dissidents have continued since that time. The Inter-American Commission on Human Rights maintained in its 2007 annual human rights report that the Cuban government's "restrictions on political rights, freedom of expression, and dissemination of ideas have created, over a period of decades, a situation of permanent and systematic violations of the fundamental rights of Cuban citizens." [11]

According to the State Department's human rights report for 2008, issued in February 2009, the Cuban government continued to commit numerous serious abuses during the year. Among the human rights problems cited in the State Department report were arbitrary arrest and detention of human rights advocates and members of independent professional organizations; harassment, beatings, and threats against political opponents by government-recruited mobs, police, and state security officials; beatings and abuse of detainees and prisoners; denial of fair trial; harsh and life-threatening prison conditions, including denial of medical care; and interference with privacy, including pervasive monitoring of private communications. As noted in the report, the government tightly controlled Internet access, with citizens only accessing it through government-approved institutions or through a few Internet facilities offered by foreign diplomatic offices. The government reviewed and censored e-mail.(See the full State Department human rights report on Cuba, available at: http://www.state.gov/g/drl/rls/hrrpt/2008/wha/119155.htm.)

In March 2003, the government conducted a severe crackdown and imprisoned 75 democracy activists, including independent journalists and librarians and leaders of independent labor unions and opposition parties. At present, 54 of the "group of 75" political prisoners remain incarcerated. On January 15, 2009, one of the detainees, Reynaldo Labrada Pena who had worked with the Varela Project, was released from prison after completing his sentence. In February 2008, Cuba released four political prisoners—union activist Pedro Pablo Alvarez Ramos, human rights activist Omar Pernet Hernández, and journalists Jose Gabriel Ramón Castillo and Alejandro González Raga—but sent them into forced exile to Spain. Prior to that, Hector Palacios was released for health reasons in December 2006.

In February 2009, the independent Cuban Commission on Human Rights and National Reconciliation (CCDHRN) documented at least 205 political prisoners, down from 234 in January 2008. The number also reflected the continued decline from previous years when the Commission estimated at least 283 prisoners at the beginning of 2007 and 333 at the beginning of 2006. The Commission maintains, however, that the government has resorted to short-term arbitrary detentions to target suspected dissidents, with more than 1,500 such detentions in 2008. [12]

Despite the reduction in the number of prisoners, human rights activists maintain that the overall situation has not improved. Cuban human rights activist Elizardo Sánchez, the head of the CCDHRN, asserts that the government is still repressing dissidents, with threats, police searches of people's homes, interrogations, and short detentions. Sánchez asserts that the police state is still in force in Cuba, reflected in almost every aspect of national life [13].

In late February 2008, Cuba signed two U.N. human rights treaties: the International Covenant on Civil and Political Rights and the International Covenant on Economic, Social, and Cultural Rights. Some considered this a positive step, but others stressed that it remains to be seen whether the Cuban government will take action to guarantee civil and political freedoms [14]. One significant step taken by the government in late March 2008 was the lifting of a ban on Cubans staying at tourist hotels. Although few Cubans will be able to afford the cost of staying in such hotels, the move is symbolically significant and ends the practices of what critics had dubbed "tourism apartheid." On the other hand, prior to the 60th anniversary of the signing of the Universal Declaration of Human Rights on December 10, 2008, up to a dozen Cuban human rights activists reportedly were detained in order to prevent them from attending planned events [15].

In April 2003, a human rights group known as the Ladies in White (Damas de Blanco) was formed by the wives, mothers, daughters, sisters, and aunts of the members of the "group of 75" dissidents arrested a month earlier in Cuba's human rights crackdown [16] The group conducts peaceful protests calling for the unconditional release of political prisoners. Dressed in white, its members attend Mass each Sunday at St. Rita's church in Havana and then walk silently through the streets to a nearby park. On April 21, 2008, ten members of the Ladies in White were physically removed from a park near the Plaza of the Revolution in Havana when they demanded the release of their husbands and the other members of the "group of 75" still imprisoned.

Although Cuban authorities continue to stifle dissent and repress freedoms, pro-democracy and human rights activists continue to call attention to Cuba's poor human rights record, and many have been recognized by the international community for their efforts. In October 2005, The Ladies in White group noted above received the Sakharov Prize for Freedom of Thought from the European Parliament.

In December 2006, independent Cuban journalist Guillermo Fariñas Hernández received the 2006 Cyber Dissident award from the Paris-based Reporters Without Borders. Fariñas went on a seven-month hunger strike in 2006, demanding broader Internet access for Cubans.

In November 2007, President Bush awarded Cuban dissident Dr. Oscar Elias Biscet with the Presidential Medal of Freedom. Biscet, who has spent most of the last eight years in jail, was sentenced in 2003 to 25 years in prison. Legislation was introduced in the 110th Congress in March 2008—H.R. 5627 (Diaz-Balart, Lincoln) and S. 2777 (Martinez)—to award the congressional gold medal to Biscet, although no action was taken on the measures.

Since late 2007, Cuban Internet blogger Yoaní Sánchez has received considerable international attention for her website, Generación Y, that includes commentary critical of the Cuban government. In May 2008, Sánchez was awarded Spain's Ortega y Gasset award for digital journalism, but the Cuban government did not provide her with an exit permit to accept the award. (Sánchez's website is available at http://www.desdecuba.com /generaciony/).

In late 2008, two international press rights groups gave awards to two Cuban independent journalists who have been imprisoned since 2003. In November 2008, the New York-based Committee for the Protection of Journalists selected Héctor Maseda Gutiérrez as a recipient of its international press freedom award, while in early December 2008, Reporters Without Borders awarded Ricardo González Alfonso its journalist of the year award. While in prison, Gutiérrez wrote a memoir that he managed to smuggle out of prison one page at a time. Before his imprisonment, González had started an association to improve independent journalism. As of December 2008, 23 journalists were imprisoned in Cuba [17].

On December 17, 2008, Cuban President Raúl Castro offered to exchange some imprisoned Cuban political dissidents for five Cubans imprisoned in the United States since 2001 for espionage. The five Cubans are serving sentences ranging from 15 years to life. Cuba's National Assembly had dubbed the so-called Cuban Five as "Heroes of the Republic," and the Cuban government has called for their return to Cuba. In response to Raúl Castro's offer, the State Department rejected the offer, insisting that the jailed dissidents in Cuba should be released immediately without any conditions [18].

Varela Project

Named for the 19th century priest, Felix Varela, who advocated independence from Spain and the abolition of slavery, the Varela Project has collected thousands of signatures supporting a national plebiscite for political reform in accordance with a provision of the Cuban Constitution. The referendum, if granted, would call for respect for human rights, an amnesty for political prisoners, private enterprise, and changes to the country's electoral law that would result in free and fair elections. The initiative is organized by Oswaldo Payá, who heads the Christian Liberation Movement [19].

In May 2002, organizers of the Varela Project submitted 11,020 signatures to the National Assembly calling for a national referendum. This was more than the 10,000 required under Article 88 of the Cuban Constitution. Former President Jimmy Carter noted the significance of the Varela Project in his May 14, 2002 address in Havana that was broadcast in Cuba. Carter noted that "when Cubans exercise this freedom to change laws peacefully by a direct vote, the world will see that Cubans, and not foreigners, will decide the future of this country." [20] In response to the Varela Project, the Cuban government orchestrated its own referendum in late June 2002 that ultimately led to the National Assembly amending the Constitution to declare Cuba's socialist system irrevocable. The Varela Project has persevered despite the 2003 human rights crackdown, which included the arrest of 21 Project activists. In October 2003, Oswaldo Payá delivered more than 14,000 signatures to Cuba's National Assembly, again requesting a referendum on democratic reforms. More recently, in October 2008, Varela Project activists launched a third campaign to collect signatures.

Economic Conditions

After the collapse of the former Soviet Union, Russian financial assistance to Cuba practically ended, and as a result, Cuba experienced severe economic deterioration from 1989-1993, with estimates of economic decline ranging from 35-50%. Since then, however, there has been considerable improvement. From 1994-2000, as Cuba moved forward with some limited market-oriented economic reforms, economic growth averaged 3.7% annually.

Economic growth was strong in the 2005-2007 period, registering an impressive 11.2% in 2005 (despite widespread damage caused by Hurricanes Dennis and Wilma), 12.1% in 2006, and 7.3% in 2007 [21] The economy benefitted from the growth of the tourism, nickel, and oil sectors, and support from Venezuela and China in terms of investment commitments and credit lines. Cuba benefits from a preferential oil agreement with Venezuela, which provides Cuba with more than 90,000 barrels of oil a day. Some observers maintain that Venezuela's oil subsidies amounted to more than $3 billion a year in 2006 [22] Venezuela also helped Cuba upgrade an oil refinery in Cienfuegos, which was inaugurated in 2007.

In 2008, economic growth slowed to an estimated 4.3%. This was prompted by several problems, including the declining price of nickel, which accounts for a major share of Cuba's exports, the rising cost of food imports, and the devastation wrought by Hurricanes Gustav and Ike, particularly in the agricultural sectors. The current global financial crisis is likely to have an effect on the Cuban economy because of lower world prices for nickel and a reduction in tourism from Canada and Europe. Cuba's reliance on Venezuela for oil could also be threatened as Venezuela faces a difficult domestic fiscal situation due to the rapid decline in the price of oil. The forecast for 2009 is for a slower economic growth rate of 3.9%. [23].

Over the years, Cuba has expressed pride for the nation's accomplishments in health and education. According to the U.N. Development Program's 2007/2008 *Human Development Report,* life expectancy in Cuba in 2005 was 77.7 years, adult literacy was estimated at almost 100%, and the infant mortality rate was 6 per 1,000 live births, the lowest rate in Latin America. For 2006 and 2007, Cuba has boasted an infant mortality rate of 5.3 [24].

When Cuba's economic slide began in 1989, the government showed little willingness to adopt any significant market-oriented economic reforms, but in 1993, faced with unprecedented economic decline, Cuba began to change policy direction. Beginning in 1993, Cubans were allowed to own and use U.S. dollars and to shop at dollar-only shops previously limited to tourists and diplomats. Self-employment was authorized in more than 100 occupations in 1993, most in the service sector, and by 1996 that figure had grown to more than 150 occupations.

Also in 1993, the government divided large state farms into smaller, more autonomous, agricultural cooperatives (Basic Units of Cooperative Production, UBPCs). It opened agricultural markets in 1994, where farmers could sell part of their produce on the open market, and it also permitted artisan markets for the sale of handicrafts. In 1995, the government allowed private food catering, including home restaurants (*paladares)*, in effect legalizing activities that were already taking place), and approved a new foreign investment law that allows fully owned investments by foreigners in all sectors of the economy with the exception of defense, health, and education.

In 1996, it authorized the establishment of free trade zones with tariff reductions typical of such zones. In 1997, the government enacted legislation to reform the banking system and established a new Central Bank (BCC) to operate as an autonomous and independent entity.

After Cuba began to recover from its economic decline, the government began to backtrack on some of its reform efforts. Regulations and new taxes made it extremely difficult for many of the nation's self-employed. Some home restaurants were forced to close because of the new regulations. In 2004, the Cuban government limited the use of dollars by state companies for any services or products not considered part of their core business. Some analysts viewed the measure as an effort to turn back the clock on economic reform measures [25].

Also in 2004, Fidel Castro announced that U.S. dollars no longer would be used in entities that at the time accepted dollars (such as stores, restaurants, and hotels). Instead, dollars had to be exchanged for "convertible pesos," with a 10% surcharge for the exchange. Dollar bank accounts are still allowed, but Cubans are not able to deposit new dollars into the accounts.

Beginning in April 2005, convertible pesos were no longer on par with the U.S. dollar, but instead were linked to a basket of foreign currencies. This reduces the value of dollar remittances sent to Cuba and provides more hard currency to the Cuban government [26].

Economic Changes under Raul

When Raúl Castro assumed provisional power in July 2006, there was some expectation that the government would be more open to economic policy changes, and a debate about potential economic reforms re-emerged in Cuba. On July 26, 2007, in a speech commemorating Cuba's revolutionary anniversary, Raúl Castro acknowledged that Cuban salaries were insufficient to satisfy needs, and maintained that structural changes were necessary in order to increase efficiency and production. He also maintained that the government was considering increasing foreign investment in the country. Some observers maintain that the speech was a forecast for economic reforms under Raúl, while others stress that only small marginal changes occurred in Raúl's first year in power [27].

In the aftermath of Raúl's July 2007 speech, Cuban public expectations for economic reform increased. Thousands of officially sanctioned meetings were held in workplaces and local PCC branches around the country where Cubans were encouraged to air their views and discuss the future direction of the country. Complaints focused on low salaries and housing and transportation problems, and some participants advocated legalization of more private businesses [28]. Raised expectations for economic change in Cuba increased the chance that the government actually would adopt some policy changes. Doing nothing would run the risk of increased public frustration and a potential for social unrest. Increased public frustration was evident in a clandestine video, widely circulated on the Internet in early February 2008, of a meeting between Ricardo Alarcón, the head of Cuba's legislature, and university students in which a student was questioning why Cuban wages are so low and why Cubans are prohibited from visiting tourist hotels (a policy subsequently changed in late March 2008) or traveling abroad. The video demonstrated the disillusionment of many Cuban youth with the poor economic situation and repressive environment in Cuba.

Since Raúl Castro officially assumed the presidency in 2008, his government has announced a series of economic changes. In his first speech as President in February 2008, Raúl promised to make the government smaller and more efficient, to review the potential revaluation of the Cuban peso, and to eliminate excessive bans and regulations that curb productivity [29]. In mid-March, the government announced that restrictions on the sales of consumer products such as computers, microwaves, and DVD and video players would be lifted. In late March, it announced that it would lift restrictions on the use of cell phones. This officially occurred in mid-April.

One of Cuba's major reform efforts under Raúl Castro in 2008 was focused on the agriculture sector, a vital issue because Cuba reportedly imports some 80% of its food needs and is paying an increasing amount for such imports due to rising food prices. In an effort to boost food production, the government began giving farmers more discretion over how to use their land and what supplies to buy. Decision-making on agriculture reportedly has shifted from the national government to the local municipal level, with government bureaucracy cut significantly [30].

In April 2008, the government announced that it would begin revamping the state's wage system by removing the limit that a state worker can earn. This is an effort to boost productivity and to deal with one of Cuba's major economic problems: how to raise wages to a level where basic human needs can be satisfied. The problem of low wages in Cuba is closely related to another major economic problem: how to unify the two official currencies circulating in the country—the Cuban convertible peso (CUC) and the Cuban peso, which traded at about 24 to 1 CUC in 2008. Most people are paid in Cuban pesos, and the minimum monthly wage in Cuba is about 225 pesos (about $9 U.S. dollars [31]), but for increasing amounts of consumer goods, convertible pesos are used. Cubans with access to foreign remittances or who work in jobs that give them access to convertible pesos are far better off than those Cubans who do not have such access.

Looking ahead, several factors could restrain the magnitude of economic policy change in Cuba. A number of observers believe that as long as Fidel Castro is around, it will be difficult for the government to move forward with any major initiatives that are viewed as deviating from Fidel's orthodox policies. Other observers point to the significant oil subsidies and investment that Cuba now receives from Venezuela that have helped spur Cuba's high economic growth levels over the past several years and maintain that such support lessens the government's impetus for economic reforms. Another factor that bodes against rapid economic policy reform is the fear that it could spur momentum for political change. Given that one of the highest priorities for Cuba's government has been maintaining social and political stability, any economic policy changes are likely to be smaller changes introduced over time that do not threaten the state's control.

There was some expectation that Raúl Castro would announce additional economic reforms in his July 26, 2008 speech on Cuba's revolutionary anniversary, but there were no such announcements. Instead, Castro acknowledged the "large number of problems that still need to be resolved, the majority of which directly affect the population" [32] Nevertheless, in an address earlier in the month to the National Assembly, Raúl pointed to the goal of increasing salaries based on job performance. According to Castro: "Socialism means social justice and equality, but equality of rights and opportunities, not salaries. Equality does not mean egalitarianism." [33]

CUBA'S FOREIGN POLICY

During the Cold War, Cuba had extensive relations with and support from the Soviet Union, with billions in annual subsidies to sustain the Cuban economy that helped fund an activist foreign policy and support for guerrilla movements and revolutionary governments abroad in Latin America and Africa. With the dissolution of the Soviet Union, an end to the Cold War, and the loss of Soviet financial support, Cuba was forced to abandon its revolutionary exploits abroad. As its economy reeled from the loss of Soviet support, Cuba was forced to open up its economy and economic relations with countries worldwide, and developed significant economic linkages with Canada, Spain, other European countries, and China. In recent years, Venezuela—under populist President Hugo Chávez—has become a significant source of support for subsidized oil imports and investment. Relations with Russia have also intensified recently, with the visit of Russian President Dmitry Medvedev to Havana in November, the visit of several Russian warships to Cuba in December 2008, and Raúl Castro's visit to Moscow in late January 2009. Chinese President Hu Jintao also visited Cuba in November signing a dozen agreements.

In Latin America, Cuba has diplomatic relations with all nations with the exception of El Salvador, and has increasingly become more engaged in Latin America beyond the already close relations with Venezuela. Brazilian President Luiz Inácio Lula da Silva visited Cuba twice in 2008, and Cuba seems especially interested in expanding relations with Brazil. Cuba became a full member of the 23 member Rio Group of Latin American and Caribbean nations in November 2008; some observers see the group, which excludes the United States, as an alternative to the Organization of American States (OAS). (Cuba's participation in the OAS has been suspended since 1962) Raúl Castro made his first foreign trip as President in December 2008, when he traveled to Venezuela, and then to Bahia, Brazil, where he attended the Latin American and Caribbean Integration and Development Summit, a regional initiative of President Lula [34].

Cuba is an active participant in international forums, including the United Nations and the controversial United Nations Human Rights Council. Cuba hosted the 14th summit of the Nonaligned Movement (NAM) in 2006, and holds the Secretary Generalship of the NAM until its next summit in 2009. It is a member of the Bolivarian Alternative for the Americas, (ALBA), a Venezuelan-led integration and cooperation scheme founded as an alternative to U.S. efforts to negotiate a region-wide Free Trade Area of the Americas (FTAA).

U.S. POLICY TOWARD CUBA

Policy Overview

In the early 1960s, U.S.-Cuban relations deteriorated sharply when Fidel Castro began to build a repressive communist dictatorship and moved his country toward close relations with the Soviet Union. The often tense and hostile nature of the U.S.-Cuban relationship is illustrated by such events and actions as U.S. covert operations to overthrow the Castro government culminating in the ill-fated April 1961 Bay of Pigs invasion; the October 1962 missile crisis in which the United States confronted the Soviet Union over its attempt to place offensive nuclear missiles in Cuba; Cuban support for guerrilla insurgencies and military support for revolutionary governments in Africa and the Western Hemisphere; the 1980 exodus of around 125,000 Cubans to the United States in the so-called Mariel boatlift; the 1994 exodus of more than 30,000 Cubans who were interdicted and housed at U.S. facilities in Guantanamo and Panama; and the February 1996 shootdown by Cuban fighter jets of two U.S. civilian planes operated by the Cuban American group, Brothers to the Rescue, which resulted in the death of four U.S. crew members.

Since the early 1960s, U.S. policy toward Cuba has consisted largely of isolating the island nation through comprehensive economic sanctions, including an embargo on trade and financial transactions. The Cuban Assets Control Regulations (CACR), first issued by the Treasury Department in July 1963, lay out a comprehensive set of economic sanctions against Cuba, including a prohibition on most financial transactions with Cuba and a freeze of Cuban government assets in the United States. The CACR have been amended many times over the years to reflect changes in policy, and remain in force today.

These sanctions were made stronger with the Cuban Democracy Act (CDA) of 1992 (P.L. 102484, Title XVII) and with the Cuban Liberty and Democratic Solidarity Act of 1996 (P.L. 104-114), the latter often referred to as the Helms/Burton legislation. The CDA prohibits U.S. subsidiaries from engaging in trade with Cuba and prohibits entry into the United States for any sea-borne vessel to load or unload freight if it has been involved in trade with Cuba within the previous 180 days. The Cuban Liberty and Democratic Solidarity Act, enacted in the aftermath of Cuba's shooting down of two U.S. civilian planes in February 1996, combines a variety of measures to increase pressure on Cuba and provides for a plan to assist Cuba once it begins the transition to democracy. Most significantly, the law codified the Cuban embargo, including all restrictions under the CACR. This provision is especially noteworthy because of its long-lasting effect on U.S. policy options toward Cuba. The executive branch is circumscribed in lifting or substantially loosening the economic embargo without congressional concurrence until certain democratic conditions are met, although the CACR includes licensing authority that provides the executive branch with some administrative flexibility (e.g. travel-related restrictions in the CACR have been eased and tightened on numerous occasions). Another significant sanction in the law is a provision in Title III that holds any person or government that traffics in U.S. property confiscated by the Cuban government liable for monetary damages in U.S. federal court. Acting under provisions of the law, however, both President Clinton and President Bush have suspended the implementation of Title III at six-month intervals.

In addition to sanctions, another component of U.S. policy, a so-called second track, consists of support measures for the Cuban people. This includes U.S. private humanitarian donations, medical exports to Cuba under the terms of the Cuban Democracy Act of 1992, U.S. government support for democracy-building efforts, and U.S.-sponsored radio and television broadcasting to Cuba. In addition, the 106th Congress approved the Trade Sanctions Reform and Export Enhancement Act of 2000 (P.L. 106-387, Title IX) that allows for agricultural exports to Cuba, albeit with restrictions on financing such exports. This led to the United States becoming Cuba's largest supplier of food and agricultural products since 2002.

Debate on the Directions of U.S. Policy

Over the years, although U.S. policymakers have agreed on the overall objectives of U.S. policy toward Cuba—to help bring democracy and respect for human rights to the island—there have been several schools of thought about how to achieve those objectives. Some have advocated a policy of keeping maximum pressure on the Cuban government until reforms are enacted, while continuing efforts to support the Cuban people. Others argue for an approach, sometimes referred to as constructive engagement, that would lift some U.S. sanctions that they believe are hurting the Cuban people, and move toward engaging Cuba in dialogue. Still others call for a swift normalization of U.S.-Cuban relations by lifting the U.S. embargo. Legislative initiatives introduced over the past decade have reflected these three policy approaches.

Dating back to 2000, there have been significant efforts in Congress to ease U.S. sanctions, with, one or both houses at times approving amendments to appropriations measures that would have eased U.S. sanctions on Cuba. Ultimately, these provisions were stripped out of final enacted measures, in part because of presidential veto threats.

In light of Fidel Castro's departure as head of government, many observers have called for a reexamination of U.S. policy toward Cuba. In this new context, there are two broad policy approaches to contend with political change in Cuba: a status-quo approach that would maintain the U.S. dual-track policy of isolating the Cuban government while providing support to the Cuban people; and an approach aimed at influencing the attitudes of the Cuban government and Cuban society through increased contact and engagement.

In general, those who advocate easing U.S. sanctions on Cuba make several policy arguments. They assert that if the United States moderated its policy toward Cuba—through increased travel, trade, and diplomatic dialogue—then the seeds of reform would be planted, which would stimulate and strengthen forces for peaceful change on the island. They stress the importance to the United States of avoiding violent change in Cuba, with the prospect of a mass exodus to the United States and the potential of involving the United States in a civil war scenario. They argue that since the demise of Cuba's communist government does not appear imminent, even without Fidel Castro at the helm, the United States should espouse a more pragmatic approach in trying to induce change in Cuba. Supporters of changing policy also point to broad international support for lifting the U.S. embargo, to the missed opportunities for U.S. businesses because of the unilateral nature of the embargo, and to the increased suffering of the Cuban people because of the embargo. Proponents of change also argue that the United States should be consistent in its policies with the world's few remaining communist governments, including China and Vietnam, and also maintain that moderating policy will help advance human rights.

On the other side, opponents of changing U.S. policy maintain that the current two-track policy of isolating Cuba, but reaching out to the Cuban people through measures of support, is the best means for realizing political change in Cuba. They point out that the Cuban Liberty and Democratic Solidarity Act of 1996 sets forth the steps that Cuba needs to take in order for the United States to normalize relations. They argue that softening U.S. policy at this time without concrete Cuban reforms would boost the Castro government, politically and economically, and facilitate the survival of the communist regime. Opponents of softening U.S. policy argue that the United States should stay the course in its commitment to democracy and human rights in Cuba, and that sustained sanctions can work. Opponents of loosening U.S. sanctions further argue that Cuba's failed economic policies, not the U.S. embargo, are the causes of Cuba's difficult living conditions.

Clinton's Administration's Easing of Sanctions

The Clinton Administration made several changes to U.S. policy in the aftermath of Pope John Paul II's 1998 visit to Cuba, which were intended to bolster U.S. support for the Cuban people. These included the resumption of direct flights to Cuba (which had been curtailed after the February 1996 shootdown of two U.S. civilian planes), the resumption of cash remittances by U.S. nationals and residents for the support of close relatives in Cuba (which had been curtailed in August 1994 in response to the migration crisis with Cuba), and the streamlining of procedures for the commercial sale of medicines and medical supplies and equipment to Cuba.

In January 1999, President Clinton announced several additional measures to support the Cuban people. These included a broadening of cash remittances to Cuba, so that all U.S. residents (not just those with close relatives in Cuba) could send remittances to Cuba; an expansion of direct passenger charter flights to Cuba from additional U.S. cities other than Miami (direct flights later in the year began from Los Angeles and New York); and an expansion of people-to-people contact by loosening restrictions on travel to Cuba for certain categories of travelers, such as professional researchers and those involved in a wide range of educational, religious, and sports activities.

Bush Administration Policy

The Bush Administration essentially continued the two-track U.S. policy of isolating Cuba through economic sanctions while supporting the Cuban people through a variety of measures. However, within this policy framework, the Administration emphasized stronger enforcement of economic sanctions and further tightened restrictions on travel, remittances, and humanitarian gift parcels to Cuba. There was considerable reaction to the Administration's June 2004 tightening of restrictions for family visits and other categories of travel, and to the Administration's February 2005 tightening of restrictions on payment terms for U.S. agricultural exports to Cuba. Nevertheless, the Bush Administration did not completely eliminate the easing of sanctions that occurred under the Clinton Administration.

For example, Americans may travel to Cuba to participate in educational activities, but these now need to be part of a structured academic program. Direct flights to Cuba also still run from Miami and New York, although flights from Los Angeles were curtailed for economic reasons in the aftermath of the tightening of travel restrictions in 2004 that reduced the number of Americans visiting Cuba.

Commission for Assistance to a Free Cuba

In October 2003, President Bush called for the establishment of an interagency Commission for Assistance to a Free Cuba, a Cabinet-level commission chaired by then - Secretary of State Colin Powell. The Commission, which had its first meeting in December 2003, was tasked with the objectives of 1) identifying additional means to help the Cuban people bring about an expeditious end to Cuba's dictatorship and 2) considering the requirements for U.S. assistance to a post-dictatorship Cuba [35].

In May 2004, President Bush endorsed the recommendations of the Commission's first report, which made recommendations for immediate measures to "hasten the end of Cuba's dictatorship" as well as longer-term recommendations to help plan for Cuba's transition from communism to democracy in various areas. The President directed that up to $59 million be committed to implement key recommendations of the Commission, including support for democracy-building activities and for airborne broadcasts of Radio and TV Marti to Cuba. The report's most significant recommendations included a number of measures to tighten economic sanctions on family visits and other categories of travel and on private humanitarian assistance in the form of remittances and gift parcels. Subsequent regulations issued by the Treasury and Commerce Departments in June 2004 implemented these new sanctions. (The full Commission report is on the State Department website at http://www.state.gov/p/wha/rt/cuba/commission/2004/.) In February 2005, the Administration continued to tighten U.S. economic sanctions against Cuba by further restricting the process of how U.S. agricultural exporters may be paid for their cash sales, a move opposed by many U.S. agricultural exporters (For more, see "Agricultural Exports and Sanctions" below).

In July 2005, Secretary of State Condoleezza Rice appointed Caleb McCarry as the State Department's new Cuba Transition Coordinator to direct U.S. government "actions in support of a free Cuba." Secretary Rice reconvened the Commission for Assistance to a Free Cuba in December 2005 to identify additional measures to help Cubans hasten the transition to democracy and to develop a plan to help the Cuban people move toward free and fair elections.

In July 2006, the Commission issued its second report, making recommendations to hasten political change in Cuba toward a democratic transition (The full report is available at http://www.cafc.gov/rpt/).

In the report, the Commission called for the United States to provide $80 million over two years for the following: to support Cuban civil society ($31 million); to fund education programs and exchanges, including university training in Cuba provided by third countries and scholarships for economically disadvantaged students from Cuba at U.S. and third country universities ($10 million); to fund additional efforts to break the Cuban government's information blockade and expand access to independent information, including through the Internet ($24 million); and to support international efforts at strengthening civil society and transition planning ($15 million). According to the Cuba Transition Coordinator, this assistance would be additional funding beyond what the Administration is already currently budgeting for these programs [36] Thereafter, the Commission recommended funding of not less than $20 million annually for Cuba democracy programs "until the dictatorship ceases to exist." This would roughly double the amount currently spent on Cuba democracy programs.

The report also set forth detailed plans of how the U.S. government, along with the international community and the Cuban community abroad, could provide assistance to a Cuban transition government to help it respond to critical humanitarian and social needs, to conduct free and fair elections, and to move toward a market-based economy. The report also outlined a series of preparatory steps in the areas of government organization, electoral preparation, and anticipating humanitarian and social needs that the U.S. government could take now, before Cuba's transition begins, so that it would be well prepared in the event that assistance was requested by the new Cuban government.

The Commission's second report received a mixed response from Cuba's dissident community. Although some dissidents, like former political prisoner Vladimiro Roca, maintain that they would welcome any U.S. assistance that helps support the Cuban dissident movement, others expressed concerns about the report. Dissident economist and former political prisoner Oscar Espinosa Chepe stressed that Cubans have to be the ones to solve their own problems. According to Chepe, "We are thankful for the solidarity we have received from North America, Europe, and elsewhere, but we request that they do not meddle in our country." [37] Miriam Leiva, a founding member of the Ladies in White, a human rights organization, expressed concern that the report could serve as a rationale for the government to imprison dissidents [38] Leiva also faulted the Commission's report for presuming what a Cuban transition must be before U.S. recognition or assistance can be provided. According to Leiva, "Only we Cubans, of our own volition ... can decide issues of such singular importance. Cubans on the island have sufficient intellectual ability to tackle a difficult, peaceful transition and reconcile with other Cubans here and abroad" [39].

U.S. Reaction to Cuba's Political Succession

In response to Fidel Castro's announcement that he was temporarily ceding power to his brother Raúl, President Bush issued a statement on August 3, 2006, that "the United States is absolutely committed to supporting the Cuban people's aspiration for democracy and freedom." The President urged "the Cuban people to work for democratic change" and pledged U.S. support to the Cuban people in their effort to build a transitional government in Cuba. U.S. officials, a the time, indicated that there were no plans for the United States to "reach out" to the new leader. Secretary of State Condoleezza Rice reiterated U.S. support for the Cuban people in an August 4, 2006, statement broadcast on Radio and TV Marti. According to Secretary Rice, "All Cubans who desire peaceful democratic change can count on the support of the United States" [40].

Although there was some U.S. concern that political change in Cuba could prompt a migration crisis, there was no unusual traffic after Castro ceded provisional power to his brother. The U.S. Coast Guard had plans to respond to such a migration crisis, with support from the Navy if needed. In her August 4, 2006, message to the Cuban people, Secretary of State Rice encouraged "the Cuban people to work at home for positive change." Department of Homeland Security officials also announced several measures to discourage Cubans from risking their lives on the open seas. U.S. officials also discouraged those in the Cuban American community wanting to travel by boat to Cuba to speed political change in Cuba. (For more, see "Migration Issues" below).

Response to Raul's Overtures

Raúl Castro asserted in an August 18, 2006, published interview that Cuba has "always been disposed to normalize relations on an equal plane," but at the same time he expressed strong opposition to current U.S. policy toward Cuba, which he described as "arrogant and interventionist."[41] In response, Assistant Secretary of State for Western Hemisphere Affairs Thomas Shannon reiterated a U.S. offer to Cuba, first articulated by President Bush in May 2002, that the Administration was willing to work with Congress to lift U.S. economic sanctions if Cuba were to begin a political opening and a transition to democracy. According to Shannon, the Bush Administration remained prepared to work with Congress for ways to lift the embargo if Cuba was prepared to free political prisoners, respect human rights, permit the creation of independent organizations, and create a mechanism and pathway toward free and fair elections [42].

In a December 2, 2006 speech, Raúl reiterated an offer to negotiate with the United States. He said that "we are willing to resolve at the negotiating table the longstanding dispute between the United States and Cuba, of course, provided they accept, as we have previously said, our condition as a country that will not tolerate any blemishes on its independence, and as long as said resolution is based on the principles of equality, reciprocity, non-interference, and mutual respect"[43].

On July 26, 2007, in a speech on Cuba's revolutionary anniversary (commemorating the 1953 attack on the Moncada military barracks), Raúl Castro reiterated for the third time an offer to engage in dialogue with the United States, and strongly criticized U.S. trade and economic sanctions on Cuba. A U.S. State Department spokesman responded that "the only real dialogue that's needed is with the Cuban people" [44].

In the second half of 2007, President Bush and other U.S. officials continued to call for a transition to democracy in Cuba. In a September 25, 2007 speech before the U.N. General Assembly, President Bush stated that "the long rule of a cruel dictator is nearing its end," and called on the United Nations to insist on free speech, free assembly, and free elections as Cuba "enters a period of transition." [45] U.S. Commerce Secretary Carlos Gutierrez stated in a speech on September 17 that "unless the regime changes, our policy will not," but indicated that the United States is "prepared to respond to genuine democratic change in Cuba"[46].

On October 24, 2007, President Bush made a policy speech on Cuba that reflected a continuation of the sanctions-based approach toward Cuba. According to the President: "As long as the [Cuban] regime maintains its monopoly over the political and economic life of the Cuban people, the United States will keep the embargo in place." In his speech, President Bush also sent a message to Cuban military, police, and government officials that "when Cubans rise up to demand their liberty," they have a choice to embrace the Cuban people's desire for change or "defend a disgraced and dying order by using force." The President conveyed to these officials that "there is a place for you in a free Cuba" [47].

Response to Raul's Official Selection as President

In the aftermath of Fidel Castro's February 19, 2008 announcement that he was officially stepping down as head of state, President Bush maintained that he viewed "this as a period of transition and it should be the beginning of a democratic transition in Cuba." State Department officials made clear that U.S. policy would not change. On February 24, 2008, the day that Raúl Castro officially became Cuba's head of state, Secretary of State Condoleezza Rice issued a statement urging "the Cuban government to begin a process of peaceful, democratic change by releasing all political prisoners, respecting human rights, and creating a clear pathway towards free and fair elections."

In remarks on Cuba policy in early March 2008, President Bush maintained that in order to improve U.S.-Cuban relations, "what needs to change is not the United States; what needs to change is Cuba." The President asserted that Cuba "must release all political prisoners ... have respect for human rights in word and deed, and pave the way for free and fair elections." [48] He reiterated these words again in a speech to the Council of the Americas on May 7, 2008 [49] On May 21, 2008, President Bush called for the Cuban government to take steps to improve life for the Cuban people, including opening up access to the Internet. He also announced that the United States would change regulations to allow Americans to send mobile phones to family members in Cuba [50].

Obama Administration Policy

During the electoral campaign, President Obama had pledged to lift restrictions on family travel to Cuba as well as restrictions on Cuban Americans sending remittances to Cuba. At the same time, he also pledged to maintain the embargo as a source of leverage to bring about change in Cuba. However, Obama also asserted that if the Cuban government takes significant steps toward democracy, beginning with the freeing of all political prisoners, then the United States would take steps to normalize relations and ease the embargo. He also maintained that, after careful preparation, his Administration would pursue direct diplomacy with Cuba without preconditions, but only when there is an opportunity to advance U.S. interests and advance the cause of freedom for the Cuban people [51].

During her Senate Foreign Relations Committee confirmation hearing for Secretary of State on January 15, 2009, Senator Hillary Clinton reiterated President Obama's pledge to lift restrictions on family travel and remittances. She indicated that the Administration did not yet have a timeline on the change, but maintained that the Administration would consult closely with Congress as it proceeds. Clinton also reiterated Obama's position that it is not time to lift the embargo since it provides an important source of leverage for further change in Cuba.

Perhaps most significantly, in response to written questions for the record regarding U.S. agricultural sales to Cuba, Cuba's retention on the State Department's state sponsors of terrorism list since 1982, and potential cooperation with Cuba on energy security and environmentally sustainable resource management, Clinton maintained that the new Administration anticipated a review of U.S. policy. She indicated that she looked forward to working with Members of Congress as the Administration moves forward in the consideration of appropriate steps to advance U.S. interests and values in the context of U.S. relations with Cuba. With regard to a question regarding a potential anti-drug agreement with Cuba, Clinton maintained the importance of anti-drug cooperation with Cuba where such cooperation is effective in stopping trafficking.

Some observers anticipate that President Obama will fulfill his campaign pledges with regard to lifting restrictions on family travel and remittances before the upcoming fifth Summit of the Americas in Trinidad and Tobago scheduled for April 17-19, 2009. Others, however, contend there might not be any Administration action on this before the summit because of a recent skirmish with Congress over Cuba provisions in the FY2009 omnibus appropriations measure [52].

During Senate consideration of the omnibus measure, several Senators expressed their opposition to provisions in the bill that would ease Cuba sanctions. In particular, there were concerns over provisions that would ease U.S. sanctions 1) on travel related to the marketing and sale of agricultural and medical exports, and 2) on payment terms for U.S. agricultural exports to Cuba. In response to Senate inquiries on how the Administration would implement these provisions, Secretary of the Treasury Timothy Geithner maintained that 1) the Administration would issue regulations providing that only a narrow class of businesses would be eligible under a new general license to travel to Cuba to market and sell agricultural and medical goods; and 2) that, with regard to payment provisions for U.S. agricultural goods, exporters would still be required to receive payment in advance of shipment [53]. While the Secretary's response ameliorated concerns of several Senators regarding the Cuba omnibus provisions, it also triggered concerns by other Senators who maintained that the Secretary's action ignores the legislative intent of the Cuba provisions to ease restrictions on agricultural sales to Cuba [54] (For further description of these provisions in the omnibus, see the legislative section in "Restrictions on Travel, Remittances, and Agricultural Exports" below).

Aftermath of 2008 Hurricanes and Tropical Storms

From mid-August through early November 2008, three hurricanes and two tropical storms caused widespread damage throughout Cuba. Tropical Storm Fay passed through central Cuba on August 18, causing severe flooding. On August 31, Hurricane Gustav struck the tobacco-growing province of Piñar del Río in western Cuba and the Isle of Youth. Tropical Storm Hanna, which did not strike Cuba directly, caused flooding in eastern Cuba in early September. Hurricane Ike made landfall in eastern Cuba on September 7 as a Category Four hurricane and severely affected both the eastern and western parts of the island, but especially the provinces of Holguin, Camaguey, and Las Tunas in the eastern part of the island. The two hurricanes caused most of the damage. Overall, just 7 people were killed, but the hurricanes severely affected the housing sector (with almost 500,000 homes damaged and over 63,000 destroyed), the power grid, and the agricultural sector [55] On November 8, 2008, Hurricane Paloma struck Cuba, devastating the town of Santa Cruz del Sur. Initially damages from the storms in August and September were estimated to amount to $5 billion, but Raúl Castro noted in the aftermath of Hurricane Paloma that overall damages from the storms since August amounted to some $10 billion [56].

The U.S. Chief of Mission at the U.S. Interests Section in Havana, Jonathan Farrar, issued a disaster declaration for Cuba on September 3, 2008, and the U.S. Agency for International Development (USAID) approved the release of $100,000 in emergency relief funds to non-governmental organizations in Cuba in response to Hurricane Gustav [57]. On September 12, in response to Hurricane Ike, the U.S. government provided another $100,000 in cash assistance to relief organizations on the ground in Cuba. The State Department maintains that the United States offered to send a humanitarian assessment team to Cuba to determine additional assistance needs, but that the Cuban government rejected the offer. U.S. officials subsequently offered a $5 million aid package for disaster relief for Cuba on September 13 that was also rejected by the Cuban government. USAID Administrator Henrietta Fore reportedly maintained that $2 million in plastic sheeting, hygiene kits, and other relief items would have been provided directly to the Cuban government, but that about $3 million in cash would still be provided through NGOs [58] The State Department made a new offer to Cuba on September 19 to supply some $6.3 million in corrugated zinc roofs, nails, tools, lumber, sheeting, and light shelter kits that would help some 48,000 people, but the Cuban government did not accept the offer [59].

In addition, according to the State Department, the U.S. government increased authorizations for U.S.-based non-governmental organizations (NGOs) to provide larger amounts of assistance to Cuba in the aftermath of the hurricanes, including expedited authorization over 90 days for up to $10 million per NGO [60].

In response to the U.S. offer to send a disaster assessment team, the Cuban government maintained that it already had a sufficient number of well-trained experts in Cuba, and noted that other countries worldwide were sending humanitarian aid without inspecting the affected areas. Instead, Cuba asked the United States to allow U.S. companies 1) to sell needed relief supplies to Cuba for the repair of housing and electrical networks; and 2) to grant private commercial credit to Cuba in order to buy food in the United States [61] In response to the U.S. offer to send $2 million in supplies to the Cuban government, the Cuban Interests Section in Washington rejected the request and called for the United States to allow U.S. companies to sell relief supplies to Cuba, if not on a permanent basis, then at least for the next six months [62].

Legislative Initiatives

In the aftermath of the hurricanes, a number of observers, including some Members of Congress, called for the temporary relaxation of restrictions on family travel and remittances (limited to $300 per quarter) as well as on the provision of gift parcels [63] to Cuba, but the Administration did not take any of these actions. Some observers also called for temporary changes to the U.S. embargo regulations to allow for unrestricted U.S. cash sales to Cuba of food and medicines, farm machinery or equipment, and relief supplies, including building materials and electrical supplies. On September 5, 2008, Chairman of the House Foreign Affairs Committee Howard Berman asked President Bush to suspend for 90 days restrictions on family visits, remittances, and gift parcels.

Several legislative initiatives were introduced in the 110th Congress that would have temporarily eased U.S. embargo restrictions in several areas. On September 15, 2008, Senator Dodd offered S.Amdt. 5581 to the Department of Defense authorization bill (S. 3001) that would have, for a 180-day period: allowed unrestricted family travel; eased restrictions on remittances by removing the limit and allowing any American to send remittances to Cuba; expanded the list of allowable items that may be included in gift parcels; and allowed for unrestricted U.S. cash sales of food, medicines, and relief supplies to Cuba. The amendment was not considered, and therefore not part of the final bill.

In the House, two legislative initiatives were introduced. On September 16, 2008, Representative Flake introduced H.R. 6913, which would have prohibited any funds from going to the Department of Commerce to implement, administer, or enforce tightened restrictions on the contents of gift parcels to Cuba that were introduced in June 2004. On September 18, 2008, Representative Delahunt introduced H.R. 6962, the Humanitarian Relief to Cuba Act, which would have, for a 180-day period: allowed unrestricted family travel; eased restrictions on remittances by removing the limit and allowing any American to send remittances to Cuba; and expanded the list of allowable items that may be included in gift parcels.

Restrictions on Travel, Remittances, and Agricultural Exports

Travel and Remittances

Restrictions on travel to Cuba have been a key and often contentious component of U.S. efforts to isolate the communist government of Fidel Castro for much of the past 40 years. Over time there have been numerous changes to the restrictions and for five years, from 1977 until 1982, there were no restrictions on travel. Restrictions on travel and remittances to Cuba are part of the CACR, the overall embargo regulations administered by the Treasury Department's Office of Foreign Assets Control (OFAC).

Major arguments made for lifting the Cuba travel ban are that it contributes to the suffering of Cuban families; it hinders efforts to influence conditions in Cuba and may be aiding Castro by helping restrict the flow of information; it abridges the rights of ordinary Americans; and Americans can travel to other countries with communist or authoritarian governments. Major arguments in opposition to lifting the Cuba travel ban are that more American travel would support Castro's rule by providing his government with potentially millions of dollars in hard currency; that there are legal provisions allowing travel to Cuba for humanitarian purposes that are used by thousands of Americans each year; and that the President should be free to restrict travel for foreign policy reasons.

Under the Bush Administration, enforcement of U.S. restrictions on Cuba travel increased, and restrictions on travel and on private remittances to Cuba were tightened. In March 2003, the Administration eliminated travel for people-to-people educational exchanges unrelated to academic course work. In June 2004, the Administration significantly restricted travel, especially family travel, and the provision of private humanitarian assistance to Cuba in the form of remittances and gift parcels.

Among the June 2004 restrictions were the following:

- Family visits were restricted to one trip every three years under a specific license and are restricted to immediate family members, with no exceptions. Under previous regulations, family visits could occur once a year under a general license, with travel more than once a year allowed, but under a specific license. Previously travel had been allowed to visit relatives to within three degrees of relationship to the traveler. The authorized per diem allowed for a family visit was reduced from the State Department per diem rate (currently $179 per day for Havana) to $50 per day.
- Cash remittances were further restricted. Quarterly remittances of $300 may still be sent, but are now restricted to members of the remitter's immediate family and may not be remitted to certain government officials and certain members of the Cuban Communist Party. The regulations were also changed to reduce the amount of remittances that authorized travelers may carry to Cuba, from $3000 to $300.
- Gift parcels were limited to immediate family members and were denied to certain Cuban officials and certain members of the Cuban Communist Party. The contents of

gift parcels may no longer include seeds, clothing, personal hygiene items, veterinary medicines and supplies, fishing equipment and supplies, or soap-making equipment.

- With the exception of informational materials, licensed travelers may not purchase or otherwise acquire merchandise and bring it back into the United States. Previous regulations allowed visitors to Cuba to import $100 worth of goods as accompanied baggage.
- Fully-hosted travel, by a person not subject to U.S. jurisdiction, was prohibited as a permissible category of travel.
- Travel for educational activities was further restricted, including the elimination of educational exchanges sponsored by secondary schools.

In April 2005, OFAC cracked down on certain religious organizations promoting licensed travel to Cuba and warned them not to abuse their license by taking individuals not affiliated with their organizations. OFAC's actions were prompted by reports that groups practicing the Afro-Cuban religion Santería had been taking large groups to Cuba as a means of skirting U.S. travel restrictions [64] In 2006, the Administration suspended the licenses of several travel service providers, including one of the largest such providers in Florida, La Estrella de Cuba. Several religious organizations also had their licenses suspended, and church groups and several Members of Congress expressed concern about more restrictive licenses for religious travel [65].

As noted above, during the electoral campaign, President Obama pledged to lift restrictions on family travel to Cuba as well as restrictions on Cuban Americans sending remittances to Cuba. Senator Hillary Clinton reiterated President Obama's pledge during her confirmation hearing for Secretary of State on January 15, 2009, but indicated that the Administration did not yet have a timeline on the change.

Congress took action on its own in the 111th Congress by including two provisions in the FY2009 omnibus appropriations measure (P.L. 111-8) that ease sanctions on travel to Cuba. Family travel once again is now allowed once every 12 months to visit a close relative for an unlimited length of stay, and the limit for daily expenditure allowed by family travelers is the same as for other authorized travelers to Cuba (State Department maximum per diem rate for Havana, currently $179 day). The definition of "close relative" is expanded to mean any individual related to the traveler by blood, marriage, or adoption, who is no more than three generations removed from that person. With regard to travel related to the marketing and sale of agricultural and medical goods to Cuba, Treasury Department's Office of Foreign Assets Control will issue be issuing regulations in the coming weeks.

Agricultural Exports and Sanctions

U.S. commercial agricultural exports to Cuba have been allowed for several years, but with numerous restrictions and licensing requirements. The 106th Congress passed the Trade Sanctions Reform and Export Enhancement Act of 2000 or TSRA (P.L. 106-387, Title IX) that allows for one-year export licenses for selling agricultural commodities to Cuba, although no U.S. government assistance, foreign assistance, export assistance, credits, or credit guarantees are available to finance such exports. TSRA also denies exporters access to U.S. private commercial financing or credit; all transactions must be conducted in cash in advance or with financing from third countries. TSRA reiterates the existing ban on importing goods from Cuba but authorizes travel to Cuba, under a specific license, to conduct business related to the newly allowed agricultural sales.

Since 2002, the United States has been Cuba's largest supplier of food and agricultural products [66] Cuba has purchased almost $2.7 billion in agricultural products from the United States since late 2001. Overall U.S exports to Cuba rose from about $7 million in 2001 to $404 million in 2004.

U.S. exports to Cuba declined in 2005 and 2006 to $369 million and $340 million, respectively, but increased to $447 million in 2007. In 2008, U.S. agricultural exports to Cuba rose to $718, far higher than in previous years, in part because of the rise in food prices and because of Cuba's increased food needs in the aftermath of several hurricanes and tropical storms that severely damaged Cuba's agricultural sector [67].

In February 2005, OFAC amended the Cuba embargo regulations to clarify that TSRA's term of "payment of cash in advance" means that the payment is received by the seller or the seller's agent prior to the shipment of the goods from the port at which they are loaded. U.S. agricultural exporters and some Members of Congress strongly objected that the action constituted a new sanction that violated the intent of TSRA and could jeopardize millions of dollars in U.S. agricultural sales to Cuba. OFAC Director Robert Werner maintained that the clarification "conforms to the common understanding of the term in international trade." [68] On July 29, 2005, OFAC clarified that, for "payment of cash in advance" for the commercial sale of U.S. agricultural exports to Cuba, vessels can leave U.S. ports as soon as a foreign bank confirms receipt of payment from Cuba. OFAC's action was aimed at ensuring that the goods would not be vulnerable to seizure for unrelated claims while still at the U.S. port. Supporters of overturning OFAC's February 22, 2005 amendment, such as the American Farm Bureau Federation, were pleased by the clarification but indicated that they would still work to overturn the February rule [69].

Some groups favor further easing restrictions on agricultural exports to Cuba. They argue that the restrictions harm the health and nutrition of the Cuban population. U.S. agribusiness companies that support the removal of restrictions on agricultural exports to Cuba believe that U.S. farmers are missing out on a market so close to the United States. Some exporters want to change U.S. restrictions so that they can sell agriculture and farm equipment to Cuba [70] Agricultural exporters who support the lifting of the prohibition on financing contend that allowing such financing would help smaller U.S. companies expand purchases to Cuba more rapidly [71]. On July 19, 2007, the U.S. International Trade Commission issued a report, requested by the Senate Committee on Finance, maintaining that the U.S. share of Cuba's agricultural, fish, and forest imports would rise from one-third to between one-half and two-thirds if trade restrictions were lifted. (See the full report available at http://www.usitc.gov/ext_relations/news_release/2007/er0719ee1.htm).

Opponents of further easing restrictions on agricultural exports to Cuba maintain that U.S. policy does not deny such sales to Cuba, as evidenced by the large amount of sales since 2001. Moreover, according to the State Department, since the Cuban Democracy Act was enacted in 1992, the United States has licensed billions of dollars in private humanitarian donations. Opponents further argue that easing pressure on the Cuban government would in effect be lending support and extending the duration of the Castro regime. They maintain that the United States should remain steadfast in its opposition to any easing of pressure on Cuba that could prolong the Castro regime and its repressive policies. Some agricultural producers that export to Cuba support continuation of the prohibition on financing for agricultural exports to Cuba because it ensures that they will be paid.

As described below, the 111th Congress recently took action by including two provisions in the FY2009 omnibus appropriations measure (P.L. 111-8) intended to ease sanctions related to the export of U.S. agricultural products to Cuba.

Legislative Initiatives

In the 111th Congress, Congress included three provisions easing Cuba sanctions in Sections 620622 of Division D of the FY2009 Omnibus Appropriations Act (H.R. 1105/P.L. 111-8) that was signed into law March 11, 2009. The provisions ease restrictions on family travel and travel for the marketing and sale of U.S. agricultural and medical exports to Cuba, and were intended to ease payment provisions for U.S. agricultural exports to Cuba.

Section 620 amends the Trade Sanctions Reform and Export Enhancement Act of 2000 to require the Secretary of the Treasury to issue regulations for travel to, from, or within Cuba under a general license for the marketing and sale of agricultural and medical goods. Such travel currently requires a specific license from OFAC, issued on a case by case basis. On March 9, 2009, Secretary of the Treasury Geithner stated in a letter published in the *Congressional Record* that the regulations issued pursuant to this provision "would provide that the representatives of only a narrow class of businesses would be eligible, under a new general license, to travel to market and sell agricultural and medical goods." The Secretary also maintained that "any business using the general license would be required to provide both advance written notice outlining the purpose and scope of the planned travel and, upon return, a report outlining the activities conducted, including the persons with whom they met, the expenses incurred, and business conducted in Cuba." [72] On March 11, 2009, OFAC maintained that it would implement this provision in the coming weeks and promulgate regulations authorizing travel under the general license for the marketing and sale of agricultural and medical goods.

Section 621 of Division D prohibits funds from being used to administer, implement, or enforce family travel restrictions that were imposed by the Bush Administration in June 2004. As noted above, those 2004 restrictions allowed family travel only to visit immediate family (grandparents, grandchildren, parents, siblings, spouses, and children) once every three years for a period not to exceed 14 days. Under the 2004 restrictions, a specific license was required from OFAC for such travel, and the authorized amount that family travelers could spend while in Cuba was limited to $50 a day. On March 11, 2009, OFAC provided guidance on its implementation of this omnibus provision that reinstated the authorization for family travel to Cuba that existed prior to the June 2004 restrictions. OFAC issued a general license authorizing family travel once every 12 months for an unlimited length of stay, and increased daily expenditure limits for family travelers to the same as all other authorized travelers to Cuba (State Department maximum per diem rate for Havana, currently $179 day). The new general license also provides for an expanded definition of "close relatives" to mean any individual related to the traveler by blood, marriage, or adoption, who is no more than three generations removed from that person (e.g. great-grandparents and second cousins). Specific licenses may be issued on a case-by-case basis for additional visits during the 12-month period or for travel to visit a close relative who is not a national of Cuba.

Section 622 of Division D prohibits funds in the Act from being used to administer, implement, or enforce an amendment to the Cuban embargo regulations on February 25, 2005 requiring that U.S. agricultural exporters using the "payment of cash in advance'" payment mechanism for selling their goods to Cuba must be paid in cash for their goods before the goods leave U.S. ports. As noted above, TSRA requires either the "payment of cash of advance" for such exports (or financing by third country financial institutions), but does not provide a definition of cash in advance. Prior to the February 2005 amendment to the Cuban embargo regulations, U.S. exporters could be paid for the goods before they were unloaded in Cuba. OFAC guidance on the implementation of this provision states that TSRA's statutory provisions remain in place that agricultural exports to Cuba be either paid for by "cash in advance" or financed using a third-country bank [73] Secretary of the Treasury Geithner provided additional guidance on the implementation of this provision in a letter published in the Congressional Record that states that, "exporters will still be required to receive payment in advance of shipment." [74] This appears to continue the Bush Administration policy imposed in February 2005. Given the Secretary's interpretation, it appears the omnibus provision will have little, if any, practical effect.

Several other legislative initiative in the 111th Congress have been introduced that would ease or eliminate restrictions on travel, remittances, and on the sale U.S. agricultural exports to Cuba.

H.R. 188 (Serrano) and H.R. 1530 (Rangel) would lift overall economic sanctions on Cuba, including all restrictions on travel, remittances, and agricultural exports. H.R. 332 (Lee) would ease restrictions on educational travel to Cuba. Identical bills, H.R. 874 (Delahunt) and S. 428 (Dorgan), would prohibit the President from regulating or prohibiting, directly or indirectly, travel to or from Cuba by U.S. citizens or legal residents, or any of the transactions incident to such travel. H.R. 1528 (Rangel) would also lift restrictions on travel. H.R. 1531 (Rangel) would lift restrictions on the sale of U.S. agricultural and medical exports to Cuba and would also lift restrictions on travel.

Trademark Sanctions [75]

For over a decade, the United States has imposed a sanction that denies protection for trademarks connected with businesses confiscated from their owners by the Cuban government. A provision in the FY1999 omnibus appropriations measure (Section 211 of Division A, Title II, P.L. 105-277, signed into law October 21, 1998) prevents the United States from accepting payment for trademark registrations and renewals from Cuban or foreign nationals that were used in connection with a business or assets in Cuba that were confiscated, unless the original owner of the trademark has consented. The provision prohibits U.S. courts from recognizing such trademarks without the consent of the original owner. The measure was enacted because of a dispute between the French spirits company, Pernod Ricard, and the Bermuda-based Bacardi Ltd. Pernod Ricard entered into a joint venture with the Cuban government to produce and export Havana Club rum, but Bacardi, whose company in Cuba was expropriated in the 1960s, maintains that it holds the right to the Havana Club name. Although Pernod Ricard cannot market Havana Club in the United States because of the trade embargo, it wants to protect its future distribution rights should the embargo be lifted.

The European Union initiated World Trade Organization dispute settlement proceedings in June 2000, maintaining that the U.S. law violates the Agreement on Trade-Related Aspects of Intellectual Property (TRIPS). In January 2002, the WTO ultimately found that the trademark sanction violated WTO provisions on national treatment and most-favored-nation obligations in the TRIPS Agreement.

On March 28, 2002, the United States agreed that it would come into compliance with the WTO ruling through legislative action by January 3, 2003 [76]. That deadline was extended several times since no legislative action had been taken to bring Section 211 into compliance with the WTO ruling. On July 1, 2005, however, in an EU-U.S. bilateral agreement, the EU agreed that it would not request authorization to retaliate at that time, but reserved the right to do so at a future date, and the United States agreed not to block a future EU request [77]. On August 3, 2006, the U.S. Patent and Trademark Office announced that Cuba's Havana Club trademark registration was "cancelled/expired," a week after OFAC had denied a Cuban government company the license that it needed to renew the registration of the trademark [78].

Two different approaches have been advocated to bring Section 211 into compliance with the WTO ruling. Some want a narrow fix in which Section 211 would be amended so that it also applies to U.S. companies instead of being limited to foreign companies. Advocates of this approach argue that it would affirm that the United States "will not give effect to a claim or right to U.S. property if that claim is based on a foreign compensation." [79] Others want Section 211 repealed altogether. They argue that the law endangers over 5,000 trademarks of over 500 U.S. companies registered in Cuba [80]. They maintain that Cuba could retaliate against U.S. companies under the Inter-American Convention for Trademark and Commercial Protection.

Several legislative initiatives were introduced during the 110th Congress reflecting these two approaches to bring Section 211 into compliance with the WTO ruling, but no action was taken on these measures. To date in the 111th Congress, H.R. 1103 (Wexler) would amend Section 211 with small fix to bring it into compliance with the WTO ruling, while H.R. 188 (Serrano) would repeal Section 211 altogether. The July 2005 EU-U.S. bilateral agreement, in which the EU agreed not to retaliate against the United States, but reserved the right to do so at a later date, has reduced pressure on Congress to take action to comply with the WTO ruling.

Offshore Oil Sector Development

The issue of Cuba's development of its deepwater offshore oil reserves in the Gulf of Mexico has been a concern among some Members of Congress. According to the U.S. Energy Information Administration, industry analysts maintain that there could be at least 1.6 billion barrels of crude oil reserves in Cuba's offshore sector; the U.S. Geological Survey estimated a mean of 4.6 billion barrels of undiscovered oil [81] In October 2008, an official of Cuba's state oil company, Cubapetroleo (Cupet), maintained there may be more than 20 billion barrels of oil in Cuba's deepwaters, but energy analysts expressed skepticism for such a claim [82].

To date, Cuba has signed agreements for seven concessions involving eight foreign oil companies for the exploration of offshore oil and gas. Repsol (Spain), Norsk-Hydro (Norway), and ONGC (India) are partners in a joint project, while Sherritt International (Canada), ONGC (India), PdVSA (Venezuela), Petronas (Malaysia), PetroVietnam, and

Petrobras (Brazil) also have additional concessions. In February 2008, Petrobras signed a wide-ranging agreement for potential exploration and production cooperation with Cuba's state oil company, Cupet. This ultimately led to an oil exploration agreement between Petrobras and Cupet signed in late October 2008. Some Members of Congress have expressed concern about oil development so close to the United States and about potential environmental damage to the Florida coast. The Repsol project has plans to drill a second well (the first was drilled in 2004) in mid-2009, and some press reports maintain that if that goes well, Cuban oil could be flowing to the market by 2013 [83].

Although there have been some claims that China is drilling in Cuba's offshore deepwater oil sector, to date its involvement in Cuba's oil sector has been focused on exploring onshore/close coastal oil extraction in Piñar del Rio province through its state-run China Petroleum and Chemical Corporation (Sinopec) [84] China does not have a concession in Cuba's offshore oil sector in the deepwaters of the Gulf of Mexico [85].

In the 110th Congress, several legislative initiatives (H.R. 1679, S. 876, and S. 2503) would have imposed sanctions related to Cuba's offshore oil development on its northern coast, while several other initiatives (S. 1268, S. 2953, H.R. 3182, H.R. 3435, and H.R. 6735) would have allowed U.S. companies to work with Cuba for the offshore exploration and extraction of oil. No action was taken on any of these initiatives.

Drug Interdiction Cooperation

Because of Cuba's geographic location, the country's waters and airspace have been used by illicit narcotics traffickers to transport drugs for ultimate destinations in the United States. Over the past several years, Cuban officials have expressed concerns over the use of their waters and airspace for drug transit as well as increased domestic drug use. The Cuban government has taken a number of measures to deal with the drug problem, including legislation to stiffen penalties for traffickers, increased training for counternarcotics personnel, and cooperation with a number of countries on anti-drug efforts. Cuba has bilateral counternarcotics agreements with 33 countries and less formal arrangements with 16 others, according to the Department of State. For several years, Cuba's Operation Hatchet has focused on maritime and air interdiction and the recovery of narcotics washed up on Cuban shores. Narcotics smuggling through Cuban territory decreased in 2006, according to both U.S. and Cuban officials [86] According to the Department of State, Cuba aggressively pursues an internal enforcement and investigation program against its incipient drug market with an effective nationwide drug prevention and awareness campaign, Operation Popular Shield.

Over the years, there have been varying levels of U.S.-Cuban cooperation on anti-drug efforts. In 1996, Cuban authorities cooperated with the United States in the seizure of 6.6 tons of cocaine aboard the Miami-bound *Limerick*, a Honduran-flag ship. Cuba turned over the cocaine to the United States and cooperated fully in the investigation and subsequent prosecution of two defendants in the case in the United States. Cooperation has increased since 1999 when U.S. and Cuban officials met in Havana to discuss ways of improving anti-drug cooperation. Cuba accepted an upgrading of the communications link between the Cuban Border Guard and the U.S. Coast Guard as well as the stationing of a U.S. Coast Guard Drug Interdiction Specialist (DIS) at the U.S. Interests Section in Havana. The Coast

Guard official was posted to the U.S. Interests Section in September 2000, and since that time, coordination has increased.

The State Department, in its February 2009 *International Narcotics Control Strategy Report*, reported that counter-narcotics cooperation, including operations in coordination with the Coast Guard DIS, continued in 2008. In July 2008, information provided by the Cuban Border Guard's operations center in Havana led the U.S. Coast Guard to a drug-laden go-fast boat in the Windward Pass. The report also noted that Cuban authorities have provided the DIS with exposure to Cuban counternarcotics efforts, including investigative criminal information, debriefings on drug trafficking cases, visits to the Cuban national canine training center and anti-doping laboratory in Havana, tours of Cuban Border Guard facilities, and access to meet with the Chiefs of Cuba's INTERPOL and Customs offices.

Cuba maintains that it wants to cooperate with the United States to combat drug trafficking, and on various occasions has called for a bilateral anti-drug cooperation agreement with the United States [87]. In January 2002, Cuba deported to the United States Jesse James Bell, a U.S. fugitive wanted on drug charges, and in early March 2002, Cuba arrested a convicted Colombian drug trafficker, Rafael Bustamante, who escaped from jail in Alabama in 1992. At the time, then Drug Enforcement Administration head Asa Hutchison expressed appreciation for Cuba's actions, but indicated that cooperation would continue on a case-by-case basis, not through a bilateral agreement [88]. In February 2007, Cuba extradited drug trafficker Luis Hernando Gómez Bustamante to Colombia, an action that drew praise from U.S. Assistant Secretary of State for International Narcotics and Law Enforcement Affairs Anne Patterson [89] Gómez Bustamante was subsequently extradited to the United States in July 2007 to face drug trafficking charges.

In April 2008, John Walters, Director of the White House Office of National Drug Control Policy, lauded U.S. anti-drug cooperation with Cuba as a good example of how cooperation has been achieved despite overall political differences between the two countries [90].

In early January 2009, Assistant Secretary of State for Western Hemisphere Affairs Tom Shannon maintained in an interview with Spain's *El País* newspaper that a drug trafficking accord with Cuba would be logical, although he could not anticipate what the next Administration would do [91].

Legislative Initiatives

Over the past several years, House and Senate versions of Foreign Operations appropriations bills have contained contrasting provisions related to funding for cooperation with Cuba on counternarcotics efforts. House bills have generally prohibited funds for such efforts, while Senate versions would have funded such efforts. Ultimately, none of these provisions were included in enacted measures.

Most recently, in the second session of the 110th Congress, the Senate Appropriations Committee version of the FY2009 State, Department, Foreign Operations, and Related Agencies Appropriations Act, S. 3288, contained a provision (section 779) that would have provided for $1 million for preliminary work by the Department of State, or other entity designated by the Secretary of State, to establish cooperation with appropriate Cuban agencies on counternarcotics matters. The money would not be available, however, if the Secretary certified that Cuba 1) does not have in place procedures to protect against the loss of innocent life in the air and on the ground in connection with the interdiction of illegal drugs; and 2) there is credible evidence of involvement of the government of Cuba in drug trafficking during the preceding 10 years. No action was taken on the measure, and no such provision was included in either the Consolidated Appropriations Act for FY2009 (P.L. 110-329) that provided foreign operations funding until March 6, 2009, or the FY2009 Omnibus Appropriations Act, (P.L. 111-8).

Cuba and Terrorism [92]

Cuba was added to the State Department's list of states sponsoring international terrorism in 1982 because of its alleged ties to international terrorism and support for terrorist groups in Latin America. Cuba had a long history of supporting revolutionary movements and governments in Latin America and Africa, but in 1992, Fidel Castro said that his country's support for insurgents abroad was a thing of the past. Cuba's change in policy was in large part due to the breakup of the Soviet Union, which resulted in the loss of billions of dollars in annual subsidies to Cuba, and led to substantial Cuban economic decline.

Cuba remains on the State Department's terrorism list. According to the State Department's *Country Reports on Terrorism 2007* report (issued April 30, 2008), Cuba has "remained opposed to U.S. counterterrorism policy, and actively and publicly condemned many associated U.S. policies and actions." The report also noted that Cuba maintains close relationships with other state sponsors of terrorism, such as Iran and Syria, and has provided safe haven for members of several Foreign Terrorist Organizations (FTOs): the Basque Homeland and Freedom (ETA) and two Colombian insurgent groups, the Revolutionary Armed Forces of Colombia (FARC) and the National Liberation Army (ELN). Colombia has publicly acknowledged that it wants Cuban mediation with the ELN.

The 2007 report also maintained that Cuba continued to permit U.S. fugitives from justice to live legally in Cuba. Most of the fugitives entered Cuba in the committing violent actions in the United States. The State Department report noted that Cuba stated in 2006 that it would no longer provide safe haven to new fugitives who may enter Cuba. In 2006, Cuba returned a U.S. fugitive who had sequestered his son and flew a stolen plane to Cuba in September. In April 2007, Cuba returned another U.S. fugitive, Joseph Adjmi, who was convicted of mail fraud in the 1960s, but disappeared before beginning his 10-year sentence. On June 13, 2008, Cuba's Ministry of Foreign Affairs announced that it deported another U.S. citizen, Leonard Auerbach, wanted in the United States for sexual exploitation of a minor and for child pornography, who had entered Cuba from Mexico in April [93]. More recently, press reports maintain that a number of fugitives from Florida accused of bilking the U.S. government of millions through Medicare fraud have fled to Cuba [94].

Critics of retaining Cuba on the terrorism list maintain that it is a holdover from the Cold War. They argue that domestic political considerations keep Cuba on the terrorism list and maintain that Cuba's presence on the list diverts U.S. attention from struggles against serious terrorist threats. Those who support keeping Cuba on the terrorism list argue that there is ample evidence that Cuba supports terrorism. They point to the government's history of supporting terrorist acts and armed insurgencies in Latin America and Africa. They point to the government's continued hosting of members of foreign terrorist organizations and U.S. fugitives from justice.

Cuba as the Victim of Terrorism

Cuba has been the target of various terrorist incidents over the years. In 1976, a Cuban plane was bombed, killing 73 people. In 1997, there were almost a dozen bombings in the tourist sector in Havana and in the Varadero beach area in which an Italian businessman was killed and several others were injured. Two Salvadorans were convicted and sentenced to death for the bombings in March 1999, and three Guatemalans were sentenced to prison terms ranging from 10-15 years in January 2002. Cuban officials maintain that Cuban exiles funded the bombings.

In November 2000, four anti-Castro activists were arrested in Panama for a plot to kill Fidel Castro. One of the accused, Luis Posada Carriles, was also allegedly involved in the 1976 Cuban airline bombing noted above [95]. The four stood trial in March 2004 and were sentenced on weapons charges in the case to prison terms ranging from seven to eight years. In late August 2004, Panamanian President Mireya Moscoso pardoned the four men before the end of her presidential term. Three of the men are U.S. citizens and traveled to Florida, where they received strong support from some in the Cuban American community, while Posada reportedly traveled to another country.

On April 13, 2005, Posada's lawyer said that his client, reportedly in the United States after entering the country illegally, would seek asylum in the United States because he has a "wellfounded fear of persecution" for his opposition to Fidel Castro [96] Posada, a Venezuelan citizen, had been imprisoned in Venezuela for the bombing of the Cuban airliner in 1976, but reportedly was allowed to "escape" from prison in 1985 after his supporters paid a bribe to the prison.

warden [97] He had been acquitted for the bombing but remained in prison pending a prosecutorial appeal [98] Posada also reportedly admitted, but later denied, involvement in the string of bombings in Havana in 1997, one of which killed an Italian tourist [99] Posada subsequently withdrew his application for asylum on May 17, 2005. Later that day, U.S. Immigration and Customs Enforcement (ICE) arrested Posada, and subsequently charged him with illegally entering the United States. A Department of Homeland Security press release indicated that ICE does not generally deport people to Cuba or countries believed to be acting on Cuba's behalf [100] Venezuela requested Posada's extradition and pledged that it would not hand Posada over to Cuba. On September 26, 2005, however, a U.S. immigration judge ruled that Posada likely faced torture in Venezuela and could not be deported in keeping with U.S. obligations under the Convention Against Torture [101].

ICE reviewed the case and determined on March 22, 2006, that Posada would not be freed from a federal immigration facility in El Paso, Texas [102]. In November 2006, however, a U.S. federal judge, who was considering Posada's plea that he be released, ordered the government to supply evidence, by February 1, 2007, justifying his continued detention. On January 11, 2007, a federal grand jury in Texas indicted Posada on seven counts for lying about how he entered the United States illegally in March 2005, whereupon he was transferred from immigration detention in El Paso to a county prison in New Mexico near the Texas border. The Cuban government responded by maintaining that Posada needs to be charged with terrorism, not just lying about how he entered the United States. Another grand jury in New Jersey is reportedly examining Posada's alleged role in the 1997 bombings in Cuba [103] Press articles in early May 2007 reported that the FBI has been gathering evidence in the 1997 bombing and that FBI agents have visited Havana as part of their investigation [104].

Posada was released from jail in New Mexico on April 19, 2007, and allowed to return to Miami under house arrest to await an upcoming trial on immigration fraud charges, but on May 9, 2007 a federal judge in Texas dismissed the charges. The judge maintained that the U.S. government mistranslated testimony from Posada and manipulated evidence [105] On June 5, 2007, Justice Department prosecutors filed a notice of appeal with the 5th U.S. Circuit Court of Appeals in New Orleans and on November 6, 2007, federal prosecutors filed a brief requesting that the court reverse the lower court's decision [106] On June 4, 2008, the appeals court heard arguments from both sides in the case; a ruling reportedly could take several months [107] Both Cuba and Venezuela strongly denounced Posada's release, contending that he is a terrorist. In late June 2008, Panama's Supreme Court ruled that Posada's 2004 pardon was unconstitutional, and in July 2008, a Panamanian court initiated a request for Posada's extradition to the Panamanian government.

U.S. Funding to Support Democracy and Human Rights

Since 1996, the United States has provided assistance—primarily through the U.S. Agency for International Development (USAID), but also through the State Department and the National Endowment for Democracy (NED)—to increase the flow of information on democracy, human rights, and free enterprise to Cuba.

USAID's Cuba program has supported a variety of U.S.-based non-governmental organizations with the goals of promoting a rapid, peaceful transition to democracy, helping develop civil society, and building solidarity with Cuba's human rights activists [108]. These efforts are largely funded through Economic Support Funds (ESF) in the annual foreign operations appropriations bill. From FY2001-FY2007, the United States provided a total of almost $71 million in funding for Cuba democracy efforts.

For FY2008, Congress fully funded the Administration's request for $45.7 million in ESF for democracy assistance for Cuba in the Consolidated Appropriations Act for FY2008 (P.L. 110161); an estimated $45.33 million, however, will be provided because of an overall 0.81% rescission. The amount was more than five times the amount requested in FY2007 ($9 million). According to the State Department's FY2008 Congressional Budget Justification (CBJ), the increase in assistance was in order to fulfill the recommendations of the July 2006 report of the Commission for Assistance to a Free Cuba to provide support for Cuban civil society, expand international awareness, break the regime's information blockade, and continue support for a democratic transition. That report, as described above, recommended $80 million over two years for a variety of measures to hasten Cuba's transition to democracy, and not less than $20 million annually thereafter for Cuba democracy programs.

Both the House- and Senate-passed versions of the FY2008 State, Foreign Operations, and Related Agencies Appropriations Act, H.R. 2764, fully funded the Administration's request for $45.7 million in ESF for Cuba democracy programs. The House committee-reported version of the bill would have provided just $9 million in ESF for such programs, but during June 21, 2007, floor consideration, the House approved H.Amdt. 351 (Diaz-Balart) by a vote of 254-170 that increased funding for ESF by $36.7 million in order to fully fund the Administration's request.

The Senate Appropriations Committee report to the bill would have provided $15 million in ESF for Cuba democracy programs. However, during September 6, 2007, floor consideration, the Senate approved S.Amdt. 2694 (Martinez) by voice vote that increased funding for Cuba democracy programs by $30.7 million to fully fund the Administration's request.

For FY2009, the Administration requested $20 million in ESF to continue to implement the program recommendations of the Commission for Assistance to a Free Cuba. The money would assist human rights activists, independent journalists, Afro-Cubans, and women, youth, and student activists. The report to the Senate Appropriations Committee version of the FY2009 State Department, Foreign Operations, and Related Agencies Appropriations Act, S, 3288 (S.Rept. 110425), recommended fully funding the Administration's request for Cuba, but also called for the State Department and USAID to conduct regular evaluations to ensure the cost effectiveness of the programs.

No final action on the appropriations measure was taken in the 110th Congress, but overall foreign operations funding was continued under a short-term continuing resolution (P.L. 110-329) until March 6, 2009. In the 111th Congress, the FY2009 Omnibus Appropriations Act (P.L. 111-8) did not include a specific earmark for the Cuba democracy funding.

Until FY2008, NED's democratization assistance for Cuba had been funded largely through the annual Commerce, Justice, and State (CJS) appropriations measure, but is now funded through the State Department, Foreign Operations and Related Agencies appropriations measure. NED funding for Cuba has steadily increased over the past several years: $765,000 in FY2001; $841,000 in FY2002; $1.14 million in FY2003; and $1.15 million in FY2004. For FY2005, NED funded 17 Cuba projects with $2.4 million.

For FY2006, NED funded 13 projects with almost $1.5 million, including $0.4 million from State Department ESF. For FY2007, NED funded 12 projects with almost $1.5 million, which included almost $1.4 million funded by the State Department.

Oversight of U.S. Democracy Assistance to Cuba

In November 2006, the Government Accountability Office (GAO) issued a report examining U.S. democracy assistance for Cuba from 1996-2005, and concluded that the U.S. program had significant problems and needed better management and oversight. According to GAO, internal controls, for both the awarding of Cuba program grants and oversight of grantees, "do not provide adequate assurance that the funds are being used properly and that grantees are in compliance with applicable law and regulations." [109] Investigative news reports on the program maintained that high shipping costs and lax oversight have diminished its effectiveness [110]. Representative William Delahunt, Chairman of the House Foreign Affairs Committee's Subcommittee on International Organizations, Human Rights, and Oversight, had requested the GAO study along with Representative Jeff Flake.

In March 2008, a White House aide to President Bush, Felipe Sixto, resigned because of alleged misuse of funds when he worked for the Center for a Free Cuba, which has been a major recipient of U.S. democracy funding [111]. On December 19, 2008, Sixto pled guilty to stealing nearly $600,000, and is expected to be sentenced in March 2009 [112]. Another group, Grupo de Apoyo a la Democracia (Group in Support of Democracy), is also under investigation by USAID for misuse of funds. Historically these two groups have been the two largest recipients of U.S. democracy funding for Cuba [113].

GAO issued a second report examining USAID's Cuba democracy program on November 24, 2008 [114]. The report lauded the steps that USAID had taken since 2006 to address problems with its Cuba program and improve oversight of the assistance. These included awarding all grants competitively since 2006, hiring more staff for the program office since January 2008; and contracting for financial services in April 2008 to enhance oversight of grantees. The GAO report also noted that USAID had worked to strengthen program oversight through pre-award and follow-up reviews, improving grantee internal controls and implementation plans, and providing guidance and monitoring about permitted types of assistance and cost sharing.

The GAO report also maintained, however, that USAID had not staffed the Cuba program to the level needed for effective grant oversight. GAO also noted the difficulty of assessing USAID's action to improve its Cuba program because most of its actions to improve the program were only taken recently. Procurement reviews completed in August 2008 by the new financial services contractor identified internal control, financial management, and procurement weaknesses at three grantees. GAO recommended that USAID: 1) ensure that its Cuba program office is staffed at the level that is needed to fully implement planned monitoring activities; and 2) periodically assess the Cuba program's overall efforts to address and reduce grantee risks, especially regarding internal controls, procurement practices, expenditures, and compliance with laws and regulations.

The Cuban American National Foundation (CANF) released a report in May 2008 maintaining that a majority of the assistance for Cuba has been spent in operating expenses by U.S.-based grantees, transition studies, and U.S.-based activities. Among the recommendations in its report, the CANF called for USAID grantees to spend a minimum of 75% of government funds in direct aid to Cuban civil society. It also called for the assistance program to provide direct cash aid to independent civil society groups, dissidents, and families of political prisoners [115].

Radio and TV Marti

U.S.-government sponsored radio and television broadcasting to Cuba—Radio and TV Martí— began in 1985 and 1990 respectively. As spelled out in the *Broadcasting Board of Governors FY2009 Budget Request*, the objectives of Radio and TV Martí are (1) to support the right of the Cuban people to seek, receive, and impart information and ideas through any media and regardless of frontiers; (2) to be effective in furthering the open communication of information and ideas through use of radio and television broadcasting to Cuba; (3) to serve as a consistently reliable and authoritative source of accurate, objective, and comprehensive news; and (4) to provide news, commentary, and other information about events in Cuba and elsewhere to promote the cause of freedom in Cuba.

Until October 1999, U.S.-government funded international broadcasting programs had been a primary function of the United States Information Agency (USIA). When USIA was abolished and its functions were merged into the Department of State at the beginning of FY2000, the Broadcasting Board of Governors (BBG) became an independent agency that included such entities as the Voice of America (VOA), Radio Free Europe/Radio Liberty (RFE/RL), Radio Free Asia, and the Office of Cuba Broadcasting (OCB), which manages Radio and TV Marti. OCB is headquartered in Miami, Florida, and operates under the BBG's International Broadcasting Bureau (IBB). Legislation in the 104th Congress (P.L. 104-134) required the relocation of OCB from Washington D.C. to south Florida. The move began in 1996 and was completed in 1998.

Radio Martí broadcasts on short and medium wave (AM) channels for 24 hours six days per week, and for18 hours one day per week utilizing transmission facilities in Marathon, Florida and Greenville, North Carolina, according to the BBG.

TV Martí broadcasts daily from its facilities in Cudjoe Key Florida, on the Hispasat satellite, and is available on the Internet 24 hours a day. It is also available on 176 cable stations throughout Latin America, according to the BBG. Until July 2005, TV Martí had also been broadcast via blimps from facilities in Cudjoe Key, Florida for four and one-half hours daily, but the aerostats were destroyed by Hurricane Dennis. From mid-2004 until 2006, TV Martí programming was transmitted for several hours once a week via an airborne platform known as Commando Solo operated by the Department of Defense utilizing a C-130 aircraft. In August 2006, OCB began to use a contracted private aircraft to transmit pre-recorded TV Martí broadcasts six days weekly, and by late October 2006 the OCB inaugurated an aircraft-broadcasting platform known as Aero Martí with the capability of transmitting live broadcasts. Aero Martí transmits broadcasts five hours daily from Monday to Saturday during the evening. According to OCB, since mid-FY2007, it has had two contracted private aircraft transmitting the broadcasts.

In December 2006, the OCB contracted with two private U.S. commercial stations to transmit Radio and TV Martí [116]. It provided a six-month contract with Radio Mambí (710 AM) in Florida, at a cost of $182,500, to broadcast one hour of Radio Martí programming five days a week from midnight to 1:00 am. Radio Mambí is a popular station in south Florida, with a 50,000 watt capacity, that is well-known for its strong anti-Castro stance. A second six-month OCB contract with WPMF (Channel 38) in Miami, known as TV Azteca, at a cost of $195,000, provided for two 30-minute TV Martí newscasts at 6 pm and 11:30 pm weekdays, along with one-minute news updates hourly over a 12 hour period weekdays. OCB chose the station because it is offered on DirecTV and because it has only a small audience in Miami. In June 2007, the two contracts were extended for an additional six months with similar terms. The contract with Radio Mambí subsequently expired in early 2008, whereas TV Martí continues to be shown on Channel 38.

Controversies

Both Radio and TV Martí have at times been the focus of controversies, including questions about adherence to broadcast standards. There have been various attempts over the years to cut funding for the programs, especially for TV Martí, which has not had much of an audience because of Cuban jamming efforts. In December 2006, press reports alleged significant problems in the OCB's operations, with claims of cronyism, patronage, and bias in its coverage [117]. In February 2007, the former director of TV Martí programming pled guilty in U.S. federal court to receiving more than $100,000 in kickbacks over a three-year period from a vendor receiving OCB contracts [118].

Over the years, there have been various government studies and audits of Radio and TV Martí, including investigations by the U.S. Government Accountability Office, by a 1994 congressionally established Advisory Panel on Radio and TV Martí, and by the State Department's and BBG's Office Inspector General offices in 1999, 2003, and 2007 [119].

The most recent State Department/BBG Office of Inspector General (OIG) report, issued in June 2007, maintained that OCB has significantly improved its operations under its current director, Pedro Roig, with an organizational realignment that has streamlined operations and has helped improve the quality of broadcasts. According to the report, "IBB quality reviews show that radio and television broadcasts have markedly improved over the past two years in production quality and content," although the report also called for greater emphasis on internal quality control to ensure that editorial standards are followed. The report lauded the introduction of new technology allowing OCB to broadcast television signals live into Cuba using airborne platforms, and maintained that there are indications that more Cubans are watching TV Martí broadcasts. It recommended that the BBG's International Broadcasting Bureau should review and assess the leases with Radio Mambí and TV Azteca at the end of the lease period to determine whether they provide additional listeners and viewers and are worth the cost, or whether they could be replaced with lease options for other stations. Looking ahead, the report maintained that OCB needs a "long-term strategic plan that anticipates the future needs of the Cuban audience, provides a template on how to compete with commercial broadcasters, and addresses what to do with OCB and its broadcasting facilities if and when uncensored broadcasting is allowed inside a democratic Cuba" [120].

One of the most controversial aspects of the OIG report, and one that has often been at the center of past congressional debate over TV Martí, is the extent to which TV Martí can be viewed in Cuba. The report maintains that there is anecdotal evidence that the Aero Martí airborne transmissions have increased viewership. The report refers to a January 2007 survey of Cuban arrivals—commissioned by Spanish Radio Productions with the cooperation of Miami Dade College—that found listening rates for Radio and TV Martí within Cuba were significantly higher than previously reported, especially for TV Martí. Although specific survey figures are not cited in the OIG report, OCB officials maintain that the survey shows that 17% of recent Cuban arrivals had watched TV Martí [121]. The OIG report also points to a February 2007 survey by the U.S. Interests Section (USINT) in Havana that reflected increased viewership. According to the BBG, that survey was completed by 500 Cuban visitors to the USINT (where TV Martí can be viewed) in January and February 2007, with 10% of the visitors indicating that they could watch TV Martí via UHF for brief periods.

Other observers contend that TV Martí can hardly be viewed in Cuba because of the government's jamming efforts. John Nichols, a Pennsylvania State University communications professor, visited Cuba in late June 2007 on a fact-finding mission sponsored by the Center for International Policy (a group that opposes current U.S. policy toward Cuba), and concluded "that the signal from the plane is essentially unusable" and that there was "no evidence of significant viewership of TV Martí." [122] In interviews with the *Associated Press*, more than two dozen Cuban immigrants to Florida contended that while Radio Martí can be heard throughout Cuba, TV Martí can rarely be seen [123] Prior BBG commissioned phone surveys in Cuba from 2003, 2005, and November 2006 estimated past week TV Martí viewership between 0.1% and 0.3% of those surveyed and past month viewership of almost 0.5%. The November 2006 survey, reportedly designed to show the early effects of the Aero Martí transmissions that began in late October, showed no statistically significant change from the 2003 and 2005 surveys. In the same surveys, Radio Martí had listenership of between 1% to 2% in the past week and 4% to 5% in the past month.

In July 2008, GAO issued a report that criticized the IBB's and OCB's practices in awarding the two contracts to Radio Mambí and TV Azteca as lacking discipline required to ensure transparency and accountability. According to GAO, the approach for awarding the Radio Mambi and TV Azteca contracts did not reflect sound business practices [124].

In January 2009, GAO issued a report asserting that the best available research suggests that Radio and TV Martí's audience is small, and cited telephone surveys since 2003 showing that less than 2% of respondents reported tuning in to Radio or TV Martí during the past week. The GAO report also cited concerns with adherence to relevant laws and standards, including the domestic dissemination of OCB programming, inappropriate advertisements during OCB programming, and TV Martí's interference with Cuban broadcasts [125].

Funding

From FY1984 through FY2007, about $564 million has been spent for broadcasting to Cuba. In recent years, funding amounted to $37.5 million in FY2006, $33.9 million in FY2007, and an estimated $33.4 million in FY2008. For FY2009, the Bush Administration requested $34.4 million for broadcasting to Cuba. Until FY2005, the Administration provided funding information for Cuba broadcasting with a breakdown of the amounts spent for Radio versus TV Martí. Since FY2005, however, the Broadcasting Board of Governors has not made such a distinction in its annual budget request.

For FY2009, the Administration requested $34.4 million for broadcasting to Cuba, slightly more than provided by Congress in FY2008. The request amount includes funding for the airborne platform that the Office of Cuba Broadcasting uses to broadcast Radio and TV Martí. The report to the Senate Appropriations Committee version of the FY2009 State Department, Foreign Operations, and Related Agencies Appropriations Act, S. 3288 (S.Rept. 110-425), recommended fully funding the Administration's request for Cuba broadcasting. The 110th Congress did not finalize FY2009 appropriations, although it did approve the Consolidated Appropriations Act for FY2009 (P.L. 110-329) that provided funding until March 6, 2009. In the 111th Congress, the FY2009 Omnibus Appropriations Act, (P.L. 111-8) provides funding for Cuba broadcasting under the Broadcasting Board of Governors' International Broadcasting Operations account, which appears to include full funding for Administration's $34.4 million request for Cuba broadcasting.

Migration Issues

1994 and 1995 Migration Accords

Cuba and the United States reached two migration accords in 1994 and 1995 designed to stem the mass exodus of Cubans attempting to reach the United States by boat. On the minds of U.S. policymakers was the 1980 Mariel boatlift in which 125,000 Cubans fled to the United States with the approval of Cuban officials. In response to Castro's threat to unleash another Mariel, U.S. officials reiterated U.S. resolve not to allow another exodus. Amid escalating numbers of fleeing Cubans, on August 19, 1994, President Clinton abruptly changed U.S. migration policy, under which Cubans attempting to flee their homeland were allowed into the United States, and announced that the U.S. Coast Guard and Navy would take Cubans rescued at sea to the U.S. naval base at Guantanamo Bay, Cuba. Despite the change in policy, Cubans continued fleeing in large numbers.

As a result, in early September 1994, Cuba and the United States began talks that culminated in a September 9, 1994 bilateral agreement to stem the flow of Cubans fleeing to the United States by boat. In the agreement, the United States and Cuba agreed to facilitate safe, legal, and orderly Cuban migration to the United States, consistent with a 1984 migration agreement. The United States agreed to ensure that total legal Cuban migration to the United States would be a minimum of 20,000 each year, not including immediate relatives of U.S. citizens. In a change of policy, the United States agreed to discontinue the practice of granting parole to all Cuban migrants who reach the United States, while Cuba agreed to take measures to prevent unsafe departures from Cuba.

In May 1995, the United States reached another accord with Cuba under which the United States would parole the more than 30,000 Cubans housed at Guantanamo into the United States, but would intercept future Cuban migrants attempting to enter the United States by sea and would return them to Cuba. The two countries would cooperate jointly in the effort. Both countries also pledged to ensure that no action would be taken against those migrants returned to Cuba as a consequence of their attempt to immigrate illegally. On January 31, 1996, the Department of Defense announced that the last of some 32,000 Cubans intercepted at sea and housed at Guantanamo had left the U.S. Naval Station, most having been paroled into the United States.

Coast Guard Interdictions

Since the 1995 migration accord, the U.S. Coast Guard has interdicted thousands of Cubans at sea and returned them to their country, while those deemed at risk for persecution have been transferred to Guantanamo and then found asylum in a third country or eventually the United States. Those Cubans who reach shore are allowed to apply for permanent resident status in one year, pursuant to the Cuban Adjustment Act of 1966 (P.L. 89-732). This so-called "wet foot/dry foot" policy has been criticized by some as encouraging Cubans to risk their lives in order to make it to the United States and as encouraging alien smuggling. Others maintain that U.S. policy should welcome those migrants fleeing communist Cuba whether or not they are able to make it to land.

The number of Cubans interdicted at sea by the U.S. Coast Guard has risen in recent years, from 666 in FY2002 to 2,712 in FY2005. In FY2006 and FY2007, Cuban interdictions rose to 2,810 and 2,868, respectively, but interdictions declined to 2,199 in FY2008 [126]. In recent years, increasing numbers of Cuban migrants attempting to reach the United States have been intercepted in Mexico. Mexico and Cuba negotiated a migration accord in October 2008 to curb the irregular flow of migrants through Mexico [127].

U.S. prosecution against migrant smugglers in Florida has increased in recent years with numerous convictions. There have been several violent incidents in which Cuban migrants have brandished weapons or in which Coast Guard officials have used force to prevent Cubans from reaching shore. In late December 2007, a Coast Guard official in Florida called on the local Cuban American community to denounce the smuggling and stop financing the trips that are leading to more deaths at sea [128] The Cuban government also has taken forceful action against individuals engaging in alien smuggling. Prison sentences of up to three years may be imposed against those engaging in alien smuggling.

In the aftermath of Fidel Castro's July 2006, announcement that he was temporarily ceding political power to his brother, Department of Homeland Security officials announced several measures to discourage Cubans from risking their lives on the open seas. On August 11, 2006, Department of Homeland Security (DHS) Deputy Secretary Michael P. Jackson urged "the Cuban people to stay on the island" and discouraged "anyone from risking their life in the open seas in order to travel to the United States." At the same time, DHS announced additional measures to discourage Cubans from turning to alien smuggling as a way to enter the United States. The measures support family reunification by increasing the numbers of Cuban migrants admitted to the United States each year who have family members in the United States, although the overall number of Cubans admitted to the United States annually will remain at about 21,000. Cubans who attempt to enter the United States illegally will be deemed ineligible to enter under this new family reunification procedure. In another change of policy, Cuban medical personnel currently conscripted by the Cuban government to work in third countries are now allowed to enter the United States; their families in Cuba are also allowed to enter the United States [129].

Migration Talks

Semi-annual U.S.-Cuban talks alternating between Cuba and the United States had been held regularly on the implementation of the 1994 and 1995 migration accords, but the State Department cancelled the 20th round of talks scheduled for January 2004, and no migration talks have been held since. According to the State Department, Cuba has refused to discuss five issues identified by the United States: (1) Cuba's issuance of exit permits for all qualified migrants; (2) Cuba's cooperation in holding a new registration for an immigrant lottery; (3) the need for a deeper Cuban port used by the U.S. Coast Guard for the repatriation of Cubans interdicted at sea; (4) Cuba's responsibility to permit U.S. diplomats to travel to monitor returned migrants; and (5) Cuba's obligation to accept the return of Cuban nationals determined to be inadmissible to the United States [130]. In response to the cancellation of the talks, Cuban officials maintained that the U.S. decision was irresponsible and that Cuba was prepared to discuss all of the issues raised by the United States [131].

Guantanamo Naval Base

The 45-square mile U.S. Naval Station at Guantanamo Bay, Cuba, has been a U.S. base since 1903, and under a 1934 treaty that remains in force, the U.S. presence can only be terminated by mutual agreement or by abandonment by the United States. When Fidel Castro assumed power in the 1959 Cuban revolution, the new government gave assurances that it would respect all its treaty commitments, including the 1934 treaty covering the Guantanamo base. Subsequently, however, as U.S.-Cuban relations deteriorated, the Cuban government opposed the presence as illegal.

The mission of the base has changed over time. During the Cold War, the base was viewed as a good location for controlling Caribbean sea lanes, as a deterrent to the Soviet presence in the Caribbean, and as a location for supporting potential military operations in the region. In 19941995, the base was used to house thousands of Cubans and Haitians fleeing their homeland, but by 1996 the last of the refugees had departed, with most Cubans paroled into the United States, pursuant to a May 1995 U.S.-Cuban migration accord. Since the 1995 accord, the U.S. Coast Guard has interdicted thousands of Cubans at sea and returned them to Cuba, while a much smaller number, those deemed at risk for persecution, have been taken to Guantanamo and then granted asylum in a third country.

Another mission for the Guantanamo base emerged with the U.S.-led global campaign against terrorism in the aftermath of the September 11, 2001, terrorist attacks in the United States. With the U.S. war in Afghanistan in 2001, the United States decided to send some captured Taliban and Al Qaeda fighters to be imprisoned in Guantanamo. Although the Cuban government has objected to the U.S. presence at Guantanamo, it did not initially oppose the new mission of housing detainees. Then Defense Minister Raúl Castro noted that, in the unlikely event that a prisoner would escape into Cuban territory, Cuba would capture the prisoner and return him to the base [132] The Cuban government, however, has expressed concerns about the treatment of prisoners at the U.S. base and has said it will keep pressing the international community to investigate the treatment of terrorist suspects [133] In January 2005, it denounced what it described as "atrocities" committed at the Guantanamo base [134]

President Obama issued Executive Order 13492 on January 22, 2009 that requires the closure of the Guantanamo detention facility (not the base itself) as soon as practicable, but no later than one year. Some Members of Congress also have called for the closure of the detention facility and have introduced legislation in the 111th Congress. Other measures have been introduced to prohibit the transfer of the enemy combatants detained at Guantanamo from being transferred to various military prisons in the United States.

With regard to the future of the Guantanamo base overall, a provision in the Cuban Liberty and Democratic Solidarity Act of 1996 (P.L. 104-114, Section 210) states that once a democratically elected Cuban government is in place, U.S. policy is to be prepared to enter into negotiations either to return the base to Cuba or to renegotiate the present agreement under mutually agreeable terms.

LEGISLATIVE INITIATIVES IN THE 111TH CONGRESS

P.L. 111-8 (H.R. 1105). Omnibus Appropriations Act, 2009. Introduced February 23, 2009; House passed (245-178) February 25, 2009; Senate passed (voice vote) March 10, 2009; signed into law March 11, 2009. Division D, Financial Services and General Government Appropriations Act, 2009, has three provisions intended to ease U.S. sanctions on Cuba. These three provisions, explained below, were identical to provisions in the S. 3260, the Senate version of the Financial Services and General Government Appropriations Act, 2009, in the 110th Congress. In addition, the Joint Explanatory Statement to the bill requires the Department of the Treasury to prepare a report within 90 days on the steps that it is taking to assess the Office of Foreign Assets Control's allocation of resources for investigating and penalizing violations of the Cuba embargo with respect to the numerous other sanctions programs it administers. As part of the report, the Treasury Department is directed to provide detailed information on OFAC's Cuba-related licensing on its enforcement of the Cuba embargo.

Section 620 of Division D amends the Trade Sanctions Reform and Export Enhancement Act of 2000 (TSRA) to require the Secretary of the Treasury to issue regulations for travel to, from, or within Cuba under a general license for the marketing and sale of agricultural and medical goods, meaning that there would be no requirement to obtain special permission from OFAC. Such travel currently requires a specific license from OFAC, issued on a case by case basis.

Section 621 of Division D prohibits funds from being used to administer, implement, or enforce family travel restrictions that were imposed by the Bush Administration in June 2004. Those 2004 restrictions allowed family travel only to visit immediate family (grandparents, grandchildren, parents, siblings, spouses, and children) once every three years for a period not to exceed 14 days. Under the 2004 restrictions, a specific license was required from OFAC for such travel, and the authorized amount that family travelers could spend while in Cuba was limited to $50 a day.

Section 622 of Division D prohibits funds in the Act from being used to administer, implement, or enforce an amendment to the Cuban embargo regulations on February 25, 2005 requiring that U.S. agricultural exporters using the "payment of cash in advance'" payment mechanism for selling their goods to Cuba must be paid in cash for their goods before the goods leave U.S. ports. Prior to the February 2005 change, the practice was for U.S. agricultural exporters to be paid in cash for their goods (as required under the TSRA), but before the actual delivery of the goods to Cuba.

Division H (Department of State, Foreign Operations, and Related Programs Appropriations Act, 2009) has two provisions related to Cuba. Section 7005 prohibits foreign assistance to the government of Cuba. Section 7015(f) provides that no funds appropriated for foreign assistance shall be obligated or expended for Cuba except as provided through the regular notification procedures of the Committees on Appropriations.

H.R. 187 (Serrano). Waives certain prohibitions with respect to nationals of Cuba coming to the United States to play organized professional baseball. Introduced January 6, 2009; referred to Committees on Foreign Affairs and Judiciary.

H.R. 188 (Serrano). Lifts the trade embargo on Cuba. Introduced January 6, 2009; referred to Committees on Foreign Affairs, Ways and Means, Energy and Commerce, Judiciary, Financial Services, Oversight and Government Reform, and Agriculture.

H.R. 332 (Lee). Provides that no funds made available to the Department of the Treasury may be used to implement, administer, or enforce regulations to require specific licenses for travel-related transactions directly related to educational activities in Cuba.

H.R. 375 (Ros-Lehtinen). Section 209 of the bill sets forth restrictions on nuclear cooperation with countries assisting the nuclear program of Venezuela or Cuba or transferring advanced conventional weapons to Venezuela or Cuba. Introduced January 9, 2009; referred to Committee on Foreign Affairs.

H.R. 874 (Delahunt)/ S. 428 (Dorgan). Identical bills would prohibit the President from regulating or prohibiting, directly or indirectly, travel to or from Cuba by U.S. citizens or legal residents, or any of the transactions incident to such travel. H.R. 874 was introduced February 4, 2009, and referred to the House Committee on Foreign Affairs. S. 428 was introduced February 12, 2009, and referred to the Senate Committee on Foreign Affairs.

H.R. 1103 (Wexler). Modifies the prohibition on recognition by U.S. courts of certain rights relating to certain marks, trade names, or commercial names. Introduced February 13, 2009; referred to the Committee on the Judiciary.

H.R. 1528 (Rangel). Allows travel between the United States and Cuba. Introduced March 16, 2009; referred to the Committee on Foreign Affairs.

H.R. 1530 (Rangel). Lift the trade embargo on Cuba. Introduced March 16, 2009; referred to the Committee on Foreign Affairs, and in addition to the Committees on Ways and Means, Energy and Commerce, the Judiciary, Financial Services, Oversight and Government Reform, and Agriculture.

H.R. 1531 (Rangel). Facilitates the export of U.S. agricultural products to Cuba as authorized by the Trade Sanctions Reform and Export Enhancement Act of 2000, removes impediments to the export to Cuba of medical devices and medicines, allows travel to Cuba by U.S. legal residents, and establishes and agricultural export promotion program with respect to Cuba.

LEGISLATION IN THE 110TH CONGRESS

Approved Measures

P.L. 110-161 (H.R. 2764). FY2008 Consolidated Appropriations Act. H.R. 2764 was originally introduced and reported by the House Committee on Appropriations (H.Rept. 110-197) on June 18, 2007 as the FY2008 State, Foreign Operations, and Related Agencies Appropriations Act. The House passed (241-178) the measure on June 22, 2007. The Senate Appropriations Committee reported the bill on July 10, 2007 (S.Rept. 110-128), and the Senate passed (81-12) it on September 6, 2007. On December 17, 2007, H.R. 2764 subsequently became the vehicle for the FY2008 Consolidated Appropriations Act, which included 11 FY2008 appropriations measures. President Bush signed the measure into law on December 26, 2007.

As signed into law, Division J of the Consolidated Appropriations Act covers State Department, Foreign Operations, and Related Agencies appropriations. The law has the following Cuba provisions:

- Similar to previous years, Section 607 of Division J prohibits direct funding for Cuba. This provision had been included in both the House and Senate versions ofthe bill.
- Section 620 of Division J adds Cuba to the list of countries requiring a special notification to the Appropriations Committees for funds obligated or expended under the act. This provision had been included in the Senate version of the bill.
- Section 691(b) of Division J provides that Cubans who supported an anti-Castro guerrilla group in the 1960s known as the Alzados are eligible for U.S. refugee status. The Senate version of the bill had included this provision.
- As set forth in the joint explanatory statement, the measure provides $45.7 million in ESF for Cuba democracy programs as requested by the Administration. Both the House- and Senate-passed versions of H.R. 2764 fully funded the Administration's request for $45.7 million in ESF for Cuba democracy programs. The House committee-reported bill would have provided $9 million in ESF for such programs, but during June 21, 2007, floor consideration, the House approved H.Amdt. 351 (Diaz-Balart) by a vote of 254-170 that increased ESF by $36.7 million in order to fully fund the Administration's request. The Senate Appropriations Committee report to the bill would have provided $15 million in ESF for Cuba democracy programs, but during September 6, 2007, floor consideration, the Senate approved S.Amdt. 2694 (Martinez) by voice vote that increased funding for Cuba democracy programs by $30.7 million to fully fund the Administration's request.
- As set forth in the joint explanatory statement, the measure provides $33.681 million for Radio and TV Marti broadcasting to Cuba, $5.019 million below theAdministration's request of $38.7 million and identical to the amount provided for FY2007. Both the House and Senate committee reports to the bill had recommended

$33.681 million for Cuba broadcasting. S.Amdt. 2695 (Martinez), which was withdrawn from consideration on September 6, 2007, would haveincreased funding by $5.019 million to fully fund the Administration's request.

- The measure does not include contrasting provisions related to counternarcotics assistance for Cuba that were included in the House and Senate versions of the bill. Section 673 of the House bill would have specifically prohibitedInternational Narcotics Control and Law Enforcement (INCLE) assistance to the Cuban government. Section 696 of the Senate bill would have provided $1 million in INCLE assistance for preliminary work by the Department of State, orsuch other entity as the Secretary of State may designate, to establish cooperation with the Cuban government on counternarcotics matters.

The final enacted measure does not include provisions easing Cuba sanctions that had been included in the House and Senate-committee versions of the FY2008 Financial Services and General Government Appropriations Act or the Senate-committee reported version of the FY2008 Agriculture Appropriations bill.

P.L. 110-96 (S. 1612). International Emergency Economic Powers Enhancement Act. Introduced and reported by the Committee on Banking, Housing, and Urban Affairs on June 13, 2007 (S.Rept. 110-82). Senate approved, amended, by unanimous consent on June 26, 2007. House approved by voice vote October 2, 2007. As approved, the bill amends the International Emergency Economic Powers Act (IEEPA) to increase the potential civil penalty imposed on any person who commits an unlawful act under the act to not exceed the greater of $250,000 (from $50,000) or an amount that is twice the amount of the transaction. The bill also increases a criminal penalty to not more than $1 million and/or 20 years imprisonment.

S.Res. 573 (Martinez). Celebrates Cuba Solidarity Day, recognizes the injustices faced by the Cuban people, and stands in solidarity with the Cuban people as they continue to work towards democratic changes in their homeland. Introduced and passed by the Senate on May 21, 2008, by unanimous consent.

Additional Condition Measures with Cuba Provisions

The following measures that received consideration contained various provisions on Cuba that would have eased U.S. sanctions, but none of these provisions made it into final enacted measures.

H.R. 2419 (Peterson). Farm, Nutrition, and Bioenergy Act of 2007. Introduced May 22, 2007; House passed July 27, 2007. Senate passed December 14, 2007. During House floor consideration on July 27, 2007, the House rejected (182-245) H.Amdt. 707 Rangel, that would have clarified the meaning of "payment of cash in advance" for the sale of agricultural commodities to Cuba; authorized direct transfer between U.S. and Cuban financial institutions for a product authorized for sale under the Trade Sanctions Reform and Export Enhancement Act of 2000; and would have authorized the issuance of U.S. visas for Cubans to conduct activities, including phytosanitary inspections, related to the export of U.S. agricultural goods to Cuba.

In the Senate, S.Amdt. 3660 (Baucus), which would have eased restrictions on U.S. agricultural sales to Cuba, was proposed on December 11, 2007, but subsequently withdrawn the same day. Several amendments regarding Cuba were submitted, but never proposed: S.Amdt. 3668 (Baucus), would have eased restrictions on U.S. agricultural exports to Cuba; S.Amdt. 3796 (Nelson, Bill), would have required a certification of certain human rights conditions in Cuba before restrictions on U.S. agricultural exports to Cuba would be eased; S.Amdt. 3792 (Martinez), would have expressed the sense of the Senate regarding the human rights situation in Cuba; and S.Amdt. 3793 (Martinez), would have prevented the easing of restrictions on U.S. agricultural exports to Cuba as long as the country is identified by the Secretary of State as a "state sponsor of terror."

H.R. 2829 (Serrano). FY2008 Financial Services and General Government Appropriations Act. Introduced and reported by House Appropriations Committee (H.Rept. 110-207) June 22, 2007. Reported by Senate Appropriations Committee July 13, 2007 (S.Rept. 110-129). House passed (240-179) June 28, 2007. As approved by the House, Section 903 would have prevented Treasury Department funds from being used to implement a February 2005 regulation that requires the payment of cash in advance prior to the shipment of U.S. agricultural goods to Cuba. The House adopted the provision during June 28, 2007 floor consideration when it approved H.Amdt. 467 (Moran, Kansas) by voice vote. The Senate Appropriations Committee version had a similar provision in Section 619, as well as another provision in Section 620 that would have allowed for travel to Cuba under a general license for the marketing and sale of agricultural and medical goods. The Cuba provisions of both the House and Senate versions of the bill were not included in the final enacted version of the measure, which was included as Division D of the FY2008 Consolidated Appropriations Act (P.L. 110-161, H.R. 2764).

H.R. 3161 (DeLauro)/ S. 1859 (Kohl). FY2008 Agricultural, Rural Development, Food and Drug Administration, and Related Agencies Appropriations Act. H.R. 3161 introduced and reported by House Appropriations Committee July 24, 2007; House passed August 2, 2007. S. 1859 introduced and reported by Senate Appropriations Committee July 24, 2007 (S.Rept. 110134). Section 741 of the Senate bill would authorize travel to Cuba under a general license for the marketing and sale of agricultural and medical goods to Cuba. The Cuba provision in the Senate version was not included in the final enacted version of the measure, which was included as Division A of the FY2008 Consolidated Appropriations Act (P.L. 110-161, H.R. 2764).

H.R. 7323 (Serrano). FY2009 Financial Services and General Government Appropriations bill. Introduced and reported by the House Appropriations Committee on December 10, 2008 (H.Rept. 110-920). The committee had approved a draft version of the bill on June 25, 2008. The bill has several provisions that would have eased Cuba sanctions. Section 621 would have prohibited funds in the Act from being used to administer, implement, or enforce new language in the Cuban embargo regulations added on February 25, 2005 (31CFR Part 515.533) that requires that U.S. agricultural exports to Cuba must be paid for before they leave U.S. ports. Section 622 would have allowed for family travel once a year (instead of the current restriction of once every three years). Section 623 would have expanded family travel to visit an aunt, uncle, niece, nephew, or first cousin (instead of the current restriction limiting such travel to visit a spouse, child, grandchild, parent, grandparent, or sibling.) The report to the bill would require the Treasury Department's Office of Foreign Assets Control (OFAC) to provide detailed information on OFAC's Cuba-related licensing and enforcement actions. None of these provisions were included in the Consolidated Appropriations Act for FY2009 (P.L. 110-329) that provided funding until March 6, 2009.

S. 3001(Levin). Duncan Hunter National Defense Authorization Act for FY2009. *S.Amdt. 5581 (Dodd),* submitted on September 15, 2008, would, for a 180-day period: allow unrestricted family travel; ease restrictions on remittances by removing the limit and allowing any American to send remittances to Cuba; expand the list of allowable items that may be included in gift parcels; and allow for unrestricted U.S. cash sales of food, medicines, and relief supplies to Cuba. The amendment was not considered and therefore not included in the final bill.

S. 3260 (Durbin). Financial Services and General Government Appropriations Act, 2009. Introduced and reported by Senate Appropriations Committee (S.Rept. 110-417) on July 14, 2008. Includes provisions easing restrictions on payment terms for the sale of agricultural goods to Cuba (section 618), travel relating to the commercial sale of agricultural and medical goods (section 619), and family travel (section 620). None of these provisions were included in the Consolidated Appropriations Act for FY2009 (P.L. 110-329) that provided funding until March 6, 2009.

S. 3288 (Leahy). Department of State, Foreign Operations, and Related Programs Appropriations Act, 2009. Introduced and reported by Senate Appropriations Committee (S.Rept. 110-425) July 18, 2008. Includes several Cuba provisions: section 706 continues a prohibition on assistance to Cuba, unless the President determines that it is in the national interest of the United States; section 719 continues the provision from FY2008 that requires that any assistance for Cuba go through the regular notification procedures of the Committees on Appropriations; section 779 provides for $1 million for preliminary work by the Department of State, or other entity designated by the Secretary of State, to establish cooperation with appropriate Cuban agencies on counternarcotics matters, although the money would not be available if the Secretary certifies that Cuba 1) does not have in place procedures to protect against the loss of innocent life in the air and on the ground in connection with the interdiction of illegal drugs; and 2) there is credible evidence of involvement of the government of Cuba in drug trafficking during the preceding 10 years. The Senate Appropriations Committee report to the bill recommended full funding for the Administration's requests of $34.392 million for Cuba broadcasting and $20 million in ESF for Cuba democracy programs, and called for the State Department and USAID to conduct regular evaluations to ensure the cost effectiveness of the programs.

S. 3289 (Kohl). Agriculture, Rural Development, Food and Drug Administration, and Related Agencies Appropriations Act, 2008. Introduced and reported by Senate Appropriations Committee (S.Rept. 110-426) July 21, 2008. Includes a provision (section 737) that would ease restrictions on travel to Cuba for the sale of agricultural and medical goods. This provision was not included in the Consolidated Appropriations Act for FY2009 (P.L. 110-329) that provided funding until March 6, 2009.

REFERENCES

[1] For more on Cuba's political succession, see CRS Report RS22742, *Cuba's Political Succession: From Fidel to Raul Castro*, by Mark P. Sullivan.

[2] Daniel Dombey, Richard Lapper, and Andrew Ward, "A Family Business, Cuban-Americans Look Beyond theHavana Handover," Financial Times, February 27, 2008.

[3] Pablo Bachelet, "New Cuban Leader Adds Military Loyalists to Team," *Miami Herald*, February 25, 2008.

[4] "Cuba: Full Text of Raúl Castro's National Assembly Address," *Cubavisión*, Havana (as translated by Open Source Center) February 24, 2008.

[5] "Text of Fidel Castro's Online Essay," *Associated Press Newswires*, January 22, 2009.

[6] Frances Robles, "Raúl Castro May Usher in More Economic Reforms," *Miami Herald*, January 15, 2009.

[7] According to Fidel, "The sweetness of power for which they had made no sacrifice awoke in them ambitions that led them to an unworthy role. The external enemy was filled with illusion about them." See: Reflections of Fidel, "Health Changes within the Council of Ministers," from *CubaDebate* as translated by *Granma International*, March 3, 2009.

[8] Wildredo Cancio Isla, "Another Leader Official Ousted," *El Nuevo Herald*, March 6, 2009.

[9] Frances Robles, "Cuban Government Undergoes Massive Restructuring," *Miami Herald*, March 3, 2009.

[10] For further discussion of potential Cuban political scenarios in the aftermath of Fidel Castro's stepping down from power in 2006 because of poor health, see CRS Report RL33622, *Cuba's Future Political Scenarios and U.S. Policy Approaches*, by Mark P. Sullivan.

[11] Organization of American States, Inter-American Commission on Human Rights, "Annual Report of the IACHR 2007," December 29, 2007, "Chapter IV, Cuba" available at http://www.cidh.org/annualrep/2007eng/Chap.4b.htm.

[12] Comision Cubana de Derechos Humanos y Reconciliacion Nacional, "Cuba en el año 2009: la situacíon de derechos civiles, políticos y económicos," February 2, 2009.

[13] Anita Snow, "Cuban Rights Group: Political Prisoners Down, But Brief Detentions of Activists Up," *AssociatedPress Newswires*, February 2, 2009; "Cuba Has Fewer Political Prisoners, Report Says," *Reuters News*, February 2, 2009; and Isabel Sanchez, "Cuba's Raúl Castro Marks 100 Days in Power," *Agence France-Presse*, June 2, 2008.

[14] James C. McKinley, Jr, "Cuban Signs Rights Pacts That It Long Had Fought," *New York Times*, March 1, 2008.

[15] Frances Robles, "Cuban Police Are Detaining Activists Prior to Human Rights Day," *Miami Herald*, December 11,2008.

[16] The website of the Damas de Blanco is available at http://www.damas deblanco.com/.

[17] Frances Robles, "Jailed Cuban Journalist Wins Prize," *Miami Herald*, December 5, 2008; and "Cuba's Repression," *Miami Herald*, November 24, 2008.

[18] Marco Sibaja, "Raul Castro Offers To Free Dissidents in Exchange for Alleged Cuban Spies Jailed in U.S.,"*Associated Press Newswires*, December 18, 2008.

[19] For further information, see the website of Oswaldo Payá, at http://www.oswaldopaya.org/es/.

[20] "Text of Jimmy Carter's Speech, Broadcast Live to Cuban People," Associated Press, May 15, 2002.

[21] "Cuba Country Report," *Economist Intelligence Unit*, February 2009.

[22] Frances Robles, "Venezuelan Oil Subsidies to Cuba Balloon," *Miami Herald*, August 2, 2007.

[23] "Cuba Country Report," *Economist Intelligence Unit*, February 2009.

[24] "Infant Mortality, 5.3 in 2007!" *Granma Internacional*, January 4, 2008.

[25] Larry Luxner, "New Decree Limits Dollar Transactions as Cuba Tightens Controls Once Again," *CubaNews*, April 2004.

[26] Larry Luxner, "Cuba's 'Convertible Peso' No Longer Linked to U.S. Dollar," *CubaNews*, April 2005, p. 3.

[27] Manuel Roig-Franzia, "Cuba's Call for Economic Detente," *Washington Post,* July 27, 2007.

[28] Frances Robles, "Cubans Urged to Vent Views," *Miami Herald*, October 2, 2007.

[29] "Cuba: Full Text of Raúl Castro's National Assembly Address," *Cubavisión*, Havana (as translated by Open Source Center) February 24, 2008.

[30] Marc Frank, "Raúl Castro Overhauls Cuba's Farm Bureaucracy," *Reuters News*, May 1, 2008.

[31] U.S. Department of State, "Country Reports on Human Rights Practices 2007, Cuba," March 11, 2008.

[32] "Cuba: Raúl Castro's 26 July Rebellion Day Speech," Havana Cubavisión (Open Source Center), July 26, 2006.

[33] "Cuba: Text of Raúl Castro's 11 July National Assembly Speech," Havana Cubavisión (Open Source Center), July 11, 2008.

[34] "Cuba: Bringing Cuba in from the cold," *Latin American Regional Report, Caribbean and Central America*, December 2008.

[35] U.S. Department of State, "Commission for Assistance to a Free Cuba," White House Fact Sheet, December 8, 2003.

[36] U.S. Department of State, Second Report of the Commission for Assistance to a Free Cuba, Briefing, July 10, 2006.

[37] Nicholas Kralev, "Bush OKs Initiative to Support Opposition," *Washington Times*, July 11, 2006.

[38] Frances Robles and Pablo Bachelet, "Plan for Change in Cuba Gets OK," *Miami Herald,* July 11, 2006.

[39] Miriam Leiva, "We Cubans Must Decide," *Miami Herald*, July 15, 2006.

[40] U.S. Department of State, "Secretary of State Condoleezza Rice Message to the People of Cuba," August 4, 2006.

[41] "No Enemy Can Defeat Us," interview of Raúl Castro by Laszar Barredo Medina, *Diario Granma*, August 18, 2006.

[42] U.S. Department of State, "U.S. Policy Toward Cuba," Thomas Shannon, Assistant Secretary for Western Hemisphere Affairs, August 23, 2006.

[43] "English Transcript of Raul Castro's Speech," *Miami Herald*, December 2, 2006.

[44] Frances Robles, "Raúl Again Offers 'Olive Branch' to U.S.," *Miami Herald,* July 27, 2007; "U.S. Government Rejects Dialogue with Cuba," *EFE*, July 27, 2007.

[45] White House, Office of the Press Secretary, "President Bush Addresses the United Nations General Assembly,"September 25, 2007.
[46] U.S. Department of Commerce, "Commerce Secretary Carlos M. Gutierrez Remarks at the Heritage Foundation,"September 17, 2007.
[47] White House, "President Bush Discusses Cuba Policy," October 24, 2007.
[48] White House, "President Bush Delivers Remarks on Cuba," March 7, 2008.
[49] "Text of Bush Speech to Council of the Americas," *Miami Herald*, May 9, 2008.
[50] White House, "President Bush Discusses Cuba, Marks Day of Solidarity," May 21, 2008.
[51] "Remarks of Senator Barack Obama, Renewing U.S. Leadership in the Americas," May 23, 2008, and "Renewing U.S. Leadership in the Americas," Factsheet, June 6, 2008, BarackObama.com
[52] Ana Radelat, "Lifting of Bush-Era Travel Rules for Exiles Could Delay Wider Policy Moves on Cuba," *Cuba News*, March 16, 2009.
[53] *Congressional Record*, March 10, 2009, pp. S2932-S2935.
[54] Caitlin Webber, "Obama Accused of Ignoring Legislators' Bid to Ease Cuba Trade Restrictions," *CQ Today*, March 18, 2009; and Jerry Hagstrom, "Bipartisan Senate Group Pushes Geithner on Cuba Trade," *Congress Daily PM, National Journal*, March 17, 2009.
[55] U.N. Office for the Coordination of Humanitarian Affairs (OCHA), "Situation Report 17 – Caribbean Hurricane Season," September 22, 2008.
[56] "Paloma Brings 2008 Hurricane Season to a Close; Damages Exceed $10 Billion,"," *CubaNews*, December 2008.
[57] USAID, Bureau for Democracy, Conflict, and Humanitarian Assistance (DCHA), Office of U.S. Foreign Disaster Assistance (OFDA), "Latin America and the Caribbean – Hurricane Season 2008, Fact Sheet #3, FY2008," September 10, 2008.
[58] Frances Robles, "Cuba Rejects U.S. Supplies, Asks for Suspension of Trade Embargo," *Miami Herald*, September 16, 2008.
[59] Frances Robles, "U.S. Offers $6.3M in Construction Materials to Cuba," *Miami Herald*, September 22, 2008; JoshuaPartlow, "Hurricanes Shift Debate on Embargo Against Cuba," *Washington Post*, September 24, 2008.
[60] U.S. Department of State, "Humanitarian Assistance to the Cuban People Following Hurricanes Gustav and Ike," September 15, 2008.
[61] Cuban Ministry of Foreign Affairs, "Cuba Asks Washington to Lift Commercial Restrictions," September 11, 2008;and "Statement by the Ministry of Foreign Affairs," September 6, 2008.
[62] Karen DeYoung, "U.S. Urges Cuba to Accept Aid; Storm Relief Would Be Sent Directly to Havana Government," *Washington Post*, September 16, 2008.
[63] In June 2004, the Department of Commerce's Bureau of Industry and Security (BIS) published changes to the Export Administration Regulations that placed new limits on gift parcels sent to Cuba. This included prohibiting the inclusion of previously-allowed items such as seeds, clothing, personal hygiene items, veterinary medicines and supplies, fishing equipment and supplies, and soap-making equipment. (*Federal Register*, June 22, 2004, pp. 34565-34567).
[64] Oscar Corral, "Is Santería Used as Ploy to Skirt Travel Rules?," *Miami Herald*, February 27, 2005.

[65] Oscar Corral, “Feds Lay Down the Law on Cuba to Travel Agents,” *Miami Herald*, April 29, 2006; Pablo Bachelet,“New Rules Impede Religious Travel,” *Miami Herald*, March 16, 2006.
[66] U.S. Department of Agriculture, Foreign Agricultural Service, Office of Global Analysis, “Cuba’s Food andAgriculture Situation Report,” March 2008.
[67] World Trade Atlas, which uses Department of Commerce Statistics.
[68] U.S. Department of the Treasury, Testimony of Robert Werner, Director, OFAC, before the House Committee on Agriculture, March 16, 2005.
[69] Christopher S. Rugaber, “Treasury Clarifies Cuba Farm Export Rule, and Baucus Relents on Nominees,”*International Trade Reporter*, August 4, 2005.
[70] “Ag Groups Split Over Trade With Cuba,” *Congress Daily AM*, National Journal, February 11, 2003.
[71] “Farm Equipment Exports Likely to Face Tough Opposition from White House, Congress,” *Cuba Trader*, Vol. III, No. 7, February 17, 2003.
[72] *Congressional Record*, March 10, 2009, p. S2933.
[73] U.S. Department of the Treasury, Office of Foreign Assets Control, “Guidance on Implementation of Cuba Traveland Trade-Related Provisions of the Omnibus Appropriations Act, 2009,” March 11, 2009.
[74] *Congressional Record*, March 10, 2009, p. S2933.
[75] For additional information, see CRS Report RS21764, *Restricting Trademark Rights of Cubans: WTO Decision and Congressional Response*, by Margaret Mikyung Lee.
[76] “U.S., EU Agree on Deadline for Complying with Section 211 WTO Finding,” *Inside U.S. Trade,* April 12, 2002.
[77] “Japan, EU Suspend WTO Retaliation Against U.S. in Two Cases,” *Inside U.S. Trade*, July 15, 2005.
[78] “PTO Cancels Cuban ‘Havana Club’ Mark; Bacardi Set to Sell Rum Under Same Mark,” *International Trade Daily*, August 10, 2006.
[79] Brian Lehman, testimony before the Senate Committee on the Judiciary, hearing on “An Examination of Section 211 of the Omnibus Appropriations Act of 1998,” July 13, 2004.
[80] “USA-Engage Joins Cuba Fight,” *Cuba Trader*, April 1, 2002.
[81] U.S. Energy Information Administration , “Country Analysis Briefs: Caribbean,” September 2007; U.S. GeologicalSurvey, “Assessment of Undiscovered Oil and Gas Resources of the North Cuban Basin, Cuba, 2004,” Fact Sheet2005-3009, February 2005.
[82] Jeff Franks, "Cuba Oil Claims Raise Eyebrows in Energy World," October 24, 2008; and Larry Luxner, “Cuba Mayhave 20 Billion Barrels of Oil But Cash Crunch Threatens Investment,” *CubaNews*, November 2008.
[83] Jorge Piñon, “Cuba’s Energy Future,” Canadian Foundation for the Americas, *FocalPoint*, April 2007, Vol. 6, No. 3; “PetroVietnam Gets Go-Ahead to Explore Seven Cuban Oil Fields,” *Dow Jones International News*, November 20, 2007; and Larry Luxner, “Cuba May have 20 Billion Barrels of Oil But Cash Crunch Threatens Investment,” *CubaNews*, November 2008.
[84] Domingo Amuchastegui, “Cuban Again Invites U.S. Oil Giants to Invest in Oil Sector,” *CubaNews*, May 2007.

[85] Lesley Clark and Erika Bolstad, "China-Cuba Rumors Fuel Renewed Offshore Drilling Debate, Rumors of China Drilling in Cuban Waters Are Rallying Support for Drilling off Florida's Coast, But Experts Say They're Untrue," *Miami Herald*, June 12, 2008.

[86] Frances Robles, "Drug-Trafficking at 11-Year Low, Cuba Says," *Miami Herald*, March 3, 2007; U.S. Department of State, International Narcotics Control Strategy Report, March 2007, p. 188.

[87] On March 12, 2002, Cuba's Ministry of Foreign Affairs and the Cuban Interests Section in Washington delivered three diplomatic notes to the U.S. Interests Section in Havana and the State Department in Washington proposing agreements on drug interdiction, terrorism, and migration issues. See "Statement from the Ministry of Foreign Affairs: Prominent Drug Trafficker Arrested in our Country," Information Office, Cuban Interests Section, March 17, 2002; "Cuba Offers to Sign Anti-Drug Pact," *Miami Herald,* April 8, 2006.

[88] Anthony Boadle, "U.S. Thanks Cuba, But Declines Anti-Drug Accord," Reuters, March 19, 2002.

[89] U.S. Department of State, Release of the 2007 International Narcotics Control Strategy Report, Anne W. Patterson, Assistant Secretary of State for International Narcotics and Law Enforcement Affairs, On-The-Record Briefing, March 1, 2007.

[90] "White House Office of National Drug Control Policy Director Waters Holds News Briefing on Emerging Transatlantic Drug Threats at the Foreign Press Center," *Newsmakers Transcripts, CQ.com*, April 28, 2008.

[91] José Manuel Calvo, "Thomas Shannon Secretario de Estado adjunto para Latinoamérica: "Sería un acuerdo contra elnarcotráfico entre Cuba y EE UU," *El País*, January 11, 2009.

[92] For further information, see CRS Report RL32251, *Cuba and the State Sponsors of Terrorism List*, by Mark P. Sullivan.

[93] Patricia Grogg, "Cuba: Government Deports U.S. Citizen Charged with Child Abuse," *Inter Press Service*, June 16,2008.

[94] Jay Weaver, "Fugitives Flee South Florida with Medicare Millions," *Miami Herald*, January 2, 2009.

[95] Frances Robles, "An Old Foe of Castro Looks Back on His Fight," *Miami Herald*, September 4, 2003.

[96] Alfonso Chardy and Nancy San Martin, "Lawyer Expects Posada to Show Soon," *Miami Herald*, April 14, 2005.

[97] Ann Louise Bardach, "Our Man's in Miami. Patriot or Terrorist?," *Washington Post*, April 17, 2005.

[98] Although Posada was acquitted by a military court, a higher court ordered a new civilian trial. Reportedly a first set of prosecutors recommended against charging Posada, but a second set of prosecutors took the case to trial, and Posadaescaped during that time in 1985. See Oscar Corral, "Debate Focuses on Escape," *Miami Herald*, June 19, 2005.

[99] Oscar Corral and Alfonso Chardy, "Victim's Kin Oppose Posada Bid for Asylum," *Miami Herald*, May 7, 2005.

[100] Department of Homeland Security, Office of Public Affairs, Statement, May 17, 2005.

[101] Alicia Caldwell, "Judge Says Cuban Militant Can't Be Deported to Venezuela," *Associated Press*, September 28, 2005.

[102] Oscar Corral, "Cuban Exile Militant Luis Posada Denied Release," *Miami Herald*, March 22, 2006.

[103] Alfonso Chardy and Jay Weaver, "Posada a Target of New Federal Probes," *Miami Herald*, November 12, 2006, and "Grand Jury Indicts Cuban Exile Militant Luis Posada Carriles," *Miami Herald*, January 12, 2007.

[104] Alfonso Chardy, Oscar Corral, and Jay Weaver, "FBI, Cuba Cooperating on Posada," *Miami Herald*, May 3, 2007;"U.S., Cuba Unite to Investigate Former CIA Op," National Public Radio, Morning Edition, May 4, 2007.

[105] Carol J. Williams, "Pressure Grows to Prosecute Cuban Exile," *Los Angeles Times*, May 10, 2007.

[106] The federal prosecutors' brief is available at http://media.miamiherald.com/ smedia/2007/11/06/20/Posada_5CA_07-50737_electronic_copy.source.prod_affiliate.56.pdf.

[107] Michael Kunzelman, "Appeals Court Hears Cuban Militant's Immigration Case," *Associated Press*, June 4, 2008.

[108] See USAID's Cuba program website: http://www.usaid.gov/locations /latin_america_caribbean/country/cuba/.

[109] U.S. Government Accountability Office, U.S. Democracy Assistance for Cuba Needs Better Management and Oversight, GAO-07-147, November 2006.

[110] Oscar Corral, "Federal Program to Help Democracy in Cuba Falls Short of Mark," *Miami Herald*, November 14, 2006, and "Is U.S. Aid Reaching Castro Foes?" *Miami Herald*, November 15, 2006.

[111] Alfonso Chardy and Pablo Bachelet, "Cuban Exile Activist Felt 'Betrayal' by Employees," *Miami Herald,* April 24, 2008.

[112] Jesse J. Holland, "Former Bush Aide Pleads Guilty to Stealing from Anti-Castro Cuban Democracy Advocates,"*Associated Press Newswires*, December 19, 2008.

[113] Frances Robles, "Hold on Funds for Cuba Democracy Project Lifted," *Miami Herald*, July 23, 2008.

[114] U.S. Government Accountability Office, *Foreign Assistance: Continued Efforts Needed to Strengthen USAID's Oversight of U.S. Democracy Assistance for Cuba*, GAO-09-165, November 2008.

[115] Alfonso Chardy, "Exile Group: Not Enough Money Getting to Cuban Dissidents," *Miami Herald*, May 15, 2008;Cuban American National Foundation, "Findings and Recommendations on the Most Effective Use of USAID-CUBAFunds Authorized by Section 109(a) of the Cuban Liberty and Democratic Solidarity (Helms-Burton) Act of 1996,"March 2008.

[116] Christina Hoag, "Radio, TV Martí To Be Aired Locally," *Miami Herald*, December 19, 2006.

[117] Oscar Corral, "Radio, TV Martí Face Another Government Audit," *Miami Herald*, December 18, 2006, and"Problems Dog Broadcaster," *Miami Herald*, December 19, 2006.

[118] Jay Weaver, "TV Martí Executive Admits Taking Kickbacks," *Miami Herald*, February 14, 2007.

[119] See the following reports and audits: U.S. General Accounting Office (GAO), *Broadcasts to Cuba, TV Marti Surveys are Flawed*, GAO/NSIAD-90-252, August 1990; U.S. GAO, *TV Marti, Costs and Compliance with Broadcast Standards and*

International Agreements, GAO/NSIAD-92-199, May 1992; U.S. GAO, Letter to Hon. Howard L. Berman and Hon. John F. Kerry regarding Radio Marti broadcast standards, GAO/NSIAD-93-126R, February 17, 1993; Advisory Panel on Radio and TV Marti, *Report of the Advisory Panel on Radio and TV Marti*, Three Volumes, March 1994; U.S. GAO, *Radio Marti, Program Review Processes Need Strengthening*, GAO/NSIAD-94-265, September 1994; U.S. GAO, *U.S. Information Agency, Issues Related to Reinvention Planning in the Office of Cuba Broadcasting*, GAO/NSIAD-96-110, May 1996; U.S. Department of State, Office of the Inspector General, *Review of Polices and Procedures for Ensuring that Radio Marti Broadcasts Adhere to Applicable Requirements*, 99-IB-010, June 1999; U.S. Department of State and the Broadcasting Board of Governors, Office of Inspector General, *Review of the Effectiveness and Implementation of Office of Cuba Broadcasting's New Program Initiatives*, Report No. IBO-A03-01, January 2003, and *Report of Inspection, Office of Cuba Broadcasting,* Report No. ISP-IB 07-35, June 2007.

[120] The State Department originally issued a two-page summary of the report on its website on June 5, 2007, and pointed out that the full report received only "limited official distribution." On July 31, 2007, the State Department issued the entire 43-page report on its website, with certain sections redacted. That version is available at http://oig.state.gov/lbry/.

[121] Pablo Bachelet, "Martí Extending Its Reach, U.S. Says," *Miami Herald*, June 20, 2007.

[122] Vanessa Bauza, "TV Martí Signal Weak in Cuba, Broadcast Specialist Says," *South Florida Sun-Sentinel*, July 31, 2007.

[123] Laura Wides-Muñoz, "Despite Expenditures, TV Martí Still Tough to See in Cuba," Associated Press, July 30, 2007.

[124] U.S. Government Accountability Office, "Broadcasting to Cuba, Weaknesses in Contracting Practices Reduced Visibility into Selected Award Decisions," GAO-08-764, July 2008.

[125] U.S. Government Accountability Office, "Broadcasting to Cuba, Actions Are Needed to Improve Strategy and Operations," GAO-09-127, January 2009.

[126] U.S. Coast Guard, Alien Migrant Interdiction, Coast Guard Office of Law Enforcement, "Total Interdictions, Fiscal Year 1982 to Present," October 15, 2008.

[127] Diego Cevallos, "Migration: More and More Cubans Entering U.S. Through Mexico," *Inter Press Service News Agency*, June 17, 2008.

[128] Laura Morales, "Exiles Urged to Stem Tide of Cubans," *Miami Herald*, December 29, 2007.

[129] Department of Homeland Security, "DHS Announces Additional Measures to Combat Alien Smuggling of Cubans," and "USCIS Will Further Strengthen Measures that Support the Reunification of Families Separated by the Castro Regime," Press Releases, August 11, 2006; Pablo Bachelet, "U.S. Program for Defecting Cuban Doctors a Success," *Miami Herald*, March 12, 2007.

[130] U.S. Department of State. State Department Regular Briefing, Richard Boucher. January 7, 2004.

[131] "Migration Talks Cancelled," *Miami Herald*, January 8, 2004.

[132] "Cuba Would Hand Over Escapees, Raúl Castro Says," *Miami Herald*, January 20, 2002.

[133] For information on terrorist suspects held at Guantanamo, see CRS Report RL31367, *Treatment of "Battlefield Detainees" in the War on Terrorism*, by Jennifer K. Elsea; and CRS Report RS22173, *Detainees at Guantanamo Bay*, by Jennifer K. Elsea.

[134] Ana Radelat, "Cuba Turns Up Rhetoric on Guantanamo as UN Condemns Human Rights Abuses," *CubaNews*, April 2005.

In: U.S. Involvement in Political, Economic and Social … ISBN: 978-1-61209-781-7
Editor: Allen P. Lowell

Chapter 3

CUBAN MIGRATION TO THE UNITED STATES: POLICY AND TRENDS

Ruth Ellen Wasem

ABSTRACT

Many of the issues surrounding Cuban migration are unique but not new. Normal immigration from Cuba has been elusive since Fidel Castro came to power. Over the past 50 years, the practice of Cubans fleeing by boat to the United States has become commonplace, and at some points reached the levels of a mass exodus. Since the last upsurge of "boat people" in the mid-1990s, the United States and Cuba worked toward establishing safe, legal immigration, which includes returning migrants interdicted by the U.S. Coast Guard. These migration policies, however, are not without critics.

The immigration of Cubans to the United States has increased since 1995, although the actual admission numbers have ebbed and flowed over this period. Cuba consistently ranks among the top 10 source countries for legal permanent residents (LPRs). Cuba ranked fifth as a top immigrant-sending country—after Mexico, China, India, and the Philippines—in FY2008. A total of 49,500 Cubans became LPRs in FY2008.

U.S. Coast Guard interdictions of Cubans have fluctuated since the mid-1990s, yet the general trend has moved upward. Cuban interdictions reached a 12-year high of 2,868 in FY2007. In FY2008, the U.S. Coast Guard reported 2,199 Cuban interdictions. Similarly, U.S. Border Patrol apprehensions of Cubans peaked at 4,295 in FY2007 and slipped to 3,351 in FY2008. Cubans who arrived at ports of entry without documents exhibited a comparable pattern, reaching a high of 13,019 in FY2007 and falling slightly to 11,278 in FY2008.

The change in leadership of both the United States and Cuba may provide openings for revisions in U.S. policy on Cuban migration. Fidel Castro's departure as head of government in July 2006 has prompted some observers to call for a reexamination of U.S. policy toward Cuba overall, and a potential opportunity to restart the migration talks that had occurred semi-annually for a decade after the 1994 U.S-Cuba Migration Accord. After serving temporarily, Raúl Castro, brother of Fidel Casto, officially assumed the Cuban presidency in February 2008. This transfer of power between the Castro brothers led some to question whether there would be much of an opening for renewed migration talks between the United States and Cuba.

During the 2008 U.S. presidential campaign, however, President Barack Obama stated he would seek to change U.S. policy by allowing unlimited family travel and remittances to Cuba, signaling to some the possibility of resuming the migration talks. In his opening speech at the Summit of the Americas on April 17, 2009, President Obama expressed the hope of "a new beginning with Cuba," specifically mentioning migration as an issue. A bipartisan group of congressional leaders are expressing support for a resumption of the migration talks with Cuba. On May 31, 2009, a U.S. State Department official reported that Cuban officials had indicated that they want to resume migration talks.

U.S. Policy toward Cuban Migrants

A watershed in U.S. immigration policy toward Cuban migrants may be on the horizon as the Obama Administration and a bipartisan group of congressional leaders weigh prospects for more open economic and diplomatic relations with Cuba [1]. A normalization of the immigration policy cast 50 years ago in response to the communist revolution in Cuba, however, is not imminent, nor is it likely to be easily achieved. This report opens with a historical analysis of the unique immigration policy that evolved with Cuba and an explanation of its nexus with other federal policies. It follows with time series analysis of Cuban migration trends. The report concludes by discussing current challenges and issues.

Evolution of the Policy

Cuba, as a communist state, has restricted many freedoms, including at various times the freedom to travel. As a result, normal immigration for Cubans has been elusive for approximately 50 years, and most Cubans have been admitted to the United States through special humanitarian provisions of the law. The first emigres who came in 1958 were, according to the history of the time, followers of General Fulgencio Batista, the dictator who had taken power in a 1952 military coup. When Fidel Castro defeated Batista and formally assumed power in Cuba in 1959, the exodus escalated, peaking at approximately 78,000 in 1962. In October of that year, Castro stopped regularly scheduled travel between the two countries, and the risky practice of asylum seekers setting sail from Cuba to Florida began [2]

Between 1962 and 1979, hundreds of thousands of Cubans entered the United States under the Attorney General's parole authority [3]. In 1980, a mass migration of asylum seekers—known as the Mariel boatlift—brought approximately 125,000 Cubans (and 25,000 Haitians) to South Florida over a six-month period. Prompted by the costs that the Mariel boatlift incurred, Congress established the "Immigration Emergency Fund" in thel 986 Immigration Reform and Control Act (IRCA) to provide federal aid to regions and communities facing more general health and safety problems due to overcrowded and unsuitable living conditions that arise when mass migration occurs. Congress also authorized that funds could be used for border enforcement costs associated with mass migration [4].

After declining for several years, Cuban "boat people" steadily rose from a few hundred in 1989 to a few thousand in 1993. After Castro made threatening speeches in 1994, riots ensued in Havana, and the Cuban exodus by boat escalated. The number of Cubans intercepted by the U.S. Coast Guard or the U.S. Border Patrol reached a post-Mariel high of almost 40,000 in 1994.

Until 1995, the United States generally had not repatriated Cubans (except certain criminal aliens on a negotiated list) under a policy established when the government became Communist within two years of the 1959 revolution. Not only has the United States been reluctant to repatriate people to a Communist country, but the Cuban government typically has also refused to accept Cuban migrants who are excludable under the Immigration and Nationality Act (INA) [5]. The key elements of current policy on Cuban immigration are the Cuban Adjustment Act of 1966, the Migration Agreements of 1994 and 1995, and the Special Cuban Migration Lottery.

Cuban Adjustment Act of 1966

Most of the undocumented Cubans who arrive in the United States are allowed to stay and adjust to permanent resident status under the Cuban Adjustment Act (CAA) of 1966 (P.L. 89-732) [6]. The CAA, as amended, provides that certain Cubans who have been physically present in the United States for at least one year may adjust to permanent resident status at the discretion of the Attorney General—an opportunity that no other group or nationality has. The alien must be eligible to receive an immigrant visa and be admissible to the United States as a legal permanent resident (LPR). Spouses and children accompanying the aliens who are applying for this adjustment are also covered by the CAA. Cubans apply to the U.S. Citizenship and Immigration Services (USCIS) in the Department of Homeland Security (DHS) to adjust as LPRs.

The CAA predates the Refugee Act of 1980, the law that incorporates refugee and asylum principles into the INA [7]. The legislative debate leading up to its enactment makes clear that persons fleeing Cuba are presumed to be refugees under international law, but the CAA does not use the language or definitions commonly used for refugee and asylee.8 Legislative efforts to "sunset" the CAA or repeal it outright have not been successful; however, in 1996 Congress enacted language stipulating that the CAA would be repealed when Cuba became a democracy [9].

Cuban Migration Agreement, September 1994

"Normalizing" migration between the two nations was the stated purpose of the migration agreement signed on September 9, 1994, when the status quo of U.S. policy toward Cuban migrants was altered significantly. The plan's objectives of safe, legal, and orderly immigration relied on six points.

- The United States agreed to no longer permit Cubans intercepted at sea to come to the United States; rather, Cubans would be placed in a safe haven camp in a third location. Justifying this policy as a "safety of life at sea" issue, Cuba also agreed to use "persuasive methods" to discourage people from setting sail.

- United States and Cuba reaffirmed their support for the United Nations General Assembly resolution on alien smuggling. They pledged to cooperate in the prevention of the illegal transport of migrants and the use of violence or "forcible divergence" to reach the United States.
- The United States agreed to admit no less than 20,000 immigrants from Cuba annually, not including the immediate relatives of U.S. citizens.
- The United States and Cuba agreed to cooperate on the voluntary return of Cubans who arrived in the United States or were intercepted at sea.
- The United States and Cuba did not reach an agreement on how to handle Cubans who are excludable under the INA, but they did agree to continue discussing the matter [10]
- The United States and Cuba agreed to review the implementation of this agreement and engage in further discussions.

It became apparent that the 20,000 minimum level per year could not be met through the INA preference system or the refugee provisions because of the eligibility criteria. In other words, few Cubans qualified for visas as family-sponsored immigrants, including immediate relatives of U.S. citizens, or as employment-based immigrants (e.g., persons of extraordinary ability, members of the professions, or skilled shortage workers) [11]. In addition to those Cubans who may qualify to immigrate through the INA preference system and who may qualify as refugees, the United States decided to use other authority in the law (i.e., parole) to allow Cubans to come to the United States and become LPRs through the CAA. As specifically discussed below, a "visa lottery" program was established to randomly select who, among the many Cubans seeking to migrate, receives a visa.

Cuban Migration Agreement, May 1995

On May 2, 1995, the Clinton administration announced a further agreement with Cuba that resolved the dilemma of the approximately 33,000 Cubans then encamped at Guantanamo [12]. This new agreement, which came at the time of year when boat people traditionally begin their journeys, had two new points. Foremost, the United States allowed most of the Cubans detained at Guantanamo to come to the United States through the humanitarian parole provisions of the INA. Cuba agreed to credit these admissions toward the minimum 20,000 LPRs per year from Cuba, with 5,000 charged annually over three years. Secondly, rather than placing Cubans intercepted at sea in safe haven camps, the United States began repatriating them to Cuba. Both parties promised to act in a manner consistent with international obligations and to ensure that no action is taken against those repatriated. U.S. officials would inform repatriated Cubans about procedures to legally immigrate at the U.S. Interests Section in Havana [13]. Those charged with alien smuggling, however, would face prison terms in Cuba.

Interdicted Cubans are given an opportunity to express a fear of persecution if returned to Cuba. Those who meet the definition of a refugee or asylee are resettled in a third country. From May 1995 through July 2003, about 170 Cuban refugees were resettled in 11 different countries, including Spain, Venezuela, Australia, and Nicaragua. The Department of State

(DOS) is required to monitor whether those migrants who are returned to Cuba are subject to reprisals [14]. In May 2004, DOS noted that it had been unable to monitor returnees outside Havana since March 2003.

As a result of this agreement, migration talks between the United States and Cuba are supposed to occur twice yearly. No migration talks have been held since January 2004, however, because DOS cancelled them due to Cuba's refusal to discuss the following key issues: Cuba's issuance of exit permits for all qualified migrants; Cuba's cooperation in holding a new registration for an immigrant lottery; the need for a deeper Cuban port utilized by the U.S. Coast Guard for the repatriation of Cubans interdicted at sea; Cuba's responsibility to permit U.S. diplomats to travel to monitor returned migrants; and Cuba's obligation to accept the return of Cuban nationals determined to be excludable from the United States [15].

As a consequence of the migration agreements and interdiction policy, a "wet foot/dry foot" practice toward Cuban migrants has evolved. Put simply, Cubans who do not reach the shore (i.e., dry land), are returned to Cuba unless they cite fears of persecution. Those Cubans who successfully reach the shore are inspected by DHS and generally permitted to stay in the United States and adjust under CAA the following year.

Special Cuban Migration Lottery

Since the 1994 migration agreement, the United States has conducted three visa lottery open seasons to implement the Special Cuban Migration Program. The three open seasons were at two- year intervals: FY1994, FY1996, and FY1998. The number of qualifying registrants increased each year, from 189,000 in 1994 to 433,00 in 1996 and to 541,00 in 1998 [16]. Cubans qualifying through the 1998 lottery continue to be paroled into the United States.

Eligible registrants must be Cuban citizens between 18 and 55 years of age. They also must be able to answer "yes" to two of the following three questions. Have you completed secondary school or a higher level of education? Do you have at least three years of work experience? Do you have any relatives residing in the United States? Once selected through the lottery, the successful applicants are given parole status with a visa that is good for six months. The medical examination, required of all potential immigrants, is good for one year. Spouses and minor children may accompany the successful registrants. Over the years, there have been reports of barriers the potential Cuban parolees face, such as exorbitantly priced medical exams, exit visa fees, and repercussions for family members who remain in Cuba.

Federal Assistance to Cuban Migrants

Cubans are among the subset of foreign nationals who are eligible for federal benefits and cash assistance. Over a decade ago, Title IV of the Personal Responsibility and Work Opportunity Reconciliation Act (PRWORA) of 1996 (P.L. 104-193) established comprehensive restrictions on the eligibility of noncitizens for means-tested public assistance and limited the eligibility of refugees and asylees to five years.17 Aliens who enter the United States without authorization are barred from any federal public benefit except the emergency services and programs expressly listed in PRWORA [18]. Amendments in P.L. 105-33 and P.L. 105-185 extended the period of food stamp/Supplemental Security Income (SSI)/Medicaid (but not Temporary Assistance for Needy Families) eligibility for refugees and asylees from five to seven years and added Cuban and Haitian Entrants to those eligible for these benefits for seven years.

Cuban-Haitian Entrants

The term "Cuban-Haitian Entrant" is not defined in the INA, but its usage dates back to 1980. Many of the Cubans and the vast majority of the Haitians who arrived in South Florida during the 1980 Mariel Boatlift did not qualify for asylum according to the individualized definition of persecution in § § 207-208 of the INA. The Carter Administration labeled Cubans and Haitians as "Cuban-Haitian Entrants" and used the discretionary parole authority of the Attorney General to admit them to the United States. Subsequently, an adjustment of status provision was included in the Immigration Reform and Control Act (IRCA) of 1986 (P.L. 99-603) that enabled the Cuban- Haitian Entrants who had arrived during the Mariel Boatlift to become LPRs [19]

While not a term of law in the INA, Congress did define Cuban-Haitian Entrant in the context of eligibility for federal assistance. Title V of the Refugee Education Assistance Act of 1980 (P.L. 96-422), commonly known as Fascell-Stone, defined Cuban and Haitian Entrants as

> (1) any individual granted parole status as a Cuban/Haitian Entrant (Status Pending) or granted any other special status subsequently established under the immigration laws for nationals of Cuba or Haiti, regardless of the status of the individual at the time assistance or services are provided; and
>
> (A) who—(i) was paroled into the United States and has not acquired any other status under the Immigration and Nationality Act [this chapter]; (ii) is the subject of removal proceedings under the Immigration and Nationality Act [this chapter]; or (iii) has an application for asylum pending with the Immigration and Naturalization Service; and
>
> (B) with respect to whom a final, nonappealable, and legally enforceable order of removal has not been entered [20]

The intent and resulting effect of the Fascell-Stone provision was to treat Cubans and Haitians in the same manner as refugees and asylees for the purposes of the federal refugee resettlement program and most other federal benefits and assistance [21]. The Office of Refugee Resettlement (ORR) uses the term "Cuban-Haitian Entrants" for Cubans who meet the Fascell-Stone definition.

Major Federal Benefit Programs

Supplemental Security Income (SSI)

Under current law, asylees, refugees, and Cuban-Haitian entrants (as well as certain aliens whose deportation/removal is being withheld for humanitarian reasons and Vietnam-born Amerasians fathered by U.S. citizens) are among categories of aliens who may be eligible for SSI for seven years after entry/grant of such status [22]. In order to receive SSI benefits, these qualified aliens must meet all the requirements for eligibility as native-born citizens. SSI eligibility requirements include meeting the definitions for age, disability, or blindness and falling below established income and resource thresholds [23]. In 2008, individual SSI beneficiaries could have received up to the maximum federal benefit rate of $637 a month, and married couples received up to $956. Cuban entrants, like other qualified aliens, are ineligible after seven years unless naturalized or if in receipt of SSI benefits as of August 22, 1996 [24]. This SSI eligibility for Cuban entrants as well as refugees, asylees, and aliens in other specified humanitarian categories was extended to nine years (during FY2009 through FY20 11) by P.L. 110-328. If qualified aliens are eligible for SSI, they are likely to be eligible for enrollment in their state's Medicaid Program [25].

Temporary Assistance for Needy Families (TANF)

Cuban Entrants are treated as refugees, and thus those families with children under 18 may be eligible for time-limited cash assistance through a state's Temporary Assistance for Needy Families (TANF) program. The Personal Responsibility Act of 1996 restricts receipt of federal TANF benefits to a 60-month lifetime limit. States may exempt up to 20% of the caseload from the time limit because of state-defined hardship, and states have the option to continue TANF benefits under special circumstances. Like other federal welfare programs, the TANF program is means-tested; however, unlike SSI, the TANF program is state-administered, and payment levels can vary widely by state [26]. In 2008, the average monthly maximum benefit level for a family of three in the median state was $389, with a range from $923 in Alaska to $170 in Mississippi [27]. Refugees and entrants participating in job training programs sponsored by the Office of Refugee Resettlement (ORR) are considered to be working toward self-sufficiency and may be exempt from certain state TANF program requirements. TANF beneficiaries may be eligible for their state's Medicaid program; however, SSI beneficiaries are generally ineligible to receive TANF in addition to SSI.

Refugee Resettlement Assistance [28]

As noted above, Cuban entrants are eligible for the federal resettlement assistance program for refugees and entrants, which is partially funded through the ORR. In addition to providing a range of social services, primarily administered by states, the ORR provides funding to states for transitional cash and medical assistance through the Transition and Medical Services program [29]. ORR resettlement assistance and services are designed to help refugees and entrants obtain self- sufficiency and social adjustment as quickly as possible. Refugees and entrants are expected to become self-sufficient within six months of arrival, and Refugee Cash Assistance (RCA) and Refugee Medical Assistance (RMA) are limited to eight months [30]

Refugees and entrants who meet the income and resource eligibility requirements for SSI, TANF, or Medicaid, but are not otherwise eligible (e.g., single males or childless females and couples), may receive benefits under the ORR-funded RCA and RMA programs [31]. Under Title V of the Refugee Education Assistance Act, participating states are fully reimbursed for cash and medical assistance to Cuban and Haitian entrants under the same conditions and to the same extent as such assistance and services for refugees under the refugee program.

Refugee Cash Assistance (RCA)

States have the option of choosing either a publically administered or public/private RCA program [32]. Most states publically administer their RCA program. By doing so, the state agency must operate its RCA program consistent with the provisions of their TANF program [33].

In publically administered RCA programs, payment levels to refugees or entrants are equivalent to a state's TANF payment levels, and thus vary across the country. The maximum RCA benefit for an individual entrant or refugee in the state of Florida, which is home to many Cuban émigrés, in 2008-2009 is $180 per month—the same payment standard as Florida TANF [34]. In Tennessee, for example, an individual could receive up to $95 a month and a family of three could receive up to $185 a month [35]. In case of California, the monthly maximum benefit for a family of three is approximately $706 or $8,448 annually [36] Public/private RCA programs have been approved by ORR in Maryland, Texas, Oregon, Louisiana, Oklahoma, and Minnesota [37]. In the Texas RCA Provider Manual, the maximum RCA payment levels for the entire eight-month RCA period are $2,680 for one-person family unit, $3,600 for a two-person family unit, and $4,560 for a three-person family unit. Under the Texas public/private model, only a portion of the RCA payment levels are distributed in cash. In months five through eight, payments are distributed in the form of vendor payments for rent and utility [38].

Refugee Medical Assistance (RMA)

Like RCA benefits, states administer their own RMA program from ORR funds, which pay for 100% of RMA costs for eligible refugees and entrants. Refugees or entrants who are not eligible for their state's Medicaid program may be eligible for RMA benefits for up to eight months. In many states, covered services under RMA are the same as covered services under their state Medicaid plan. Costs of RMA per refugee vary due to variables such as age, health of the beneficiary, and services provided. The state of Florida, for example, estimated the average 2007 RMA monthly benefit per person at $165.29 [39].

ANALYSIS OF MIGRATION TRENDS [40]

Despite a history of travel restrictions imposed by the Castro government, Cuba was one of the top immigrant-sending countries during the last half of the 20th century and is one of the top immigrant-sending countries thus far in the 21st century [41]. In FY2008, there were 49,500 Cubans who became legal permanent residents (LPRs)—surpassed only by LPRs from Mexico, China, India, and the Philippines [42]. Yet, very few Cubans have arrived in the United States through the legal immigration avenues proscribed by the INA. An analysis of the trends in Cuban migrants— and how their patterns have changed over time—follows.

U.S. Coast Guard Interdictions

Since the May 1995 agreement, the U.S. Coast Guard interdictions of Cubans have fluctuated, but trended upward over time. Interdictions were low during the first few years after the migration agreement (e.g., 411 in FY1996 and 421 in FY1997). The number of Cuban interdictions more than doubled between FY1997 and FY1998—when 903 Cubans were interdicted—and reached 1,619 in FY1999. Interdictions gradually dipped from 1,000 in FY2000 to 666 in FY2002. Interdictions hit a 12-year high of 2,868 in FY2007. In FY2008, the U.S. Coast Guard interdicted 2,199 Cubans [43]. Figure 1 presents this time series.

Unauthorized Cubans Arriving in the United States

Although the vast majority of foreign nationals apprehended by the U.S. Border Patrol agents are Mexican nationals, apprehensions of unauthorized migrants from other countries have more than quadrupled in recent years [44]. Consistent with this trend, Cuban apprehensions have steadily escalated since a low point of 819 in FY2004.

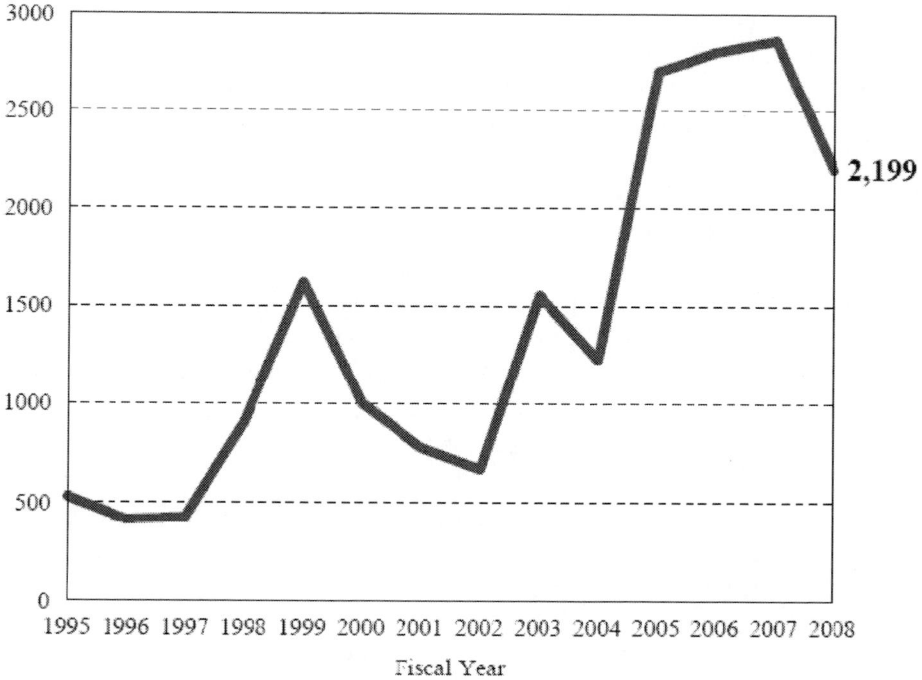

Source: CRS presentation of U.S. Coast Guard data.

Figure 1. Maritime Interdictions of Cubans, FY1995-FY2008.

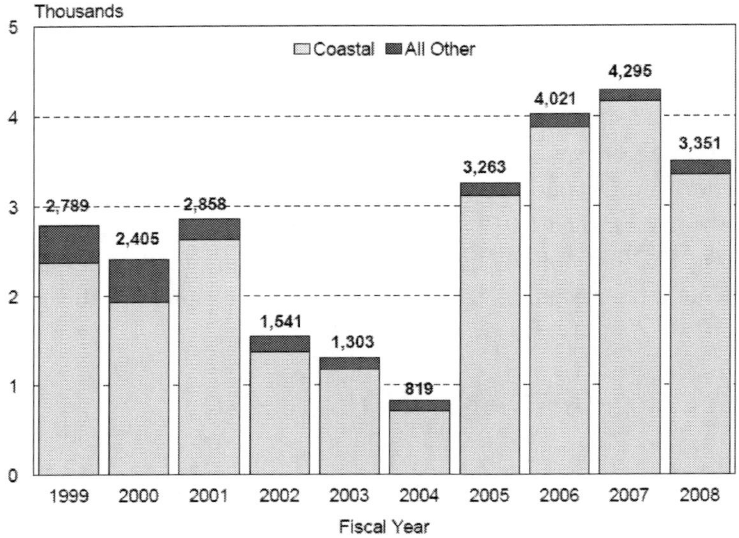

Source: CRS presentation of U.S. Border Patrol data.

Figure 2. U.S. Border Patrol Apprehensions of Cubans, FY1999-FY2008.

In FY2007, Cuban nationals comprised 4,295 of the 68,016 apprehensions of aliens from countries other than Mexico [45]. The number of Cubans that the U.S. Border Patrol apprehended dipped slightly to 3,351 in FY2008. It is important to note, as Figure 2 depicts, that the U.S. Border Patrol apprehends most Cubans in coastal areas rather than along the southern land borders.

As discussed above, Cubans migrants have traditionally traveled by sea through the Florida Straits toward the coast of South Florida. Other Cubans have been seeking alternate travel routes. In a more western passage, migrants sail from Cuba coming ashore somewhere along Mexico's Yucatan Peninsula and eventually making their way over land to the U.S. border. According to media reports, many Cuban migrants have been landing on the coast of Mexico's Quintana Roo state, approximately 120 miles from the Cuban coast. According to a report published in one of Mexico's leading daily newspapers, La Jornada, Mexico had become the principal route for Cuban migration to the United States in 2007 [46].

Cubans who arrived at ports of entry without documents appear to exhibit a pattern over time that is comparable to Coast Guard interdictions and Border Patrol apprehensions, although a complete 1995-2008 time series is not available..Inadmissible Cubans arriving at ports of entry reached a high of 13,019 in FY2007 and fell slightly to 11,278 in FY2008, as Figure 3 illustrates. The Laredo CBP field office reported the largest number of inadmissible Cubans during this period, FY2004-FY2008, with the Miami CBP field office following at a distant second.

Mexico would began to repatriate Cubans who arrive in Mexico with proper documents [47]. The director of the Cancun regional office of the National Institute of Migration in Mexico, Luis Alberto Molina Rios, explained the policy change: "The option of repatriation will reduce the number of Cubans arriving in Mexico." Effective November 20, 2008, the Mexican Navy has reportedly added Cuban interdiction and repatriation to the duties of their vessels patrolling Mexico's eastern coast [48].

If confirmed Cuban nationals present themselves at an official land port of entry at the U.S border with Mexico, they are inspected by CBP regardless of whether the Cuban national has valid immigration documents. Cubans are expressly exempt from the expedited removal provisions in the INA, which allow CBP agents to remove any alien who lacks proper documentation from the United States without any further hearings or review, unless the alien indicates a fear of persecution [49]. CBP officers generally parole Cuban nationals into the United States, and ultimately the Cuban parolees adjust to LPR status under the CAA.50 As a result, unauthorized Cuban migrants who enter through Mexico are more likely to identify themselves to CBP officers than are other unauthorized aliens [51].

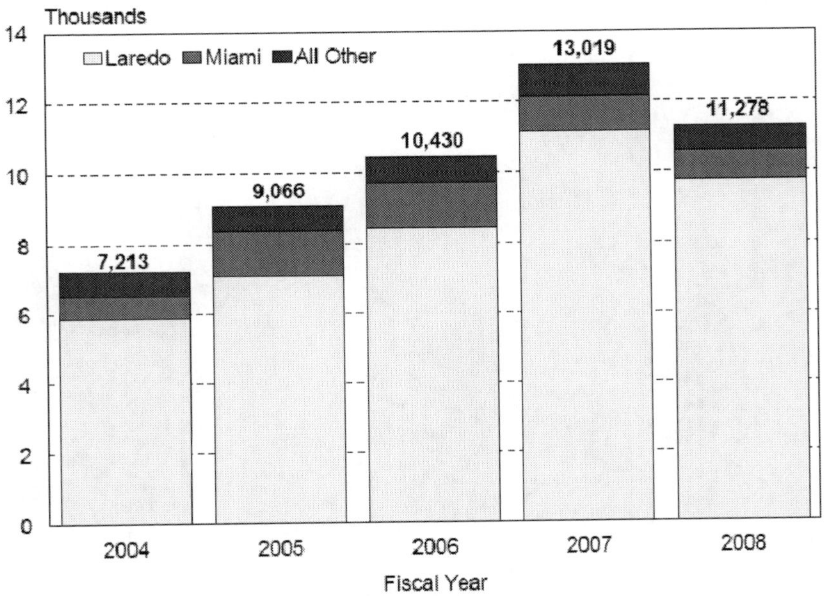

Source: CRS presentation of data from CBP's Borderstat database.

Notes: CBP officers label Cubans who lack proper immigration documents as inadmissible, as are all other foreign nationals who attempt entry without proper documents. In most instances, the Cubans are paroled in the United States.

Figure 3. Inadmissible Cubans Arriving at Ports of Entry, FY2004-FY2008 Laredo, Miami, and all other field offices.

In-country Refugee Processing

The United States has conducted in-country refugee processing in Cuba since the 1994-1995 migration talks [52]. Cubans are eligible to apply for admission to the United States through the in- country refugee program under what is known as the Priority 2 (P-2) category [53]. The P-2 category of Cubans specifically includes:

- former political prisoners;
- members of persecuted religious minorities;
- human rights activists;
- forced labor conscripts during the period 1965-1968;

- persons deprived of their professional credentials or subjected to other disproportionately harsh or discriminatory treatment resulting from their perceived or actual political or religious beliefs; and
- persons who have experienced or fear harm because of their relationship—family or social—to someone who falls under one of the preceding categories [54]

All refugee processing and admissions by the United States dropped precipitously when new security procedures were implemented after the September 11, 2001 terrorist attacks, and refugee processing of Cubans were no exception [55].

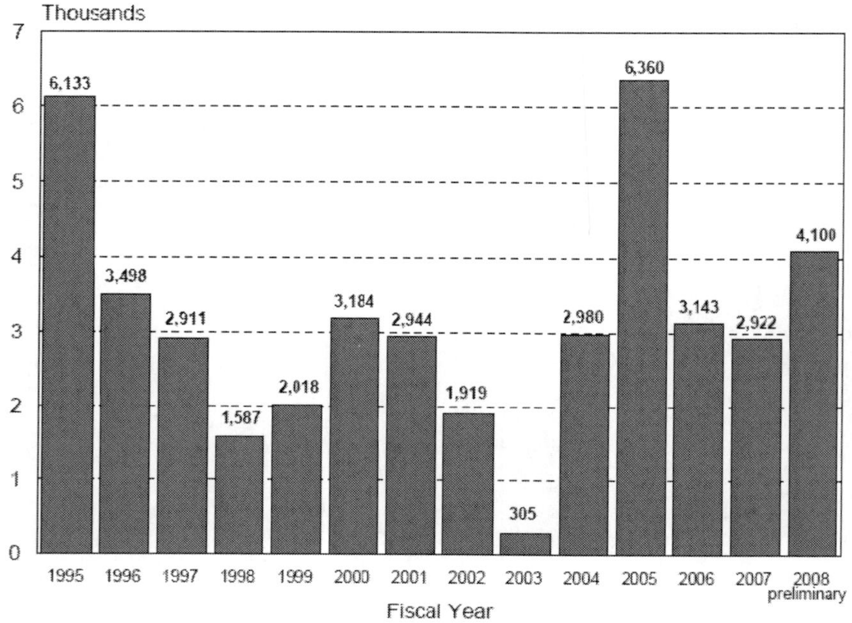

Source: CRS presentation of data from the DHS Office of Immigration Statistics and preliminary data from the USCIS Office of Refugee, Asylum, and International Operations.

Notes: Cubans approved in one fiscal year may not arrived in the United States until the following year.

Figure 4. Refugee Arrivals from Cuban In-country Processing, FY1999-FY2008.

As Figure 4 indicates, there were only 305 Cuban refugee arrivals in FY2003, primarily the result of the difficulties in conducting security clearances and background checks. During this period, there were reported problems obtaining exit visas from the Cuban government for the refugees. The U.S. Citizenship and Immigration Services (USCIS) provided data for FY2004 that detailed this situation. USCIS considered 8,658 Cubans for refugee status and approved 5,670 (65%) in FY2004. Only 2,980 Cuban refugees, however, actually arrived in the United States in FY2004 [56]. The refugee processing logjam appears to have eased by the end of FY2005, as Figure 4 depicts 6,260 Cuban refugee arrivals. The in-country refugee program reportedly approved over 4,200 Cubans during FY2008, and 4,100 Cubans were expected to arrive in FY2008 [57].

In terms of total immigration from Cuba (i.e., as immediate relatives of U.S. citizens, as legal immigrants through the preference system, as refugees, as parolees or other adjustments through CAA or through the Nicaraguan Adjustment and Central American Relief Act), approximately half of a million Cubans have become LPRs since FY1981. Of that number, well over half have become LPRs since the 1994-1995 migration agreements went into effect. Although actual admission numbers have been jagged over this period, the trend line has moved upward.

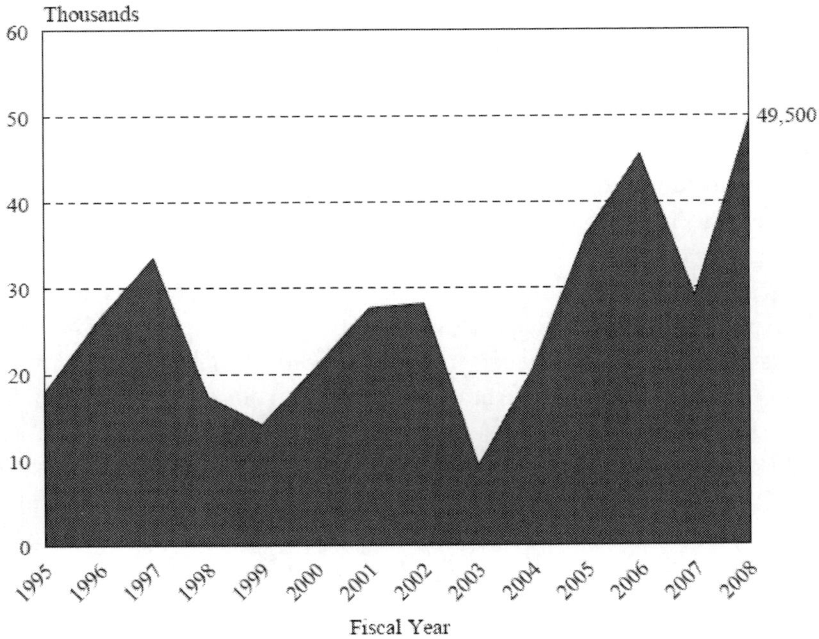

Source: CRS presentation of DHS Office of Immigration Statistics data.

Figure 5. Cubans Becoming LPRs, FY1995-FY2008.

Cuba consistently ranks among the top 10 source countries for LPRs. A total of 49,500 Cubans became legal permanent residents in FY2008. Cuba ranked fifth as a top immigrant-sending country—after Mexico, China, India, and the Philippines—in FY2008 [58].

CURRENT CHALLENGES AND ISSUES

U.S. immigration policy toward Cuban migrants juggles immigration control and humanitarian compassion within a larger policy framework that remains quite contentious. The change in leadership of both the United States and Cuba may provide openings for revisions in U.S. policy on Cuban migration. A normalization of immigration policies, however, is not imminent nor is it likely to be easily achieved. Some of the major challenges and issues that bear on U.S. policy on Cuban migrants are discussed below.

Interdiction and Repatriation

Some consider the migrant interdiction and repatriation policy to be at odds with the rescue mission of the U.S. Coast Guard, while others view it as integral to maritime security role of the U.S. Coast Guard. A series of events in 1999 illustrate the difficulties balancing these priorities. A well-publicized incident in June 1999 provoked outrage when the U.S. Coast Guard used pepper spray and a water cannon to prevent six Cubans from reaching Surfside Beach in Florida. A few weeks later, a woman drowned when a boat capsized during interdiction. Notably in late November 1999, the U.S. Coast Guard opted to bring six-year old Elian Gonzalez and two other survivors of an ill-fated journey to the United States rather than taking them to Cuba as the migration agreement provides. For the first five months Elian Gonzalez was in the United States, he was in the temporary care of his father's uncle, Lazaro Gonzalez, who lives in Miami. When Elian's father, Juan Miguel Gonzalez, arrived in the United States in April 2000 to assume custody of his son, Lazaro Gonzalez defied a federal government order to turn over the child. Then-Attorney General Janet Reno ordered federal law enforcement officers to remove Elian from the home of Lazaro Gonzalez in the pre-dawn hours of April 22, 2000 [59].

Several incidents in 2003 offer further examples of the interdiction and repatriation dilemma. On April 11, 2003, the Cuban government executed three men who had hijacked a ferry in Havana on April 2 in an attempt to reach the United States. The men were executed by firing squads after summary trials that were held behind closed doors. International human rights groups, such as Amnesty International and Human Rights Watch, and a number of countries, including Mexico, the European Union, and the 15-nation Caribbean Community, condemned the crackdown and the executions [60]. In July 2003, a dozen people reportedly stole a Cuban-flagged boat from the marina where it was docked in Cuba and kidnapped the three watchmen guarding the marina in the process. When the boat was in international waters allegedly on route to Florida, the U.S. Coast Guard officials tried to intercept it and reportedly faced violent resistance when they interdicted the vessel.

All 15 persons on board were taken to the U.S. Coast Guard cutter and interviewed by a USCIS asylum officer. The three watchmen indicated a desire to return to Cuba. When the Cuban government offered to sentence the 12 persons implicated in crimes (purportedly boat theft, kidnapping, and assaulting federal officers) to 10 years in prison, the United States agreed to return them [61].

The reach of the interdiction policy became clear on January 5, 2006, when the U.S. Coast Guard found 15 Cubans, including 4 women and 2 children, on an old Key West bridge that was no longer connected to land. The decision to repatriate the Cubans was made by the Coast Guard's legal office in conjunction with DHS Immigration and Customs Enforcement. The Coast Guard stated that the Cubans "were determined to be feet-wet and processed in accordance with standard procedure." [62]. By 2006, migrant interdiction and repatriation had become the keystone in the designing of Operation Vigiliant Sentry (OVS), the DHS coordinated plan for response to a Caribbean mass migration. OVS was reportedly exercised throughout 2006 to prepare for a potential migration in the event of instability in Cuba [63].

Supporters of these repatriation decisions argue that it is critical to deter illegal and dangerous migration of Cubans who flee on unseaworthy or overcrowded vessels [64].

Some further maintain that the prison sentences of the 12 Cubans who stole a boat in 2003, which the Cuban government apparently negotiated with the United States, were essential to prevent a repeat of summary executions that occurred to the hijackers in April of that year. Critics of these decisions assert that both countries (United States and Cuba) are denying these people their rights to due process and a hearing [65]. Some called for a full investigation of these incidents, and some sought an end to the current interdiction and repatriation policy [66].

Cuban Adjustment Act

Some maintain the 1966 Cuban Adjustment Act is obsolete and locked into the mind set of the Cold War era, as well as unnecessary since Cubans may seek asylum under the refugee laws enacted since 1966. The CAA, as discussed above, permits Cubans who have been physically present in the United States for at least one year to become LPRs. Over the decades since its enactment, it has enabled most Cubans to enter the United States regardless of whether they have proper immigration documents. Some opponents of the CAA assert that it is discriminatory because it gives Cubans an immigration advantage that foreign nationals from no other country have. Immigration control proponents have argued that it serves as a magnet attracting Cubans who would not otherwise qualify for admission. Just as there are efforts in Congress to liberalize economic policies (especially travel and agricultural) with Cuba since Raul Castro assumed power, some argue that it is time to regularize immigration policy with Cuba [67].

Opponents of repealing or revising the CAA say that it would send the wrong message to Cubans during this critical period. It is not necessary and may be unwise, some maintain, to alter the law now that Fidel Castro has transferred power to his brother Raul Castro. Supporters of the CAA point out that the success of the migration agreement—particularly its commitment to admit at least 20,000 Cubans annually—depends on the ability to adjust the parolees under the CAA. If the CAA were repealed, supporters point out, only Cubans who met the refugee definition or who qualified for visas as family-sponsored immigrants or as employment-based immigrants would be able to immigrate to the United States, and the backlogs for immigrant visas would grow [68].

Cash Benefits

Confusion over the extent of federal cash assistance available to Cuban migrants prompted allegations that Cubans were receiving cash payments in excess of amounts normally available to other program beneficiaries. Some allege further that Cuban migrants use these federal cash payments to pay smugglers to shepherd them into the United States. Media reports have indicated that smugglers can charge Cuban migrants up to $15,000 each [69]

The RCA payments available to Cuban entrants, however, are not issued in a lump sum, and the payment levels provide only basic monthly assistance to refugees without income or assets with which to support themselves for a maximum period of eight months. In the state of Florida, for example, a single Cuban entrant—as other eligible refugees and asylees—who meets the federal and state eligibility requirements for RCA in Florida would be eligible to receive between $95 to $180 a month [70]. More broadly, some questions why all Cubans—rather than those who enter as refugees—are afforded the same set of federal benefits as refugees. Most LPRs who enter the United States are barred from federal benefits for at least five years according to comprehensive restrictions on the eligibility of noncitizens for means-tested public assistance [71]. Others maintain that Cubans are refugees, regardless of whether they adjust through the CAA or the refugee provisions in the INA.

Migration Talks

Whether the United States should resume migration talks with Cuba is central to the policy debate. Semi-annual migration talks between Cuba and the United States had been held regularly on the implementation of the 1994 and 1995 migration accords for a decade. The U.S. State Department, however, had cancelled the 20th round of talks scheduled for January 2004, and no migration talks were held since. According to the State Department, Cuba had refused to discuss issues integral to the migration agreement [72]. In response to the cancellation of the talks, Cuban officials maintained that the decision of the United States was irresponsible and that Cuba was prepared to discuss all of the issues raised by the United States [73].

Fidel Castro's departure as head of government in July 2006 has prompted some observers to call for a reexamination of U.S. policy toward Cuba overall, and a potential opportunity to restart the migration talks. After serving temporarily, Raúl Castro, brother of the former dictator, officially assumed the Cuban presidency in February 2008. This transfer of power between the Castro brothers led some to question whether there would be much of an opening for renewed migration talks between the United States and Cuba.

During the 2008 presidential campaign, however, President Barack Obama stated he would seek to change U.S. policy by allowing unlimited family travel and remittances to Cuba, signaling to some the possibility of resuming the migration talks. In his opening speech at the Summit of the Americas on April 17, 2009, President Obama expressed the hope of "a new beginning with Cuba," specifically mentioning migration as an issue [74].

Supporters of resuming the migration talks maintain that the talks are a key element. In February, the ranking member of the Committee on Foreign Relations, Senator Richard Lugar, released a staff report that specifically called for a resumption of the migrations talks.

> Regarding migration, staff recommends the revival of US.-Cuban biannual migrations talks, which have been suspended since 2004. These talks provide an important venue for discussing the shared problem of illegal migration. The USG should remain committed to fully implementing its agreements under the 1994 Joint Communique and the 1995 Joint Statement (collectively known as the U.S.-Cuba Migration Accords) as effective tools for promoting safe, legal, and orderly migration.
>
> In addition, staff suggests an executive branch review of the "wet-foot, dry-foot policy." Under this policy, Cubans who are intercepted at sea are sent back to Cuba or to a third country while those who make it to U.S. soil are allowed to remain in the United States. The review should assess whether this policy has led to the inefficient use of U.S. Coast Guard resources and assets as well as the potential to redirect these resources to drug interdiction efforts [75].

Some of those challenging the resumption of the migration talks argue that Cuba should address the five areas of concern (listed above) before the United States moves forward. The State Department spokesman during the George W. Bush Administration, Richard Boucher, made this point in 2004: "The point is not just to have a meeting," Boucher said, "the point is to deal with the serious issues involved." Whether to even negotiate with the current government of Cuba is an issue raised by others. Roger Noreiga, of the American Enterprise Institute and formerly the Assistant Secretary of State for Western Hemisphere Affairs, offered this argument in 2008:

> Some of those counseling "stability" may be concerned about a mass migration of Cubans fleeing chaos. It is time to rethink that argument, which is usually wielded by those policymakers counseling a "go slow" approach. The best hope for avoiding a dangerous mass migration of Cubans to our shores in a post-Fidel world is to help them press for real change at home. If we stand by as their dreams of a new future are dashed by Raúl, we are inviting a burst of migration by a new generation of desperate Cubans.... In this post-Fidel period, any clumsy word or deed suggesting that the United States accepts the transfer of power from one dictator to another would snuff out the nascent hopes for freedom and consign 1 1million Cubans to additional years of hopeless dictatorship [76].

On May 31, 2009, an official at the U.S. Department of State reported that the Cuban government had indicated that it wants to resume talks on the legal immigration of Cubans to the United States [77]. Migration talks with Cuba, however meaningful, would likely be incremental in scope. The objectives of such talks would be striving toward safe, legal, and orderly immigration.

ACKNOWLEDGMENTS

Janice Cheryl Beaver of the Knowledge Services Group contributed research and text to an earlier draft of this report.

REFERENCES

[1] For example, see U.S. Congress, Senate Committee on Foreign Relations, *Changing Cuba Policy—In the United States National Interest*, committee print, 111th Cong., 1st sess., February 23, 2009, S. Prt. 111-5 (Washington: GPO, 2009).

[2] U.S. Congress, Senate Committee on Judiciary, *Review of U.S. Refugee Resettlement Programs and Policies*, committee print, prepared by Congressional Research Service, 96th Cong., 2nd sess., 1980.

[3] "Parole" is a term in immigration law which means that the alien has been granted temporary permission to be present in the United States. Parole does not constitute formal admission to the United States and parolees are required to leave when the terms of their parole expire, or if otherwise eligible, to be admitted in a lawful status.

[4] §113 of IRCA is §404(b) of INA; 8 U.S.C. 1101, note.

[5] Cubans who have been convicted of crimes in the United States pose complex problems, as Cuba is among a handful of nations that do not generally accept the return of criminal aliens. For a discussion of the broader issue, see CRS Report RL32480, *Immigration Consequences of Criminal Activity*, by Yule Kim and Michael John Garcia.

[6] Act of Nov. 2, 1966; 80 Stat 1161. The original statute was amended by the Immigration and Nationality Act Amendments of 1976 (P.L. 94-57 1), which exempted these adjustments from numerical limits of the preference system, and by the Refugee Act of 1980 (P.L. 96-2 12), which reduced the length of the physical presence requirement from two years to one year.

[7] As a signatory to the United Nations Protocol Relating to the Status of Refugees, the United States agrees not to return an alien to a country where his life or freedom would be threatened.

[8] A refugee is a person who is unwilling or unable to return to his home country because of a well-founded fear of persecution on account of race, religion, nationality, or membership in a particular social group or political opinion. The notable difference between a refugee and asylee is the physical location of the person seeking the status. Those in the United States apply for asylum, while those abroad apply for refugee status.

[9] Section 606 of the Illegal Immigration Reform and Immigrant Responsibility Act of 1996, Division C of P.L. 104- 208.

[10] Grounds for removal include health-related grounds, criminal grounds, national security grounds, Nazi persecution grounds, public charge grounds, illegal entry and immigration law violations, and lack of proper immigration documents. §212(a) of INA; 8 U.S.C. 1182(a).

[11] For further explanation of these criteria, see CRS Report RL32235, *U.S. Immigration Policy on Permanent Admissions*, by Ruth Ellen Wasem.

[12] President George H.W. Bush began using facilities at the U.S. Naval Air Station in Guantanamo, Cuba, to detain Haitians who tried to flee to the United States in 1991 as a result of the military coup in Haiti. DHS's Immigration and Customs Enforcement (ICE) continues to operate the Migrant Operations Center at Guantanamo. There are reportedly no more than 20-40 interdicted migrants detained at Guantanamo at any one time.

[13] The United States and Cuba do not have formal diplomatic relations, and as a result, U.S. interests in Cuba are conducted through the Embassy of Switzerland in Havana, Cuba. The U.S. Interests Section in Havana is staffed by United States Foreign Service personnel who operate independently of the Swiss in virtually all but protocol respects. According to the Department of State website: "The functions of USINT are similar to those of any U.S. government presence abroad: Consular Services, a Political and Economic Section, a Public Diplomacy Program, and Refugee Processing unique to Cuba." http://havana.usint.gov/about_the_embassy.html last access May 6, 2009.

[14] Pursuant to § 2245 of P.L. 105-277, DOS makes a semi-annual report to Congress on the treatment of those returned.

[15] U.S. Department of State, State Department Regular Briefing, Richard Boucher, January 7, 2004.

[16] Communication with staff at Office of International Affairs in the Immigration and Nationalization Service and the Cuba Desk at the State Department, July 9, 2001.

[17] CRS Report RL33809, *Noncitizen Eligibility for Federal Public Assistance: Policy Overview and Trends*, by Ruth Ellen Wasem.

[18] CRS Report RL34500, *Unauthorized Aliens' Access to Federal Benefits: Policy and Issues*, by Ruth Ellen Wasem.

[19] § 202 of the Immigration Reform and Control Act of 1986 (P.L. 99-603).

[20] §501(e)(1) of the Refugee Education Assistance Act of 1980 (P.L. 96-422).

[21] §501(a)(1) of P.L. 96-422 states: "The President shall exercise authorities with respect to Cuban and Haitian entrants which are identical to the authorities which are exercised under chapter 2 of title IV of the Immigration and Nationality Act."

[22] In most cases, an officer of the U.S. Citizenship and Immigration Services from DHS determines if a non-citizen is granted status in one of the qualified alien categories.

[23] Countable resource limit for SSI eligibility is $2,000 for individuals and $3,000 for couples. See CRS Report RS20294, *SSI Income and Resource Limits: A Fact Sheet*, by Scott Szymendera for additional information on income and resource limits and exclusions.

[24] CRS Report RL33809, *Noncitizen Eligibility for Federal Public Assistance: Policy Overview and Trends*, by Ruth Ellen Wasem.

[25] Thirty-two states link federal eligibility for SSI with state-administered Medicaid eligibility by automatically qualifying SSI recipients for Medicaid. Other states either follow the Social Security Administration's(SSA) SSI eligibility rules and require a separate Medicaid application, or they establish their own Medicaid eligibility rules outside of the SSA. For more information, see the Social Security Administration's Medicaid Information at http://www.socialsecurity.gov/disabilityresearch /wi/medicaid.htm, accessed on February 21, 2008.

[26] In some states, TANF applications are filed at the county level and benefit levels can vary by county.

[27] CRS Report RL32760, *The Temporary Assistance for Needy Families (TANF) Block Grant: Responses to Frequently Asked Questions*, by Gene Falk.

[28] For a fuller discussion of refugee resettlement, see CRS Report RL31269, *Refugee Admissions and Resettlement Policy*, by Andorra Bruno.

[29] ORR cannot reimburse states for TANF, SSI, or Medicaid programs.

[30] E-mail correspondence from the Administration for Children and Families, Office of Legislative Affairs and Budget, February 1, 2008.

[31] U.S. Department of Health and Human Services, Administration for Children and Families, Annual ORR Reports to Congress-2005, at http://www.acf.hhs.gov/programs/orr/data/arc.htm, accessed on February 24, 2008

[32] In 2000, ORR published a final rule amending the requirements governing RCA. States were given a choice in how RCA services would be administered in their states. Codified at 45 CFR Part 400.

[33] *Annual ORR Reports to Congress-2005.*

[34] Fiscal Year 2008-2009 RCA and TANF payment standard for Florida provided to CRS by the Florida Department of Children and Families, Feb. 11, 2008.

[35] E-mail correspondence from the Administration for Children and Families, Office of Legislative Affairs and Budget, February 1, 2008.

[36] Data on TANF cash assistance benefits levels are available through the National Center for Children in Poverty at http://www.ncp.org, accessed on Feb. 26, 2008. Also see Table 6 in CRS Report RL32760, *The Temporary Assistance for Needy Families (TANF) Block Grant: Responses to Frequently Asked Questions*, by Gene Falk.

[37] As reported in the *Annual ORR Reports to Congress-2005.*

[38] Information obtained from the *Texas Refugee Cash Assistance (RCA) Manual* at http://www.dads.state.tx.us/ handbooks/rca/, accessed on February 25, 2008.

[39] Information provided to CRS by the Florida Department of Children and Families, Febrary 11, 2008.

[40] CRS sought times series data from the lead DHS agencies beginning in FY1995 (beginning of the Migration Agreement) for each of the migration avenues analyzed in this section of the report. The U.S. Coast Guard and the U.S. Citizenship and Immigration Services have provided the time series data. The U.S. Customs and Border Protection does not have complete times series data available for this analysis.

[41] For further data analysis, see CRS Report RL32235, *U.S. Immigration Policy on Permanent Admissions*, by Ruth Ellen Wasem.

[42] Randall Monger and Nancy Rytina, U.S. Legal Permanent Residents: 2008, DHS Office of Immigration Statistics, Annual Flow Report, Washington, DC, March 2009, http://www.dhs.gov/xlibrary/assets/statistics/publications/ lpr_fr_2008.pdf.

[43] For interdiction data, see http://www.uscg.mil/hq/cg5/cg53 1/AMIO/FlowStats/currentstats. asp (accessed March 31, 2009)

[44] For background on this issue, see CRS Report RL33097, *Border Security: Apprehensions of "Other Than Mexican" Aliens*, coordinated by Blas Nuñez-Neto.

[45] Information provided by DHS Customs and Border Protection, Customs and Border Protection, Office of Border Patrol.

[46] Gerardo Arreola, "Mexico, Principal Route for Illegal Migration from Cuba to the U.S.," *LaJornada*, October 2, 2007. Translated from Spanish to English by Mabel Gracias.

[47] "Cuban migrants risk repatriation," *Los Angeles Times*, October 20, 2008.

[48] Sara Miller Llana, "New Cuban Escape Route: via Mexico," *The Christian Science Monitor*, November 5, 2008.

[49] Aliens subject to expedited removal must be detained until they are removed and may be released only due to medical emergency or if necessary for law enforcement purposes. In addition, aliens who have been expeditiously removed are barred from returning to the United States for five years. CRS Report RL33109, *Immigration Policy on Expedited Removal of Aliens*, by Alison Siskin and Ruth Ellen Wasem.

[50] Ibid.

[51] Information provided by the Refugee Affairs Division, Office of Refugee, Asylum and International Operations, U.S. Citizenship and Immigration Services, March 27, 2008.

[52] Cubans who have gone to a third country may be considered for refugee resettlement if referred by the United Nationals High Commissioner for Refugees (UNHCR) or a U.S. Embassy.

[53] For further discussion of refugee processing and admissions, see CRS Report RL3 1269, *Refugee Admissions and Resettlement Policy*, by Andorra Bruno.

[54] U.S. Department of State, Population, Refugees, and Migration, *Refugee Admissions Program for Latin America and the Caribbean*, February 6, 2009.

[55] CRS Report RL31269, *Refugee Admissions and Resettlement Policy*, by Andorra Bruno, and Jeanne Batalova, *Spotlight on Refugees and Asylees in the United States*, Migration Policy Institute, Migration Information Source, Washington, DC, August 2006.

[56] E-mail correspondence from the Office of Refugee Affairs, USCIS, DHS, January 17, 2006.

[57] U.S. Department of State, Population, Refugees, and Migration, *Refugee Admissions Program for Latin America and the Caribbean*, February 6, 2009.

[58] Randall Monger and Nancy Rytina, *U.S. Legal Permanent Residents: 2008*, DHS Office of Immigration Statistics, Annual Flow Report, Washington, DC, March 2009, http://www.dhs.gov/xlibrary/assets/statistics/publications/ lpr_fr_2008.pdf

[59] Much of the debate surrounding Elian Gonzalez played out in the courts. On March 21, 2000, the U.S. Federal District Court held that the Attorney General has sufficiently broad authority to refuse to consider Elian's asylum application. Elian's Miami relatives appealed that decision to the U.S. Court of Appeals for the 1 1th Circuit, which issued a temporary stay preventing Elian's return to Cuba, but ultimately unanimously rejected the family's appeal on June 1. On June 28, the U.S. Supreme Court upheld the lower court's ruling and cleared the way for Elian to return to Cuba with his immediate family later that day. For a full account of the Elian Gonzalez case, see CRS Report RS20450, *The Case of Elian Gonzalez: Legal Basics*, by Larry M. Eig, and CRS Report RL3 0570, *Elian Gonzalez: Chronology and Issue*s, by Ruth Ellen Wasem and Barbara A. Salazar (archived, available on request).

[60] CRS Report RL32730, *Cuba: Issues for the 109th Congress*, by Mark P. Sullivan.

[61] CRS Report RL32730, *Cuba: Issues for the 109th Congress*, by Mark P. Sullivan.

[62] *Florida Sun-Sentinel*, "Cubans repatriated after feds say abandoned Keys bridge is not U.S. soil," by Madeline Baró Diaz, January 10, 2006.

[63] OVS lays out a large-scale and coordinated response of over thirty federal, state, and local organizations to safely interdict migrants and prevent a humanitarian crisis. In particular, Coast Guard vessels and CBP aircraft would establish a "perimeter" around the country experiencing the flood of emigration. Former DHS Secretary Michael Chertoff approved OVS on August 21, 2007. Robert B. Watts, "Caribbean Maritime Migration: Challenges for the New Millennium," *Homeland Security Affairs*, no. 2 (2008); Danielle Barav, *Mass Migration from Cuba: How likely?* World Security Project, U.S.-Cuba Cooperative Security Project, March 25, 2008.

[64] U.S. Congress, House Committee on Transportation and Infrastructure, Subcommittee on Coast Guard and Maritime Transportation, *Overview of Coast Guard Drug and Migrant Interdiction*, hearing, 111th Cong., 1st sess., March 11, 2009.

[65] John-Thor Dahlberg, "Return of Migrants Roils Cuban-Americans," *Latin American Herald Tribune*, January 2003.

[66] Human Rights First (formerly Lawyers Committee for Human Rights), *U.S. Should Change Its Interdiction Practices*, Asylum Protection News. No. 18. 2003.

[67] CRS Report R40193, *Cuba: Issues for the 111th Congress*, by Mark P. Sullivan.

[68] For further explanation of these criteria, see CRS Report RL32235, *U.S. Immigration Policy on Permanent Admissions*, by Ruth Ellen Wasem.

[69] See, for example, *Reuters*, "Cuban Migrants Have it Easier on the U.S.-Mexico Border," by Robin Emmott, October 11, 2007, and *New York Times*, "Fleeing to U.S., Cubans' First Stop is Often Mexico," by Marc Lacey, October 16, 2007.

[70] Information provided to CRS by the Florida Department of Children and Families, Febrary 11, 2008.

[71] CRS Report RL33809, *Noncitizen Eligibility for Federal Public Assistance: Policy Overview and Trends*, by Ruth Ellen Wasem.

[72] U.S. Department of State. State Department Regular Briefing, Richard Boucher, January 7, 2004.

[73] "Migration Talks Cancelled," *Miami Herald*, January 8, 2004.

[74] William E. Gibson , "President Barack Obama Seeks 'a new beginning' with Cuba," *Fort Lauderdale Sun Sentinel*, April 18, 2009.

[75] For example, see U.S. Congress, Senate Committee on Foreign Relations, *Changing Cuba Policy—In the United States National Interest*, committee print, 111th Cong., 1st sess., February 23, 2009, S. Prt. 111-5 (Washington: GPO, 2009), p. 8.

[76] Roger Noreiga, *Oh, Brother! Another Castro Clings to Power in Cuba*, American Enterprise Institute, Latin American Outlook, March 12, 2008.

[77] Merle David Kellerhals Jr., "U.S., Cuba Agree to Resume Talks on Immigration, Direct Mail," America.gov, June 1, 20009.

In: U.S. Involvement in Political, Economic and Social … ISBN: 978-1-61209-781-7
Editor: Allen P. Lowell

Chapter 4

CUBA: U.S. RESTRICTIONS ON TRAVEL AND REMITTANCES

Mark P. Sullivan[#]

ABSTRACT

Restrictions on travel to Cuba have been a key and often contentious component in U.S. efforts to isolate Cuba's communist government for much of the past 40 years. Under the Bush Administration, restrictions on travel and on private remittances to Cuba were tightened. In March 2003, the Administration eliminated travel for people-to-people educational exchanges unrelated to academic coursework. In June 2004, the Bush Administration further restricted family and educational travel, eliminated the category of fully-hosted travel, and restricted remittances so that they could only be sent to the remitter's immediate family. Initially there was mixed reaction to the Bush Administration's June 2004 tightening of Cuba travel and remittance restrictions, but opposition to the policy grew, especially within the Cuban American community regarding the restrictions on family travel and remittances.

Dating back to 2000, there have been numerous legislative efforts to ease restrictions on travel to Cuba in various ways. From 2000-2004, one or both houses of Congress approved amendments to appropriations bills that would have eased restrictions on travel, but these provisions ultimately were stripped out of final enacted measures. The Bush Administration regularly threatened to veto legislation if it contained provisions weakening Cuba sanctions. In the 110th Congress, several House and Senate committee versions of appropriations bills (H.R. 2829, S. 1859, H.R. 7323, S. 3260, and S. 3289) had provisions that would have eased restrictions on travel to Cuba in various ways, but no final action was taken before the end of the Congress.

During the 2008 electoral campaign, President Obama pledged to lift restrictions on family travel to Cuba as well as restrictions on Cuban Americans sending remittances to Cuba. Senator Hillary Clinton reiterated President Obama's pledge during her confirmation hearing for Secretary of State on January 15, 2009, but indicated that the Administration did not yet have a timeline on the change. A number of observers expect

[#] E-mail: msullivan@crs.loc.gov

that the Administration will fulfill President Obama's campaign pledge before the upcoming fifth Summit of the Americas in Trinidad and Tobago scheduled for April 17-19, 2009.

The 111th Congress, however, already has taken action to ease some restrictions on travel to Cuba by including two provisions in the FY2009 omnibus appropriations measure (P.L. 111-8), signed into law on March 11, 2009. The first provision eases restrictions on family travel, which the Treasury Department implemented by issuing a general license for such travel as it existed prior to the Bush Administration's tightening of family travel restrictions in June 2004. Family travel is now allowed once every 12 months for an unlimited length of stay to visit a close relative who is no more than three generations removed from the traveler. The second provision eases travel restrictions related to the marketing and sale of agricultural and medical goods to Cuba, and requires the Treasury Department to issue a general license for such travel. The Treasury Department maintained that it would issue regulations in the coming weeks.

Several additional initiatives have been introduced in the 111th Congress that would ease restrictions on travel to Cuba: H.R. 188 and H.R. 1530 would lift the embargo, including travel restrictions; H.R. 1531 would facilitate the export of U.S. agricultural products to Cuba and also prohibit restrictions on travel to Cuba; H.R. 874/S. 428 and H.R. 1528 would prohibit restrictions on travel to Cuba; and H.R. 332 would ease restrictions on educational travel.

Most Recent Developments

On March 11, 2009, President Obama signed into law the Omnibus Appropriations Act, 2009 (P.L. 111-8), which included two provisions easing restrictions on family travel to Cuba and travel related to the marketing and sale of agricultural and medical goods to Cuba. The House had approved the measure on February 25, while the Senate approved the measure on March 10.

On January 15, 2009, during her Senate Foreign Relations Committee confirmation hearing for Secretary of State, Senator Hillary Clinton reiterated President-elect Obama's pledge to lift restrictions on family travel and remittances, but also indicated that the Administration did not have a timeline on the change.

On September 18, 2008, the House Foreign Affairs Committee's Subcommittee on International Organizations, Human Rights, and Oversight held a hearing on U.S. restrictions on Cuban-American travel to Cuba.

From mid-August through September 10, 2008, four major storms (Hurricanes Gustav and Ike, and Tropical Storms Hanna and Fay) caused widespread damage throughout Cuba. In the aftermath of the hurricanes, a number of observers, including some Members of Congress, called for the temporary relaxation of restrictions on family travel and remittances as well as on the provision of gift parcels to Cuba. On September 5, 2008, Chairman of the House Foreign Affairs Committee Howard Berman asked President Bush to suspend for 90 days restrictions on family visits, remittances, and gift parcels. Several legislative initiatives were introduced that would have temporarily eased U.S. embargo restrictions in these areas: S.Amdt. 5581 (Dodd) to S. 3001, H.R. 6913 (Flake), and H.R. 6962 (Delahunt). (See "Legislative Initiatives in the Aftermath of 2008 Hurricanes" below)

On August 28, 2008, a U.S. Federal district judge in Miami stuck down a 2006 Florida state law that prohibited Florida state colleges from using state and nonstate funds for travel to countries on the State Department's state sponsors of terrorism list, which includes Cuba.

On July 21, 2008, the Senate Appropriations Committee reported its version of the FY2009 Agriculture Appropriations bill, S. 3289 (S.Rept. 110-426), with a provision that would ease restrictions on travel to Cuba for the sale of agricultural and medical goods. It would allow for a general license for such travel instead of a specific license that requires permission from the Treasury Department. The measure had been approved by the Committee on July 17, 2008.

On July 14, 2008, the Senate Appropriations Committee reported its version of the FY2009 Financial Services and General Government Appropriations bill, S. 3260 (S.Rept. 110-417), which includes provisions easing restrictions on family travel and on travel to Cuba relating to the commercial sale of agricultural and medical goods. With regard to family travel, the bill would provide that no funds may be used to administer, implement, or enforce the Administration's June 2004 tightening of restrictions related to travel to visit relatives in Cuba. With regard to travel for agricultural or medical sales, the bill would allow for a general license for such travel instead of a specific license that requires permission from the Treasury Department.

On June 30, 2008, a group of south Florida travel agencies specializing in travel to Cuba filed suit in U.S. federal court in Miami challenging a recent Florida state law related to Cuba travel. That law requires travel agencies that sell trips to countries on the State Department's list of state sponsors of terrorism (currently Cuba, Iran, Syria, Sudan, and North Korea, which could be removed this summer) to pay annual fees up to $2,500 and to post up to a $250,000 bond required for the agencies to operate in Florida.

On June 25, 2008, the House Appropriations Committee approved its version of the FY2009 Financial Services and General Government Appropriations bill that includes provisions easing restrictions on family travel and U.S. agricultural exports to Cuba. The bill would liberalize family travel to Cuba by allowing for such travel once a year (instead of the current restriction of once every three years) and by allowing such travel to visit aunts, uncles, nieces, nephews, and first cousins. The bill subsequently was introduced as H.R. 7323 (Serrano) and reported (H.Rept. 110-920) on December 10, 2008).

On March 5, 2008, Cuban Americans living in Vermont filed a complaint in U.S. federal court in Burlington, Vermont, that U.S. restrictions on family travel to Cuba violate their civil rights. Affiliates of the American Civil Liberties Union of Florida, Massachusetts, and Vermont filed a brief in support of the complaint on May 16, 2008.

Background to Travel Restrictions

Since the United States imposed a comprehensive trade embargo against Cuba in the early 1960s, there have been numerous policy changes to restrictions on travel to Cuba. The embargo regulations do not ban travel itself, but place restrictions on any financial transactions related to travel to Cuba, which effectively result in a travel ban. Accordingly, from 1963 until 1977, travel to Cuba was effectively banned under the Cuban Assets Control Regulations (CACR) issued by the Treasury Department's Office of Foreign Assets Control (OFAC) to implement the embargo. In 1977, the Carter Administration made changes to the regulations that essentially lifted the travel ban. In 1982, the Reagan Administration made other changes to the CACR that once again restricted travel to Cuba, but allowed for travel-related transactions by certain categories of travelers. Under the Clinton Administration, there were several changes to the Treasury Department regulations, with some at first tightening the restrictions, and others later loosening the restrictions.

Under the Bush Administration, the travel regulations were tightened significantly, with additional restrictions on family visits, educational travel, and travel for those involved in amateur and semi-professional international sports federation competitions. In addition, the categories of fully-hosted travel and people to people educational exchanges unrelated to academic coursework were eliminated as permissible travel to Cuba. The Bush has also cracked down on those traveling to Cuba illegally, further restricted religious travel by changing licensing guidelines for such travel, and suspended the licenses of several travel service providers in Florida for license violations. The regulations that remain in place today are less restrictive than those in place from 1963 to 1977, but more restrictive than those in place from 1977-1982 when the travel ban was essentially lifted.

Chronology of Cuba Travel Restrictions

1960—In the first trade restrictions on Cuba after the rise to power of Fidel Castro, President Eisenhower placed most U.S. exports to Cuba under validated license controls, except for nonsubsidized food, medicines, and medical supplies. The action did not include restrictions on travel.

1962/1963—In February 1962, President Kennedy imposed a trade embargo on Cuba because of the Castro regime's ties to the Soviet Union. Pursuant to the President's directive, the Department of the Treasury's Office of Foreign Assets Control (OFAC) issued the Cuban Import Regulations. On July 9, 1963, OFAC issued a more comprehensive set of prohibitions, the Cuban Assets Control Regulations, which effectively banned travel by prohibiting any transactions with Cuba.

1977—In March, the Carter Administration announced the lifting of restrictions on U.S. travel to Cuba that had been in place since the early 1960s. The Carter Administration lifted the travel ban by issuing a general license for travel-related transactions for those visiting Cuba. Direct flights were also allowed.

1982—In April, the Reagan Administration re-imposed restrictions on travel to Cuba, although it allowed for certain categories of travel, including travel by U.S. government officials, employees of news or film making organizations, persons engaging in professional research, or persons visiting their close relatives. It did not allow for ordinary tourist or business travel that had been allowed since the Carter Administration's 1977 action.

1984—On June 28, the Supreme Court, in a 5-4 decision in the case of Regan v. Wald, rejected a challenge to the ban on travel to Cuba and asserted the executive branch's right to impose travel restrictions for national security reasons.

1993—The Clinton Administration, in June 1993, slightly amended restrictions on U.S. travel to Cuba. Two additional categories of travel were allowed: travel to Cuba "for clearly defined educational or religious activities"; and travel "for activities of recognized human rights organizations." In both categories, travelers were required to apply for a specific license from OFAC.

1994—In August, President Clinton announced several measures against the Cuban government in response to an escalation in the number of Cubans fleeing to the United States. Among these measures, the Administration tightened travel restrictions by prohibiting family visits under a general license, and allowing specific licenses for family visits only "when extreme hardship is demonstrated in cases involving extreme humanitarian need" such as terminal illness or severe medical emergency. Such visits required a specific license from OFAC. In addition, professional researchers were required to apply for a specific license, whereas since 1982 they had been able to travel freely under a general license. (Federal Register, August 30, 1994, pp. 44884-44886).

1995—In October, President Clinton announced measures to ease some U.S. restrictions on travel and other activities with Cuba, with the overall objective of promoting democracy and the free flow of ideas. The new measures included authorizing general licenses for transactions relating to travel to Cuba for Cuban Americans making yearly visits to close relatives in "circumstances that demonstrate extreme humanitarian need." This reversed the August 1994 action that required specific licenses. However, those traveling for this purpose more than once in a 12-month period would need to apply to OFAC for a specific license. In addition, the new measures allowed for specific licenses for free-lance journalists traveling to Cuba. (Federal Register, October 20, 1995, pp. 54194-54198).

1996—On February 26, following the shootdown of two U.S. civilian planes two days earlier by Cuban fighter jets, President Clinton took several measures against Cuba, including the indefinite suspension of charter flights between Cuba and the United States. Qualified licensed travelers could go to Cuba, provided their flights were routed through third countries.

1998—On March 20, following Pope John Paul II's January trip to Cuba, President Clinton announced several changes in U.S. policy toward Cuba, including the resumption of licensing for direct charter flights to Cuba. On July 2, OFAC issued licenses to nine air charter companies to provide direct passenger flights from Miami International Airport to Havana's Jose Marti Airport.

1999—On January 5, President Clinton announced several measures to support the Cuban people that were intended to augment changes implemented in March 1998. Among the measures introduced was the expansion of direct passenger charter flights from additional U.S. cities other than Miami. In August, the State Department announced that direct flights to Cuba would be allowed from New York and Los Angeles. In addition, President Clinton also announced in January 1999 that measures would be taken to increase people-to-people exchanges. As a result, on May 13, 1999, OFAC issued a number of changes to the Cuba embargo regulations that effectively loosened restrictions on certain categories of travelers to Cuba. Travel for professional research became possible under a general license, and travel for a wide range of educational, religious, sports competition, and other activities became possible with specific licenses authorized by OFAC on a case-by-case basis. In addition, those traveling to Cuba to visit a close family member under either a general or specific license only needed to "demonstrate humanitarian need," as opposed to "extreme humanitarian need" that had been required since 1995 (Federal Register, May 13, 1999, pp. 25808-25820).

2000—In October, Congress approved and the President signed the Trade Sanctions Reform and Export Enhancement Act of 2000 (Title IX of P.L. 106-387), which included a provision that prohibited travel-related transactions for "tourist activities," which as set forth in Section 910(b)(2) of the act are defined as any activity not authorized or referenced in the existing travel regulations (31 CFR 515.560, paragraphs (1) through (12)). The congressional action appeared to circumscribe the authority of the OFAC to issue specific travel licenses on a case-by-case basis that do not fit neatly within the categories of travel already allowed by the regulations.

2001—On July 12, 2001, OFAC published regulations pursuant to the provisions of the Trade Sanctions and Export Enhancement Act of 2000 (Title IX of P.L. 106-387)that prohibited travel-related transactions for "tourist activities." (Federal Register, July 12, 2001, pp. 36683-36688). On July 13, 2001, President Bush announced that he had asked the Treasury Department to enhance and expand the capabilities of OFAC to prevent, among other things, "unlicensed and excessive travel."

2003—On January 29, 2003, OFAC published proposed enforcement guidelines (as an appendix to 31 CFR Part 501) for all its economic sanctions programs and additional guidelines (as an appendix to 31 CFR Part 515) for the Cuba sanctions program. The general guidelines provide a procedural framework for OFAC's enforcement of economic sanctions, while the Cuba specific guidelines consists of penalties for different embargo violations. (Federal Register, January 29, 2003, pp. 4422-4429).

On March 24, 2003, OFAC announced that the Cuba travel regulations were being amended to ease travel to Cuba for those visiting close relatives (Federal Register, March 24, 2003, pp. 14141-14148). Travel is now permitted to visit relatives to within three degrees of relationship of the traveler and is not restricted to travel in circumstances of humanitarian need. The new regulations also increased the amount a traveler may carry, up to $3,000 (compared to $300 previously), although the limit of $300 per quarter destined for each household remains. Finally, the regulations were tightened for certain types of educational travel. People-to-people educational exchanges unrelated to academic coursework are no longer allowed. Some groups have lauded the restriction of these educational exchanges because they believe they have become an opportunity for unrestricted travel; others criticize the Administration's decision to restrict the second largest category of travel to Cuba in which ordinary people have been able to travel and exchange with their counterparts on the island.

On October 10, 2003, President Bush instructed the Department of Homeland Security, as part of a broader initiative on Cuba, to increase inspections of travelers and shipments to and from Cuba in order to more strictly enforce the trade and travel embargo.

2004—On February 26, 2004, President Bush ordered the Department of Homeland Security to expand its policing of the waters between Florida and Cuba with the objective of stopping pleasure boating traffic (Federal Register, March 1, 2004, pp. 9315-9517).

On June 16, 2004, OFAC published changes to the CACR implementing the President's directives to implement certain recommendations of the Commission for Assistance to a Free Cuba. The new regulations tightened travel restrictions in several ways. Fully-hosted travel was eliminated as a legal category of permissible travel. Family visits were restricted to one trip every three years under a specific license to visit only immediate family (grandparents, grandchildren, parents, siblings, spouses, and children) for a period not to exceed 14 days. The daily amount of money that family visitors can spend while in Cuba was reduced from the State Department per diem rate (currently $179) to $50. Specific licenses for visiting non-Cuban nationals in Cuba (such as a student) are now limited to when the family member visited is in "exigent circumstances." The general license for amateur or semi-professional athletic teams to travel to Cuba to engage in sports competitions was eliminated; such travel now requires a specific license. (Federal Register, June 16, 2004, pp. 33768-33774)

Specific licenses for educational activities were further restricted in several ways: the institutional licenses are restricted to undergraduate and graduate institutions, while the category of educational exchanges sponsored by secondary schools was eliminated; the duration of institutional licenses was shortened from two to one year; three types of licensed educational activities—structural education programs in Cuba offered as part of a course at the licensed institution, formal courses of study offered at a Cuban academic institution; and teaching at a Cuban academic institution—are required to be no shorter than 10 weeks.

The new regulations also further restricted sending cash remittances to Cuba. Quarterly remittances of $300 may still be sent, but are now restricted to members of the remitter's immediate family and may not be remitted to certain government officials and certain members of the Cuban Communist Party. The regulations were also changed to reduce the amount of remittances that authorized travelers may carry to Cuba, from $3000 to $300. This reversed OFAC's March 2003 changes to the regulations that had increased the amount that authorized travelers could carry to $3000.

On June 22, 2004, the Department of Commerce's Bureau of Industry and Security (BIS) published regulations related to the recommendations of the Commission for Assistance to a Free Cuba. The new regulations placed new limits on gift parcels sent to Cuba and personal baggage of travelers going to Cuba. Gift parcels may no longer contain items such as seeds, clothing, personal hygiene items, veterinary medicines and supplies, fishing equipment and supplies, and soap-making equipment. Baggage is now limited to 44 pounds. (Federal Register, pp. 34565-34567) On July 8, 2004, the U.S. Coast Guard published regulations requiring U.S. vessels less than 100 meters to have a Coast Guard permit to enter Cuban territorial waters (Federal Register, pp. 41367-41374).

2005—On March 31, 2005, OFAC made changes to its guidelines for license applications related to religious travel. Specific licenses issued under CFR 515.566(b) for religious organizations now only authorize up to 25 individuals to travel to Cuba no more than once per calendar quarter. The specific licenses under this section will not be valid for more than one year. (OFAC, Comprehensive Guidelines for License Applications to Engage in Travel-related Transactions Involving Cuba, Revised September 2004, p. 40, the relevant paragraph was updated March 31, 2005).

2009—On March 11, 2009, President Obama signed into law the Omnibus Appropriations Act, 2009 (P.L. 111-8), with two provisions easing restrictions on travel to Cuba.

Section 620 of Division D amends the Trade Sanctions Reform and Export Enhancement Act of 2000 (TSRA) to require the Secretary of the Treasury to issue regulations for travel to, from, or within Cuba under a general license for the marketing and sale of agricultural and medical goods, meaning that there would be no requirement to obtain special permission from OFAC. Such travel currently requires a specific license from OFAC, issued on a case-by-case basis. OFAC maintained that it would issue regulations in the coming weeks, although a letter from Secretary of the Treasury Timothy Geithner published in the Congressional Record stated that the new regulations "would provide that the representatives of only a narrow class of businesses would be eligible, under a new general license, to travel to market and sell agricultural and medical goods." The Secretary also maintained that "any business using the general license would be required to provide both advance written notice outlining the purpose and scope of the planned travel and, upon return, a report outlining the activities conducted, including the persons with whom they met, the expenses incurred, and business conducted in Cuba." (Congressional Record, March 10, 2009, p. S2933.)

Section 621 of Division D prohibits funds from being used to administer, implement, or enforce family travel restrictions that were imposed by the Bush Administration in June 2004. OFAC implemented this provision by reinstating a general license for family travel as it existed prior to the Bush Administration's tightening of restrictions in June 2004. Travel is now allowed once every 12 months to visit a close relative for an unlimited length of stay, and the limit for daily expenditure allowed by family travelers is the same as for other authorized travelers to Cuba (State Department maximum per diem rate for Havana, currently $179 day). The new general license also expands the definition of "close relative" to mean any individual related to the traveler by blood, marriage, or adoption who is no more than three generations removed from that person.

CURRENT PERMISSIBLE TRAVEL TO CUBA

The travel regulations can be found at 31CFR 515.560, which references other sections of the Cuban Assets Control Regulations for travel-related transaction licensing criteria. (For an overview of the Treasury Department regulations on travel to Cuba, see OFAC's website http://www.treas.gov/offices/enforcement/ofac/). At present, certain categories of travelers may travel to Cuba under a general license, which means that there is no need to obtain special permission from OFAC. In addition, a wide variety of travelers engaging in family visits, and educational, religious, humanitarian, and other activities may be eligible for specific licenses. Applications for specific licenses are reviewed and granted by OFAC on a case by case basis. Some specific licenses may authorize multiple trips to Cuba over an extended period of time.

The general license categories include the following:

- Persons visiting a close family relative who is a national of Cuba (defined as any individual related to the traveler by blood, marriage, or adoption who is no more than three generations removed from the traveler or form a common ancestor with the traveler) once every 12 months for an unlimited length of stay. (31 CFR 515.561; OFAC, General License for Visits to Close Relatives in Cuba, March 11, 2009.)
- Officials of the U.S. government, foreign governments, and certain inter-governmental organizations traveling on official business (31 CFR 515.562);
- Persons regularly employed as journalists by a news reporting organization or by persons regularly employed as supporting broadcast or technical personnel (31 CFR 515.563); and
- Full-time professionals conducting professional research in their areas (provided that the research is of a noncommercial, academic nature, that the research comprises a full work schedule in Cuba, and that the research has a substantial likelihood of public dissemination) or attending professional meetings or conferences in Cuba organized by an international professional organization, institution, or association that regularly sponsors meetings or conferences in other countries (31 CFR 515.564).

The specific license categories include the following:

- Persons visiting a close family relative who is a national of Cuba for additional visits during a 12-month period (31 CFR 515.561; OFAC, Guidance on Implementation of Cuba Travel and Trade-Related Provisions of the Omnibus Appropriations Act, 2009, March 11, 2009);
- Persons visiting an immediate family member who is not a national of Cuba and is in exigent circumstances, provided the person being visited is in Cuba pursuant to OFAC authorization, the exigency has been reported to the U.S. Interests Section in Havana, and the license would support the mission of the U.S. Interests Section (31 CFR 515.561; OFAC, Guidance on Implementation of Cuba Travel and Trade-Related Provisions of the Omnibus Appropriations Act, 2009, March 11, 2009);
- Free-lance journalists (31 CFR 515.563);
- Professional researchers undertaking research or attending professional meetings who do not qualify for a general license (31 CFR 515.564);
- Specific institutional licenses (up to one year) for students and full-time employees of undergraduate or graduate degree-granting academic institutions to participate in educational activities. These activities include participation in a structured educational program in Cuba as part of a course offered at the licensed institution (not less than 10 weeks); noncommercial academic research in Cuba specifically related to Cuba for the purpose of obtaining a graduate degree;
- Participation in a formal course of study at a Cuban institution (not less than 10 weeks) provided it will be accepted for credit toward the student's undergraduate or graduate degree at the licensed U.S. institution; teaching at a Cuban academic institution (not less than 10 weeks); and sponsorship of a Cuban scholar to teach or engage in other scholarly activity at the licensed institution. (CFR 515.565);
- U.S. religious organizations, for its members undertaking religious activities in Cuba (31 CFR 515.566); [Note: According to OFAC, specific licenses under515.566(a), which does not limit the number of travelers or the frequency of trips, are for smaller religious organizations, such as individual churches and congregational units; larger religious organizations, such as national associations of churches, may now obtain a license under 515.566(b), which, according to revised March 2005 licensing guidelines "will only authorize up to twenty-five (25) individuals to travel to Cuba per trip and will permit no more than one trip per calendar quarter."[1]
- Amateur or semi-professional athletes participating in competitions, provided that the competition is held under the auspices of the international sports federation for the relevant sport, that U.S. participants are selected by the U.S. federation for the relevant sport, and that the competition is open for attendance, and in relevant situations, for the Cuban public. Those involved in public performances, athletic and other competitions, and exhibitions, provided that the event is open for attendance, and in relevant situations, participation by the Cuban public, and that all profits are donated to an independent nongovernmental organization in Cuba or a U.S.-based charity (31 CFR 515.567);
- Those traveling for activities in support of the Cuban people, such as activities of recognized human rights organizations, activities designed to promote a rapid,

peaceful transition to democracy, and activities intended to strengthen civil society (31 CFR 515.574);

- Those involved in humanitarian projects in Cuba, such as medical and health-related projects, construction projects, intended to benefit legitimately independent civil society groups, environmental projects, projects involving non-formal educational training, within Cuba or off island, on topics including civil education, journalism, advocacy and organizing, adult literacy and vocational skills, community-based grass roots projects, projects suitable to the development of small-scale enterprise, projects related to agricultural and rural development that promote independent activity, and projects involving the donation of goods to meet basic human needs (31 CFR 515.575);
- Those involved in activities of private foundations or research or education institutes that have an established interest in international relations to collect information related to Cuba for noncommercial purposes (31 CFR 515.576);
- Those involved in the importation, exportation, or transmission of informational materials (31CFR 515.545); and
- Those involved in activities related to marketing, sales negotiation, accompanied delivery, or servicing of exports to Cuba authorized by the Department of Commerce or engaged in by U.S. owned or controlled foreign firms (31CFR515.533 and 31 CFR 515.559). Note: The Omnibus Appropriations Act, 2009 (P.L. 111-8), signed into law March 11, 2009, directed the Treasury Department to issue regulations authorizing, by general license, travel-related transactions for travel to, from, or within Cuba for the marketing and sale of agricultural and medical goods. The Treasury Department maintains that it will implement this provision in the coming weeks, but until new regulations are issued, such travel must continue to be authorized by specific license as set forth in 31CFR 515.533. (OFAC, Guidance on Implementation of Cuba Travel and Trade-Related Provisions of the Omnibus Appropriations Act, 2009, March 11, 2009.)

Current Restrictions on Remittances

U.S. cash remittances to Cuba account for an estimated \$400-\$800 million per year, according to the 2004 report of the Commission for Assistance to a Free Cuba, although the report also noted that some estimates were as high as \$1 billion annually [2]. According to a November 2007 GAO report, no reliable data exist for cash remitted directly or indirectly from the United States to Cuba although it maintained that data from several sources showed that worldwide remittances to Cuba amounted to between \$900 million and \$1 billion [3].

Restrictions on such remittances are regulated by the Cuban Assets Control Regulations (CACR) and have changed over time. Pursuant to OFAC's June 16, 2004, amendments to the CACR, a total of \$300 per quarter may be sent to nationals of Cuba who are members of the remitter's immediate family (spouse, child, grandchild, parent, grandparent, or sibling) (CFR 515.570). Remittances to certain officials of the Cuban government and certain members of the Cuban Communist Party are not allowed. Up to \$300 in remittances may be carried by an authorized traveler to Cuba (CFR 515.560(c)(4)).

Prior to OFAC's June 16, 2004, changes to the CACR, remittances were not restricted to members of the remitter's immediate family but could be sent to any household in Cuba, provided the household did not include a senior-level Cuban government official or senior-level Communist Party official. Authorized travelers also could carry up to $3,000 in cash remittances.

An additional tightening of remittance policy was that the general OFAC license authorizing banks to send individual remittances to Cuba was eliminated. Banks now need to be specifically licensed by OFAC in order to become a remittance-forwarding service provider. OFAC is responsible for regulating 103 licensed remittance-forwarding service providers [4].

Reaction to the June 2004 Tightening of Travel and Remittance Restrictions

There was mixed reaction to the Bush Administration's June 2004 tightening of Cuba travel and remittance restrictions, including within the Cuban American community. The President maintained that such restrictions would "prevent the regime from exploiting hard currency of tourists and remittances to Cubans to prop up their repressive regime." [5] Supporters of the tightened restrictions argued that both educational and family travel to Cuba had become fronts for tourist travel. Tightening up on such travel, they argued, would deny the regime with dollars that help maintain its repressive control. (According to the Commission for Assistance for a Free Cuba, some 125,000 family visits to Cuba in 2003 resulted in about $96 million in hard currency for the government [6]) Another argument made by some supporters of the tightened restrictions is that the limiting of family travel to once every three years helps ensure that such travel is limited to family emergencies. Along these lines, some argue that limiting family travel makes travelers more sensitive to political repression on the island and highlights that Cuban Americans are political refugees, not economic immigrants. Some supporters of the additional remittance restrictions argue that the Bush Administration demonstrated a continuation of the compassionate policy of supporting the Cuban people by not cutting the level of remittances allowed, $300 per quarter. They emphasize that the Administration only took action to ensure that the remittances would be restricted to immediate family members and not benefit certain members of the Cuban government and Cuban Communist Party.

Opponents of the tightened travel and remittance restrictions make a number of policy arguments. They maintain the restrictions are anti-family and threaten the basic principle of family reunification. Some in the Cuban American community argue that the policy of restricting family visits is inhumane and will only result in more suffering for Cuban families. They especially oppose the additional restrictions that do not allow travel to visit cousins, aunts, uncles, and more-distant relatives. Another argument opposing restrictions on travel and private remittances is that the steps will have no effect on reducing repression in Cuba or weakening the government's instruments of repression. Opponents of the tightened restrictions maintain that the new restrictions are opposed by several prominent Cuban dissidents, including Oswaldo Paya of the Varela Project and Elizardo Sanchez of the Cuban Commission for Human Rights and National Reconciliation. Miriam Leiva, one of the founders of the Ladies in White human rights group maintains that the policy punishes dissidents and their families; she compared the U.S. restrictions to the situation faced by Cubans, who cannot travel without permission from the Cuban government [7]. Former political prisoner Oscar Espinosa Chepe, released from prison in December 2004, called the U.S. policy "absurd," maintaining that "what we need is to create space for dialogue." [8]

There were also concerns that the new restrictions were drafted without considering the full consequences of their implementation. For example, the elimination of the category of fully-hosted travel raised concerns about the status some 70 U.S. students receiving full scholarships at the Latin American School of Medicine in Havana. The school has more than 3,000 students from 23 countries and consists of a six-month pre-med program and a six-year medical school program. Members of the Congressional Black Caucus, who were instrumental in the establishment of the scholarship program for U.S. students, expressed concern that the students may be forced to abandon their medical education because of the new OFAC regulations. As a result of these concerns, OFAC ultimately licensed the medical students in August 2004 to continue their studies and engage in travel-related transactions.

In the aftermath of the Administration's tightening of travel restrictions, there was increased opposition to the policy and several groups were established opposing the Administration's actions. A group know as ENCASA, the Emergency Network of Cuban American Scholars and Artists for Change in Cuba Policy, launched a media campaign in 2006 opposing the travel restrictions [9] In June 2006, another group of some 450 scholars known as the Emergency Coalition to Defend Educational Travel (ECDET) filed suit in U.S. federal court in Washington against the Treasury Department, maintaining that travel restrictions violate academic freedom [10] (On November 4, 2008, the U.S. Court of Appeals for the District of Columbia found that the travel restrictions do not violate the right to academic freedom [11]).

With regard to family travel, a group in Miami, the Association of Christian Women in Defense of the Cuban Family, organized several protests against the tightened family travel restrictions [12] In March 2008, Cuban Americans living in Vermont filed a complaint in U.S. federal court in Burlington, Vermont, that U.S. restrictions on family travel to Cuba violate their civil rights. Affiliates of the American Civil Liberties Union of Florida, Massachusetts, and Vermont subsequently filed a brief in support of the complaint. Human Rights Watch maintains that the U.S. travel policies inflict harm on Cuban families and undermine the freedom of movement of hundreds of thousands of Cuban Americans [13]. In a 2005 report, Human Rights Watch cited numerous cases of family hardships after the tightened family travel restrictions went into effect, including the inability to visit children, sick or dying parents, or to attend funerals [14].

A 2007 Florida International University poll examining attitudes of the Cuban American community in South Florida showed that about 64% of respondents would like to return to the less restrictive polices on travel and remittances that were in place in 2003. Moreover, 55.2% of respondents supported allowed unrestricted travel overall, not just family travel [15].

Estimates of U.S. Travelers to Cuba

Estimates of U.S. citizens traveling to Cuba vary considerably as reported by U.S. and Cuban government sources. According to a November 2007 GAO report, U.S. and Cuban government data on U.S. travel to Cuba are incomplete and cover different populations, and as a result there are no reliable estimates of total U.S. travel to Cuba [16] Nevertheless, travel service providers maintain that the elimination of the people-to-people trips in 2003 and significant restrictions on family travel in 2004 have significantly reduced the number of Americans visiting Cuba.

In terms of U.S. figures, the inter-agency Commission for Assistance to a Free Cuba estimated in May 2004 that some 160,000-200,000 legal and illegal travelers visited Cuba from the United States annually over the past decade. According to the Commission, the largest category of legal travel consisted of Cuban Americans visiting their families, amounting to 125,000 out of a total of 160,000 Americans visiting Cuba in 2003 [17] In July 2007, the U.S. International Trade Commission (ITC) issued a report examining the effect of U.S. restrictions on travel (as well as restrictions on U.S. agricultural sales). As a baseline, the ITC report estimated that about 171,000 American traveled to Cuba in 2005 (a figure considerably higher than Cuban government estimates cited below). The ITC concluded that lifting travel restrictions would result in travel by U.S. citizens to Cuba rising to between 550,000 and 1 million [18].

Cuban officials maintain that overall U.S. travel to Cuba has dropped considerably over the past four years because of the tightening of U.S. travel restrictions, from 200,859 Americans in 2003, to 108,172 in 2004, 101,000 in 2005 and 96,000 in 2006. This reflects a decline of over 52% in U.S. travelers to Cuba from 2003 to 2006. Looking at the number of Cuban Americans traveling to Cuba, the Cuban government estimates that 115,050 visited Cuba in 2003, 57,145 in 2004, 62,000 in 2005, and 59,000 in 2006 [19].

OFAC Review of Travel and Carrier Service Providers

OFAC is responsible for regulating the activities of licensed travel and carrier service providers (travel agencies, tour operators, and airline companies) around the country. As of January 2009, there were about 155 licensed travel and carrier service providers, the majority of which are concentrated in Florida, down from over 190 such providers in mid-2008 [20] The licensed service providers must keep records for each transaction, including transactions between service providers. The record keeping must include details about individual travelers and their circumstances sufficient to allow identification and verification that the transactions comply with the Cuban Assets Control Regulations (CACR) implemented by OFAC. Individuals traveling to Cuba under the authorization of OFAC must maintain records of all travel transactions for five years [pursuant to 31 CFR Parts 501.601 and 501.602].

The CACR spells out the requirements for travel service providers (TSP) and carrier service providers (CSP) to put procedures in place to establish that each customer is in full compliance with the regulations [21]. The regulations require such providers to demonstrate that they require each customer to attest, in a signed statement, to his or her qualification for authorized travel. The statement must provide facts supporting the customer's belief that he or she qualifies for travel to Cuba according to the categories of travel set forth in the CACR.

As part of the compliance process, licensed travel agencies must provide details about travelers to the air carriers prior to the air carriers accepting a reservation or selling a seat on a flight. This information consists of the passenger's full name, mother's maiden name, address, date of birth, passport number and country of issuance, airport of departure from the

United States, and whether travel is under a general or specific license. The licensed air carrier in turn must provide detailed information to OFAC in Washington by electronic mail 48 to 72 hours prior to departure of the flight. This consists of (1) the information provided by the travel service provider (TSP) on each authorized traveler; (2) U.S. departure and return dates; and (3) the name of the TSP who arranged for the travel. Generally what happens is that travelers fill out a travel affidavit with the TSP providing the information, including what type of license they are traveling under, and the TSP then provides information to the carrier service provider before a reservation is actually made.

Passengers on direct flights to Cuba need to fill out an OFAC Outbound Declaration Card (entitled Travel to Cuba). Carrier Service Providers are required to ensure that every passenger receives one of the cards as part of the check-in procedure at the ticket counter assigned to the charter. CSPs must collect the completed and signed cards before the passenger boards the plane, and must make the completed cards available to the U.S. Customs Service inspector at the departure gate for review. If no inspector is present or if the inspector returns the cards to the CSP, then the cards must be forwarded to the OFAC-Miami office.

In January 2006, OFAC suspended a South Florida travel agency, La Estrella de Cuba, from booking travel to Cuba. The agency reportedly was one of the largest licensed travel agencies, booking some 300 to 500 passengers monthly to Cuba. According to a Treasury Department spokesman, OFAC had plans to conduct 25 on-site audits in 2006 at agencies that do business with Cuba [22] In addition to La Estrella de Cuba, OFAC suspended the service activities of several other companies in 2006, including Baby Envios Travel, Fortuna Travel Services, Cubatur Express, La Perla del Caribe, Summit Jet Corporation, Adventure Tours and Travel, Art Quest International, Super Travel Services, Caribbean Air Service, Discovery Travel, and Cuba Familia Envios [23].

ENFORCEMENT OF CUBA TRAVEL RESTRICTIONS

Enforcement of U.S. restrictions on Cuba travel increased considerably under the Bush Administration. The major agencies involved in enforcing the travel restrictions include the Treasury Department's OFAC, which in addition to licensing travelers and licensing and monitoring travel-service providers, also investigates suspected travel violations and imposes civil fines; the Department of Homeland Security's Customs and Border Protection (CBP), which inspects passengers to and from Cuba and screens passengers on other international flights for compliance with U.S. travel restrictions; and the Department of Justice, which prosecutes criminal violations of the Cuba embargo.

President Bush announced in July 2001 that he had asked the Treasury Department to enhance and expand the enforcement capabilities of the Office of Foreign Assets Control. The President noted the importance of upholding and enforcing the law in order to prevent, among other things, "unlicensed and excessive travel" and to ensure that humanitarian and cultural exchanges actually reach pro-democracy activists in Cuba [24] On October 10, 2003, President Bush instructed the Department of Homeland Security to enforce the trade and travel embargo more strictly. As a result, the CBP's inspections of passengers traveling to and from Cuba were stepped up.

In 2004, the Bush Administration moved to tighten enforcement of Cuba travel restrictions in several ways. In February and March 2004, OFAC identified 11 companies in

Cuba, Argentina, the Bahamas, Canada, Chile, the Netherlands, and England (10 travel companies and one gift forwarder), blocked their assets under U.S. jurisdiction, and prohibited any transactions with these companies [25] On February 26, 2004, President Bush ordered the Department of Homeland Security to expand its policing of the waters between Florida and Cuba with the objective of stopping pleasure boating traffic [26]. In early May 2004, the President endorsed the recommendations of Commission for Assistance to Free Cuba. These included increased inspections of travelers and shipments to Cuba and an increase in both maritime surface patrols and air sorties in the region by law enforcement agencies in order to locate and prosecute pleasure boaters who travel to Cuba illegally.

Beginning in 2005, the Bush Administration tightened restrictions on religious travel to Cuba, not by making changes to the CACR, but by changing the guidelines for specific license applications for religious travel. According to OFAC, after restrictions on family travel were tightened in June 2004, it noticed an increase in the improper use of licenses by large religious organizations, which solicited participation in trips to Cuba beyond their own organizations. As a result, OFAC implemented a new policy of more tightly restricting the licenses of larger national religious organizations. Previously these organizations were licensed under Section 515.566(a) of the CACR without restriction on the number of travelers or the frequency of trips.

Under the new policy, larger religious organizations are now required to obtain a license under the more restrictive Section 515.566(b) of the CACR, which as of March 31, 2005, limits trips to four per year (one per quarter), each of which are limited to 25 individuals. Smaller religious organizations, such as individual churches and congregational units, may continue to apply for a specific license under Section 515.566(a), which does not limit the number of travelers or trips under the license.

More than 100 Members of Congress sent a letter to the Treasury Department in March 2006 questioning OFAC's actions that further restricted religious travel to Cuba. Church groups such as Church World Service, the National Council on Churches, American Baptist Churches USA, the Alliance for Baptists, and the Presbyterian Church have expressed strong opposition to the new restrictions [27]. Visits by members of Catholics and Jewish organizations have also diminished because of the tightened restrictions [28].

There were further indications in 2006 of the Bush Administration's strict enforcement of travel restrictions. Press reports in January indicated that OFAC sent letters to some 200 travelers from two U.S. groups—Pastors for Peace (which organizes caravans of aid from the United States to Cuba via Mexico) and the Venceremos Brigade—both of which have long organized trips to Cuba in defiance of U.S. sanctions [29].

Moreover, as described above, OFAC suspended the licenses of several companies providing travel and remittances services. In October 2006, the U.S. government established an inter-agency Cuban Sanctions Enforcement Task Force, chaired by the U.S. Attorney for the Southern District of Florida, with support from the FBI, and the Treasury, Homeland Security, and Commerce Departments. The primary goals of the task force are the investigation of Cuba embargo violations and enforcement through federal criminal prosecutions.

Civil Penalties

Beginning in April 2003, OFAC began making available a regular listing of civil penalties enforcement information for its sanctions programs, including violations of the Cuba travel regulations [30] According to a Treasury Department spokesmen, the information was being made available to make the process more transparent to the public. Under the Trading with the Enemy Act, the Secretary of the Treasury may impose civil fines up to $55,000 per violation of the Cuban Assets Control Regulations. According to OFAC, typical individual penalties range from $3,000 to $7,500, but the majority of cases are settled for less [31] Penalties against companies are generally much larger.

Since April 2003, enforcement actions for the Cuba travel regulations have included penalties against the following companies: Metso Minerals, Zim American Israeli Shipping Company, Playboy Enterprises, Omega World Travel, Mr. Travel, Havanatur & Travel Service, American Airlines, Cuba Paquetes, MRP Group Inc., Air Jamaica, Trek Tours (Rhode Island), Premiere Travel of Ohio, Hialeah Gardens Immigration Agency, Only Believe Ministries (Ohio), the Salvation Army (Texas Division), Beau Rivage Resorts Inc. (Mississippi), E & J Gallo Winery (California), the Four Oaks Foundation (New York), Pioneer Valley Travel (Massachusetts), the International Bicycle Fund (Washington state), Augsburg College (Minnesota), the U.S./Cuba Labor Exchange (Michigan), Coda International Tours Inc. (Florida), Travelocity.com (Texas), American Express Company (Mexico), Lakes Community Credit Union (Michigan), Sonida International (New York), Journey Corporation Travel Management (New York), RMO Inc. (Colorado), Tours International America (California), Aerovacations Inc. (California), Agoda Company (Thailand), Center for Cross Cultural Study Inc. (Massachusetts), Priceline.com (Connecticut), and Magic USA Tours (Florida). A number of other companies have received penalties for violating other aspects of the Cuba embargo regulations.

In addition, the listing shows that numerous individuals have had civil penalties assessed or reached informal settlements for alleged violations of various restrictions under the Cuban Assets Control Regulations. Since 2004, according to the information provided on OFAC's website, almost 900 individuals either have been assessed a penalty or reached an informal settlement for violations of the Cuba regulations (not just travel-related restrictions) with more than $1.1 million in penalties. The number of individuals penalized by OFAC has fallen considerably since 2006. a. A total of 290 individuals were penalized in 2004, 579 in 2005, 21 in 2006, and 17 in 2007. In 2008, OFAC reported that 32 individuals were penalized, with the majority for the purchase of Cuban cigars over the Internet.

GAO Report on Enforcement of Cuba Sanctions [32]

In late November 2007, the GAO issued a report on U.S. enforcement of the Cuba embargo. The report called into question whether U.S. efforts to enforce the Cuba embargo were having a detrimental effect on CBP's ability to carry out its primary mission of keeping terrorists, criminals and inadmissible aliens out of the country, and on OFAC's ability to administer more than 20 other sanctions programs. As such, the report recommended: (1) that the Secretary of Homeland Security direct CBP to re-evaluate its level of resources dedicated to inspecting passengers from Cuba at the Miami International Airport; and (2) that the

Treasury Department direct the OFAC to reassess the allocation of resources for investigating and penalizing violations of the Cuba embargo with respect to its administration of other sanctions programs.

ARGUMENTS FOR LIFTING CUBA TRAVEL RESTRICTIONS

Those who argue in favor of lifting restrictions on travel to Cuba contend that the travel ban hinders U.S. efforts to influence political and economic conditions in Cuba. Supporters of a change in Cuba travel policy argue that U.S. support for democracy in Latin America has been augmented by person-to-person contact and exchanges. The exception to democracy in the region is Cuba, where the United States continues to maintain a policy of isolation. They argue that the best way to realize change in Cuba is to lift restrictions, allowing a flood of U.S. citizens to travel and engage in conversations with average Cubans. They point to the influence of person-to-person contact in Russia and Eastern European nations which they argue ultimately helped lead to the fall of communism in the Soviet bloc. They maintain that restricting travel by ordinary Americans prevents interaction and information exchanges with ordinary Cubans, exchanges that can help break down the Cuban government's tight control and manipulation of news; that the current travel ban actually supports the Cuban government in its efforts to restrict information provided to the Cuban people; and that it in effect supports Castro's totalitarian control over Cuba.

A second argument made by those who want to lift travel restrictions is that the ban abridges the rights of ordinary Americans to travel. They argue that the U.S. government should not be requiring Cuban Americans to apply for a license to travel more than once a year to visit sick or dying family members. They contend that such restrictions on the right to travel subvert the first amendment right of free speech.

Those in favor of lifting the travel ban also argue that U.S. citizens can travel to other communist or authoritarian governments around the world, such as the People's Republic of China, Vietnam, Burma, and Iran. They point out that Americans could travel to the Soviet Union before its breakup. Supporters of changing travel policy toward Cuba argue that their proposals would still allow the President to prohibit such travel in times of war or armed hostilities, or if there were imminent danger to the health or safety of Americans. They argue that these conditions do not exist with regard to Cuba, and point to a May 1998 Defense Intelligence Agency report that concluded that "Cuba does not pose a significant military threat to the U.S. or to other countries in the region" [33].

Those arguing for lifting travel restrictions also point to human rights activists in Cuba who themselves argue for the lifting of such sanctions. According to the prominent Cuban human rights activist Elizardo Sanchez: "The more Americans on the streets of Cuban cities, the better for the cause of a more open society in Cuba" [34].

Supporters of lifting the travel ban maintain that such a move would not lift the underlying U.S. embargo on trade and financial transactions with Cuba. They point to the 1977-82 period when the travel ban was essentially lifted, but the overall embargo remained in place.

Finally, some supporters of lifting the travel restrictions argue that the U.S. economy would benefit from increased demand for air and cruise travel, which reportedly would expand U.S. economic output. According to a report prepared for the Center for International

Policy, a policy group that advocates lifting the embargo, U.S. economic output would expand by $1.18-$1.61 billion, with the creation of between 16,888 and 23,020 jobs if travel restrictions were lifted [35].

Arguments for Maintaining Cuba Travel Restrictions

Those favoring the continuation of current restrictions on travel to Cuba point out that there are already significant provisions in U.S. law permitting Americans to travel there for legitimate reasons that support the Cuban people and not the Cuban government. They point out that thousands of Americans travel to Cuba legally under the various provisions of the Cuban embargo regulations, many of whom are Cuban Americans visiting family members. Other categories of travel allowed include students, journalists, researchers, artists, musicians, and athletes.

A second argument made for maintaining current restrictions on travel to Cuba is that lifting the travel ban entirely will open the floodgates to American tourist travel that will support Castro's rule by providing his government with millions in tourist receipts. Advocates of restricting travel oppose any loosening that could prolong the Castro regime by propping it up with increased income. In contrast to those supporting tourist travel, they believe that continued travel restrictions will help influence Cuba's policy. They argue that since the collapse of the Soviet Union and the loss of Soviet subsidies to Cuba, the travel and embargo regulations have contributed to Castro's decision to cut the military's size and budget by half since 1989 and to introduce limited economic reforms. Lifting travel restrictions, they argue, would eliminate the U.S. leverage on Cuba to enact further reforms. Those favoring the maintenance of current travel restrictions argue that the reality of the human rights situation dispels the notion that American tourists would be engaging in exchanges with ordinary Cubans. They maintain that the thousands of European, Canadian, and other tourists who travel to Cuba each year largely stay in tourist hotels that are off limits to most Cubans and thus have no discernable effect on the human rights situation in Cuba.

Some opposed to lifting travel restrictions argue that there should be tourist travel as long as Cuba provides refuge to violent criminals who have escaped U.S. justice. The State Department maintains that more than 70 fugitives from U.S. justice are hiding out in Cuba, including convicted murderer Joanne Chesimard, who killed a New Jersey state trooper in 1973.

Finally, many opponents of legislation to lift the Cuba travel restrictions argue that the authority to impose such restrictions is an important foreign policy tool for the President. They point out that the President has the authority to restrict travel when it is in the national security or foreign policy interests of the United States, and has utilized that policy tool when needed. They point to past instances of restricting travel to Libya, Vietnam, and North Korea. With regard to Cuba, they point to the 1984 Supreme Court decision in the case of *Regan v. Wald* that upheld restrictions on travel to Cuba imposed by the Reagan Administration.

LEGISLATIVE INITIATIVES IN THE 111TH CONGRESS

On March 11, 2009, President Obama signed into law the Omnibus Appropriations Act, 2009 (P.L. 111-8), with two provisions easing restrictions on travel to Cuba. (The provisions were identical to provisions that had been included in the Senate Appropriations Committee version of the FY2009 Financial Services and General Government Appropriations bill in the 110th Congress, S. 3260).

In the enacted bill, Section 620 of Division D, Financial Services and General Government Appropriations Act, 2009, amends the Trade Sanctions Reform and Export Enhancement Act of 2000 (TSRA) to require the Secretary of the Treasury to issue regulations for travel to, from, or within Cuba under a general license for the marketing and sale of agricultural and medical goods, meaning that there would be no requirement to obtain special permission from OFAC. Such travel currently requires a specific license from OFAC, issued on a case-by-case basis. OFAC maintained that it would issue regulations in the coming weeks.

Section 621 of Division D prohibits funds from being used to administer, implement, or enforce family travel restrictions that were imposed by the Bush Administration in June 2004. OFAC implemented this provision by reinstating a general license for family travel as it existed prior to the Bush Administration's tightening of restrictions in June 2004. Travel is now allowed once every 12 months to visit a close relative for an unlimited length of stay, and the limit for daily expenditure allowed by family travelers is the same as for other authorized travelers to Cuba (State Department maximum per diem rate for Havana, currently $179 day). The new general license also expands the definition of "close relative" to mean any individual related to the traveler by blood, marriage, or adoption who is no more than three generations removed from that person.

The joint explanatory statement to P.L. 111-8 also requires the Department of the Treasury to prepare a report within 90 days on the steps that it is taking to assess OFAC's allocation of resources for investigating and penalizing violations of the Cuba embargo with respect to the numerous other sanctions programs it administers. As part of the report, the Treasury Department is directed to provide detailed information on OFAC's Cuba-related licensing on its enforcement of the Cuba embargo.

Several other legislative initiatives have been introduced in the 111th Congress that would ease restrictions on travel to Cuba: H.R. 188 (Serrano) and H.R. 1530 (Rangel) would lift the overall embargo on trade and financial transaction with Cuba, including travel restrictions. H.R. 1531 (Rangel) would facilitate the export of U.S. agricultural products to Cuba and also prohibit restrictions on travel to Cuba. H.R. 874 (Delahunt)/S. 428 (Dorgan) and H.R. 1528 (Rangel) prohibit restrictions on travel to Cuba. H.R. 332 (Lee) would ease restrictions on educational travel by providing that no funds made available to the Department of the Treasury may be used to implement, administer, or enforce regulations to require specific licenses for travel-related transactions directly related to educational activities in Cuba.

LEGISLATIVE INITIATIVES IN THE 110TH CONGRESS

In the 110th Congress, several House and Senate committee versions of appropriations bills had provisions that would have eased restrictions on travel to Cuba in various ways, but none of these provisions were included in final enacted legislation. Numerous other bills were introduced that would have eased restrictions on travel and remittance in various ways, but no action was taken on these measures.

First Session Action

In the first session of the 110th Congress, two Senate Appropriations Committee reported-versions of appropriations bills had provisions that would have eased restrictions on travel to Cuba for the marketing and sale of agricultural and medical goods, but ultimately these provisions were not included in the FY2008 Consolidated Appropriations Act (P.L. 110-161). The Senate version of the FY2008 Financial Services and General Government appropriations bill, reported July 19, 2007, H.R. 2829, had a provision in Section 620 that would eased such travel restrictions, while the Senate version of the FY2008 Agriculture appropriations bill, S. 1859, reported July 24, 2007, had such a provision in Section741.

Second Session Action

In the second session, several versions of House and Senate appropriations bills had provisions easing Cuba travel restrictions and other Cuba sanctions, but none of these were included in the FY2009 continuing resolution. The House Appropriations Committee approved its version of the Financial Services and General Government Appropriations bill for FY2009 on June 25, 2008, which contained provisions in Title VI that would have eased restrictions on the sale of U.S. agricultural exports to Cuba and on family travel to Cuba. The committee ultimately introduced and reported the bill, H.R. 7323, on December 10, 2008 (H.Rept. 110-920). With regard to family travel, Section 622 would have allowed for such travel once a year (instead of the current restriction of once every three years), while Section 623 would have expanded such travel by a person to visit an aunt, uncle, niece, nephew, or first cousin (instead of the current restriction limiting such travel to visit a spouse, child, grandchild, parent, grandparent, or sibling).

On July 14, 2008, the Senate Appropriations Committee reported its version of the FY2009 Financial Services and General Government Appropriations bill, S. 3260 (S.Rept. 110-417), which included provisions easing restrictions on family travel and on travel to Cuba relating to the commercial sale of agricultural and medical goods. With regard to family travel, Section 620 would have provided that no funds could be used to administer, implement, or enforce the Administration's June 2004 tightening of restrictions related to travel to visit relatives in Cuba. With regard to travel for agricultural or medical sales, Section 619 would have allowed for a general license for such travel instead of a specific license that requires permission from the Treasury Department.

On July 21, 2008, the Senate Appropriations Committee reported its version of the FY2009 Agriculture Appropriations bill, S. 3289 (S.Rept. 110-426), with a provision in

Section 737 that would have eased restrictions on travel to Cuba for the sale of agricultural and medical goods. The provision would have allowed for a general license for such travel instead of a specific license that requires permission from the Treasury Department. The measure had been approved by the Committee on July 17, 2008.

Additional Initiatives in the 110th Congress

A number of other initiatives introduced in the 110th Congress would have eased Cuba travel restrictions. H.R. 654 (Rangel), S. 721 (Enzi), and Section 254 of S. 554 (Dorgan) would prohibit the President from regulating or prohibiting travel to Cuba or any of the transactions incident to travel. Two bills that would lift overall economic sanctions—H.R. 217 (Serrano) and H.R. 624 (Rangel)—would also lift travel restrictions. H.R. 177 (Lee) would ease restrictions on educational travel to Cuba. H.R. 757 (Delahunt) would lift restrictions on family travel and the provision of remittances for family members in Cuba. H.R. 1026 (Moran, Jerry), which would facilitate the sale of U.S. agricultural products to Cuba, includes a provision that would provide for general license authority for travel-related transactions for people involved in agricultural sales and marketing activities or in the transportation of such sales. H.R. 2819 (Rangel) and S. 1673 (Baucus), which would ease restrictions on U.S. agricultural and medical exports to Cuba, would also lift restrictions on travel to Cuba. The Senate Committee on Finance held a hearing on S. 1673 on December 11, 2007.

Legislative Initiatives in the Aftermath of 2008 Hurricanes

In the aftermath of the Hurricanes Gustav and Ike that struck Cuba in late August and early September 2008, several legislative initiatives were introduced that would have temporarily eased U.S. embargo restrictions in several areas, including restrictions on family travel, remittances, the provision of gift parcels, and the sale of relief supplies to Cuba. On September 15, 2008, Senator Dodd offered S.Amdt. 5581 to the Department of Defense authorization bill (S. 3001) that would have, for a 180-day period: allowed unrestricted family travel; eased restrictions on remittances by removing the limit and allowing any American to send remittances to Cuba; expanded the list of allowable items that may be included in gift parcels; and allowed for unrestricted U.S. cash sales of food, medicines, and relief supplies to Cuba. The amendment was not considered, and therefore not part of the final bill.

In the House, two legislative initiatives were introduced in the aftermath of the hurricanes that would have temporarily eased restrictions in various ways. On September 16, 2008, Representative Flake introduced H.R. 6913, which would have prohibited any funds from going to the Department of Commerce to implement, administer, or enforce tightened restrictions on the contents of gift parcels to Cuba that were introduced in June 2004. On September 18, 2008, Representative Delahunt introduced H.R. 6962, the Humanitarian Relief to Cuba Act, which would have, for a 180-day period: allowed unrestricted family travel; eased restrictions on remittances by removing the limit and allowing any American to send remittances to Cuba; and expanded the list of allowable items that may be included in gift parcels.

Legislative Initiatives in the 109th Congress

In the 109th Congress, several amendments to FY2006 and FY2007 appropriations bills that would have eased Cuba travel restrictions in various ways and restrictions on sending gift parcels to Cuba were defeated. Several bills were introduced that would have lifted or eased restrictions on travel and the provision of remittances to Cuba, but no action was taken on these measures.

First Session Action

On June 30, 2005, the House rejected three amendments easing Cuba sanctions to H.R. 3058, the FY2006 Transportation, Treasury, Housing and Urban Development, Judiciary, District of Columbia, and Independent Agencies Appropriations Act. The amendments failed during House floor consideration: H.Amdt. 420 (Davis) on family travel, by a vote of 208-211; H.Amdt. 422 (Lee) on educational travel, by a vote of 187-233; and H.Amdt. 424 (Rangel) on the overall embargo, by a vote of 169-250. An additional amendment on religious travel, H.Amdt. 421 (Flake), was withdrawn, and an amendment on family travel by members of the U.S. military, H.Amdt. 419 (Flake), was ruled out of order for constituting legislation in an appropriations bill. The introduction of H.Amdt. 419 was prompted by the case of a U.S. military member who served in Iraq, Sgt. Carlos Lazo, who was prohibited from visiting his two sons in Cuba because he last visited there in 2003.

During June 29, 2005, Senate consideration of H.R. 2361, the FY2006 Interior, Environment, and Related Agencies Appropriations Act, the Senate rejected (60-35; a two-thirds majority vote was required) a motion to suspend the rules with respect to S.Amdt. 1059 (Dorgan), which would have allowed travel to Cuba under a general license for the purpose of visiting a member of the person's immediate family for humanitarian reasons. The amendment was then ruled out of order. Its introduction had also been prompted by the case of Sgt. Carlos Lazo who wants to visit his sons in Cuba, one of whom was gravely sick.

On June 15, 2005, the House rejected (210-216) H.Amdt. 270 (Flake) to H.R. 2862, the FY2006 Science, State, Justice, Commerce, and Related Agencies Appropriations Act. The amendment would have prohibited the use of funds to implement, administer, or enforce June 2004 tightened restrictions on sending gift parcels to Cuba. H.Amdt. 269 (McDermott), which would have prohibited the use of funds in the bill to prosecute any individual for travel to Cuba, was offered but subsequently withdrawn.

During April 6, 2005, Senate floor consideration of the FY2006 and FY2007 Foreign Affairs Authorization Act, S. 600, the Senate considered S.Amdt. 281 (Baucus) and a second-degree amendment, S.Amdt. 282 (Craig) that would have facilitated the sale of U.S. agricultural products to Cuba. The language of the amendments consisted of the provisions of S. 328 (Craig), the Agricultural Export Facilitation Act of 2005, which included a provision for a general license for travel transactions related to the marketing and sale of agricultural products, as opposed to the current requirement of a specific license for such travel transactions. Neither action on the amendments nor on S. 600 was completed.

Second Session Action

On June 14, 2006, the House rejected two amendments to the FY2007 Transportation/ Treasury appropriation bill, H.R. 5576, that would have eased Cuba travel restrictions. H.Amdt. 1050 (Rangel), rejected by a vote of 183-245, would have prohibited funds from being used to implement the overall economic embargo of Cuba. H.Amdt. 1051 (Lee), rejected by a vote of 187-236, would have prohibited funds from being used to implement the Administration's June 2004 tightening of restrictions on educational travel to Cuba. An additional Cuba amendment, H.Amdt. 1032 (Flake), would have prohibited the use of funds to amend regulations relating to travel for religious activities in Cuba; it was withdrawn from consideration.

In other action, on June 22, 2006, the Senate Appropriations Committee reported its version of the FY2007 Agriculture appropriations bill, H.R. 5384 (S.Rept. 109-266), which contained a provision (Section 755) liberalizing travel to Cuba related to the sale of agricultural and medical goods. The provision would have provided for such travel under a general license, instead of under a specific license as currently allowed, issued on a case-by-case basis by the Treasury Department. Final action on the appropriations measure was not completed by the end of the 109th Congress. Similar Senate provisions in FY2004 and FY2005 agricultural appropriations bills were stripped out of the final enacted measures.

Additional Initiatives in the 109th Congress

A number of other legislative initiatives were introduced in the 109th Congress that would have eased restrictions on travel and remittances to Cuba. Two bills—S. 894 (Enzi) and H.R. 1814 (Flake)—would have specifically lifted overall restrictions on travel to Cuba. H.R. 2617 (Davis) would have prohibited any additional restrictions on per diem allowances, family visits to Cuba, remittances, and accompanied baggage beyond those that were in effect on June 15, 2004. H.R. 3064 (Lee) would have prohibited the use of funds available to the Department of the Treasury to implement regulations from June 2004 that tightened restrictions on travel to Cuba for educational activities. H.Con.Res. 206 (Serrano), introduced in the aftermath of Hurricane Dennis that struck Cuba in July 2005 (causing 16 deaths and significant damage), would have expressed the sense of Congress that the President should temporarily suspend restrictions on remittances, gift parcels, and family travel to Cuba to allow Cuban-Americans to assist their relatives.

Two bills—H.R. 208 (Serrano) and H.R. 579 (Paul)—would have lifted the overall embargo on trade and financial transactions with Cuba, including restrictions on travel and remittances to Cuba.

Finally, two identical bills dealing with easing restrictions on exporting agricultural commodities to Cuba—H.R. 719 (Moran of Kansas) and S. 328 (Craig)—included provisions that would have provided for a general license for travel transactions related to the marketing and sale of agricultural products, as opposed to the current requirement of a specific license for such travel transactions.

LEGISLATIVE INITIATIVES IN THE 108TH CONGRESS [36]

In the 108th Congress, several FY2004 and FY2005 appropriations bills had provisions that would have eased Cuba travel restrictions in various ways, but ultimately these provisions were not included in final appropriations measures. The Administration had threatened to veto legislation if it contained provisions weakening Cuba sanctions. In addition, several bills in the 108th Congress were introduced that specifically would have lifted or eased restrictions on travel to Cuba, but no action was taken on these measures.

First Session Action

Since action on FY2003 Treasury Department appropriations was not completed before the end of the 107th Congress, the 108th Congress faced early action on it and other unfinished FY2003 appropriations measures. The final version of the FY2003 omnibus appropriations measure, H.J.Res. 2 (P.L. 108-7), which included Treasury Department appropriations, did not include provisions affecting restrictions on travel to Cuba. The White House had threatened to veto the measure if it contained provisions weakening the embargo. While the Senate version did not include the Senate Appropriations Committee provision from the 107th Congress that would have eased travel restrictions by prohibiting any funding for enforcing the Cuba travel regulations, it did include a provision (contained in Division J, Section 124) that would have expedited action on travel applications for travel by OFAC within 90 days of receipt. Ultimately, however, the Senate provision was dropped in the conference report (H.Rept. 108-10) on the omnibus measure.

Both the House and Senate versions of the FY2004 Transportation-Treasury appropriations bill, H.R. 2989, had nearly identical provisions that would have prevented funds from being used to administer or enforce restrictions on travel or travel-related transactions. But the provisions were dropped in the conference report to the FY2004 Consolidated Appropriations Act, P.L. 108-199 (H.R. 2673, H.Rept. 108-401, filed November 25, 2003), which incorporated seven regular appropriations acts, including Transportation-Treasury appropriations. The conference also dropped two Cuba provisions from the House version of H.R. 2989 that would have eased restrictions on remittances and on people-to-people educational exchanges. The White House again threatened to veto any legislation that would weaken economic sanctions against Cuba.

The House provisions had been approved during September 9, 2003, House floor consideration of the H.R. 2989: H.Amdt. 375 (Flake), approved by a vote of 227-188, would have prevented funds from enforcing travel restrictions (Section 745 of the House version); H.Amdt. 377 (Delahunt), approved by a vote of 222-196, would have prevented funds from enforcing restrictions on remittances (Section 746); and H.Amdt. 382 (Davis), approved by a vote of 246-173, would have prohibited funds from being used to eliminate the travel category of people-to-people educational exchanges (Section 749).

During Senate floor consideration of H.R. 2989 on October 23, 2003, the Senate approved by voice vote S.Amdt. 1900 (Dorgan), nearly identical to the Flake amendment noted above that would have prevented funds from being used to administer or enforce restrictions on travel or travel-related transactions (Section 643 of the Senate version). A motion to table the Dorgan amendment was defeated by a vote of 59-36. The Senate approved the bill by a vote of 91-3. The only difference between the Senate and House language was that the Dorgan amendment, as amended by S.Amdt. 1901 (Craig), provided that the section would take effect one day after enactment of the bill.

In other action, the conference on the FY2004 Consolidated Appropriations Act, P.L. 108-199 (H.R. 2673), also dropped a provision in the Senate version of the FY2004 agriculture appropriations bill that would have allowed travel to Cuba under a general license for travel related to the sale of agricultural and medical goods. On July 17, 2003, the Senate Appropriations Committee approved its version of the FY2004 agriculture appropriations bill, S. 1427, that included a provision (Section 760) allowing travel to Cuba under a general license (which does not require applying to the Treasury Department) for travel related to the commercial sale of agricultural and medical goods. The Senate included this provision when it approved H.R. 2673 on November 6, 2003. The House-passed version of the bill, H.R. 2673, had no such provision.

At present, such travel to Cuba is allowed with OFAC's approval of a specific license. In early June 2003, the Treasury Department rejected an application to travel to Cuba for organizers of a second U.S. food and agribusiness fair in Havana [37]. The first such trade fair, held in September 2002, featured some 288 exhibitors from more than 30 states and resulted in millions in U.S. agricultural sales to Cuba [38].

Second Session Action

Several FY2005 appropriations measures had provisions that would have eased Cuba sanctions, but these were dropped in the FY2005 omnibus appropriations measure (H.R. 4818, H.Rept. 108-792).

The House-passed version of the FY2005 Commerce, Justice, and State appropriations bill, H.R. 4754, approved July 8, 2004 (397-18), included a provision (Section 801) that would have prohibited funds from being used to implement, administer, or enforce recent amendments to the Cuba embargo regulations that tightened restrictions on gift parcels and baggage taken by individuals for travel to Cuba. The provision was added by a Flake amendment, H.Amdt. 647, approved by a vote of 221-194 on July 7, 2004. The Senate version of the bill, S. 2809, as reported out of committee, did not include such a provision.

Both the House-approved version of the FY2005 Transportation/Treasury appropriations bill, H.R. 5025, and the Senate Appropriations Committee version of the bill, S. 2806, had provisions that would have eased Cuba sanctions in various ways. In its statement of policy on H.R. 5025, the Administration indicated that the President would veto the measure if it contained provisions weakening Cuba sanctions.

The House-passed version of H.R. 5025 had three provisions that would have eased Cuba sanctions. During floor consideration on September 21, 2004, by a vote of 225-174, the House approved a Davis (of Florida) amendment (H.Amdt. 769), which provided that no funds could be used to administer, implement, or enforce the Bush Administration's June 2004 tightening of restrictions on visiting relatives in Cuba. On September 22, 2004, the House approved two additional Cuba amendments by voice vote, a Waters amendment (H.Amdt. 770) that would have prohibited funds from being used to implement any sanction imposed on private commercial sales of agricultural commodities or medicine or medical supplies to Cuba and a Lee amendment (H.Amdt. 771) that would have prohibited funds from being used to implement, administer, or enforce the Bush Administration's June 2004 tightening of restrictions on travel for educational activities. The House also rejected a Rangel amendment (H.Amdt. 772) on September 22, 2004, by a vote of 225-188 that would have more broadly prohibited funds from being used to implement, administer, or enforce the economic embargo of Cuba. During September 15, 2004 House floor consideration of H.R. 5025, Representative Jeff Flake announced his intention not to offer an amendment, as he had for the past three years, that would have prohibited funds from being used to administer or enforce restrictions on travel or travel-related transactions.

The Senate version of the FY2005 Transportation/Treasury appropriations bill, S. 2806, as reported out of the Senate Appropriations Committee (S.Rept. 108-342) on September 15, 2004, had a provision (Section 222) that would have prohibited funds from administering or enforcing restrictions on Cuba travel or travel-related transactions. That provision, which was proposed by Senator Byron Dorgan, was unanimously approved by the Subcommittee on Transportation, Treasury, and General Government on September 9, 2004.

The Senate version of the FY2005 Agriculture Appropriation bill, S. 2803, as reported by the Senate Appropriations Committee (S.Rept. 108-340), had a provision (Section 776) that would have directed the Secretary of the Treasury to promulgate regulations allowing for travel to Cuba under a "general license" when it was related to the commercial sale of agricultural and medical products. The House-passed version of the bill, H.R. 4766, had no such provision. In its statement of policy on the bill, the Administration stated that the President would veto the measure if it contained a provision weakening Cuba sanctions.

Additional Initiatives in the 108th Congress

Among other initiatives introduced in the 108th Congress, but not acted upon, two bills would specifically have lifted restrictions on travel to Cuba: S. 950 (Enzi), introduced April 30, 2003, and H.R. 2071 (Flake), introduced May 13, 2003. H.R. 3422 (Serrano), introduced October 30, 2003, would, among other provisions, have lifted restrictions on travel to Cuba. Three broad legislative initiatives were introduced that would have lifted all Cuba embargo restrictions, including those on travel: H.R. 188 (Serrano), introduced January 7, 2003, S. 403 (Baucus), introduced February 13, 2003, and H.R. 1698 (Paul), introduced April 9, 2003. Another initiative, S. 2449 (Baucus)/H.R. 4457 (Otter), introduced respectively on May 19 and 20, 2004, would have required yearly congressional approval for the renewal of trade and travel restrictions with respect to Cuba. Finally, H.R. 4678 (Davis of Florida), introduced June 24, 2004, in the aftermath of the President's tightening of Cuba sanctions, would have barred certain additional restrictions on travel and remittances to Cuba.

Legislative Initiatives in the 107TH Congress [39]

In the 107th Congress, although various measures were introduced that would have eliminated or eased restrictions on travel to Cuba and the House voted in both the first and second sessions to prohibit spending to administer the travel regulations, no legislative action was completed by the end of the second session.

First Session Action

During July 25, 2001 floor action on H.R. 2590, the FY2002 Treasury Department appropriations bill, the House approved an amendment that would prohibit spending for administering Treasury Department regulations restricting travel to Cuba. H.Amdt. 241, offered by Representative Flake (which amended H.Amdt. 240 offered by Representative Smith), would prohibit funding to administer the Cuban Assets Control Regulations (administered by OFAC) with respect to any travel or travel-related transaction. The amendment was approved by a vote of 240 to 186, compared to a vote of 232-186 for a similar amendment in last year's Treasury Department appropriations bill.

The Senate version of H.R. 2590, approved September 19, 2001, did not include any provision regarding U.S. restrictions on travel to Cuba, and the provision was not included in the House-Senate conference on the bill (H.Rept. 107-253). During Senate floor debate, Senator Byron Dorgan noted that he had intended to offer an amendment on the issue, but that he decided not to because he did not want to slow passage of the bill. He indicated that he would support the House provision during conference, but ultimately, however, the House-Senate conference report on the bill did not include the Cuba provision. In light of the changed congressional priorities in the aftermath of the September 11 attacks on New York and Washington, conference negotiators reportedly did not want to slow passage of the bill with any controversial provisions. The Bush Administration had threatened to veto the Treasury bill if it included the Cuba travel provision.

Second Session Action

The Cuba travel issue received further consideration in the second session of the 107th Congress. A bipartisan House Cuba working group of 40 Representatives vowed as one of its goals to work for a lifting of travel restrictions. On February 11, 2002, the Senate Appropriations Committee's Subcommittee on Treasury and General Government held a hearing on the issue, featuring Administration and outside witnesses.

The travel issue was part of debate during consideration of the FY2003 Treasury Department appropriations bill (H.R. 5120 and S. 2740). Secretary of State Colin Powell and Secretary of the Treasury Paul O'Neill said they would recommend that the President veto legislation that includes a loosening of restrictions on travel to Cuba (or a weakening of restrictions on private financing for U.S. agricultural exports to Cuba) [40]. The White House also stated that President Bush would veto such legislation [41].

In July 23, 2002 floor action on H.R. 5120, the House approved three Cuba sanctions amendments, including one on the easing of travel restrictions offered by Representative Jeff Flake. The House approved the Flake travel amendment (H.Amdt. 552), by a vote of 262-167, that would provide that no funds could be used to administer or enforce the Treasury Department regulations with respect to travel to Cuba. The Flake amendment would not prevent the issuance of general or specific licenses for travel to Cuba. Some observers raised the question of whether the effect of this amendment would be limited since the underlying embargo regulations restricting travel would remain unchanged; enforcement action against violations of the relevant embargo regulations could potentially take place in future years when the Treasury Department appropriations measure did not include the funding limitations on enforcing the travel restrictions [42].

During consideration of H.R. 5120, the House also rejected two Cuba amendments. A Rangel amendment (H.Amdt. 555), rejected by a vote of 204-226, would have prevented any funds in the bill from being used to implement, administer, or enforce the overall economic embargo of Cuba, which includes travel. A Goss amendment (H.Amdt. 551), rejected by a vote of 182-247, would have provided that any limitation on the use of funds to administer or enforce regulations restricting travel to Cuba or travel-related transactions would only apply after the President certified to Congress that certain conditions were met regarding biological weapons and terrorism [43] The rule for the bill's consideration, H.Res. 488 (H.Rept. 107-585), had provided that the Goss amendment would not be subject to amendment.

The House subsequently passed H.R. 5120 on July 24, 2002, by a vote of 308-121, with the three Cuba amendments, including the Flake Cuba travel amendment.

The Senate version of the Treasury Department appropriations measure, S. 2740, as reported by the Senate Committee on Appropriations on July 17, 2002 (S.Rept. 107-212), included a provision, in Section 516, that was similar, although not identical, to the Flake amendment described above. It provided that no funds may be used to enforce the Treasury Department regulations with respect to any travel or travel-related transactions, but would not prevent OFAC from issuing general and specific licenses for travel to Cuba. In addition, Section 124 of the Senate bill stipulated that no Treasury Department funds for "Departmental Offices, Salaries, and Expenses" may be used by OFAC, until OFAC has certain procedures in place to expedite license applications for travel to Cuba.

Congress did not complete action on the FY2003 Treasury Department appropriations measure before the end of the 107th Congress, so action was deferred until the 108th Congress.

Additional Legislative Initiatives in the 107th Congress

Several other initiatives were introduced in the 107th Congress that would have eased U.S. restrictions on travel to Cuba, but no action was taken on these measures.

H.R. 5022 (Flake), introduced June 26, 2002, would have lifted all restrictions on travel to Cuba.

Several broad bills would have lifted all sanctions on trade, financial transactions, and travel to Cuba: H.R. 174 (Serrano), the Cuban Reconciliation Act, introduced January 3, 2001, and identical bills S. 400 (Baucus) and H.R. 798 (Rangel), the Free Trade with Cuba Act, introduced February 27 and 28, 2001, respectively.

S. 1017 (Dodd) and H.R. 2138 (Serrano), the Bridges to the Cuban People Act of2001, introduced June 12, 2001, would, among other provisions, have removedall restrictions on travel to Cuba by U.S. nationals or lawful permanent residentaliens.

Several bills would, among other provisions, have repealed the travel restrictionsimposed in the 106th Congress by the Trade Sanctions Reform and ExportEnhancement Act of 2000 (P.L. 106-387, Title IX, Section 910). These includeidentical bills S. 402 (Baucus) and H.R. 797 (Rangel), the Cuban HumanitarianTrade Act of 2001, introduced February 27 and 28, 2001; S. 171 (Dorgan), introduced January 24, 2001; and S. 239 (Hagel), the Cuba Food and Medicine Access Act of 2001, introduced February 1, 2001.

LEGISLATIVE INITIATIVES IN THE 106TH CONGRESS

The only action completed by the 106th Congress relating to Cuba travel involved a tightening of travel restrictions. The final version of the FY2001 agriculture appropriations measure (P.L. 106-387, Title IX, Trade Sanctions Reform and Export Enhancement Act of 2000) included a provision that restricts travel to Cuba to those categories of non-tourist travel already allowed by the Treasury Department regulations. Section 910 of the law provides that neither general nor specific licenses for travel to Cuba can be provided for activities that do not fit into the 12 categories expressly authorized in the Cuban Assets Control Regulations, Section 515.560 (a) of Title 31, CFR, paragraphs (1) through (12).

As noted in the law, the Secretary of the Treasury may not authorize travel that is not expressly authorized in the 12 categories of the regulations. The provision prevents the Administration from loosening the travel restrictions to allow tourist travel. This, in effect, strengthens restrictions on travel to Cuba and somewhat circumscribes the authority of OFAC to issue specific travel licenses on a case-by-case basis under Section 515.560 (b) of Title 31, CFR. OFAC in the past has utilized that section to provide specific licenses for activities that do not fit neatly within the categories of travel set forth in 515.560 (a), including such travel for medical evacuations of Americans legally in Cuba and for U.S. contractors servicing the needs of the U.S. Interests Section (Regulations implementing the provision of the law were issued by OFAC on July 12, 2001).

In other legislative action, the Senate considered the issue of travel to Cuba in June 30, 1999 floor action on the FY2000 Foreign Operations Appropriations bill, S. 1234. An amendment was introduced by Senator Christopher Dodd that would have terminated regulations or prohibitions on travel to Cuba and on transactions related to such travel in most instances [44]. The Senate defeated the amendment by tabling it in a 55-43 vote on June 30, 1999. On November 10, 1999, Senator Dodd introduced identical language as S. 1919, the Freedom to Travel to Cuba Act of 2000, but no action was taken on the bill.

The House took up the issue of travel to Cuba when it considered H.R. 4871, the Treasury Department appropriations bill, on July 20, 2000. A Sanford amendment was approved (232-186) to prohibit funds in the bill from being used to administer or enforce the Cuban Assets Control Regulations with respect to any travel or travel-related transaction. Subsequently, the language of the amendment was dropped from a new version of the FY2001 Treasury Department appropriations bill, H.R. 4985, introduced on July 26. H.R. 4985 was appended to the conference report on the Legislative Branch appropriations bill—H.R. 4516, H.Rept. 106-796—in an attempt to bypass Senate debate on its version of the Treasury appropriations bill, S. 2900. The Senate initially rejected this conference report on September 20, 2000, by a vote of 28-69, but later agreed to the report, 58-37, on October 12. The House had agreed to the conference report earlier, on September 14, 2000, by a vote of 212-209.

REFERENCES

[1] U.S. Department of the Treasury, Office of Foreign Assets Control, "Comprehensive Guidelines for License Applications to Engage in Travel-Related Transactions

Involving Cuba," September 2004 (although the guidelines note that these limits on religious travel were added on March 31, 2005).
[2] Commission for Assistance to a Free Cuba, Report to the President, May 2004. p. 34.
[3] U.S. Government Accountability Office, *Economic Sanctions: Agencies Face Competing Priorities in Enforcing the U.S. Embargo on Cuba,* GAO-08-80, November 30, 2007, p. 34.
[4] U.S. Department of the Treasury, Office of Foreign Assets Control, *List of Authorized Providers of Air, Travel, and Remittance Forwarding Services to Cuba,* May 5, 2008.
[5] President George W. Bush, "Remarks After Meeting with the Commission for Assistance for a Free Cuba," U.S.Department of State, May 6, 2004.
[6] Commission for Assistance to a Free Cuba, Report to the President, May 2004. p. 37.
[7] Miriam Leiva, "Whose Country Is It, Anyway?" May 24, 2004, http://Salon.com; and "Why Deal with North Korea and Not Cuba," *Miami Herald*, March 1, 2008.
[8] David Adams, "Dissidents Say It's Time to Open Talks," *St Petersburg Times*, December 18, 2006.
[9] Oscar Corral, "Scholars, Artists Rip Embargo," *Miami Herald*, April 26, 2006.
[10] "Cuba's Campus Attrition," *CQ Weekly*, July 24, 2006; also see ECDET's website available at http://www.ecdet.org/
[11] Jack Chang, "Court Upholds Limits on Student Trips to Cuba," *Miami Herald*, November 5, 2008.
[12] Laura Morales, "Protesters Call for Family-Friendly Cuban Travel," *Miami Herald*, August 27, 2006.
[13] Human Rights Watch, *World Report 2008*, January 2008.
[14] Human Rights Watch, Families Torn Apart, *The High Cost of U.S. and Cuban Travel Restrictions*, October 2005.
[15] "2007 FIU Cuba Poll," Institute for Public Opinion Research and Cuban Research Institute, Florida InternationalUniversity.
[16] U.S. Government Accountability Office, *Economic Sanctions: Agencies Face Competing Priorities in Enforcing the U.S. Embargo on Cuba,* GAO-08-80, November 30, 2007, p. 31.
[17] Commission for Assistance to a Free Cuba, Report to the President, May 2004. pp. 28 and 36.
[18] U.S. International Trade Commission, U.S. Agricultural Sales to Cuba: Certain Economic Effects of U.S. Restrictions, USITC Publication 3932, July 2007. See the text of the report at
[19] Vanessa Arrington, "Number of Americans Traveling to Cuba Drops Amid Tougher U.S. Stance, Cuban Government Says," *Associated Press*, September 28, 2005; Gary Marx, "Tougher U.S. Policy Curtails Aid to Cubans," *Chicago Tribune*, October 10. 2005; Vanessa Arrington, "Cuban Official: Embargo Losses Are More than $4 Billion," *Associated Press*, October 3, 2006; and information provided to CRS by the Cuba Interests Section, Washington, DC, October 4, 2007.
[20] OFAC also regulates the activities of companies that forward remittances to Cuban according to the restrictions set forth in the Cuban Assets Control Regulations. Most companies that forward remittances are also travel service providers. See U.S. Department of the Treasury, Office of Foreign Assets Control, *List of Authorized*

Providers of Air, Travel, and Remittance Forwarding Services to Cuba, January 16, 2009.

[21] 31 CFR 515.572. In addition, OFAC has a circular outlining responsibilities of travel and carrier service providers for Cuba travel. See U.S. Department of the Treasury, Office of Foreign Assets Control, *Circular 2006, Travel, Carrier and Remittance Forwarding Service Provider Program*, March 2006.

[22] Oscar Corral, "Cuba Travel Curtailed Further," *Miami Herald*, January 27, 2006.

[23] Wilfredo Cancio Isla, "Aprietan las restricciones para los viajes a Cuba," *El Nuevo Herald* (Miami), April 28, 2006, and "Cierran en Miami otra agencia de viajes a Cuba," *El Nuevo Herald*, June 6, 2006; U.S. Department of the Treasury, Office of Foreign Assets Control, *List of Authorized Providers of Air, Travel, and Remittance Forwarding Services to Cuba,* November 29, 2006.

[24] White House, "Statement by President Bush on Cuba: Toward a Democratic Cuba," July 13, 2001.

[25] U.S. Department of State, International Information Programs, Washington File, "Treasury Dept. Identifies 10 Entities for Cuban Embargo Violations," February 9, 2004, and "U.S. Continues Crackdown on Illegal Travel to Cuba," March 18, 2004.

[26] Presidential Proclamation 7757 of February 26, 2004, *Federal Register*, March 1, 2004, p. 9515; Carol Rosenberg, "New Rule Restricts American Boaters from Sailing to Island," *Miami Herald*, February 27, 2004.

[27] Adelle M. Banks, "Restrictions on Religious Travel to Cuba Questioned," *Religion News Service*, March 7, 2006.

[28] Oscar Corral, "Religious Groups Feel Cut Off from Cuba," *Miami Herald*, February 14, 2007.

[29] Pablo Bachelet, "U.S. Gets Tougher on Groups Defying Cuba Travel Rules," *Miami Herald*, January 12. 2006; Meghan Clyne, "Bush Enforcing Cuba Embargo in New Push," *New York Sun*, January 12, 2006.

[30] See OFAC's website for information on civil enforcement actions: http://www.treas.gov/offices/enforcement/ofac/ civpen/.

[31] "Hearing of the Senate Foreign Relations Committee: Challenges for U.S. Policy Toward Cuba," Federal News Service, October 2, 2003.

[32] U.S. Government Accountability Office, *Economic Sanctions: Agencies Face Competing Priorities in Enforcing the U.S. Embargo on Cuba,* GAO-08-80, November 30, 2007. A copy of the report is available at http://www.gao.gov/docsearch/abstract.php?rptno=GAO-08-80

[33] Defense Intelligence Agency. Report on Cuban Threat to U.S. National Security. May 6, 1998.

[34] Congressional Record, July 25, 2001, p. H4599.

[35] *The Impact on the U.S. Economy of Lifting Restrictions on Travel to Cuba*, The Brattle Group, Washington, D.C. Prepared by Dorothy Robyn, James D. Reitzes, and Bryan Church. July 15, 2002.

[36] For a complete listing and discussion of all Cuba bills in the 108th Congress, see CRS Report RL31740, *Cuba: Issues for the 108th Congress*, by Mark P. Sullivan.

[37] Nancy San Martin, "U.S. Pulls Plug on Cuba Expo," *Miami Herald*, June 18, 2003.

[38] Nancy San Martin, "U.S. Official Dampens Trade-Show Enthusiasm with Talks of Cuban Credit," *Miami Herald*, September 29, 2002.

[39] For a complete listing and discussion of all Cuba bills in the 107th Congress, see CRS Report RL30806, *Cuba: Issues for the 107th Congress*, by Mark P. Sullivan and Maureen Taft-Morales.

[40] U.S. Department of State, International Information Programs, Washington File, "Bush Administration OpposesLegislative Efforts to Amend Cuba Policy," July 16, 2002.

[41] White House, Press Briefing by Ari Fleischer, July 24, 2002.

[42] "House Approves Limits on Treasury Enforcement of Cuba Embargo," *Inside U.S. Trade*, July 26, 2002.

[43] For further information on the issues of biological weapons and terrorism as they relate to Cuba, see CRS Report RL30806, *Cuba: Issues for the 107th Congress*, by Mark P. Sullivan and Maureen Taft-Morales.

[44] The Dodd amendment allowed for travel restrictions to be imposed if the United States is at war with Cuba, if armed hostilities are in progress, or when threats to physical safety or public health exist. Under current law, the Secretary of State has the same authority to restrict travel (22 USC 211a).

In: U.S. Involvement in Political, Economic and Social … ISBN: 978-1-61209-781-7
Editor: Allen P. Lowell

Chapter 5

EL SALVADOR: POLITICAL, ECONOMIC, AND SOCIAL CONDITIONS AND U.S. RELATIONS

Clare Ribando Seelke[#] and Peter J. Meyer

ABSTRACT

Throughout the last few decades, the United States has had a strong interest in El Salvador. During the 1 980s, El Salvador was the largest recipient of U.S. aid in Latin America as its government struggled against the Farabundo Marti National Liberation Front (FMLN) insurgency during a 12-year civil war. A 1992 negotiated peace accord brought the war to an end and formally assimilated the FMLN into the political process as a political party. After the peace accords were signed, U.S. involvement shifted towards helping the government rebuild democracy and implement market-friendly economic reforms.

Successive National Republican Alliance (ARENA) governments, including that of the current president, Tony Saca, have maintained close ties with the United States. The Saca Administration has cooperated in counter-narcotics operations, supported the U.S. coalition forces in Iraq, and implemented the Dominican Republic-Central America-United States Free Trade Agreement (CAFTA-DR). However, ARENA governments—including the Saca Administration—have struggled to reduce violence and poverty in El Salvador.

FMLN candidate Mauricio Funes won a close election for El Salvador's presidency in March 2009, marking the first FMLN presidential victory and the first transfer in political power between parties since the end of El Salvador's civil war. Funes' victory followed strong showings by the FMLN in the January 2009 municipal and legislative elections, in which the party won a plurality of the seats in National Assembly and the largest share of the municipal vote. Funes will take power in June 2009 and has pledged to govern in a moderate fashion. He will likely need to confront the high levels of violence and poverty in the country as well as deal with the effects of the global financial crisis.

Although some Members of Congress have expressed reservations about working with an FMLN administration, relations between El Salvador and the United States will likely remain friendly during the Obama Administration. President-elect Funes has

[#] Specialist in Latin American Affairs, E-mail: cseelke@crs.loc.gov pledged to remain in CAFTA-DR and expressed his willingness to work with the United States on immigration and counter- narcotics issues. Following his election, the Obama Administration congratulated President-elect Funes for his victory and pledged to work with him to build on the already strong ties between the United States and El Salvador.

BACKGROUND

El Salvador, nearly the size of Massachusetts, is the smallest nation in Central America, and the most densely populated, with some 7.1 million people. With a per capita income of $2,540, it is considered by the World Bank to be a lower-middle-income country. Since the early 1990s, El Salvador has posted economic growth, held free and fair elections, and survived a series of natural disasters. Significant problems remain, however, such as endemic poverty and rampant gang violence. These social problems, as well as a polarized political system, are inextricably linked to the country's devastating civil war, which lasted throughout the 1980s and resulted in some 75,000 deaths [1].

POLITICAL SITUATION

The current president of El Salvador, Antonio (Tony) Saca of the conservative ARENA party, was elected in March 2004, along with Ana Vilma de Escobar, El Salvador's first female vice president. Saca, a well-known businessmen and sports announcer, won the Salvadoran presidential election handily in the first round with 57.7% of the vote. His nearest rival, Shafick Handal of the FMLN, a 73-year-old former guerrilla and Communist party member, obtained 35.7% of the vote. Neither of the two third-party candidates received even 5% of the vote. President Saca's first round victory was a serious setback for the FMLN, which had gone into the campaign with high expectations based on its strong performance in the March 2003 legislative elections. In 2005, tensions within the party resulted in defections to a new party, the Democratic Revolutionary Front (FDR). However, in the March 2006 legislative elections, the FMLN, recaptured left-leaning electoral support from the FDR, winning 32 of 84 legislative seats [2]. The FMLN's electoral fortunes continued in 2009 as the party won a plurality in the legislature with 35 seats and its presidential candidate, Mauricio Funes, won the presidency.

Legislative Record

Early in his term, President Saca garnered broad support for criminal justice reforms and used multiparty negotiations to facilitate passage of some aspects of his reform agenda, including an anti-terrorism law and electoral reform. Saca used support from third parties in order to ratify the Dominican Republic-Central America-United States Free Trade Agreement (CAFTA-DR) over FMLN objections. He also used that support to secure passage of sweeping legislative reforms backed by the United States as prerequisites for CAFTA-DR implementation [3]. President Saca has since struggled, however, to gain legislative approval for some of his budget proposals and foreign loans, which has left some social programs underfunded. There are also mounting frustrations that neither President Saca nor the Legislative Assembly has effectively addressed the country's persistent crime problem. Legislative activity stalled in late 2008 as attention shifted towards the 2009 elections [4].

2009 Elections

Municipal and Legislative Elections

Municipal and legislative elections were held in El Salvador on January 18, 2009. Sporadic political confrontations and the murders of three activists—two supporters of the FMLN and one of the FDR—in the weeks leading up to the elections raised fears of violence at the polls [5] However, the elections were conducted largely without incident under the supervision of 110 observers from the Organization of American States (OAS), 80 observers from the European Union (EU), and observers from a variety of other organizations including the Association of Election Bodies from Central America and the Caribbean and the Inter-American Union of Election Bodies. The FMLN won a plurality in the 84-seat National Assembly with 35 seats, three more than it previously held. ARENA won 32 seats, the rightwing National Conciliation Party (PCN) won 11, the centrist Christian Democratic Party (PDC) won 5, the center-left Democratic Change (CD) won 1, and the FDR dissolved after failing to win a single seat. The new legislators will take their seats for three year terms on May 1, 2009.

At the local level, ARENA won 122 municipalities, the FMLN won 96 (21 in alliances with the PDC and/or CD), and minor parties won the other 44. While ARENA won more municipalities than the FMLN—including a surprise upset in the capital, San Salvador—the FMLN won 49.5% of the municipal vote to ARENA's 40% and was the only party to increase its representation nationally. Although turnout exceeded that of several recent non-presidential elections in which nearly 60% of the population abstained, only half of the eligible population voted [6].

Presidential Election

The presidential election was held on March 15, 2009. Despite some concerns about potential fraud and some inter-party violence in the run up to the vote, the election was conducted relatively peacefully. Some 5,000 national and international electoral observers supervised the proceedings while 20,000 members of the Salvadoran military and police provided security [7]. The chief electoral observer of the European Union asserted that the election functioned more smoothly than the January municipal and legislative vote and declared that allegations of fraud were unfounded [8]. Around 61% of the Salvadoran population turned out to vote, giving Mauricio Funes of the FMLN a narrow 51.3%-48.7% victory over Rodrigo Ávila of ARENA [9]. Funes will begin his five year term on June 1, 2009.

The electoral campaign was extremely polarizing, with Ávila and Funes both seeking to moderate their own images while simultaneously raising doubts about their opponents. Ávila presented a somewhat populist plan of governance in order to convince Salvadorans that he would do more to address social inequities than previous ARENA administrations. Ávila and ARENA also argued that Funes would be controlled by the more orthodox members of the

FMLN, such as his running mate and former guerilla Salvador Sánchez Cerén. In addition, they asserted that a Funes victory would lead to deterioration in relations with the United States and the installation of a political system like that of Venezuela, Cuba, or Nicaragua. Funes, a former television journalist and the first FMLN presidential candidate who did not participate in the country's civil war, attempted to project a moderate image throughout the campaign while calling for a change in government and an end to ARENA's 20-year rule [10].

Prospects for Governance

President-elect Funes will have to deal with a closely divided legislature when he takes office. Since the FMLN will hold only 35 of the 84 seats in the National Assembly for the next three years and ARENA's 32 legislators will likely form a solid opposition, smaller parties such as the PCN, PDC, and CD will likely play crucial roles in determining what legislation passes. Although the PCN and PDC are ideologically closer to ARENA and have formed governing alliances with it in the past, they may be willing to strike bargains with the FMLN and Funes. Indeed, many mayors and other party leaders of the PCN and PDC endorsed Funes despite the formal endorsement of Ávila by their parties' leaderships [11]. Given that a two-thirds vote is needed to pass some measures—including the national budget—the new president will also need to work with members of ARENA. Furthermore, Funes also will likely have to reign in the more orthodox factions of his own party, making political negotiation and compromise keys to the success of the administration [12].

Throughout his campaign and in his first interviews following the election, President-elect Funes pledged to govern as a moderate. He has cited President Lula of Brazil as a model for his administration, praising Lula's ability to maintain macroeconomic stability and combat poverty. Funes has called for national unity and a new social pact, saying that the problems El Salvador faces as a result of the global economic downturn can only be resolved through a joint effort of all sectors of society. During the campaign, Funes pledged to maintain the dollarization of the economy, continue to recognize El Salvador's sovereign debt obligations, and remain in all trade agreements, including CAFTA-DR. Since his election, Funes has restated his desire to work with President Obama and forge closer relations with the United States [13].

Economic and Social Conditions

In the 1990s, El Salvador achieved notable stability and economic growth. The Salvadoran government embraced a "neo-liberal" economic model, cutting government spending, privatizing state-owned enterprises, and adopting the dollar as its national currency. El Salvador is now one of the most open economies in the world, but, after posting strong growth rates in the 199 0s, it registered only 2% growth from 2000-2004. Between 2000 and 2003, El Salvador's economic stagnation was linked to disruptions that resulted from Hurricane Mitch in 1998, two major earthquakes in 2001, a decline in coffee prices, and the slowdown in the U.S. economy following September 11, 2001.

El Salvador has posted moderate economic growth rates in recent years, but high food and energy prices, as well as the current slowdown in the U.S. economy are likely to have a negative impact on the Salvadoran economy. While remittances, agricultural exports, and reconstruction projects increased in 2005, high oil prices, natural disasters (including Tropical Storm Stan), and a slump in the maquiladora sector (large assembly plants operating in free-trade zones) kept growth at a moderate 2.8% in 2005. GDP growth in El Salvador accelerated to roughly 4% in 2006, spurred by the implementation of the CAFTA-DR, diversification of the country's export sector, and high global prices for coffee and sugar. The economy again expanded by an estimated 4.7% in 2007, but analysts estimate that GDP growth slowed to roughly 3.2% in 2008. Remittances, largely sent from Salvadorans living in the United States, now contribute roughly 18% of El Salvador's annual GDP, making the country's economy increasingly dependent on the U.S. economy [14]. As the U.S. economy slows, remittances, investment, and U.S. demand for Salvadoran goods will decline. Analysts estimate El Salvador's economy will grow by just 1.1% in 2009 and 1.9% in 2010 [15] Although most decisions on how to confront the economic crisis will be left to the next President due to election season legislative inaction, El Salvador signed for a loan of $400 million from the Inter-American Development Bank (IDB) in December 2008, which will be used to ensure access to credit for El Salvador's productive sectors [16].

El Salvador's economy has fared better than some other countries in the hemisphere, but the country's growth rates have not been high enough to produce dramatic improvements in standards of living. With 48% of the population living in poverty and more than 25% reportedly feeling they must migrate abroad in search of work, some critics have argued that the average Salvadoran household has not benefitted from neoliberalism. Dollarization has raised the cost of living while its primary benefits, lower interest rates and easier access to capital markets, have not resulted in an overall decline in poverty levels. Between 1989 and 2004, poverty levels rose from 47% to 51%. Additionally, the fruits of stable economic growth have not been equitably distributed as the income of the richest 10% of the population is 47 times higher than that of the poorest 10%. Although migration has reduced rural unemployment and infused some households with extra income in the form of remittances, it has caused social disruptions and resulted in a "passive and dangerous dependency" in some communities [17].

Gangs and Violence [18]

Pervasive poverty and inequality, unemployment and underemployment, drug trafficking, corruption, and illicit firearms have contributed to the related problems of crime and violence that have plagued El Salvador since its civil war. As many as 30,000 Salvadoran youth belong to maras (street gangs). Salvadoran National Police officials have estimated that gangs are responsible for up to 60% of homicides, but evidence to support this assertion is lacking [19] Gangs are increasingly involved in human trafficking, drug trafficking, and kidnapping, and threaten the country's stability.

In response to the gang problem, El Salvador's Congress passed tough mano dura ("firm hand") anti-gang reforms in 2003 and 2004 that outlawed gang membership, enhanced police power to search and arrest suspected gang members, and stiffened penalties for convicted gang members. Changes in legislation have been accompanied by the use of joint military and police patrols to round up gang suspects. The Salvadoran government reported that its tough anti-gang legislation initially led to a 14% drop in murders in 2004, but murder rates and gang-related crimes have remained at elevated levels since that time. Many youth arrested under mano dura provisions have been subsequently released for lack of evidence that they committed any crime. Gang roundups have exacerbated prison overcrowding and inter-gang violence within the prisons has resulted in several inmate deaths. There have been credible reports that extrajudicial youth killings by vigilante groups have occurred since mano dura took effect. Moreover, in response to mano dura, gangs are changing their behavior to avoid detection [20].

Relations with the United States

Throughout the last two decades, the United States has maintained a strong interest in the political and economic situation in El Salvador. During the 1980s, El Salvador was the largest recipient of U.S. aid in Latin America as its government struggled against the armed FMLN insurgency. After the 1992 peace accords were signed, U.S. involvement in El Salvador shifted towards helping the government transform the country's economy into a model of free-market economic development. In the 1990s, total U.S. foreign assistance to El Salvador declined from wartime levels ($570.2 million in 1985), and shifted from military aid towards development assistance and disaster relief. Military aid to El Salvador reached a peak of $196.6 million in 1984, but fell to $0.4 million a decade later. Successive ARENA governments have maintained close ties with the United States.

Some analysts had predicted that a Funes victory would complicate U.S.-Salvadoran relations. Indeed, a number of Members of Congress expressed dismay over alleged links between the FMLN and countries such as Venezuela, Russia, and Iran and suggested that a Funes victory may necessitate strict control over remittances to El Salvador and the termination of Temporary.

Protected Status for Salvadorans living in the United States [21]. However, other Members of Congress expressed their hopes that the Obama Administration would respect the will of the Salvadoran people by working constructively with whoever was democratically elected [22]. The Obama Administration reaffirmed its neutrality in the days before the election and announced it would respect the result [23]. Following the election, the Obama Administration and President-elect Funes both reiterated their desires to work together and forge stronger relations between the United States and El Salvador [24].

U.S. Foreign Aid

El Salvador received an estimated $28.6 million in regular U.S. assistance in FY2008, as well as roughly $6 million in FY2008 supplemental assistance for counternarcotics and anticrime efforts as part of the Administration's Mérida Initiative [25]. The FY2009 request for El Salvador was for $37.0 million in bilateral assistance, as well as roughly $17.3 million of the $100 million in Mérida funds requested for the Central American region. An enacted continuing resolution (P.L. 110-329) funded U.S. programs in El Salvador at FY2008 levels through March 6, 2009, while a recently enacted FY2009 omnibus appropriations measure (P.L. 111-8) funds foreign aid through the end of the fiscal year [26].

Millennium Challenge Account (MCA) Compact

In late November 2006, El Salvador signed a five-year, $461 million compact with the Millennium Challenge Corporation to develop its northern border region, where more than 53% of the population lives in poverty. The compact includes (1) $88 million for technical assistance and financial services to farmers and rural businesses; (2) $100 million to strengthen education and training and improve public services in poor communities; and (3) $233 million to rehabilitate the Northern Transnational Highway and some secondary roads. The MCC compact has been designed to complement the CAFTA-DR and regional integration efforts. Although many have praised its potential, some have questioned why the compact was not designed to encourage communities to channel remittance flows into collective projects that could generate employment and improve local infrastructure [27].

Counter-Narcotics Issues

Not a major producer of illicit drugs, El Salvador serves as a transit country for narcotics, mainly cocaine and heroin, cultivated in the Andes and destined for the United States. El Salvador, along with Ecuador, Aruba, and the Netherlands Antilles, serves as a Forward Operating Location (FOL) for U.S. anti-drug forces. It is also the home of the U.S.-backed International Law Enforcement Academy (ILEA), which provides police management and specialized training to the region. In 2008, El Salvador's National Civilian Police seized 1.35 metric tons of cocaine, 430 kilograms of marijuana, and 8.4 kilograms of heroin [28].

Support for U.S. Military Operations in Iraq

El Salvador sent 360 soldiers to Iraq to support the U.S.-led coalition in August 2003 and maintained a constant troop presence there for five and a half years, the longest contribution of any Latin American nation. President Saca announced in December 2008 that the last contingent of Salvadoran soldiers would leave Iraq following the expiration of the U.N. Security Council mandate on December 31, 2008 [29]. The final Salvadoran soldiers to serve in Iraq—the 200 members of the 11th Contingent of the Cuscatlan Battalian—returned to El Salvador in February 2009. During their time in Iraq, the 11 Salvadoran contingents carried out 30 reconstruction projects worth $1.2 million in the cities of Al Hillah and Al Kut. Five Salvadoran soldiers were killed and 20 were wounded [30]. The FMLN continually opposed sending Salvadoran soldiers to support the U.S.-led coalition, and most polls indicate that a majority of Salvadorans were against sending troops to Iraq [31].

Migration Issues

The United States responded to the natural disasters in El Salvador in 2001 by granting Temporary Protected Status (TPS) to eligible Salvadoran migrants living in the United States [32]. In October 2008, the U.S. government extended the TPS of an estimated 220,000 eligible Salvadoran migrants living in the United States until September 9, 2010. TPS is an important bilateral issue for El Salvador, whose migrants living in the United States sent home some $3.9 billion in remittances in 2008, an increase from 2007 [33]. The exodus of large numbers of poor migrants to the United States has also eased pressure on the Salvadoran social service system and labor market. In contrast, observers are concerned about the impact Salvadoran deportees from the U.S. are having on the country's gang problems. In FY2008, 20,959 Salvadorans were deported from the United States [34].

U.S. Trade and the CAFTA-DR

The United States is El Salvador's main trading partner, purchasing 48% of its exports and supplying close to 34% of its imports. More than 300 U.S. companies currently operate in El Salvador, many of which are based in the country's 13 free trade zones. Since the 1980s, El Salvador has benefitted from preferential trade agreements, such as the Caribbean Basin Initiative and later the Caribbean Basin Trade Partnership Act (CBTPA) of 2000, which have provided some of its exports, especially apparel and related items, duty-free entry into the U.S. market. As a result, the composition of Salvadoran exports to the United States has shifted from agricultural products, such as coffee and spices, to apparel and textiles. Since the expiration of global textile quotas on December 31, 2004, Salvadoran apparel producers have had trouble competing with goods from cheaper Asian producers.

On December 17, 2004, despite strong opposition from the FMLN, El Salvador became the first country in Central America to ratify CAFTA-DR. In December 2005, the Salvadoran Legislative Assembly passed a package of sweeping legislative reforms, including tighter intellectual property restrictions, which were backed by the United States as prerequisites for CAFTA-DR implementation. On March 1, 2006, El Salvador became the first country to implement the CAFTA-DR. Salvadoran officials have attributed recent increases in some jobs, exports, and investments to CAFTA-DR. In 2006, although apparel exports to the United States declined, El Salvador saw a 21% increase of non-apparel exports to the United States—including ethanol, food stuffs, and metal products—much of which has been attributed to CAFTA-DR. A slight recovery in some textile and apparel exports to the United States combined with increases in nontraditional exports to result in a 10% increase in Salvadoran exports to the United States in 2007 and a 9% increase in 2008. At the same time, U.S. exports to El Salvador increased by 16% in 2006, 7.5% in 2007, and 6.5% in 2008 [35]. The Saca government expects CAFTA-DR to continue encouraging foreign investments in information technology, communications, and other growth sectors.

Critics are concerned, however, that the inability of some Salvadoran farmers to compete with U.S. agricultural producers may offset the job and investment gains that are resulting from the agreement. Proponents maintain that the MCC compact, as well as existing trade capacity building programs funded by the United States and other donors, should help ensure that vulnerable sectors benefit from the agreement. Critics also argue that although CAFTA-

DR has provisions providing for the enforcement of domestic labor and environmental laws and creating cooperative ways to bring those laws up to international standards, the penalties for countries not enforcing their laws are relatively weak. Some have challenged the assertion that labor rights and working conditions have improved in the region as a result of CAFTA-DR.

REFERENCES

[1] Central Intelligence Agency, "World Factbook," 2009.

[2] "Country Profile: El Salvador," *Economist Intelligence Unit,* 2008.

[3] For more information on CAFTA-DR, see CRS Report RL31870, *The Dominican Republic-Central America-United States Free Trade Agreement* (CAFTA-DR), by J. F. Hornbeck.

[4] "Country Report: El Salvador," *Economist Intelligence Unit*, November 2008.

[5] "Asesinan a dos militantes del FMLN en El Salvador," *Agencia Mexicana de Noticias*, January 11, 2009.

[6] "Arena and FMLN both claim victory," *Latin American Caribbean and Central America Report*, January 2009; "Country Report: El Salvador," *Economist Intelligence Unit*, February 2009; "FMLN falls short of legislative majority," *Latin American Weekly Report*, January 22, 2009.

[7] "El Salvador prepares to vote," *Latin News Daily*, March 13, 2009; "El Salvador: 20,000 policías y soldados en comicios," *Associated Press*, March 4, 2009.

[8] "Destaca UE normalidad en elecciones salvadoreñas," *Agencia Mexicana de Noticias*, March 17, 2009.

[9] "FMLN wins in El Salvador," *Latin News Daily*, March 16, 2009.

[10] Maureen Meyer, "Presidential Elections in El Salvador: Expectations for Change and the Challenges Ahead," *Washington Office on Latin America*, March 12, 2009.

[11] "Country Report: El Salvador," *Economist Intelligence Unit*, February 2009; "El Salvador Election Bulletin," *National Democratic Institute*, March 11, 2009; Marcos Aleman, "El Salvador: militares y ex rebeldes unidos contra Arena," *Associated Press*, March 10, 2009.

[12] "El Salvador politics: Leftists on the ascent," *Economist Intelligence Unit*, January 27, 2009.

[13] Ibid; Alberto Fajardo, "Funes quiere gobernar cerca Brasil y EEUU," *Reuters*, March 16, 2009; "Presidente electo El Salvador propone pacto social ante crisis," *Reuters*, March 16, 2009.

[14] "Government to Promote Inscription to Preferential Immigration Status for Salvadorans in the U.S." *Global Insight*, July 6, 2007.

[15] "Country Report: El Salvador," *Economist Intelligence Unit*, February 2009.

[16] "El Salvador: recursos del BID disponibles para sector productivo," *Associated Press*, February 12, 2009.

[17] Dovelyn Agunias, "Remittance Trends in Central America," *Migration Policy Institute*, April 2006; Sarah Gammage, "Exporting People and Recruiting Remittances: A Development Strategy for El Salvador?," *Latin American Perspectives*, November 2006.

[18] For more information, see CRS Report RL34112, *Gangs in Central America*, by Clare Ribando Seelke.

[19] "2,576 Homicidios en el 2004 en El Salvador," *Agence France Presse*, January 5, 2004; United Nations Office on Drugs and Crime (UNODC), *Crime and Development in Central America: Caught in the Crossfire*, May 2007.

[20] "Central America: Maras Pose Greater Threat Than Ever," *Latin American Weekly Report*, February 7, 2008; United Nations Development Program (UNDP), "*Maras y Pandillas: Comunidad y Policia en Centroamérica*," October 2007; "Youth Gangs in Central America," Washington Office on Latin America, November 2006.

[21] "Funes critica amenaza de quitar TPS a salvadoreños," *Associated Press*, March 12, 2009. For more information on Temporary Protected Status, see "Migration Issues".

[22] "Piden legisladores de EU a Obama respeto electoral en El Salvador," *Agencia Mexicana de Noticias*, March 5, 2009.

[23] EEUU dice que respetará resultado de elección en El Salvador," *Associated Press,* March 12, 2009.

[24] "Robert Wood, "Daily Press Briefing," *U.S. Department of State*, March 16, 2009; Blake Schmidt, "El Salvador's president-elect seeks close U.S. ties," *Miami Herald*, March 17, 2009.

[25] See CRS Report RS22837, *Merida Initiative: U.S. Anticrime and Counterdrug Assistance for Mexico and Central America*, by Colleen W. Cook and Clare Ribando Seelke.

[26] It is unclear how much bilateral and Mérida Initiative assistance El Salvador will receive in FY2009 since the omnibus appropriation does not fund foreign aid accounts at the same levels as the FY2009 request.

[27] The MCC compact also includes $45 million to cover program administration and evaluation. See http://www.mcc.gov/documents/factsheet-112906-elsalvador.pdf; Marcela Sánchez, "Putting Remittances to Work," *Washington Post*, December 9, 2006.

[28] U.S. Department of State, *International Narcotics Control Strategy Report*, February 27, 2009.

[29] "Presidente de El Salvador anuncia retiro de tropas de Irak," *Reuters*, December 23, 2008.

[30] "200 Soldiers of last El Salvador detail in Iraq return home," *EFE News Service*, February 7, 2009.

[31] "El Salvador to cut Small Troop Presence in Iraq," *Reuters*, August 7, 2008.

[32] For more information on TPS, see CRS Report RS20844, *Temporary Protected Status: Current Immigration Policy and Issues*, by Ruth Ellen Wasem and Karma Ester.

[33] "Latin America: Remittances slide," *Economist Intelligence Unit Business Latin America*, January 26, 2009.

[34] Information provided to CRS by the Department of Homeland Security, Immigration and Customs Enforcement, Office of Detention and Removal.

[35] U. S. Department of Commerce statistics, as presented by *World Trade Atlas*, 2009.

In: U.S. Involvement in Political, Economic and Social ... ISBN: 978-1-61209-781-7
Editor: Allen P. Lowell

Chapter 6

HONDURAN-U.S. RELATIONS

Peter J. Meyer and Mark P. Sullivan

ABSTRACT

The Central American nation of Honduras, one of the hemisphere's poorest countries, faces significant challenges in the areas of crime, human rights, and improving overall economic and living conditions. While traditional agricultural exports of coffee and bananas are still important for the economy, nontraditional sectors, especially the maquiladora, or export-processing industry, have grown significantly over the past decade. Among the country's development challenges are a poverty rate over 60%, high infant mortality, and a significant HIV/AIDS epidemic. Despite these challenges, increased public spending on health and education have reaped significant improvements in development indicators over the past decade.

Current President Manuel Zelaya of the Liberal Party won a four-year term in the November 2005 elections. The country has enjoyed 27 years of uninterrupted elected civilian democratic rule. The economy, which grew 6.3% in 2007 and is expected to have grown 4% in 2008, has benefitted from significant debt reduction by the international financial institutions that is freeing government resources to finance poverty-reduction programs. The U.S. recession and global financial crisis, however, are expected to slow Honduran economic growth sharply in 2009.

The United States has a close relationship with Honduras, characterized by an important trade partnership, a U.S. military presence in the country, and cooperation on a range of transnational issues. In addition to being a party to the Dominican Republic-Central America Free Trade Agreement (DR-CAFTA), Honduras has cooperated extensively with the United States on counternarcotics and port security. Some 78,000 Hondurans living in the United States have been provided temporary protected status (TPS) since the country was devastated by Hurricane Mitch in 1998.

U.S. foreign aid to Honduras amounted to $44 million in FY2008 and an estimated $47 million in FY2009. Honduras is also likely to receive a portion of the $105 million in assistance dedicated to Central America in 2009 under the Mérida Initiative, which was designed to boost the region's capabilities to interdict the smuggling of drugs, arms, and people and support a regional anti-gang strategy. For FY2010, the Obama Administration requested over $68 million in assistance for Honduras as well as an additional $100 million for the continuation of the Mérida Initiative in Central

America. Beyond traditional foreign assistance, the Millennium Challenge Corporation approved a five-year $215 million compact with Honduras in 2005.

RECENT DEVELOPMENTS

On March 24, 2009, President Zelaya issued a decree calling for a popular referendum on the convocation of a national constituent assembly to amend the constitution (See "Constitutional Referendum" below).

On March 14, 2009, Honduras announced an economic stimulus plan totaling $250 million (1.7% of GDP). The plan includes a new credit line for the private sector, funds for social services, and increased and accelerated spending on public infrastructure projects.

On March 11, 2009, President Obama signed into law the Omnibus Appropriations Act of 2009 (P.L. 111-8), which included $105 million for the Mérida Initiative in Central America to support the region's fight against drug trafficking, gangs, and organized crime.

On January 9, 2009, President Zelaya signed a letter of agreement with the United States concerning the Mérida Initiative.

On November 30, 2008, Honduras held primary elections to determine the candidates for the November 2009 elections. Porfirio Lobo Sosa, the opposition National Party's 2005 presidential nominee, once again won the support of his party. The Liberal Party's presidential nominee will be former Vice President Elvin Santos (See "November 2009 Elections" below).

On October 9, 2008, the Honduran Congress ratified the country's membership in the Bolivarian Alternative of the Americas (ALBA), an initiative launched by Venezuelan President Hugo Chávez in 2004 and signed onto by President Zelaya in August 2008. ALBA is a socially oriented trade block that includes cooperation in a range of areas such as health, education, culture, investment, and finance. Other ALBA members include Venezuela, Bolivia, Cuba, Dominica, and Nicaragua. The agreement follows the Honduran government's January 2008 decision to participate in PetroCaribe, the Venezuelan program that provides oil at preferential discounted rates to Caribbean countries.

On October 1, 2008, the U.S. Secretary of Homeland Security announced that the United States would extend temporary protected status (TPS) by 18 months for more than 70,000 eligible Hondurans in the United States. TPS for Hondurans was scheduled to expire on January 5, 2009. It originally was provided in the aftermath of Hurricane Mitch in 1998, and has now been extended seven times (See "Migration Issues" below).

On September 19, 2008, President Zelaya accredited the new U.S. Ambassador to Honduras, Hugo Llorens, after a one week delay that the Honduran President maintained was to show solidarity with Bolivia in its diplomatic spat with the United States. Bolivia had expelled the U.S. Ambassador for allegedly inciting opposition protests.

POLITICAL AND ECONOMIC CONDITIONS

A Central American nation with a population of about 7.4 million, Honduras has enjoyed 27 years of uninterrupted civilian democratic rule since the military relinquished power in

1982 after free and fair elections. With a per capita income of $1,600 (2007), Honduras is classified by the World Bank as a lower middle income developing economy, and remains one of the poorest countries in the hemisphere [1]. Traditional agricultural exports of coffee and bananas are still important for the Honduran economy, but nontraditional sectors, such as shrimp farming and the maquiladora, or export-processing industry, have grown significantly over the past decade. Among the country's development challenges are an estimated poverty rate over 60%; an infant mortality rate of 31 per 1,000; and chronic malnutrition for one out of three children under five years of age. Honduras also has a significant HIV/AIDS crisis, with an adult infection rate of 1.5% of the population. The Garifuna community (descendants of freed black slaves and indigenous Caribs from St. Vincent) concentrated in northern coastal areas has been especially hard hit by the epidemic. Despite these challenges, the World Bank maintains that increased public spending on health and education has reaped significant improvements in development indicators over the past decade [2].

Current President Manuel Zelaya of the Liberal Party won the November 2005 election 49.9% to 46.17%, narrowly defeating his National Party rival Porfirio Lobo Sosa, the head of the Honduran Congress. While the process was deemed free and fair, technical difficulties caused a delay in the official vote count, and resulted in Lobo waiting until December 7, 2005, to concede defeat.

The Liberal (PL) and National (PN) parties traditionally have been the country's two dominant political parties. Both are considered center-right parties, and there appear to be few major ideological differences between the two. During the 2005 campaign, both candidates broadly supported the direction of the country's market-oriented economic policy, but they emphasized different approaches in dealing with crime perpetrated by youth gangs. Lobo called for tougher action against gangs by reintroducing the death penalty (which was abolished in 1957) and increasing prison sentences for juvenile delinquents, whereas Zelaya opposed the death penalty and emphasized a more comprehensive approach that would include job creation and training. Zelaya also campaigned for more citizen involvement and transparency in government and promised to increase social programs and combat corruption.

Manuel Zelaya

Born in 1952, José Manuel "Mel" Zelaya Rosales hails from Olancho department in rural eastern Honduras. Zelaya studied civil engineering in college, but left his studies for business, investing in timber and cattle. He owns a ranch in Olancho. Zelaya joined the Liberal Party in 1970, and became party coordinator for the departments of Olancho and Colón in 1980. He was first elected to Congress in 1985 and won three additional terms. He served as head of the Honduran Social Investment Fund from 1994-1997 and again from 1998-2001 in two Liberal Party Administrations. He founded a progressive faction of the Liberal Party, and won the party's presidential primary in February 2005 before winning the general election.

Sources: "Manuel Zelaya," Biography Resource Center Online, Gale, 2006; People Profile Manuel "Mel" Zelaya, LatinNews.com, November 15, 2006.

Challenges for the Zelaya Government

Inaugurated to a four-year term on January 27, 2006, Zelaya succeeded President Ricardo Maduro of the National Party, who was elected in 2001. During his tenure, Zelaya has faced longstanding challenges in the areas of crime, human rights, and improving overall economic and living conditions in one of the hemisphere's poorest countries. In the 2005 legislative elections that were held simultaneously with the presidential elections, Zelaya's Liberal Party won 62 seats in the 128-member Congress, just short of a majority. This has made it more difficult for the Zelaya government to enact its legislative agenda.

Zelaya enjoyed high approval ratings early in his administration, buoyed by the strong performance of the economy, his efforts to fulfill campaign pledges of free school enrollment and an increase in teachers' pay, and his efforts to curb rising fuel costs [3]. Public support for Zelaya has evaporated, however, as his Administration has struggled to achieve concrete results on a number of issues of importance. Most Hondurans have not seen an improvement in their living standards as poverty, unemployment, and inflation have remained high. Violent crime has also increased. According to the United Nations Development Program, the country's 2008 murder rate reached 57.9 per 100,000 inhabitants, a 25.2% increase from 2007 and one of the highest rates in the world [4]. In May 2008, some 30,000 Hondurans marched in protest in of high crime rates in San Pedro Sula, the country's second largest city. Although he has advocated transparency in government, Zelaya has faced several corruption scandals during his term. A number of high ranking officials have been forced to resign and the transparency law passed by his Administration has been criticized as having too many loopholes [5].

November 2009 Elections

President Zelaya's governing agenda has begun to be overshadowed by the upcoming November 2009 elections. Primary elections to select the parties' nominees were held in November 2008. Although the primaries were deemed free and fair, four politicians—three members of the PL and one member of the PN—were killed by masked gunmen in the weeks before the elections. It is unclear whether the murders were political, drug-related (one politician was a member of the congressional committee on security and narco-trafficking), or random acts of violence [6]. Porfirio Lobo Sosa won 81% of the primary vote to once again claim the PN presidential nomination. Former Vice President Elvin Santos is the PL presidential nominee.

In August 2008, the Supreme Electoral Tribunal (TSE) had ruled that Santos was constitutionally ineligible for the presidency because he had served as president during Zelaya's absences from the country and the constitution prohibits presidential re-election. Nonetheless, Santos continued to campaign and registered his lawyer, Mauricio Villeda, as a stand-in candidate. Villeda then surprisingly defeated Zelaya's favored candidate, head of congress Roberto Micheletti, 52%-32% in the PL primary [7]. Following Santos' resignation as Vice President and congressional approval of a decree that stated a vice president could only be barred from running for president if he or she had served as president within the last 6 months of his or her mandate, the PL registered Santos as its official presidential candidate. Although Micheletti originally refused to recognize Santos as the party nominee, he relented after Santos offered him the presidency of the PL leadership committee. Santos represents the traditional conservative faction of the Liberal Party [8].

Constitutional Referendum

In March 2009, President Zelaya issued a decree calling on the National Statistics Institute (INE) to hold a popular referendum by the end of June 2009 to determine if the country should include an additional ballot question in the November 2009 general elections on whether Honduras should convoke a national constituent assembly to amend the constitution. Zelaya has argued that presidential reelection should be possible and that the constitution—drafted in 1982 — must be made to reflect the "substantial and significant changes" that have taken place in Honduran society in recent years [9].

The proposal was immediately criticized by officials from across the Honduran political spectrum. The PL head of congress expressed firm opposition, the presidential candidates of both the PL and the PN accused Zelaya of trying to perpetuate himself in power, and the attorney general's office charged that Zelaya was violating the constitution—which states that the prohibition on presidential reelection cannot be amended under any circumstances. Both presidential candidates have slightly reversed themselves, however, as Lobo now wants a referendum in November 2009 for a constituent assembly in July 2010 and Santos is open to a referendum occurring sometime in 2010. In order for a referendum to occur, 86 of the 128 legislators in the Honduran Congress would have to approve the request. The TSE could then call a referendum, which would need 51% of the electorate to participate for the result to be valid [10]. Given the strong opposition within both major parties, it is unlikely any referendum will occur until Zelaya is out of office. Nonetheless, Zelaya has continued to push forward, maintaining that "it is going to happen and nothing will stop it" [11].

Economic Situation

Honduras was devastated by Hurricane Mitch in 1998, which killed more than 5,000 people and caused billions of dollars in damage. The gross domestic product declined by 1.4% in 1999, and the country felt the effects of the storm for several years, with roads and bridges washed out, the agricultural sector hard hit, and scores of orphaned children, many of whom joined criminal gangs. Spurred on by substantial U.S. foreign assistance, however, the economy rebounded by 6% in 2000, and has remained positive ever since. More recently, the economy registered growth rates of 4.1% in 2005, 6.3% in 2006 and 2007, and an estimated 4% in 2008 [12].

Despite this economic improvement, Honduras remains one of the most impoverished nations in Latin America. It has a poverty rate over 60% and according to a 2005 study by the National Institute of Statistics, only 26% of the economically active population works in non-subsistence positions with non-precarious salaries [13].

In April 2008, Honduras signed a $64 million standby agreement with the International Monetary Fund (IMF) designed to support the government's economic policy program of continuing high growth levels, containing inflation, and reforming the electricity sector. The government maintained the agreement would open up more than $225 million in foreign loans for the country. In past years, Honduras had negotiated three poverty reduction and growth facility (PRGF) agreements with the IMF that imposed fiscal and monetary targets on the government to maintain firm macroeconomic discipline and to develop a comprehensive poverty reduction strategy. The most recent PRGF agreement, which expired in February 2007, made Honduras eligible for about $1 billion in debt relief under the IMF and World Bank's Highly Indebted Poor Countries (HIPC) Initiative. The Inter-American Development Bank (IDB) also announced a debt forgiveness program in late 2006 for its poorest members, including Honduras, which benefitted from a reduction of $1.4 billion in foreign debt, freeing government resources to finance poverty- reduction programs [14].

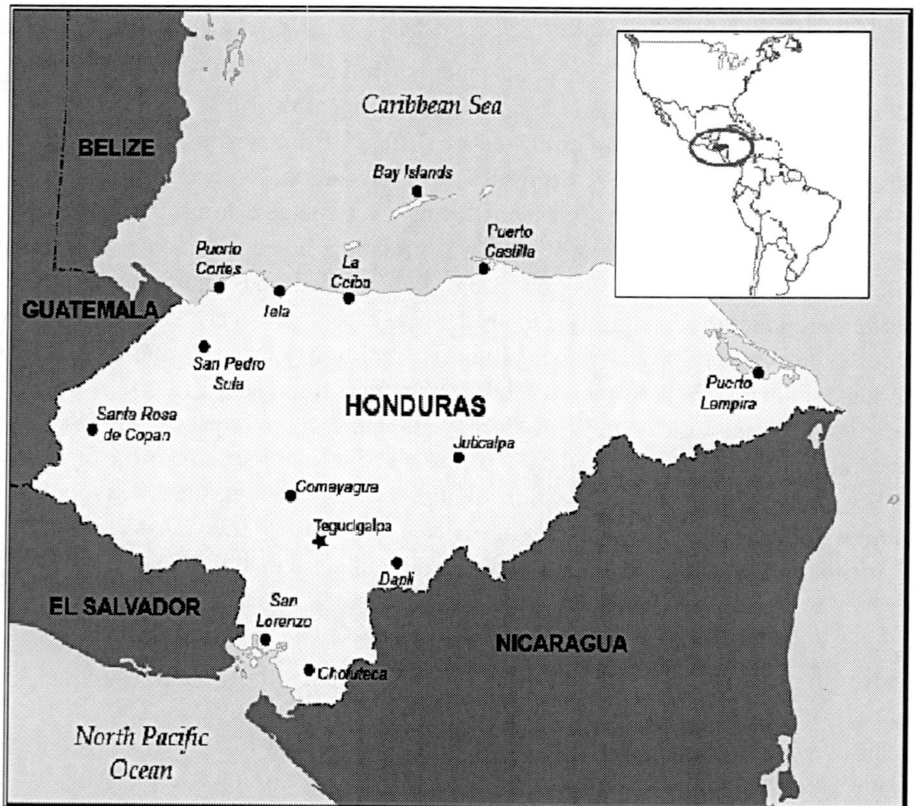

Source: Map Resources. Adapted by CRS Graphics.

Figure 1. Map of Honduras.

The global financial crisis and U.S. economic slowdown have taken a toll on the Honduran economy as remittances, foreign investment, and demand for Honduran exports have fallen sharply. Remittances are expected to decline by $112 million in 2009, a loss of 1% of GDP [15]. Likewise, exports were down 15% in the first quarter of 2009 [16]. Unemployment is also rising. Over 180,000 Hondurans have lost their jobs since October 2008 [17]. To confront the economic downturn, the Honduran government announced a plan to spend $250 million (1.7% of GDP) in public and private funds to stimulate the economy. Among other provisions, the plan includes a credit line for the private sector, capital for the banking sector, new funds for social services, and increased and accelerated spending on public infrastructure projects [18]. The International Monetary Fund (IMF) expects the Honduran economy to grow by just 1.5% in 2009 and 1.9% in 2010 [19].

ISSUES IN U.S.-HONDURAN RELATIONS

The United States has had close relations with Honduras over many years, characterized by significant foreign assistance, an important trade relationship, a U.S. military presence in the country, and cooperation on a range of transnational issues. The bilateral relationship became especially close in the 1980s when Honduras returned to democratic rule and became the lynchpin for U.S. policy in Central America. At that time, the country became a staging area for U.S.-supported excursions into Nicaragua by anti-Sandinista opponents known as the contras.

Today, overall U.S. policy goals for Honduras include a strengthened democracy with an effective justice system that protects human rights and promotes the rule of law, and the promotion of sustainable economic growth with a more open economy and improved living conditions. The United States also cooperates with Honduras to deal with such transnational issues as narcotics trafficking, money laundering, the fight against terrorism, illegal migration, and trafficking in persons, and supports Honduran efforts to protect the environment and combat HIV/AIDS. There are some 800,000 to 1 million Hondurans residing in the United States, who sent an estimated $2.8 billion in remittances to Honduras in 2008, roughly a fourth of the country's gross domestic product [20].

According to some analysts, President Zelaya has jeopardized Honduras' traditional close relations with the United states by forging closer relations with Venezuelan President Hugo Chávez and his allies [21]. In addition to joining Venezuela's PetroCaribe and Bolivarian Alternative for the Americas (ALBA), Zelaya delayed the accreditation of U.S. Ambassador to Honduras Hugo Llorens by one week in September 2008 in order to show solidarity with Bolivia in its diplomatic spat with the United States. President Zelaya reportedly took a softer tone in his first official meeting with Ambassador Llorens, however, and described the United States "as an ally and friend." Zelaya maintains that he has been forced to turn to Venezuela for assistance in addressing high food and energy prices as a result of insufficient U.S. support [22].

Economic Linkages

U.S. trade and investment linkages with Honduras have increased greatly since the early 1980s. In 1984, Honduras became one of the first beneficiaries of the Caribbean Basin Initiative (CBI), the unilateral U.S. preferential trade arrangement providing duty-free importation for many goods from the region. In the late 1980s, Honduras benefitted from production-sharing arrangements with U.S. apparel companies for duty-free entry into the United States of certain apparel products assembled in Honduras. As a result, maquiladoras or export-assembly companies flourished, most concentrated in the north coast region. The passage of the Caribbean Basin Trade Partnership Act in 2000 (CBTPA), which provided Caribbean Basin nations with NAFTA-like preferential tariff treatment, further boosted Honduran maquiladoras. Trade relations expanded again following the implementation of the

Dominican Republic-Central America-United States Free Trade Agreement (CAFTA-DR), which entered into force with Honduras in April 2006.

The United States is by far Honduras' largest trading partner. In 2008, the United States was the destination of about 37% of Honduran exports and the origin of about 37% of its imports. Honduras is the largest Central American exporter to the United States and the top Latin American exporter of knit apparel to the United States. In 2008, U.S. exports to Honduras amounted to about $4.8 billion, up 31% from 2006. Knit and woven apparel inputs accounted for a substantial portion, as did machinery and petroleum. U.S. imports from Honduras amounted to about $4 billion in 2008, with knit and woven apparel (assembled products from the maquiladora sector) accounting for the lion's share. Other Honduran exports to the United States include coffee, seafood, bananas, electrical wiring, gold, and tobacco [23]. In terms of investment, the stock of U.S. foreign direct investment in Honduras amounted to $968 million in 2007, concentrated in the manufacturing sector [24]. More than 150 U.S. companies operate in Honduras, with investments in the maquila or export assembly sector, fruit production, tourism, energy generation, shrimp farming, animal feed production, telecommunications, fuel distribution, cigar manufacturing, insurance, brewing, food processing, furniture manufacturing, and numerous U.S. restaurant franchises [25].

Despite the increases in trade and investment that have occurred since the implementation of CAFTA-DR, a number U.S. and Honduran officials have expressed concerns about the agreement. Honduran officials are concerned about the loss of agricultural jobs in the corn, rice, beef, poultry, and pork sectors since the country opened its market to U.S. agricultural products. Some fear that the loss of agricultural employment could lead to social unrest if not addressed properly through long-term investment.

While CAFTA-DR has provisions to enforce domestic labor codes and improve labor rights, a number of U.S. officials maintain that the provisions are inadequate given the history of non-compliance with labor laws in many Central American nations. The U.S. State Department's 2008 Country Reports on Human Rights Practices for Honduras found credible evidence that employees engaged in union duties were blacklisted within the maquiladoras and that union leaders were occasionally targeted with threats and violence [26].

U.S. Foreign Assistance

The United States has provided considerable foreign assistance to Honduras over the past three decades. In the 1980s, the United States provided about $1.6 billion in economic and military aid as the country struggled amid the region's civil conflicts. In the 1990s, U.S. assistance to Honduras began to wane as regional conflicts subsided and competing foreign assistance needs grew in other parts of the world. Hurricane Mitch changed that trend as the United States provided almost $300 million in assistance to help the country recover from the 1998 storm. As a result of the new influx of aid, total U.S. assistance to Honduras for the 1 990s amounted to around $1 billion. With Hurricane Mitch funds expended by the end of 2001, U.S. foreign aid levels to Honduras again began to decline.

Recent foreign aid funding to Honduras amounted to about $49 million in FY2006, almost $44 million in FY2007, and $40.5 million in FY2008 (see Table 1). For FY2009, an estimated $43 million in regular foreign aid funding is being provided. In addition, Honduras will likely receive a portion of the $105 million allocated to Central America through the

Mérida Initiative to boost the region's narcotics interdiction capabilities and support a regional anti-gang strategy. For FY2010, the Obama Administration requested over $68 million in foreign aid for Honduras, including over $53 million in Development Assistance, $12 million in Global Health and Child Survival assistance, and $1.3 million in Foreign Military Financing. U.S. assistance in FY2010 will support a variety of projects designed to enhance security, strengthen democracy, improve education and health systems, conserve the environment, and build trade capacity.

In addition to the $68 million in bilateral assistance requested, Honduras would also likely receive a portion of the $100 million requested for Central America in FY2010 for the continuation of the Mérida Initiative.

Additional foreign assistance is provided to Honduras through the Peace Corps, which has been active in the country since 1963, and the Millennium Challenge Corporation (MCC), which signed a five-year $215 million compact for Honduras in June 2005. The MCC compact has two components, a rural development project and a transportation project.

Table 1. U.S. Foreign Aid to Honduras, (U.S. $ in thousands)

Account	FY2006	FY2007	FY2008	FY2009 (est.)	FY2010 (req.)
Global Health and Child Survival (USAID)[a]	13,140	12,034	12,035	11,750	11,000
Global Health and Child Survival (State)[b]	—	750	1,000	1,000	1,000
Development Assistance	20,604	15,540	15,149	21,382	53,434
Economic Support Funds	—	175	—	—	—
Foreign Military Financing	891	675	496	400	1,300
International Military Education & Training	1,218	1,404	936	700	700
International Narcotics Control & Law Enforcement	—	—	744	—	800
Nonproliferation, Antiterrorism & Demining	315	268	—	—	—
Food Aid (P.L. 480)	13,105	13,005	10,150	8,000	—
Total	49,273	43,851	40,510	43,232[c]	68,234[d]

[a] This foreign aid account used to be called "Child Survival and Health," but was re-labeled with the FY2010 budget request. The majority of U.S. assistance to combat HIV/AIDS has been provided under this account.

[b] This foreign aid account used to be called "Global HIV/AIDS Initiative," but was re-labeled with the FY2010 budget request.

[c] The Omnibus Appropriations Act, 2009 (P.L. 111-8) provides $105 million for Central America under the Mérida Initiative, some of which will likely go to Honduras.

[d] The Obama Administration's FY2010 request includes $100 million to continue the Mérida Initiative in Central America. Honduras would likely receive some of these funds.

Sources: U.S. Department of State, Congressional Budget Justification, Foreign Operations, FY2008-FY2010; Peace Corps, Congressional Budget Justification, FY2007-2009.

The rural development project involves providing Honduran farmers with the skills needed to grow and market horticultural crops. The transportation project will improve a highway linking the Atlantic port of Puerto Cortés to Pacific ports and major production centers in Honduras, El Salvador, and Nicaragua. It will also involve improvements to main highways, secondary, and rural roads to enable farmers and other businesses to get their products to markets more efficiently [27].

U.S. Military Presence

The United States maintains a troop presence of about 550 military personnel known as Joint Task Force (JTF) Bravo at Soto Cano Air Base. JTF Bravo was first established in 1983 with about 1,200 troops, who were involved in military training exercises and in supporting U.S. counterinsurgency and intelligence operations in the region. Today, U.S. troops in Honduras support such activities as disaster relief, medical and humanitarian assistance, counternarcotics operations, and search and rescue operations that benefit Honduras and other Central American countries. Regional exercises and deployments involving active duty and reserve components provide training opportunities for thousands of U.S. troops. In the aftermath of Hurricane Mitch in 1998, U.S. troops provided extensive assistance in the relief and reconstruction effort. JTF Bravo has responded to a number of natural disasters in the region in recent years, most recently deploying two disaster relief teams to Panama and Costa Rica to assist victims of severe flooding and landslides in November and December 2008 [28].

Crime

Honduras, along with neighboring El Salvador and Guatemala, has become fertile ground for gangs, which have been fueled by poverty, unemployment, leftover weapons from the conflicts of the 1980s, and the U.S. deportation of criminals to the region. The two major gangs in Honduras—Mara Salvatrucha, or MS-13, and the 18th Street gang, or M-18—were first established in Los Angeles in the 1980s by Salvadoran immigrants who were excluded from Mexican-American gangs. The U.S. deportation of criminals back to the region in the 1990s may have helped lay the foundation for the development of MS- 13 and M- 18 in Central America [29]. Although estimates of the number of gang members in Central America vary widely, the U.S. Southern Command maintains that there are some 70,000, concentrated largely in Honduras, El Salvador, and Guatemala [30]

During his term, President Maduro (2002-2006) increased the number of police officers and signed legislation that made maras (street gangs) illegal and gang membership punishable with 12 years in prison.

Although the crackdown won popular support and initially reduced crime, its success was short-lived. Following his election, President Zelaya replaced the previous administration's zero-tolerance policy with dialogue and other outreach techniques designed to convince gang members to give up violence and reintegrate into society [31]. Failure to achieve concrete results, however, led the Zelaya Administration to shift its emphasis toward more traditional anti-gang law enforcement operations. The Administration increased the number of police and military troops in the streets and conducted raids against suspected criminals. Nonetheless, crime and violence in Honduras have continued unabated [32].

Several U.S. agencies have been involved in assisting Honduras and other Central American countries in dealing with the gang problem [33]. On the law enforcement side, the

FBI and the U.S. Immigration and Customs Enforcement (ICE) have worked closely with Honduran law enforcement and the United States has provided anti-gang training for Honduran police and prosecutors [34].

The U.S. Agency for International Development, while not having a specific program focusing on gangs, supports several programs that attack the risk factors associated with gang membership and violence. These include a program to provide basic education skills to at- risk youths and a program to improve the effectiveness and transparency of the justice system [35].

In July 2007, the United States pledged $4 million to help Central American governments draft a regional security strategy to fight street gangs and drug trafficking [36].

As noted above, Congress has also provided funding to Central through the Mérida Initiative to boost the region's counternarcotics capabilities and support the development of a regional anti-gang strategy. In the 110th Congress, H.Res. 564 (Engel), approved by the House on October 2, 2007 by voice vote, recognizes that violence poses an increasingly serious threat to peace and stability in Central America and supports expanded cooperation between the United States and the countries in the region, including Honduras, to deal with youth gangs in Central America.

Migration Issues

Temporary Protected Status

In the aftermath of Hurricane Mitch in 1998, the United States provided temporary protected status (TPS) to eligible Hondurans who may otherwise have been deported from the United States. Originally slated to expire in July 2000, TPS status has now been extended seven times due to the U.S. government's assessment that Honduras would have difficulty in coping with the deportees returns. The most recent TPS extension came in October 2008, when then-Secretary of Homeland Security Michael Chertoff announced that the U.S. would continue provide TPS for an additional 18 months, expiring on July 5, 2010. Homeland Security officials maintain that the TPS extension was necessary because Honduras continues to face social and economic challenges in its efforts to restore the nation to normalcy despite the significant progress the country has made in terms of recovery and rebuilding. Some 78,000 Hondurans benefit from TPS [37].

Deportations [38]

Deportations to Honduras have increased significantly over the past decade. About 30,000 Hondurans were deported from the United States in both FY2007 and FY2008, making Honduras one of the top recipients of deportees on a per capita basis [39]. Increasing deportations from the United States have been accompanied by similar increases in deportations from Mexico, a transit country for Central American migrants bound for the United States. Honduran policymakers are concerned about their country's ability to absorb the large volume of deportees as it is often difficult for those returning to the country to find gainful employment. Individuals who do not speak Spanish, who are tattooed, who have criminal records, and/or who lack familial support face additional difficulties re-integrating into Honduran society. In addition to these social problems, leaders are concerned that remittances may start to fall if the current high rates of deportations continue [40]. In March 2007, the Honduran Congress approved a motion calling for the United States to halt deportations of undocumented Honduran migrants who live and work in the United States [41].

Some analysts contend that increasing U.S. deportations of individuals with criminal records has exacerbated the gang problem in Honduras and other Central American countries. By the mid-1990s, the civil conflicts in Central America had ended and the United States began deporting unauthorized immigrants, many with criminal convictions, back to the region. Between 2000 and 2004, an estimated 20,000 criminals were sent back to Central America, many of whom had spent time in prisons in the United States for drug and/or gang-related offenses. Some observers contend that gang-deportees have "exported" a Los Angeles gang culture to Central America, and that they have recruited new members from among the local populations [42]. Although a recent United Nations study says that there is little conclusive evidence to support their claims, the media and many Central American officials have attributed a large proportion of the rise in violent crime in the region to gangs, particularly gang-deportees from the United States [43]. In July 2007 testimony before the House Subcommittee on the Western Hemisphere, the Honduran Ambassador to the United States asserted that although the United States provides information to countries on the criminal background of deportees, the information does not include whether the repatriated nationals are gang members. About 19% of Hondurans deported from the United States in FY2008 were removed on criminal grounds [44].

Drug Trafficking

Honduras is a transit country for cocaine and heroin flowing from the Andean region of South America to the United States and Europe. It is also increasingly a transshipment point for precursor chemicals used in the production of methamphetamine. Remote and poorly controlled areas of Honduras along the country's north coast are natural safe havens for drug traffickers, providing them with isolated areas for trafficking operations, such as refueling maritime assets and making boat-to-boat transfers.

The U.S. State Department's 2009 International Narcotics Control Strategy Report acknowledges the government of Honduras for its ongoing cooperation with the United States on counternarcotics efforts, noting that successful joint operations led to an increase in narcotics arrests and seizures. In 2008, the government of Honduras seized 6.5 metric tons of cocaine, 2 kilograms of crack cocaine, 19.6 kilograms of heroin, 3 metric tons of marijuana, 3.5 million pseudoephedrine pills, and over five tons of precursor chemicals. These seizures also led to 721 arrests and the confiscation of $6.7 million in assets. The United States has supported a variety of anticorruption, police training, and maritime operations programs intended to improve Honduras' counternarcotics capabilities [45].

Honduras' counternarcotics efforts continue to face a number of obstacles, however, including funding constraints, official corruption, and insufficient precursor chemical controls. Additionally, Mexican drug cartels have now expanded their reach to Honduras. It has been reported that the Gulf and Sinaloa cartels now engage in direct and indirect operations within Honduras, especially along the northern and Atlantic coast, and that Los Zetas have cells in every department of the country [46].

In October 2008, President Zelaya became the first Latin American president to openly suggest the legalization of drugs. He argued that narcotics trafficking has led to increased violence and that supporting addict treatment programs would be a better use of the government's resources [47]. Nonetheless, Honduras has continued its counternarcotics efforts. In January 2009, President Zelaya signed a letter of agreement with the United States to implement the Mérida Initiative, and in February 2009, the United States began construction on a counternarcotics base in the Honduran department of Gracias a Dios, which borders Nicaragua and the Caribbean and is a major corridor for traffickers.

Human Trafficking

According to the State Department's 2008 Trafficking in Persons (TIP) Report, Honduras is a source and transit country for women and children trafficked for the purpose of commercial sexual exploitation. Many victims are trafficked from rural areas to tourist and urban locales such as San Pedro Sula, the north Caribbean coast, and the Bay Islands. Destination countries for trafficked Honduran women and children include the United States, Mexico, Guatemala, and El Salvador. There are also foreign victims of commercial sexual exploitation in Honduras, most having been trafficked from neighboring countries, including economic migrants en route to the United States that have been victimized by traffickers.

While the State Department maintains that Honduras does not fully comply with the minimum standards for the elimination of trafficking, it notes that the government is making significant efforts to do so. As a result, Honduras is considered a so-called "Tier 2" country. The report recognizes the Honduran government's increased efforts to investigate trafficking crimes. While, Honduras opened just 24 trafficking-related investigations in 2006, it opened 74 in 2007, leading to 13 prosecutions and 8 convictions. The report also recognized the government's progress in trafficking prevention. In addition to conducting TV and radio awareness-raising campaigns, the Honduran government conducted 50 anti-trafficking training sessions for more than 3,000 government officials, civil society members, students, and journalists in 2007. Nonetheless, the report indicates a number of areas in which Honduras can do more to combat trafficking. It recommends that the Honduran government increase its shelter aid and victims services, amend anti-trafficking laws to prohibit labor trafficking, increase criminal investigations of corrupt public officials involved in trafficking activities, and enhance international collaboration to prosecute foreign tourists engaging in the exploitation of trafficked women and children [48].

Port Security

Honduras and the United States have cooperated extensively on port security. For the United States, port security emerged as an important element of homeland security in the aftermath of the September 11, 2001 terrorist attacks. Honduras views such cooperation as important in order to ensure the speedy export of its products to the United States, which in turn could increase U.S. investment in the country.

In March 2006, U.S. officials announced the inclusion of the largest port in Honduras, Puerto Cortés, in the U.S. Container Security Initiative (CSI). CSI is operated by the U.S.

Customs and Border Protection (CBP) of the Department of Homeland Security, and uses a security regime to ensure that all containers that pose a potential risk for terrorism are identified and inspected at foreign ports before they are placed on vessels destined for the United States. Honduras also participates in the Department of Energy's Megaports Initiative, which supplies ports with equipment capable of detecting nuclear or radioactive materials, and the Secure Freight Initiative (SFI), which deploys equipment capable of scanning containers for radiation and information risk factors before they are allowed to depart for the United States. Puerto Cortés was one of six ports around the world chosen to be part of the first phase of the SFI [49].

REFERENCES

[1] World Bank, World Development Report, 2009.

[2] "Honduras Country Profile," *Economist Intelligence Unit*, 2008; World Bank, "Honduras Country Brief," September 2006, and "Fighting Malnutrition in Central America," December 19, 2006; U.N. Economic Commission for Latin America and the Caribbean, "Social Panorama of Latin America 2007," August 2008; Also see CRS Report RL32713, *Afro-Latinos in Latin America and Considerations for U.S. Policy*, by Clare Ribando Seelke and June S. Beittel.

[3] "Un 57 Pct de Hondureños Aprueba Gestión Presidente Zelaya," Reuters, January 24, 2007; "Honduras Country Report," *Economist Intelligence Unit*, January 2007.

[4] "Honduras report signals rising violence," *Latin News Daily*, February 22, 2009.

[5] Thelma Meja, "Corruption: Honduras Grapples with Murky Transparency Law," *Global Information Network*, February 23, 2007.

[6] "Honduras: Primaries turn bloody," *Latin News Weekly Report*, November 27, 2008.

[7] "Divisive primaries split ruling PL," *Latin American Caribbean & Central America Report*, December 2008.

[8] "Honduras' Vice President Regains the Right to Run; Elvin Santos is Partido Liberal Presidential Candidate," *Latin America Data Base NotiCen*, March 5, 2009.

[9] "Constitutional reform or power grab?," *Latin American Weekly Report*, March 26, 2009.

[10] "Country Report: Honduras," *Economist Intelligence Unit*, April 2009.

[11] "Honduras: Zelaya could face impeachment," *Latin American Weekly Report*, April 2, 2009.

[12] "Honduras: Country Report," *Economist Intelligence Unit*, September 2008 and January 2009.

[13] "Honduras Country Profile," *Economist Intelligence Unit*, 2008.

[14] "Honduras: Country Report," *Economist Intelligence Unit*, April 2007; Nestor Ikeda, "Inter-American Development Bank Forgives Debt of 5 Nations," *Associated Press*, March 17, 2007.

[15] "Downturn in the US leads to first decline in remittances by migrants," *Latin American Weekly Report*, May 21, 2009.

[16] "Honduras: Trade down, budget problems and elections loom," *Latin American Economy & Business*, May 2009.

[17] "Desempleo aumentará a causa de crisis económica," *La Prensa* (Honduras), May 22, 2009.
[18] "Honduras: Country Report," *Economist Intelligence Unit*, April 2009.
[19] International Monetary Fund, "World Economic Outlook," April 2009.
[20] U.S. Department of State, "Background Note: Honduras," June 2008; "Latin America: Remittances slide," *Economist Intelligence Unit*, January 26, 2009.
[21] "Honduras: Zelaya Risks ALBA Membership," *Oxford Analytica*, September 16, 2008.
[22] Freddy Cuevas "Honduran Leader: U.S. Apathy Made Him Turn to Chávez," *Associated Press Newswires*, September 19, 2008.
[23] U.S. Department of Commerce statistics, as presented by *Global Trade Atlas*, 2009.
[24] U.S. Department of Commerce, Bureau of Economic Analysis, "Survey of Current Business," September 2008.
[25] U.S. Department of State, "Background Note: Honduras," June 2008.
[26] U.S. Department of State, Bureau of Democracy, Human Rights, and Labor, "2008 Country Reports on Human Rights Practices," February 25, 2009.
[27] Millennium Challenge Corporation, "Honduras Overview," available at http://www.mcc.gov/countries/honduras/ index.php
[28] "Stavridis Praises U.S.-Honduran Cooperation in Confronting Mutual Threats," *U.S. Fed News*, January 30, 2009.
[29] Ana Arana, "How the Street Gangs Took Central America," *Foreign Affairs*, May 1, 2005.
[30] House Armed Services Committee, Posture Statement of Gen. Bantz Craddock, Commander, U.S. Southern Command, March 9, 2005.
[31] "Honduran Government Reaches Out to Rehabilitate Gangs," *ACAN-EFE*, January 30, 2006.
[32] Marion Barbel, "Homicide Rate Confirms Honduras as One of Region's Most Violent Nations," *Global Insight Daily Analysis*, September 11, 2008.
[33] See CRS Report RL34112, *Gangs in Central America*, by Clare Ribando Seelke.
[34] House Committee on International Relations, Subcommittee on the Western Hemisphere, Statement of John P. Torres, U.S. Immigration and Customs Enforcement, U.S. Department of Homeland Security, Hearing on "Gangs and Crime in Latin America," April 20, 2005.
[35] U.S. Agency for International Development, "Central America and Mexico Gang Assessment, Annex 3: Honduras Profile," April 2006.
[36] "U.S. Offers Funds to Help Fight Central America Gangs," *Reuters,* July 18, 2007.
[37] U.S. Department of Homeland Security, Citizenship and Immigration Services, "Extension of the Designation of Honduras for Temporary Protected Status," October 1, 2008. For background on TPS, see CRS Report RS20844, *Temporary Protected Status: Current Immigration Policy and Issues*, by Ruth Ellen Wasem and Karma Ester.
[38] Clare Ribando Seelke contributed information to this section. Also see CRS Report RL34112, *Gangs in Central America*, by Clare Ribando Seelke.
[39] Information Provided to CRS by the Department of Homeland Security, Immigration and Customs Enforcement, Office of Detention and Removal.

[40] Pamela Constable, "Deportees' Bittersweet Homecoming; Migration is Boon, Bane for Honduras," *Washington Post*, June 27, 2007.

[41] "CN Pide a EEUU que Cesen las Deportaciones de Compatriotas," *La Tribuna* (San Pedro Sula, Honduras), March 14, 2007.

[42] Ana Arana, "How the Street Gangs Took Central America," *Foreign Affairs*, May/June 2005.

[43] United Nations Office on Drugs and Crime (UNODC), *Crime and Development in Central America: Caught in the Crossfire*, May 2007.

[44] Information Provided to CRS by the Department of Homeland Security, Immigration and Customs Enforcement, Office of Detention and Removal.

[45] U.S. Department of State Bureau for International Narcotics and Law Enforcement Affairs, "2009 International Narcotics Control Strategy Report (INCSR)," February 27, 2009.

[46] "Carteles mexicanas azotan a Honduras," *La Prensa* (Honduras), August 27, 2008; "Los Zetas hondureños, nueva pesadilla para los inmigrantes," *Tiempo* (Honduras), March 18, 2009.

[47] "Honduras floats drug legalisation," *Latin News Daily*, October 14, 2008.

[48] U.S. Department of State Office to Monitor and Combat Trafficking in Persons, "Trafficking in Persons Report," June 2008.

[49] U.S. Department of Homeland Security, "DHS and DOE Launch Secure Freight Initiative," Press Release, December 7, 2006, and "Secure Freight Initiative Becomes Fully Operational in United Kingdom, Pakistan, and Honduras," *Press Release*, October 12, 2007.

In: U.S. Involvement in Political, Economic and Social ... ISBN: 978-1-61209-781-7
Editor: Allen P. Lowell

Chapter 7

HAITI: CURRENT CONDITIONS AND CONGRESSIONAL CONCERNS

Maureen Taft-Morales

ABSTRACT

Haiti shares the island of Hispaniola with the Dominican Republic. Since the fall of the Duvalier dictatorship in 1986, Haiti has struggled to overcome its centuries-long legacy of authoritarianism, extreme poverty, and underdevelopment. While some progress has been made in developing democratic institutions, they remain weak. Economic and social stability have improved considerably. But poverty remains massive and deep, and economic disparity is wide.

In May 2006, René Préval began his second five-year term as President of Haiti. During his first two years in office, Préval began to establish internal political stability by attempting to strengthen democratic institutions and creating an environment that would attract private investment and spur job creation. Haiti's fragile stability has been repeatedly shaken, however, if not by political problems, then by climatic ones. In 2008, a worsening food crisis led to violent protests and the removal of Haiti's Prime Minister. Parliament rejected Préval's first two choices for a new prime minister, but finally confirmed Michele Pierre-Louis, a highly-regarded educator and economist, as Prime Minister in September 2008. In the summer of 2008, four major storms caused widespread devastation in Haiti.

Haiti remains the poorest country in the western hemisphere. Over half the population of 8.2 million people live in extreme poverty. Since Haiti's developmental needs and priorities are many, and deeply intertwined, the Haitian government and the international donor community are implementing an assistance strategy to address these many needs simultaneously. The Préval administration presented a revised strategy at a donors' conference on April 14. Haiti received aid commitments of $353 million. The United States pledged $68 million in new FY2009 assistance, including $20 million in targeted budget support. The United Nations Stabilization Mission in Haiti (MINUSTAH) has been in Haiti to help restore order since the collapse of former President Jean-Bertrand Aristide's government in 2004. MINUSTAH's current strength is 9,089 troops.

The main priorities for U.S. policy regarding Haiti are to strengthen fragile democratic processes, continue to improve security, and promote economic development.

Other concerns include the cost and effectiveness of U.S. aid; protecting human rights; combating narcotics, arms, and human trafficking; addressing Haitian migration; and alleviating poverty. The FY2009 aid request for Haiti was $246 million. The Omnibus Appropriations Act of 2009 (P.L. 111-8) provided for an additional $41 million in bilateral economic and international security assistance for Haiti. The FY20 10 aid request for Haiti is $293 million.

The 111th Congress may consider the balance and scope of assistance to Haiti. Members have already requested that the Obama Administration grant Temporary Protected Status (TPS) to Haitians living in the United States. Of immediate concern to Congress may be ensuring that second round elections scheduled for June 21 for 11 Haitian Senate seats are free, fair, and—in light of recent violent protests—peaceful. Prohibited from running on technicalities, former President Aristide's Lavalas party boycotted the first round vote; turnout nationwide averaged 11%. Congress may take up debt relief for Haiti again.

Current law related to Haiti includes P.L. 111-8, P.L. 110-161, P.L. 110-246, and P.L. 109-432. Pending legislation related to Haiti includes H.Con.Res. 17, H.R. 144, H.R. 264, H.R. 331, H.R. 416, H.R. 417, H.R. 1567, S. 730, and S. 1183; for details see sections on Legislation.

POLITICAL BACKGROUND

Haiti shares the island of Hispaniola with the Dominican Republic; Haiti occupies the western third of the island. Since the fall of the Duvalier dictatorship in 1986, Haiti has struggled to overcome its centuries-long legacy of authoritarianism, extreme poverty, and underdevelopment. While significant progress has been made in improving governance, democratic institutions remain weak. Poverty remains massive and deep, and economic disparity is wide. Attempts at democratic rule have been intermittent and only partially successful. In 1991, a military coup interrupted the first term of Haiti's first democratically-elected President, Jean-Bertrand Aristide; the threat of a U.S. military intervention allowed him to return three years later and finish his term.

In 1996, the first transition between two democratically elected presidents in Haitian history occurred when René Préval assumed the presidency. Five years later, in 2001, Aristide was re- elected. Political conflict led to the collapse of his government in 2004, which was followed by an interim government. Charges of corruption against Aristide, dissolution of the parliament by Préval in his first term, questions of the interim government's legitimacy, and flawed elections under all of them contributed to their inability to establish a fully accepted or functioning government.

Since 2004, however, Haiti has made what the International Monetary Fund (IMF) and others call "remarkable progress" toward political stability and economic stabilization [1]. The government has conducted democratic presidential and parliamentary elections, and enacted wide-ranging reforms, especially in economic governance.

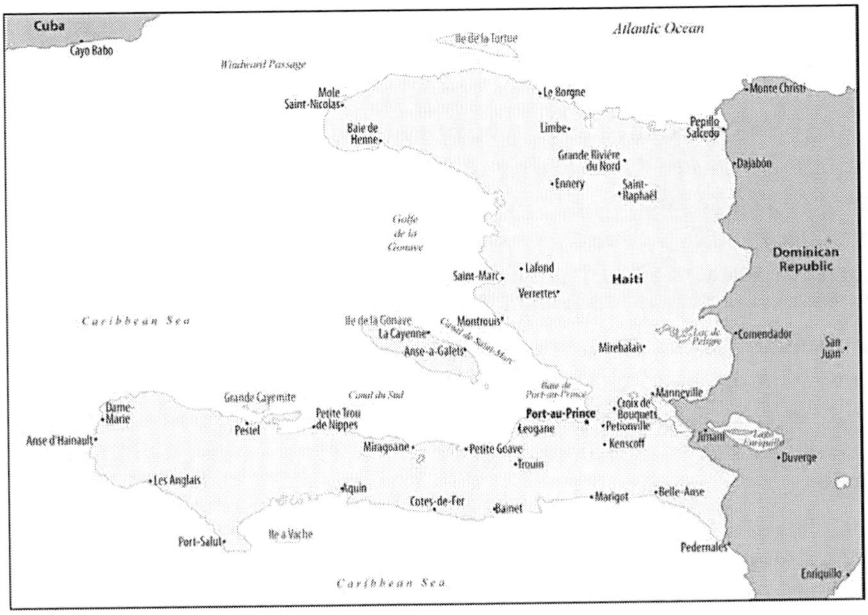

Source: Map Resources. Adapted by CRS.

Figure 1. Map of Haiti.

Although crime and violence continue to undermine Haitian development, security has improved significantly enough that the United Nations Stabilization Mission in Haiti (MINUSTAH) is shifting the focus of its biggest contingent from security to development. The fundamental inequality of Haitian society has remained basically unchanged, though, and Haiti remains the poorest country in the hemisphere.

In proximity to the United States, and with such a chronically unstable political environment and fragile economy, Haiti has been a constant policy issue for the United States. The U.S. Congress views the stability of the nation with great concern and commitment to improving conditions there.

In May 2006, René Préval began his second five-year term as President of Haiti. During his first three years in office, Préval has established relative internal political stability. He outlined two main missions for his government: (1) to build institutions, and (2) to establish favorable conditions for private investment in order to create jobs. In November 2007, his Administration published its Poverty Reduction Strategy, a key step in meeting IMF requirements for debt relief. International donors pledged more than $1.5 billion in economic assistance to Haiti. With the support of the MINUSTAH, which arrived in Haiti in 2004, security conditions have improved and reform of the country's police force has begun. Former President George W. Bush praised Préval for his efforts to improve economic conditions and establish the rule of law in Haiti. Préval pledged to cooperate with U.S. counternarcotics efforts. Both President Barack Obama and Secretary of State Hillary Clinton have met with President Préval and indicated strong support for development in Haiti.

The Préval government worked with international donors and agencies to update its poverty reduction strategy to take into account the damage done by the hurricanes and storms and the reconstruction that is being done. The government presented the revised strategy and received $353 million in new aid commitments at a donors' conference on April 21, 2009.

Haiti's fragile stability has been repeatedly shaken, however, if not by political problems, then by climatic ones. In April 2008, a worsening food crisis led to violent protests and the removal of Haiti's Prime Minister. UN officials said political opponents and armed gangs infiltrated the protests and fired at UN peacekeepers in an effort to weaken the government. Without a Prime Minister, Haiti could not sign certain agreements with foreign donors or implement programs to address the crisis for over four months. Parliament, having rejected Préval's first two choices for a new prime minister, finally confirmed Michele Pierre-Louis, a highly-regarded educator and economist who has worked on behalf of Haitian poor and youths, as Prime Minister in September 2008. They were spurred to act in part so that the government could respond to natural disasters: in late August and September, four major storms directly hit or passed close to Haiti, causing widespread devastation. There are some 19 political parties in the legislature competing for influence and positioning themselves for legislative and presidential elections in 2010 and 2011, respectively, further complicating governability.

In June, student protests against university budget cuts expanded into broader protests demanding the departure of United Nations forces in Haiti and that President Préval sign a bill increasing the minimum wage raising the minimum wage from about $1.75 to $5.00 a day. The Congress passed the law in May, but it does not become law until the President signs it. Some critics believe he is bowing to pressure from textile manufacturers to delay the bill's implementation.

The average daily wage for textile assembly workers is $5.25, above the new minimum wage. Some manufacturers, noting that they would have to raise wages proportionally, had asked for a gradual implementation of the law so that they could negotiate new contracts incorporating the new wages into their costs. The Congress passed the bill with no transition phase in it.

The Haitian Parliament and 2009 Elections

After the collapse of the Aristide government in 2004, the Parliament was not fully functioning. It was reestablished with elections in April 2006. The Haitian parliament comprises a Senate, with 30 seats, and the Chamber of Deputies, with 99 seats. One-third of the Senate is elected every two years; the Senate has operated with only one-third of its members for about a year and a half, as unrest, hurricanes, and divisions with the electoral council delayed elections for the other two- thirds. Préval dissolved the electoral council last year and formed a new one.

Since then, technical preparations for the elections went well, but the process was fraught with political tensions. The provisional electoral council, with the support of MINUSTAH and donors, completed the election preparation, including voter registration, ballot printing, and training of election workers. But the council also caused controversy by barring former President Jean- Bertrand Aristide's Fanmi Lavalas party from participating for mostly technical reasons. Part of the problem is that two rival factions submitted separate lists of candidates.

The council rejected both lists because neither faction had documents signed by the party's head, Aristide. Aristide lives in exile in South Africa. Although technically correct, some observers felt the decision had a politically motivated element, to prevent the once powerful Lavalas from gaining more seats. A UN Security Council delegation in Haiti praised the Lavalas party for seeking a reversal of the decision through legal means, and urged a resolution to the impasse to avoid yet another electoral crisis, of which Haiti has had many in the last couple of decades.

In the end, Lavalas was still not allowed to run, and Lavalas supporters boycotted the elections. For 12 of the Haitian Senate's 30 seats that were held on April 19, 2009. About 4,000 electoral security workers and 6,500 UN peacekeepers helped maintain order on election day. The process was relatively peaceful, but protests and the shooting of a poll official led the government to cancel the vote in one rural department. Apathy, the boycott, and the closing of public transportation out of concern for security contributed to extremely low voter turnout, averaging 11% nationwide.

Only one candidate won a majority of the vote, so a runoff vote is scheduled to be held on June 21. A clash between the ruling party and an opposition party, the Struggling People's Organization, OPL, resulted in the death of one person, increasing concerns about violence around the elections. Opposition parties have filed claims of voting fraud, and at least four have vowed to vote against seating the winners of the elections. Some critics have called for the election to be postponed.

The elections could give President Préval's coalition, Lespwa ("Hope" in Haitian Creole), a majority in the Senate. Lespwa currently controls one-third of the chamber's seats. Lespwa candidates in the runoff could give the party five to nine more seats. Préval hopes such wins would give him the support he needs in Parliament to pass constitutional reforms and support his economic agenda. Lingering disputes over the elections could dampen that support, however. In addition, several members of Parliament have defected recently from the coalition. He also wishes to strengthen the executive, which some in Parliament oppose.

Elections for the Chamber of Deputies are due to be held in 2010. There are no term limits for either chamber; re-election rates are extremely low, however. Parliamentarians are already positioning themselves for the next presidential elections in 2011 as well.

SOCIOECONOMIC CONDITIONS

Plagued by chronic political instability and frequent natural disasters, Haiti remains the poorest country in the Western Hemisphere. Haiti's poverty is massive and deep. Over half the population (54%) of 9 million people live in extreme poverty, living on less than $1 a day; 78% live on $2 or less a day, according to the World Bank. Poverty among the rural population is even more widespread: 69% of rural dwellers live on less than $1 a day, and 86% live on less than $2 a day. Hunger is also widespread: 81% of the national population and 87% of the rural population do not get the minimum daily ration of food defined by the World Health Organization. In remote parts of Haiti, children are dying of malnutrition [2]

In order to reach its Millennium Development Goal of eradicating extreme poverty and hunger by 2015, Haiti's Gross Domestic Product (GDP) would have to grow 3.5% per year, a goal the International Monetary Fund (IMP) says Haiti is not considered likely to achieve.

Over the past 40 years, Haiti's per capita real GDP has declined by 30%. Therefore, economic growth, even if it is greater than population growth, is not expected to be enough to reduce poverty. Haiti has experienced economic growth since 2004. Economic growth for FY2007 was 3.2%, the highest rate since the 1 990s, but the forecasted growth for FY2008-

2009 is only 1.9%, reflecting the impact of recent storms and the global economic crisis. The global economic crisis has also led to a drop of about 10% in remittances from Haitians abroad, which last year amounted to about $1.65 billion, more than a fourth of Haiti's annual income [3].

The likelihood that economic growth will contribute to the reduction of poverty in Haiti is further reduced by its enormous income distribution gap. Haiti has the second largest income disparity in the world. Over 68% of the total national income accrues to the wealthiest 20% of the population, while less than 1.5% of Haiti's national income is accumulated by the poorest 20% of the population. When the level of inequality is as high as Haiti's, according to the World Bank, the capacity of economic growth to reduce poverty "approaches zero" [4].

HAITI'S DEVELOPMENT CHALLENGES AND INTERNATIONAL ASSISTANCE STRATEGY [5]

Strategy for Growth and Poverty Reduction

In November 2007, the Préval government issued a "Growth and Poverty Reduction Strategy Paper," one of the qualifications for debt relief through the World Bank's Heavily Indebted Poor Country (HIPC) initiative and the IMF's Poverty Reduction and Growth Facilities [6]. Its implementation cost for 2007 to 2010 is just under $4 billion; the international community has contributed or pledged about half of that amount. The poverty reduction strategy focuses on three "priority pillars." The first is areas for growth, focusing on agriculture and rural development; tourism; infrastructure modernization; and science, technology and innovation. The second pillar is human development, concentrating on education and training; health; water and sanitation; persons with disabilities; childhood poverty; young people; HIV/AIDS; and gender equity. The third pillar calls for investment in democratic governance, focusing on the establishment of an equitable justice system; creation of a climate of security; modernization of the state; and political and economic decentralization.

Post-Disaster Assessment of Needs

In August and September 2008, four major hurricanes or tropical storms directly struck or passed close to Haiti, killing hundreds of Haitians and affecting hundreds of thousands more. The storms caused flooding in all ten of the country's departments. Tropical Storm Fay struck Haiti on August 16 while Hurricane Gustav struck on August 26 with heavy rains and winds. In the first days of September, Tropical Storm Hanna brought more torrential rain, causing floods as deep as almost ten feet in Gonaives. Hurricane Ike did not directly strike Haiti, but significantly increased water levels in areas that were already flooded. Overall, almost 500 people died.

At the time, Haiti was already experiencing a food crisis, and the impact of the storms greatly exacerbated the problem, mainly due to flooding. The storms destroyed approximately one-third of the country's rice crop, essentially used for domestic consumption, as well as livestock, other crops, seeds, and farm equipment. The storms hit during harvest season, meaning that farmers would not have had capital from that crop to reinvest in future crops [7]

The Growth and Poverty Reduction Strategy—and its budget—was developed prior to the devastating hurricanes of 2008. World Bank Group President Robert Zoellick visited Haiti in October 2008, and called on the Haitian government and donors to reinvigorate short-term recovery and reconstruction efforts and long-term development programs, and promote a new "vision" for medium-term growth and development. To help it do this, the Haitian government requested a Post-Disaster Needs Assessment that was published in November 2008 [8]. Damages and losses were estimated at almost $900 million ($897.39 million). The greatest damage was done to agricultural production, with almost $200 million in damages and losses, and housing, with about $180 million in damages and losses. Needs were assessed at approximately $269 million for immediate relief efforts, and approximately $494 million for reconstruction and rehabilitation, for a total of $763 million.

Priorities for immediate relief projects are food security, social welfare, and watershed protection, The overarching goal of the reconstruction and rehabilitation projects is to rebuild better, so that the living conditions of communities affected by the storms are better than they were beforehand. That is, to reestablish the basic infrastructure while also fostering economic development and reducing the risks of the next disasters.

Some analysts argue that Haiti needs its own economic stimulus package, an extraordinary level of aid committed over a long period of time to establish security and achieve poverty reduction. According to Hedi Annabi, the UN's envoy to Haiti, Haiti needs $3 billion over the next two to three years to recover from the hurricanes, if the $570 million spent yearly on the UN peacekeeping mission is to be at all effective.

The President of the Inter-American Development Bank (IDB), Luis Moreno, has also called for extraordinary assistance from the international community for Haiti. Calling Haiti the most fragile of IDB's member countries, Moreno said that no other nation in Latin America and the Caribbean is as vulnerable to economic shocks and natural disasters as is Haiti. In December 2008 the IDB offered Haiti an additional $50 million in assistance for 2009. The World Bank approved an additional $25 million in emergency grants for Haiti in November 2008 to finance rebuilding of key infrastructure, water and sanitation works, and technical assistance to incorporate disaster risk management into Haiti's overall development strategy. The United Nations designates Haiti one of the 50 "least developed countries" in the world, facing a higher risk than other countries of failing to come out of poverty, and therefore needing the highest degree of attention from the international community.

Relations with Donors and Donors Conference

Since Haiti's developmental needs and priorities are many, and deeply intertwined, the Haitian government and the international donor community are implementing an assistance strategy that attempts to address these many needs simultaneously. The challenge is to accomplish short-term projects that will boost public and investor confidence, while also pursuing long-term development plans to improve living conditions for Haiti's vast poor population. The challenge has been made more daunting by developments such as rising food and gasoline prices world- wide, internal political crises, and natural disasters. Préval has criticized the donor community for not dispersing funds quickly enough. Some international donors have complained that Préval's government keeps changing priorities -first children's needs, then road-building, then security issues such as high rates of crime and kidnapping, leading Préval's government and MINUSTAH to focus on improving security.

There are other frustrations on the part of both donors and the Haitian government regarding foreign assistance. The Haitian government is frustrated that U.S. and other foreign aid is provided through non-governmental organizations (NGOs) rather than directly to the government. The Préval Administration indicates it wants more accountability by NGOs, so that the government knows what projects are being carried out. Donors are worried about the lack of Haitian capacity to design and implement programs, as well as corruption. Furthermore, Préval's style of leadership is viewed by many as a mixed blessing. He encourages national dialogue to develop consensus on strategies rather than imposing policy from above—a welcome departure from Haiti's traditionally autocratic style of leadership—but his lack of forceful leadership means progress on many fronts is limited. Some of these issues were addressed at the international donors' conference held in the spring of 2009.

April 2009 Donors Conference [9]

International donors asked Haiti to update the Growth and Poverty Reduction Strategy, to clarify priorities and reflect post-hurricane conditions and needs. The government of Haiti presented such a revised strategy incorporating the findings of both the Post-Disaster Needs Assessment and the UN's "Haiti: From Natural Catastrophe to Economic Security" report, at a donors conference held April 21, 2009 in Washington, DC. The Haitian government outlined the priorities of its new two-year plan, "Haiti: a New Paradigm," which include investing in strategic infrastructure, improving economic governance and the business environment, improving the provision of basic services, and ensuring environmental sustainability [10]. The government and donors hope to generate up to 150,000 jobs through such actions, and by taking advantage of the investment opportunities created by the HOPE II Act (P.L. 110-246), the trade law that grants trade preferences for U.S. imports of Haitian apparel. The government's new plan also calls for job creation through higher productivity in agriculture.

Donors from 28 countries and multilateral organizations pledged $353 million in new aid to Haiti over the next two years. Although the amount was less than the Haitian government had said it needed, Prime Minister Pierre-Louis said that, considering the global economic crisis, it was more than she had expected, and pledged to use the funds properly. Donors agreed to coordinate assistance more effectively, with each other and with the Haitian government. World Bank President Robert Zoellick urged donors to reduce the burden on Haiti's government by working with the Haitian government to track results and accountability of foreign assistance better, and by developing joint benchmarks, and conducting joint assessments [11].

One of the government's immediate priorities was to get pledges to help bridge its $125 million budget gap; according to the Inter-American Development Bank, Haiti received about $83 million in such support for FY2008 to FY2010. The United States pledged $68 million in new FY2009 assistance, including $20 million in targeted budget support, in addition to the $245.9 million already requested for FY2009.

Some analysts emphasize that the Haitian government and civil society must be partners in designing any development strategy if they are to succeed and be sustainable. They also warn that job creation and other development efforts must occur not only in the cities, but also in rural areas, to reduce urban migration, dependence on imported food, and environmental degradation.

As mentioned above, economic growth alone is unlikely to reduce poverty in Haiti. Therefore, the Haitian government and many in the international donor community maintain that donors must continue to make a long-term commitment to Haitian development. Furthermore, in order to reduce poverty across the board, some observers say that development strategies must specifically target improving the living conditions of the poor, and address the inequities and prejudices that have contributed to Haiti's enormous income disparity [12].

Outlook Regarding Haitian Development

Despite the current economic and social problems currently existing in Haiti and the comprehensive and complex challenges facing the country today, prominent analysts note with optimism the progress Haiti has made and its potential for sustainable development. The UN Security Council conducted a fact-finding visit to Haiti in March 2009, and noted that the country had made significant improvements in security and judicial reform, although it still needs to contend with widespread poverty and susceptibility to natural disasters. Both the Préval and the preceding interim government also made progress toward goals outlined in Haiti's international assistance strategy, including improved macroeconomic management, procurement processes, and fiscal transparency; increased voter registration; and jobs creation. Although the natural disasters caused setbacks, the government had also made progress in providing broader access to clean water and other services. The UN Security Council delegation's leader said, “[I]t does appear that there is a window of opportunity to enable the consolidation of stability and the undertaking of a process of sustainable development.” [13]

In addition to the Security Council visit to Haiti, the UN Secretary-General commissioned a report, published in January 2009, that recommends a strategy to move Haiti beyond recovery to economic security [14]. According to the UN report, “the opportunities for [economic development in] Haiti are far more favorable than those of the 'fragile states' with which it is habitually grouped.” The report's author, economist Paul Collier, is known for his book, The Bottom Billion, which explores why there is poverty and how it can be reduced. Among his reasons for optimism regarding Haiti: Haiti is part of a peaceful and prosperous region, not a conflictive one; and while political divisions and limited capacity make governing difficult, Collier believes that Haiti's leadership is “good by the standards of most post-conflict situations. Both the President and the Prime Minister have integrity, experience and ability, and a deep concern with the maintenance of social peace.” The UN report recommends that modest and focused actions be taken to build economic security on the foundation of social stability that has been built in Haiti over the past five years. Because that stability is fragile, the report mentions such actions should be taken immediately and should focus on strengthening security by creating jobs, especially in the garment and agricultural sectors, providing basic services, enhancing food security, and fostering environmental sustainability.

Collier and other analysts note that Haiti has an important resource in the 1.5 million Haitians living abroad, for funds, technical skills, and political lobbying. Eighty percent of the

Haitian diaspora remitted $1.65 billion to Haiti in 2006—double Haiti's national budget, and about a third of its gross domestic product [15]. The world economic recession has led to about a 10% drop in Haitian remittances so far in 2009, however.

The efforts of Haitian-Americans and others lobbying on Haiti's behalf led to another advantage Haiti has the most advantageous access to the U.S. market for apparel of any country through the HOPE II Act (the Haitian Hemispheric Opportunity through Partnership Encouragement Act, P.L. 110-246; see Legislation section below). Supporters say the HOPE Act will provide jobs and stimulate the Haitian economy. Critics worry that it will exploit Haitians as a source of cheap labor for foreign manufacturers, and hurt the agricultural economy by drawing more people away from farming. According to the U.S. embassy in Haiti, the HOPE II Act has helped create about 11,000 jobs.

The United Nations Stabilization Mission in Haiti (MINUSTAH)

The United Nations Stabilization Mission in Haiti (MINUSTAH), has been in Haiti to help restore order since the collapse of former President Jean-Bertrand Aristide's government. Armed rebellion and diminished international support for Aristide led him to flee into exile in February 2004. An international force authorized by the UN arrived shortly after his departure, and was replaced by MINUSTAH in June 2004. MINUSTAH worked closely with the interim government from 2004 to 2006 when, after several delays, elections were held. The Mission has continued to work closely with the Préval Administration since then. Although some Haitians call for the removal of foreign troops, President Préval supports the mission's presence, saying that he "will not adopt a falsely nationalist position," and that MINUSTAH should stay until Haiti is ready to assume responsibility for security [16]

MINUSTAH's mandate includes three basic components: (1) to help create a secure and stable environment; (2) to support the political process by fostering effective democratic governance and institutional development, supporting government efforts to promote national dialogue and reconciliation and to organize elections; and (3) to support government and non-governmental efforts to promote and protect human rights, as well as to monitor and report on the human rights situation. MINUSTAH has played a key role in emergency responses to natural disasters, including facilitating the delivery of emergency humanitarian assistance. As part of its work, the Mission has also conducted campaigns to combat gangs and drug-trafficking with the Haitian police.

The Force Commander is Major-General Carlos Alberto Dos Santos Cruz of Brazil. Brazil also supplies 1,200 troops, the Mission's largest contingent. Sixteen other countries contribute military personnel, and 42 countries supply police personnel. MINUSTAH's current troop strength is 9,055 total uniformed personnel, consisting of 7,044 troops and 2,011 police. They are supported by 506 international civilian personnel; 1,255 local civilian staff; and 194 United Nations volunteers. The Mission's budget for this year (July 1, 2008-June 30, 2009) is $601.58 million. Brazilian officials recently announced that security had improved to the point that their troops would be shifting their focus to development work instead [17]. MINUSTAH's mandate has been extended another year, to October 2009, and will likely be extended again.

U.S. Policy Objectives and Assistance

The main priorities for U.S. policy regarding Haiti are to strengthen fragile democratic processes, continue to improve security, and promote economic development. Other concerns include the cost and effectiveness of U.S. aid; protecting human rights; combating narcotics, arms, and human trafficking; addressing Haitian migration; and alleviating poverty. Some Members expressed concern about the Bush Administration's October 2006 decision to lift partially the 15- year-old arms embargo against Haiti in order to allow arms and equipment to be provided to Haitian security units. The Obama Administration has said that Haiti is an important issue, deserving of support, and has called for a full review of policy toward the country.

Both President Préval and Prime Minister Pierre-Louis have asked that the United States change its travel warning on Haiti, arguing that it discourages the foreign investment the United States says it is trying to promote through the HOPE II Act and other forms of assistance. The current advisory warns U.S. citizens of the risks of travel to Haiti and recommends deferring nonessential travel until further notice, citing ongoing security concerns [18].

U.S. Assistance to Haiti

U.S. assistance for Haiti in FY2007 totaled $225 million. Estimated foreign assistance in FY2008, not including emergency food and humanitarian aid, was approximately $234 million. Among other provisions affecting aid to Haiti, the FY2008 Consolidated Appropriations Act (H.R. 2764/P.L. 110-161) stipulated that not less than $201.5 million in economic and military assistance be provided to Haiti. The former Bush Administration' s FY2008 request for Haiti included $83 million to combat HIV/AIDS and $25.5 million for an integrated conflict mitigation program to target urban crime. The previous Administration contributed $45 million in emergency food aid in response to the April food crisis. Humanitarian assistance in response to the 2008 hurricanes was about $33.7 million in FY2008 and FY2009 funds.

The estimate for FY2009 is for $287 million, including $18 million and $91 million for Global Health and Child Survival under USAID and State Department, respectively; $121 million in Economic Support Funds; $35.5 million in P.L. 480 food aid; $17.5 million for International Narcotics Control and Law Enforcement; $0.22 million for International Military Education and Training, and $0.4 million in Foreign Military Financing. The Omnibus Appropriations Act of 2009 (P.L. 111-8), signed into law on March 11, 2009, provides "not less than $25 1.126 million" in bilateral economic and international security assistance for Haiti, providing $41 million more than the original request. About $2 million will be provided to Haiti through the Merida Initiative for counter narcotics efforts.

The request for FY20 10 assistance for Haiti is for $293 million, including $21 million and $91 million for Global Health and Child Survival under USAID and State Department, respectively; $125 million in Economic Support Funds; $35.5 million in P.L. 480 food aid; $18.5 million for International Narcotics Control and Law Enforcement; $0.22 million for

International Military Education and Training, and $1.6 million in Foreign Military Financing.

Hurricane Damage and U.S. Assistance

In August and September 2008, four major storms directly hit or passed close to Haiti, causing widespread devastation. The hurricanes caused an estimated $1 billion in damage—equivalent to about 15% of Haiti's GDP—and set back much of any progress that had been made in recent years. The U.S. government provided $30 million in humanitarian assistance to affected Haitian populations in response to the hurricanes in Haiti in FY2008, and another $2million in FY2009, for a total of $33 million. Congress provided not less than $100 million for hurricane relief and reconstruction assistance for Haiti and other Caribbean countries in the FY2009 continuing appropriations resolution (P.L. 110-329) signed into law September 30, 2008. $96 million of this is directed to Haiti.

Haiti was already experiencing a food crisis; the impact of the storms has greatly exacerbated the problem, mainly due to flooding. The storms destroyed approximately one-third of the country's rice crop. Haiti's rice crop is essentially used for domestic consumption, and reportedly is a lifeline for many Haitians. Livestock, other crops, seeds, and farm equipment were destroyed as well. The storms hit during harvest season, meaning that farmers will not have capital from this crop to reinvest in future crops. Some observers worry that additional food shortages and price increases could again lead to riots, like the ones in April 2008 that killed several people and contributed to the dismissal of the Prime Minister at the time, and to higher incidences of children dying of malnutrition.

Temporary Protected Status

Haitians have repeatedly sought Temporary Protected Status (TPS), which would allow them to remain in the United States without threat of deportation, after various domestic crises, arguing that the return of deportees would contribute to instability and be a further drain on already inadequate services. After last summer's devastating tropical storms and hurricanes, President Préval publicly requested that illegal Haitian migrants in the United States be granted TPS. Over 30,000 Haitians are currently in detention facing deportation. The former Bush Administration turned down the request at the end of its term.

While visiting Haiti on April 16, Secretary of State Hillary Clinton said the Obama Administration was considering granting TPS to Haitians. Proponents argue that Haiti is ill-equipped to absorb thousands of deportees, and depends on the remittances they send back to Haiti. Opponents of TPS have argued that granting it could encourage a wave of new immigrants. Clinton said if granted, the policy would only apply to Haitians already in the U.S. before President Obama's election. She also said the policy of interdicting Haitian migrants on the high seas and returning them to Haiti would continue.

CONGRESSIONAL RESPONSE AND CONCERNS

There was bipartisan support in the 110th Congress to assist the Préval government. Responding to the food crisis and Préval's earlier calls for increased U.S. investment in Haiti, Congress passed the second Haitian Hemispheric Opportunity through Partnership Encouragement (HOPE) Act as part of the 2008 farm bill in June 2008 (Title XV, P.L. 110-246) [19]. The law expands trade preferences for U.S. imports of Haitian apparel first provided in the 2006 version of the HOPE Act (P.L. 109-432, Title V). In late June 2008, Congress amended the Merida Initiative, an aid package for Mexico and Central America that was part of the FY2008 Supplemental Appropriations Act, H.R. 2642 (P.L. 110-252), to include counternarcotics funds for Haiti.

The 111th Congress may consider not only the balance of financial support for democracy building, security enhancement, counternarcotics, development assistance, police and judicial reform, and disaster recovery and prevention, but also the scope of the assistance.

Several Members have already requested that the Obama Administration grant Temporary Protected Status (TPS) to Haitians living in the United States because of the disastrous conditions in Haiti. The Bush Administration decided that Haiti did not currently warrant a TPS designation, and was criticized by some Members and human rights advocates for renewing deportations of Haitians after a three-month reprieve in the aftermath of the hurricanes. Deportations have continued under the Obama Administration. The Haitian Protection Act of 2009 (H.R. 144), a bill that would require the Secretary of Homeland Security to designate Haiti as a country whose qualifying nationals may be eligible for temporary protected status was introduced January 6, 2009.

Another issue of immediate concern to Congress is likely to involve an effort to ensure that free fair, and safe elections are held for the Haitian Senate runoff races on June 21, 2009. As discussed in the "Political Background" section above, tensions remains over the exclusion of former President Jean-Bertrand Aristide's Fanmi Lavalas party from the elections on technical grounds.

Congress may once again take up debt relief for Haiti. In the 110th Congress the House passed an amendment to the Jubilee Act [H.Amdt. 993 to H.R. 2634] in April 2008 recommending immediate cancellation of Haiti's outstanding debts to multilateral institutions). Much of Haiti's $1.7 billion foreign debt is owed to multilateral institutions.

LEGISLATION IN THE 111TH CONGRESS

P.L. 111-8. In the Omnibus Appropriations Act, 2009, sec. 7045(b) deals expressly with Haiti, stating that (1) the Government of Haiti shall be eligible to purchase defense articles and services under the Arms Export Control for the Coast Guard; (2) of the funds appropriated by this Act under Title III, Bilateral Economic Assistance, and Title IV, International Security Assistance, not less than $251.1 26 million shall be made available for assistance for Haiti; and (3) none of the funds made available by this Act under the heading 'International Narcotics Control and Law Enforcement' may be used to transfer excess weapons, ammunition or other lethal property of an agency of the U .S. Government to the Government of Haiti for use by the Haitian National Police until the Secretary of State reports to the Committees on Appropriations that any members of the Haitian National Police who have been credibly alleged to have committed serious crimes, including drug trafficking and violations of internationally recognized human rights, have been suspended.

The omnibus act contains several other provisions related to Haiti as well. For the federal prison system, up to $20 million shall remain available until expended for expenses authorized by section 501(c) of the Refugee Education Assistance Act of 1980 (8 U.S.C. 1522 note), for the care and security in the United States of Haitian [and Cuban] entrants. International Military Education and Training funds for Haiti may only be provided through the regular notification procedures of the Committees on Appropriations and any such notification must include a detailed description of the proposed activities. No Foreign Military Financing Program funds may be made available for Haiti, except pursuant to the regular notification procedures of the Committees on Appropriations. None of the funds appropriated under Title 1 II—Bilateral Economic Assistance; Title IV—International Security Assistance; Title V—Multilateral Assistance; or Title VI—Export and Investment Assistance—may be obligated or expended for assistance for Haiti, except through the regular notification procedures of the Committees on Appropriations. Signed into law March 11, 2009.

H.Con.Res. 17. Expressing the sense of Congress with regard to providing humanitarian assistance to countries of the Caribbean devastated by Hurricanes Gustav and Ike and Tropical Storms Fay and Hanna.. Introduced and referred to the House Committee on Foreign Affairs January 9, 2009.

H.R. 144. The Haitian Protection Act of 2009 would require the Secretary of Homeland Security to designate Haiti as a country whose qualifying nationals may be eligible for temporary protected status. Introduced January 6, 2009; referred to the House Judiciary Committee's Subcommittee on Immigration, Citizenship, Refugees, Border Security, and International Law February 9, 2009.

H.R. 264. The Save America Comprehensive Immigration Act of 2009 would amend the Immigration and Nationality Act (INA) to provide increased protections and eligibility for family- sponsored immigrants, including to authorize adjustment of status for certain nationals or citizens of Haiti. Introduced January 7, 2009, referred to House Judiciary; House Homeland Security; House Oversight and Government Reform Committees; referred to the Subcommittee on Immigration, Citizenship, Refugees, Border Security, and International Law February 9, 2009.

H.R. 331. Would establish a Congressional Independent Commission to examine the U.S. government's role in the February 2004 coup d'etat in the Republic of Haiti. Would terminate the Commission 60 days after submission of its final report to Congress and the President. Introduced and referred to the House Committee on Foreign Affairs January 8, 2009.

H.R. 416. Would authorize the Secretary of State to establish the Shirley Chisholm United States- Caribbean Educational Exchange Program under which scholars and secondary, undergraduate, graduate, and post-graduate students from communities demonstrating the greatest need within certain Caribbean countries, including Haiti, would attend U.S. schools and participate in activities designed to promote a greater understanding of U .S. values and culture. Students would be expected to invest the knowledge and experiences they gain in the United States back into CARICOM (Caribbean Community and Common Market) countries. Would also authorize the Secretary, through the United States Agency for International Development (USAm), to establish a program to improve primary and secondary education in such countries by enhancing teacher training, strengthening curriculum and instructional materials, and assisting improvements in school management and public administration of education. Introduced and referred to the House Committee on Foreign Affairs January 9, 2009.

H.R. 417. The Next Steps for Haiti Act of 2009 would authorize the Director of Foreign Assistance, in consultation with the government of Haiti and Haitian civil society organizations, to establish the Haiti Professional Exchange Program to assign qualified Haitian Americans and others to provide technical assistance to help Haiti improve in areas vital to its growth and development, including education, energy, environment, health care, infrastructure, security, transportation, and disaster preparedness. Directs the Secretary of State to implement a student loan forgiveness program for program participants. Introduced and referred to the House Committee on Foreign Affairs January 9, 2009.

H.R. 1567. The Haitian Refugee Immigration Fairness Act (HRIFA) Improvement Act of 2009 would amend the 1998 HRIFA to (1) require determinations with respect to children to be made using the age and status of an individual on October 21, 1998 (enactment date of the HRIFA of 1998); (2) permit an application based upon child status to be filed by a parent or guardian if the child is present in the United States on such filing date; and (3) include document fraud among the grounds of inadmissibility which shall not preclude an otherwise qualifying Haitian alien from permanent resident status adjustment. It would also permit new status adjustment applications to be filed for a limited time period. Introduced March 17, 2009, referred to the House Judiciary Committee's Subcommittee on Immigration, Citizenship, Refugees, Border Security, and International Law on April 27, 2009.

S. 730. The Affordable Footwear Act of 2009 would amend the Caribbean Basic Economic Recovery Act to provide footwear imported directly from Haiti into the United States with the same preferential treatment that is provided to certain imported footwear under the Dominican Republic-Central America-United States Free Trade Agreement. Introduced and referred to the Senate Committee on Finance on March 26, 2009.

S. 1183. The Haiti Reforestation Act of 2009 would authorize the Secretary of Agriculture to provide assistance to the Government of Haiti to end within 5 years the deforestation in Haiti and restore within 30 years the extent of tropical forest cover in existence in Haiti in 1990. Introduced and referred to the Senate Committee on Foreign Relations June 4, 2009.

ENACTED LEGISLATION IN THE 110TH CONGRESS

P.L. 110-161. FY2008 Consolidated Appropriations Act. Division J includes the provision of not less than $201.5 million in total economic and military assistance to Haiti. The act provides that the Government of Haiti is eligible to purchase defense articles for the Coast Guard; states that IMP funds and FMF may only be provided to Haiti through the regular notification procedures; and includes a restriction on certain INCLE funding to Haiti. The joint explanatory statement to the act recommends providing $5 million to support USAID's watershed reforestation program in Haiti. Introduced on June 18, 2007 as the State Department Foreign Operations and Related Agencies Appropriations Act, H.R. 2764. The House Appropriations Committee issued its report on the bill, H.Rept. 110-197, on June 18, and the House passed the bill on June 22. The Senate Appropriations Committee approved its version of the bill, S.Rept. 110-128, on June 28, and the Senate passed it on September 6, approving the same level of total funding as the House bill. On December 17, 2007, H.R. 2764 became the vehicle for the FY2008 Consolidated Appropriations Act, with Division J providing for foreign aid appropriations. The bill was signed into law on December 26, 2007.

P.L. 110-181. Section 1023 of the National Defense Authorization Act for Fiscal Year 2008 requires the President to submit a report on counternarcotics assistance for the government of Haiti within 120 days of the enactment of this law. The report is to provide a description and assessment of the counternarcotics assistance provided to the Government of Haiti by the Departments of Defense, State, Homeland Security, and Justice; (2) A description and assessment of any impediments to increasing counternarcotics assistance to the Government of Haiti; (3) An assessment of the potential for the provision of counternarcotics assistance for the Government of Haiti through the United Nations Stabilization Mission in Haiti. Signed into law January 28, 2008.

P.L. 110-329. The Consolidated Security, Disaster Assistance, and Continuing Appropriations Act, 2009 was a FY2009 continuing resolution that continued funding at FY2008 levels through March 6, 2009. Introduced on June 8, 2007, it was signed into law on September 30, 2008.

P.L. 110-252. In the Supplemental Appropriations Act, 2008, Sec. 1407 states that $65 million in International Narcotics Control and Law Enforcement (INCLE), Foreign Military Financing Program (FMF), Nonproliferation, Anti-Terrorism, Demining and Related Programs, and Economic Support Funds, may be made available for assistance to Central America, Haiti, and the Dominican Republic only to combat drug trafficking and related violence and organized crime, and for judicial reform, institution building, anti-corruption, rule of law activities, and maritime security, providing that $2.5 million in INCLE funds shall be made available for assistance for Haiti, and that none of the funds shall be made available for budget support or as cash payments. Requires the Secretary of State to submit a detailed spending plan of those funds within 45 days of the bill's enactment.

Fifteen percent of the INCLE and FMF funds for Haiti may not be obligated until the Secretary of State reports in writing to the Committees on Appropriations that the government is 1) establishing police complaints commissions with authority and independence to receive complaints and carry out effective investigations; (2) implementing reforms to improve the capacity and ensure the independence of the judiciary; and (3) investigating and prosecuting members of the federal police and military forces who have been credibly alleged to have committed violations of human rights. Signed into law June 30, 2008.

P.L. 110-246. The HOPE II Act, or the second Haitian Hemispheric Opportunity through Partnership Encouragement Act, is Title XV of the Food, Conservation, and Energy Act of 2008, or farm bill. The law expands trade preferences for U.S. imports of Haitian apparel first provided in the 2006 version of the HOPE Act (P.L. 109-432, Title V). It was enacted over veto into law on June 18, 2008.

ENACTED LEGISLATION IN THE 109TH CONGRESS

P.L. 109-13. Emergency Supplemental Appropriations Act for Defense, the Global War on Terror, and Tsunami Relief, for the fiscal year ending September 30, 2005. Makes $20 million in Economic Support Funds available for Haiti, of which $2.5 million should be made available for criminal case management, case tracking, and the reduction of pre-trial detention in Haiti, notwithstanding any other provision of law. Introduced March 11, 2005 (H.Rept. 109-72), signed into law May 11, 2005.

P.L. 109-53. Dominican Republic-Central America-United States Free Trade Agreement Implementation Act. Contains a side letter indicating the Administration's intent to work with Congress to allow benefits available under the Caribbean Basin Trade Partnership Act for articles co-produced by Haiti and the Dominican Republic to continue once CAFTA is implemented. Introduced June 23, 2005 (H.Rept. 109-182); passed Senate 54-45 June 30; signed into law August 2, 2005.

P.L. 109-95. Amends the Foreign Assistance Act of 1961 to provide assistance for basic care for orphans and other vulnerable children in developing countries. Introduced March 17, 2005. Signed into law November 8, 2005.

P.L. 109-102. Department of State, Foreign Operations and Related Programs Appropriations Act, 2006. International Military Education and Training funds and Foreign Military Financing may only be provided to Haiti through the regular notification procedures. Section 549 makes available for Haiti (1) $20 million from Child Survival and Health Programs Fund; (2) $30 million from Development Assistance; (3) $50 million from Economic Support Fund; (4) $15 million from International Narcotics Control and Law Enforcement; (5) $1 million from Foreign Military Financing Program; and (6) $215,000 from International Military Education and Training. It also continues to allow the government of Haiti to purchase defense articles and services under the Arms Export Control Act for the Coast Guard. Section 549 (c) prohibits any 'International Narcotics Control and Law Enforcement' funds from being used to transfer excess weapons, ammunition, or other lethal property of an agency of the United States government to the government of Haiti for use by the Haitian National Police until the Secretary of State certifies to the Committees on Appropriations that (1) the United Nations Mission in Haiti (MINUSTAH) has carried out the vetting of the senior levels of the Haitian National Police and has ensured that those credibly alleged to have committed serious crimes, including drug trafficking and human rights violations, have been suspended; and (2) the Transitional Haitian National Government is cooperating in a reform and restructuring plan for the Haitian National Police and the reform of the judicial system as called for in United Nations Security Council Resolution 1608 adopted on June 22, 2005. Introduced June 24, 2005, referred to House and Senate Committees on Appropriations (H.Rept. 109-152; S.Rept. 109-96). Signed into law November 14, 2005.

The conference report expresses concern about members of the Haitian National Police or other individuals unlawfully using weapons, ammunition, and other lethal materiel that has been provided or sold by the United States Government and therefore requires the certification included in Section 549(c). The conferees understand that investigations into extrajudicial killings and other alleged incidents of human rights abuses by the police were currently underway but were severely limited by the lack of investigative capacity within the HNP. The conferees request that not later than 60 days after the date of enactment of this act, the State Department report to the appropriate congressional committees the findings of these investigations, including information on whether any United States-supplied or provided weapon or ammunition was used during those incidents. Directs the Secretary of State to submit a report to the Committees on Appropriations within 30 days of enactment of the act which (1) describes in detail the steps taken by the Haitian Transitional Government and the United Nations Stabilization Mission to provide adequate security to permit free and fair elections with broad based participation by all political parties, and to demobilize, disarm and reintegrate armed groups, and (2) provides an assessment of the effectiveness of such steps. Conference report (H.Rept. 109-265) agreed to in House 358-39, November 4, 2005.

P.L. 109-108. Departments of Commerce and Justice, Science and Related Agencies Appropriations Act, 2006. Provides that an amount not to exceed $20 million shall remain available until expended to make payments in advance for grants, contracts and reimbursable agreements, and other expenses authorized by Section 501(c) of the Refugee Education Assistance Act of 1980, for the care and security in the United States of Haitian (and Cuban) entrants. Introduced June 10, 2005. H.Rept. 109-118; S.Rept. 109-88; conference report (H.Rept. 109-272). Signed into law November 22, 2005.

P.L. 109-162. Violence Against Women and Department of Justice Reauthorization Act of 2005. Amends Violence Against Women Act of 2002, provides for aliens or children of aliens who qualify for relief under the Haitian Refugee Immigration Fairness Act of 1998 to petition for certain protections of battered and trafficked immigrants. Introduced July 22, 2005. H.Rept. 109- 233. Signed into law January 5, 2006.

P.L. 109-234. Emergency Supplemental Appropriations Act for Defense, the Global War on Terror, and Hurricane Recovery, 2006. Provides an additional $22.5 million for Haiti. Includes $5 million in Child Survival and Health funds and $17.5 million in Economic Support Funds for police and judicial reform programs and job creation programs. Introduced March 13, 2006. Signed into law June 15, 2006.

P.L. 109-432. The HOPE Act, or the Haitian Hemispheric Opportunity through Partnership Encouragement Act of 2006 (H.R. 6142), was incorporated into the Tax Relief and Health Care Act of 2006 as Title V. Allows duty-free entry to specified apparel articles 50% of which were made and/or assembled in Haiti, the United States, or a country that is either a beneficiary of a U.S. trade preference program, or party to a U.S. free trade agreement (for the first three years; the percentage would be higher after that). Requires ongoing Haitian compliance with certain conditions, including making progress toward establishing a market-based economy, the rule of law, elimination of trade barriers, economic policies to reduce poverty, a system to combat corruption, and protection of internationally recognized worker rights. It also stipulates that Haiti not engage in activities that undermine U.S. national security or foreign policy interests, or in gross violations of human rights. Introduced, referred to House Committee on Ways and Means September 21, 2006. Signed into law December 20, 2006.

REFERENCES

[1] Ugo Fasano, “Haiti's Economic, Political Turnaround,” IMF Survey Magazine: Countries & Regions, Sept. 17, 2007; and World Bank, “Haiti Country Brief,” Sept. 2008, at http://go.worldbank.org/55NM6XlVQ0. See also, “Remarks by United Nations Secretary-General Ban Ki-Moon at a High-Level Donor Conference on Haiti (as released by the UN),” and “Statement by Ambassador Susan E. Rice, United States Permanent Representative to the United Nations, in the UN Security Council (as released by the US Mission to the UN in New York,” Federal News Service, April 21, 2009.

[2] “Rural Haitian Children Starving,” *Associated Press*, Nov. 2 1,2008.

[3] Mike Blanchfield, "In recession, Haitians abroad send less money home," *Canwest News Service*, Mar. 17, 2009.

[4] World Bank, "Income Distribution, Inequality, and Those Left Behind," *in Global Economic Prospects 2007: Managing the Next Wave of Globalization*, p. 83. December 1, 2006.

[5] For further information, see CRS Report RL34029, *Haiti's Development Needs and a Statistical Overview of Conditions of Poverty*, by Maureen Taft-Morales and Demond Alexander Drummer; for background on the 2004-2007 strategy, see CRS Report RL33 156, *Haiti: International Assistance Strategy for the Interim Government and Congressional Concerns*, by Maureen Taft-Morales.

[6] Growth and Poverty Reduction Strategy Paper available at http://siteresources.worldbank.org/INTHAITIINFRENCH/ Resources/HaitiDSNCRPEnglish.pdf.

[7] For further information, see CRS Report RS22975, *Haiti: Post-Hurricane Conditions and Assistance*, by Maureen Taft-Morales and Mark P. Sullivan.

[8] *Le Rapport d'Evaluation des Besoins Apres Desastre Cyclones Fay, Gustav, Hanna et Ike (Haiti Post-Disaster Needs Assessment, PDNA),* Prepared for the Government of the Republic of Haiti with the support of the World Bank, the United Nations System, and the European Commission, November 2008. Author's translation. Available in French at http://gfdrr.org/docs/Haiti_PDNA_2008.pdf.

[9] Information on the donors conference, including documents and a chart of donor pledges, is available at [http://events.iadb.org/calendar/eventDetail.aspx? source=press&lang=en&id=525].

[10] "Haiti: a New Paradigm" is available at http://idbdocs.iadb.org/WSDocs/ getDocument.aspx?DOCNUM=1942794].

[11] "Robert B. Zoellick at Conference on Haiti's Social and Economic Development-Remarks by Robert B. Zoellick, President, the World Bank," *ENP Newswire*, April 16, 2009.

[12] See for example, Robert Maguire, "Paul Collier's Report on Economic Security in Haiti," March 2009. Focal Point, Vol. 8, Issue 2.

[13] "Haiti: UN Council Mission reports strides in security, worrisome poverty," *States News Service*, Mar. 19, 2009.

[14] Paul Collier, "Haiti: From Natural Catastrophe to Economic Security, A Report for the Secretary-General of the United Nations," Jan. 2009, available at http://www.securitycouncilreport.org

[15] Mike Blanchfield, "In recession, Haitians abroad send less money home," *Canwest News Service*, Mar. 17, 2009.

[16] "Haiti: MINUSTAH to Stay on for 2 to 3 Years," Latinnews Daily, Mar. 13, 2006

[17] Jonathan M. Katz, "Largest UN force in Haiti to focus on development," *Associated Press*, April 25, 2009.

[18] Travel warning as of June 17, 2009, from [http://travel.state.gov/travel/cis_pa_tw/ tw/tw_917.html].

[19] For more information see CRS Report RL34687, *The Haitian Economy and the HOPE Act*, by J. F.

In: U.S. Involvement in Political, Economic and Social … ISBN: 978-1-61209-781-7
Editor: Allen P. Lowell

Chapter 8

CHILE: POLITICAL AND ECONOMIC CONDITIONS AND U.S. RELATIONS

Peter J. Meyer

ABSTRACT

Following a violent coup against democratically elected Marxist President Salvador Allende in 1973, Chile experienced 17 years of military rule under General Augusto Pinochet before reestablishing its elected civilian democracy in 1990. A center-left coalition of parties known as the Concertación has governed Chile for the nearly two decades since the end of the dictatorship. The coalition has enacted a number of constitutional changes to strengthen civilian control of the military and to undertake the prosecution of those alleged to be responsible for human rights violations during the Pinochet-era. Chile has made significant economic progress under the Concertación's free market economic policies and moderate social programs, which have produced notable economic growth and considerable reductions in poverty.

Current President Michele Bachelet has faced a number of challenges since her 2006 election. Widespread demonstrations over education, increased militancy by indigenous groups, and opposition control of the legislature have hindered President Bachelet's ability to govern. The global financial crisis is President Bachelet's latest challenge, though the government's timely decision to save recent fiscal surpluses has allowed Chile to pursue counter-cyclical policies and minimize the effects of the economic downturn. The government will likely spend much of 2009 coping with the effects of the financial crisis while political parties prepare for the December presidential and legislative elections.

Chile has enjoyed close relations with the United States since its transition back to democracy. Both countries have emphasized similar priorities in the region, designed to strengthen democracy, improve human rights, and advance free trade. Chile and the United States have also maintained strong commercial ties, which have become more extensive since the bilateral free trade agreement between them entered into force in 2004. Additionally, U.S. officials have expressed appreciation for Chile's leadership and moderating influence in a region increasingly characterized by political unrest and anti-American populism.

Political and Economic Background

Allende Era

Chile declared independence from Spain in 1810, but did not achieve full independence until 1818. By 1932, Chile had established a mass electoral democracy, which endured until 1973. During much of this period, Chile was governed by presidents who pursued import-substitution industrialization (ISI), the expansion of the welfare state, and other statist economic policies. These policies were expanded following the election of Eduardo Frei of the Christian Democratic Party (PDC) in 1964. Frei's government took majority ownership of the copper mines, redistributed land, and improved access to education. Despite these actions, some Chileans felt more radical policies were needed.

In 1970, Salvador Allende, a Socialist and the leader of the Popular Unity coalition, was elected president. Allende accelerated and furthered the changes of the previous administration by fully nationalizing firms, expanding land reform, and generally socializing the economy. While Allende's supporters pushed him to move more quickly, the political center, represented by the PDC, joined with the parties of the right to block Popular Unity initiatives in the legislature.

This ideological difference prevented the Chilean government from addressing the faltering economy and served to further radicalize supporters on both ends of Chile's already polarized society. When the situation continued to deteriorate following the indecisive 1973 legislative elections, the military intervened [1].

Pinochet Era

On September 11, 1973, the Chilean military, under the control of General Augusto Pinochet, deposed the Allende government in a violent coup and quickly consolidated control of the country. The military junta closed Congress, censored the media, declared political parties in recess, and regarded the organized left as an internal enemy of the state. Within the first few months of military rule, over 1,200 people in Chile were killed or disappeared for political reasons, nearly 20,000 were imprisoned, and many of them were tortured. By the end of the dictatorship in 1990, the number of killed or disappeared had risen to at least 2,279 and the number of imprisoned and tortured is said to have exceeded 30,000 [2]. General Pinochet emerged as the figurehead of the junta soon after the coup and won a tightly controlled referendum to institutionalize his regime in 1978. Pinochet reversed decades of statist economic policies by rapidly implementing a series of changes that liberalized trade and investment, privatized firms, and dismantled the welfare state. Pinochet won another tightly controlled referendum in 1980, which approved the Constitution that continues to govern Chile today. The new constitution called for a plebiscite to take place in 1988 in which Chileans would have the opportunity to reelect Pinochet to another 8-year term or reject him in favor of contested elections. Although the Chilean economy enjoyed a period of rapid economic growth between 1976 and 1981, a banking crisis from 1981 to 1984 sparked widespread protests [3]. Following these initial demonstrations, Chilean civil society groups became more active in criticizing the policies of the Pinochet regime. At the same time, political parties began to reemerge to challenge the government. In 1988, several civil society groups and political parties formed a coalition in opposition to Pinochet's reelection. In the plebiscite, 55% of the Chilean people voted against another 8-year term for Pinochet, triggering the election campaign of 1989 [4].

Return to Democracy

The 1989 elections created the political dynamics that prevail in Chile today. Two major coalitions of parties were formed to contest the elections. The center-left "Coalition of Parties for Democracy," or Concertación, united 17 groups that were opposed to the Pinochet dictatorship. The major parties in the coalition were the centrist PDC and the center-left Radical Party (PR), Social Democratic Party (PSD) and Party for Democracy (PPD), which was created by Socialists in 1987 to circumvent the Pinochet regime's ban on Marxist parties. The center-right "Democracy and Progress" coalition included the center-right National Renovation (RN) and the rightist Independent Democratic Union (UDI). A third coalition, the "Broad Party of the Socialist Left," was composed of leftist parties unwilling to participate in the Concertación, including the Communist Party (PC). Patricio Alwyn, a Christian Democrat and the candidate of the Concertación, won the presidency with 55% of the vote and the Concertación won majorities in the Chamber of Deputies and among the elected members of the Senate [5].

The Concertación coalition has governed Chile continuously since the transition to democracy and has undergone few changes. The coalition is now composed of the PDC, the PPD, the Socialist Party (PS), which officially began contesting elections as a part of the Concertación in 1993, and the Radical Social Democratic Party (PRSD), which was created through a merger of the PR and PSD in 1994. Eduardo Frei Ruiz-Tagle of the PDC was elected president in 1993, followed by Ricardo Lagos of the PPD in 1999, and Michelle Bachelet of the PS in 2006. Concertación governments have pushed through a number of constitutional reforms that strengthened civilian control over the military, eliminated the institution of unelected senators, and reduced presidential terms from 6 years to 4. They have been unable to eliminate the binomial election system, which has historically inflated conservative representation as a result of two-member districts that require a coalition to win by 2-1 margins in order to secure both seats [6]. Although the center-right coalition has never won the presidency, it gained control of both legislative houses for the first time in 2008. It has undergone a number of name changes, most recently becoming the "Alliance for Chile," or Alianza. The leftist coalition that includes the PC is now called "Together We Can Do More" (JPM), and has never elected a Member of Congress.

All of the Concertación administrations have generally maintained the open economic policies of the Pinochet regime and promoted export-led development through their pursuit of free trade agreements and encouragement of new export sectors such as forestry products, salmon, fresh fruit, wine, and methanol. Chile now has over 50 bilateral or regional trade agreements, more than any other country, and has established a diverse economy much less reliant on its traditional copper exports [7]. Concertación administrations have also implemented some redistribution policies to address poverty and inequality in Chile. Although income distribution remains virtually unchanged since the dictatorship, economic growth and the social programs of the Concertación have been successful in reducing poverty.

The percentage of Chileans living in poverty fell from 39% in 1990 to 13.7% in 2006. The World Bank classifies Chile as an upper middle income developing country based on its 2007 per capita income of $8,350 [8]. Chile is also the only country in Latin America and the Caribbean on pace to meet all eight of the United Nations (UN) Millennium Development Objectives by 2015 [9].

Recent Political and Economic Developments

2005 Presidential and Legislative Elections

The most recent presidential and legislative elections were held in December 2005. Michelle Bachelet, the Concertación candidate for president and a member of the PS, won 45.9% of the first round vote. The Alianza split its vote, with the RN's Sebastián Piñera taking 25.2% and Joaquín Lavín of the UDI winning 23.2%. Since no candidate won a majority, a run-off election was held in January of 2006 in which Bachelet defeated Piñera 53.5% to 46.5%. Bachelet is the first female president in Chile's history. The Concertación also won majorities in both legislative houses, with 65 of the 120 seats in the Chamber of Deputies and 20 of the 38 seats in the Senate [10]. As a result of the 2005 constitutional reform that eliminated the institution of unelected senators, the Concertación established true majorities in both legislative houses for the first time.

Loss of Concertación Control over Legislature

The Concertación has struggled in the legislature since the 2005 election. A number of corruption scandals involving missing public funds and falsified election campaign financial reports hit the coalition in late 2006. These scandals led to the Concertación losing two deputies to corruption charges, one from the PPD and one from the PS. Soon after, the PPD expelled one of the party's founders, Deputy Jorge Schaulsohn, for accusing the Concertación of having a culture of corruption. This expulsion led to two other high profile members of the party, Deputy Javier Etcheberry and Senator Fernando Flores, leaving the party and the Concertación. Senator Flores and Deputy Schaulsohn have since created a new party, Chile Primero [11].

In November 2007, President Bachelet requested a new public subsidy for the failing Transantiago transportation system. Senator Adolfo Zaldívar of the PDC joined with Senator Flores, and the senators of the Alianza to defeat the proposal. The PDC expelled Senator Zaldívar from the party for his lack of party discipline on an issue of importance to the ruling coalition, leading 5 deputies from Zaldivar 's faction of the PDC to leave the party and the Concertacíon [12].

After all of the corruption charges, expulsions, and resignations, the Concertación was left with only 56 of the 120 seats in the Chamber of Deputies and 18 of the 38 seats in the Senate [13]. The Alianza reached an agreement with the unaffiliated members of the Senate to make Senator Zaldívar the Senate President in 2008 in exchange for making a member of the Alianza the Senate President in 2009. The Chamber of Deputies decided to allow the Concertación to remain in control of the Presidency in 2008 but hand control to the Alianza in

2009 [14]. In March 2009, Jovino Novoa—a member of the UDI and a controversial figure who served as general sub- secretary in the Pinochet government from 1979 to 1 982—was elected president of the Senate and Rodrigo Alvarez, also of the UDI, was elected president of the Chamber of Deputies. This is the first time that the Alianza has had control of both houses since the transition to democracy.

2008 Municipal Elections

In the municipal elections held on October 26, 2008, Chileans overwhelmingly voted for a change of direction, with more than half of the country's 345 mayors being replaced. For the first time, the Concertación split into two smaller coalitions to contest council seats, the Democratic Concertación, composed of the PDC and PS, and the Progressive Concertación, consisting of the PPD and the PRSD. The four parties contested mayoral races as a single coalition. The Alianza, JPM, and "For a Clean Chile"—a new coalition that included Chile First, the Regional Party of Independents (PRI), and the Ecological Party—also took part in the elections.

Although the Concertación won more council and mayoral seats than the Alianza, the Alianza won a larger share of the national vote than the Concertación for the first time. The Alianza won 40.5% of the vote with 38.4% going to the Concertación, 6.4% to JPM, 4% to For a Clean Chile, and 10% to independents. When considering only votes for council seats, the Democratic Concertación took 27.9% of the national vote and the Progressive Concertación took 17.3% [15].

2009 Presidential and Legislative Elections

Presidential and legislative elections will take place on December 13, 2009. Since presidents are ineligible to serve consecutive terms in Chile, President Bachelet will not be running for reelection. Half of the seats in the Senate and the entire Chamber of Deputies will also be up for election. Some analysts believe the 2008 municipal election results suggest that the Alianza is in a strong position while the Concertación is weaker than it has been at any point since the return to democracy [16]. With Pinochet gone, democracy consolidated, and human rights violations being prosecuted, a number of observers—both within and outside the Concertación—believe there is no longer a common purpose holding the coalition together [17] Others contend that the Chilean left may well unite behind the Concertación presidential candidate in the event of a second round runoff and that the coalition's prospects for maintaining power are improving as a result of the public's approval of President Bachelet's handling of the economic crisis [18].

A number of analysts consider Sebastián Piñera, a wealthy businessman and the 2005 candidate of the center-right RN, to be the front-runner for the election [19]. Piñera has sought to broaden his political support by creating the "Coalition for Change," which includes several smaller parties, such as Chile Primero, the Christian Humanist Movement, and the Force of the North, in addition to the parties of the Alianza (RN and UDI). He has pledged to generally continue the economic policies of the Concertación while improving education and the efficiency of the state. While most polls continue to show him in the lead, he has drawn considerable criticism as a result of his failure to place all of his financial investments in a blind trust [20].

Observers had expected that President Eduardo Frei (1994-2000), a member of the centrist PDC and the presidential candidate of the ruling Concertación, would be Piñera's main opposition. In April 2009, Frei—who had been endorsed by the PDC, PPD, and PS—defeated Senator José Antonio Gómez of the center-left PRSD 64.6% to 35.4% in the first of nine scheduled Concertación primaries. Since he won by more than 20%, Frei was given the Concertación nomination and was able forgo the rest of the primaries [21]. Frei has sought to capitalize on strong public support for President Bachelet's handling of the economic crisis and contrast himself with Piñera by emphasizing his belief that the state should play a major role in addressing the downturn. He also named a youthful campaign team in hopes of deflecting charges that he represents the political establishment.

Frei and Piñera will face a number of other presidential candidates, all of whom are dissident members of the Concertación. Senator Adolfo Zaldívar—formerly of the PDC—is the candidate of the centrist PRI, Senator Jorge Arrate—formerly of the PS—is the candidate of the leftist JPM, Senator Alejandro Navarro—formerly of the PS—will be the candidate of the leftist Progressive Pole of the Left, and Deputy Marco Enríquez-Ominami of the PS is running as an independent. As previously noted, Zaldivar was expelled from the PDC for his lack of party unity. Arrate and Navarro have criticized the PS for abandoning its principles and advocating centrist policies. Enríquez-Ominami decided to run after the PS refused to hold a presidential primary.

While Zaldivar, Arrate, and Navarro are all polling in the low single digits, support for EnríquezOminami has surged, stunning the Chilean political scene. A June 2009 poll found that Enríquez-Ominami had the support of 26% of Chileans, placing him behind Piñera at 35%, but ahead of Frei at 24% [22]. Enríquez-Ominami is the 35-year-old son of leftwing guerilla Miguel Enríquez— who founded the Movement of the Revolutionary Left and was killed fighting against the Pinochet regime—and the step-son of Carlos Ominami, a PS senator. He claims to represent a younger generation of Chileans that are tired of traditional politicians [23]. While he is generally seen as a leftist—he opposes the Hidroaysén hydroelectric project on environmental grounds, wants to legalize abortion, and would boost education and health spending—Enríquez-Ominami has suggested cutting the top personal income tax rate and partially privatizing state companies. In order to stand as an independent candidate, Enríquez-Ominami will need to resign from the PS and collect 36,037 signatures from non-affiliated voters by July 12, 2009 [24]. If no presidential candidate receives an outright majority, the top two candidates will proceed to a runoff election.

Education Demonstrations

Since the transition to democracy, many Chileans have called on the government to address inequality in the education system that activists contend is a result of Pinochet-era privatization reforms. Despite successive Concertación governments' lack of action, students had high hopes following Bachelet's election since she had based her campaign around themes of social justice. When President Bachelet neglected to even mention education during a state of the nation speech in May 2006, Chilean students organized the largest social demonstrations in the country since the return to democracy. With nearly 75% of the public backing them, students filled the streets, took over schools, and organized rallies that drew as many as 800,000 people [25]. The resulting street violence and near complete shut down of Chile's education system forced President Bachelet to shuffle her cabinet, replacing the education, economy, and interior ministers. President Bachelet also increased education spending and created a commission to consider education reform. The Administration eventually put forward the General Education Law (LGE), which was designed to better regulate the current system. Student groups and teachers unions have protested the new law, saying it fails to address the privatization of education, which they contend is the root problem [26].

Mapuche Activism

Confrontation with the Mapuche population has been a persistent problem for the Bachelet Administration. The Mapuche are Chile's largest indigenous group and comprise approximately 4% of the population or 660,000 of Chile's 16.5 million citizens [27]. They are mainly located in the central and southern regions of Bíobío, Araucanía, Los Ríos, and Los Lagos (See Figure 1 for a map of Chile). The Mapuche have long sought official recognition as a people, protection of indigenous rights, and restoration of full ownership of their ancestral lands. Mapuche groups have pursued these ends through a variety of means. Some pushed for the ratification of convention 169 of the International Labour Organization (ILO) on indigenous rights, which President Bachelet promulgated in September 2008 [28]. Others, such as the Arauco-Malleco Coordinating Committee (CAM), have pursued more militant actions, occupying ancestral Mapuche lands and burning vehicles, machinery, and buildings on them, frequently targeting logging companies. Despite promises from successive Concertación governments to rectify Chile's relationship with its indigenous groups, Mapuche groups maintain that action has been slow, both in terms of the transfer of lands to Mapuche communities and land titling.

CAM has increased its militant actions in recent years, because of its dissatisfaction with the government's efforts on indigenous issues.

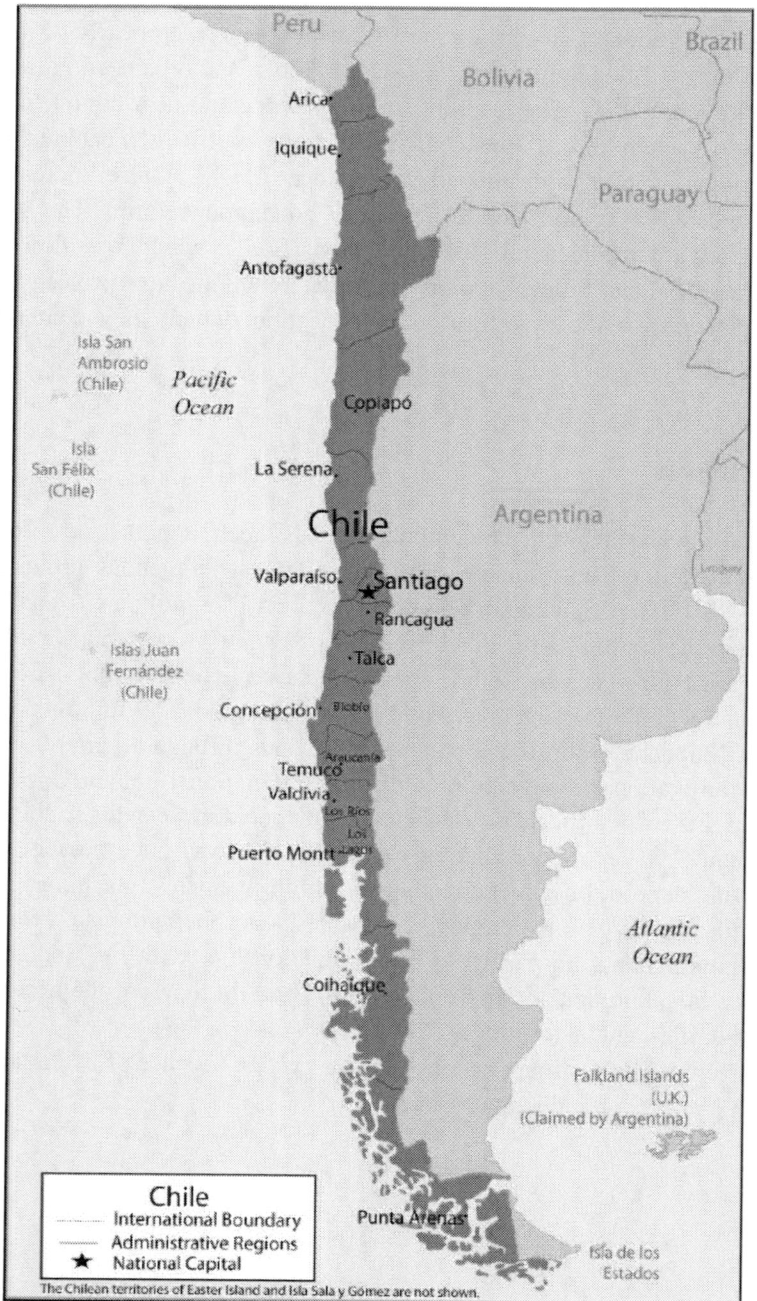

Source: Map Resources. Adapted by CRS Graphics.

Figure 1. Map of Chile.

As a result, the Bachelet Administration has captured and imprisoned many of CAM's leaders. Nonetheless, conservative politicians and media have accused the government of inaction and alleged connections between the Mapuche and foreign terrorist organizations like the Revolutionary Armed Forces of Colombia (FARC) and Basque Homeland and Freedom (ETA) in Spain. The government insists that there is no credible evidence of operational links between these groups, and CAM denies having any foreign ties. Human rights groups have also criticized the Bachelet Administration, accusing Chile's carabineros (police force) of arbitrary arrests, torture, and beatings of Mapuche people and condemning the government's use of Pinochet-era anti-terrorism laws to prosecute Mapuche activists [29]. In April 2009, 130 police officers raided three Mapuche communities, seizing documents and arresting 11 members of CAM in connection to an October 2008 attack on a public prosecutor. While CAM denounced the raid as "extremely violent and abusive," the Chilean government maintained that the operation had been conducted "impeccably" [30].

Human Rights

In recent years, Chile has continued to address human rights violations from the Pinochet era. In September 2005, the Chilean Supreme Court upheld a court of appeals ruling that stripped Pinochet of immunity and allowed him to stand trial for his role in the killing of 119 political dissidents who were found dead in Argentina in 1975. In January 2006, an appeals court again stripped Pinochet of his immunity from prosecution for his role in the killing of two of Allende's bodyguards in 1973. Pinochet was stripped of immunity a third time in September 2006 by Chile's Supreme Court so that he could stand trial for the abuses at the Villa Grimaldi detention center, an infamous center for torture whose victims included President Bachelet. In December 2006, after having several charges dropped because of his failing health (but still under indictment in two human rights cases and on tax evasion), Pinochet died of complications from a heart attack [31]. The Chilean government is currently trying to recover $26 million in public funds that Pinochet allegedly deposited in U.S. banks [32].

Other dictatorship-era officials have also been prosecuted for human rights violations. Former intelligence chief, retired General Manuel Contreras, was sentenced to two life prison terms in July 2008 for organizing the 1974 double assassination of General Carlos Prats and his wife in Buenos Aires, Argentina. Contreras was already imprisoned as a result of convictions stemming from other dictatorship-era crimes, including the 1976 assassination of former Ambassador to the United States, Orlando Letelier and his American associate, Ronni Moffitt, in Washington, D.C. [33]. Sergio Arellano Stark, the commander of the so-called "Caravan of Death" that executed 80 political prisoners of the dictatorship shortly after the coup in 1973, was sentenced to 6 years in prison in October 2008 [34]. In May 2009, two Chileans were arrested in connection to the 1973 torture and execution of Chilean singer-songwriter Victor Jara [35]. In all, over 100 former members of the Chilean military have been convicted for their dictatorship-era crimes [36]. Family members of the disappeared and other human rights advocates continue to push for greater transparency concerning the actions of the dictatorship and for those responsible to be brought to justice.

Energy Challenges

As a result of limited domestic energy resources and increasing demand due to its strong economic growth, Chile has become heavily dependent upon foreign energy imports. Over the past decade, Chilean demand for electricity grew at an average rate of 6% per year [37]. In order to satisfy this demand, primary energy imports increased from 45% to 67% of the total supply between 1990 and 2006. Chile now imports about 99% of its crude oil, 72% of its natural gas, and 92% of its coal [38]. While Chile has tried to secure sufficient energy resources through its open economic policies, its supply has been threatened by a number of regional developments.

In 2004, Argentina cut its natural gas exports to Chile as a result of a domestic energy crisis. Since then, Argentine natural gas exports to Chile have fluctuated considerably, nearly leading to electricity rationing in early 2008 [39].

These export cutbacks have adversely impacted Chilean economic activity and have forced Chile to reconsider its energy options. Chile is now focusing on diversifying both its energy suppliers and supplies. The Chilean government and private firms began developing liquefied natural gas (LNG) terminals in 2006. The first LNG terminal is expected to start operations in central Chile in July 2009. Given the feasibility of establishing power plants close to ports and the diversity of countries that export coal, Chile has begun to increase its reliance on coal-fired power plants. These plants are expected to produce a quarter of all Chilean electricity by 2020, up from 15% at present. Domestic renewable sources of energy are also receiving increased attention. Chile has begun construction on a number of new hydroelectric plants, is studying geothermal and tidal energy potential, and is installing wind farms. A 2008 law requires energy providers to generate 5% of their electricity from renewable sources by 2010 and 10% by 2024 [40].

Global Financial Crisis

The global financial crisis and economic slowdown have taken a toll on Chile's economy. Real gross domestic product (GDP) growth slowed from 5.1% in 2007 to an estimated 3.2% in 2008 [41]. The Santiago Stock Exchange (IPSA), like those in many emerging markets, suffered considerable losses in the second half of 2008. Additionally, the price of copper—which provides 40% of the government's revenues—fell below $2 per pound for the first time in three years in October 2008 [42]. As a result, government earnings from copper fell by 23% in 2008 and total government revenue fell 0.6% for the year [43]. The trend continued into the first quarter of 2009 as Chile experienced its first economic contraction in 10 years. GDP fell by 2.1% and unemployment reached 9.2%. [44].

Nonetheless, Chile's economy has begun to show signs of recovery. The Chilean government invested $20.3 billion (12% of GDP) from fiscal surpluses generated by high copper prices in recent years in two sovereign wealth funds. These funds have allowed the government to pursue counter-cyclical policies and inject liquidity in the financial sector.

In January 2009, President Bachelet announced a $4 billion (2.8% of GDP) economic stimulus package. The plan includes temporary tax cuts for small businesses, increased benefits for poor Chileans, $700 million for infrastructure projects, and $1 billion for Codelco, the state-owned copper company. The independent Chilean Central Bank has also cut the benchmark interest rate to a record low of 1.25%. [45].

As of May 2009, the IPSA index was up 25% on the year and had recovered to its May 2008 levels. International copper prices have also rebounded, increasing 56% on the year and once again exceeding $2 per pound. The Chilean Central Bank, however, is forecasting an economic contraction of 0.75% for 2009 [46].

CHILE-U.S. RELATIONS

The United States and Chile have enjoyed close relations since Chile's transition back to democracy. The countries maintain strong commercial ties and share common commitments to democracy, human rights, and free trade.

Both countries have demonstrated these commitments by supporting the implementation of the Inter-American Democratic Charter, signing a bilateral free trade agreement, and supporting the proposed Free Trade Area of the Americas (FTAA) [47].

The Obama Administration has described Chile as one the United States' closest allies in the region and Vice President Biden visited the country in March 2009 during his first trip to Latin America [48].

U.S. Assistance

In order to promote economic development and prevent the election of a communist government, the United States provided Chile with extensive assistance during the 1950s and 1960s. President Kennedy made Chile the centerpiece of his "Alliance for Progress," providing the country with $293 million in economic assistance between 1961 and 1963 [49].

Assistance declined following the election of Allende and has generally remained low since then, increasing briefly during the early years of the Pinochet dictatorship and again following the transition to democracy. Chile received $1.4 million in U.S. assistance in FY2008, is scheduled to receive $1.2 million in FY2009, and would receive $2.3 million in FY2010, if Congress funds the Administration's request [50].

The majority of U.S. assistance to Chile is focused on modernizing the Chilean military by improving its capacity to act as a peacekeeping force and its ability to conduct joint operations with the U.S. military. U.S. assistance also goes to programs that deter weapons of mass destruction, improve civilian control over the military, and upgrade military equipment.

The 110th Congress passed the Naval Vessel Transfer Act of 2008 (H.R. 7177, P.L. 110-429, signed into law on October 15, 2008), which contains a provision that authorizes the President to transfer by grant a Kaiser class oiler, Andrew J. Higgins (AO- 190), to the government of Chile.

Free Trade Agreement

The United States and Chile signed a bilateral free trade agreement (FTA) on June 6, 2003. Following the House and Senate passage of the U.S.-Chile Free Trade Implementation Act, President Bush signed the bill into law on September 3, 2003 (P.L. 108-77). The FTA established immediate duty-free treatment for 85% of bilateral trade in consumer and industrial products, increasing market access for both countries [51].

Since the agreement went into force on January 1, 2004, bilateral trade between the United States and Chile has more than tripled, totaling $20.3 billion in 2008. U.S. imports from Chile grew from $3.7 billion in 2003 to $8.1 billion in 2008 while U.S. exports to Chile grew from $2.7 billion in 2003 to $12.1 billion in 2008. The United States was Chile's top source of imports and the second largest destination for Chile's exports while Chile was the 25th largest export market for U.S. goods in 2008 [52].

Regional Leadership

Chile has been an active participant and frequent leader in multilateral engagement at both the regional and global levels. Chile has joined with the United States as part of the multinational peacekeeping force in Haiti since 2004, first as a part of the Multinational Interim Force-Haiti (MIFH) and subsequently as a part of the UN Stabilization Mission in Haiti (MINUSTAH). Chile has committed more human and material resources to MINUSTAH than it has to any previous peacekeeping mission and the country's early presence in the MIFH encouraged a number of other countries in the region to play a role in MINUSTAH [53].

The United States and Chile also worked together as members of the so-called "Group of Friends of Venezuela," to foster discussion between President Hugo Chávez and the political opposition [54]. Chile has taken on the role of regional leader in fora that do not involve the United States as well, such as the emergency summit of the Union of South American Nations (UNASUR) called by President Bachelet in September 2008 in order to resolve the political turmoil in Bolivia.

Table 1. Chilean Political Acronyms

Acronym	Political Organization	Description
CAM	Arauco-Malleco Coordinating Committee	Militant Mapuche organization
JPM	Together We Can Do More	Leftist coalition of parties
PC	Communist Party	Leftist member party of JPM
PDC	Christian Democratic Party	Centrist member party of the Concertación[a]
PPD	Party for Democracy	Center-left member party of the Concertación
PR	Radical Party	Center-left member party of the Concertación at return to democracy
PRI	Regional Party of Independents	Centrist party formed in merger of two regional parties,
PRSD	Radical Social Democratic Party	Center-left member party of the Concertación, merger of PR and PSD
PS	Socialist Party	Center-left member party of the Concertación
PSD	Social Democratic Party	Center-left member party of the Concertación at return to democracy
RN	National Renovation	Center-right member party of the Alianza[b]
UDI	Independent Democratic Union	Rightist member party of the Alianza

Source: Compiled by CRS.

Notes:

[a] The Concertación is a center-left coalition of parties.

[b] The Alianza is a center-right coalition of parties.

Narcotics and Human Trafficking

Although Chile is not a drug producing country, it is increasingly used as a transshipment point for Andean cocaine destined for Europe and, to a lesser extent, the United States. It is also a source for precursor chemicals used in the processing of cocaine. The United States provides support to the Chilean government for anti-narcotics programs focused on police intelligence capabilities, interagency cooperation, anti-money laundering efforts, and maritime security. Through September 2008, Chilean officials had seized 1,421 kilograms of cocaine; 3,200 kilograms of cocaine paste; and 7,087 kilograms of marijuana. Chile is providing regional leadership in counternarcotics as the President of the Inter-American Drug Abuse Control (CICAD) for 2009 [55].

Chile is also a source, transit, and destination country for trafficking in persons for commercial sexual and labor exploitation. The U.S. Department of State's 2008 Trafficking in Persons (TIP) Report states that Chile does not fully comply with the minimum standards for the elimination of trafficking because its statutory framework does not specifically prohibit labor trafficking. Chile made significant efforts to fully comply with the U.S. standards during the 2007-2008 reporting period, however, introducing anti-trafficking legislation, opening a significant number of trafficking investigations, and improving assistance for trafficking victims. As a result, the U.S. Department of State designated Chile a "Tier 2" country [56].

References

[1] *Chile: A Country Study*, ed. Rex A. Hudson, (Washington, D.C.: Library of Congress, 1994).

[2] Report of the National Commission for Truth and Reconciliation, February 1991; Report of the National Commission on Political Imprisonment and Torture, November 2004.

[3] For more information on the Chilean financial crisis and its comparisons to the U.S. financial crisis, see CRS Report RS22961, *The U.S. Financial Crisis: Lessons From Chile*, by J. F. Hornbeck.

[4] Alan Angell & Benny Pollack, "The Chilean Elections of 1989 and the Politics of the Transition to Democracy," *Bulletin of Latin American Research*, Volume 9 (1), 1990.

[5] Ibid. Prior to a 2005 constitutional reform, former presidents served as "senators-for-life" and nine senators were designated by the armed forces and other bodies.

[6] Peter M. Siavelis, "Electoral System, Coalitional Disintegration, and the Future of Chile's Concertación," *Latin American Research Review*, Volume 40 (1), 2005.

[7] Central Intelligence Agency, "World Factbook," September 2008.

[8] World Bank, "World Development Indicators Database," September 2008.

[9] The objectives work toward the goals of eradicating extreme hunger and poverty, achieving universal primary education, promoting gender equality, reducing child mortality, improving maternal health, combating disease, ensuring environmental stability, and developing a global partnership for development; "Chile: Leading the Millennium Objectives League," *Latin American Brazil & Southern Cone Report*, September 2008.

[10] "Chile: Country Report," *Economist Intelligence Unit*, January 2006; February 2006.
[11] "Chile: Concertación Faces Schism," *Latin News Weekly Report*, May 10, 2007.
[12] "Chile: DC Crisis Sets Scene for 2009 Contest," *Latin American Brazil & Southern Cone Report*, December 2007.
[13] "Defections Leave Chile's Ruling Coalition in Precarious Situation," *Latin American Brazil & Southern Cone Report*, January 2008.
[14] "Chile: Zaldívar Assumes Presidency of Senate," *Latin News Weekly Report*, March 19, 2008.
[15] "Chileans Vote for Change," *Latin News Daily*, October 27, 2008.
[16] Benjamin Witte, "Chile: Municipal Elections Show Governing Concertación Suffering Signs of Wear and Tear," *Latin America Data Base NotiSur*, November 21, 2008; "Conservatives Boost Presidential Hopes," *Latin America Monitor Southern Cone*, December 2008; Romain Le Cour Grandmaison "Chile: A Fading Concertación on the Road to Losing the Presidency," *Council on Hemispheric Affairs*, January 29, 2009.
[17] Jack Chang, "Chile's Ruling Coalition Faces Struggles," *McClatchy News Service*, July 17, 2008.
[18] "Concertación Courts Communists," *Latin American Weekly Report*, February 5, 2009; "Bachelet Rings the Changes," *Latin American Weekly Report*, March 19, 2009.
[19] "Chile: Piñera Front-Runner in December Elections," *Oxford Analytica*, June 2, 2009.
[20] Ibid.
[21] "Chile: Frei Seals Victory and Squares Up to Piñera," *Latin American Weekly Report*, April 8, 2009.
[22] The same poll gave Zaldívar 2%, Arrate 1.2% and Navarro 0.5%. "Supera Enríquez-Ominami a Candidato Presidencial Oficialista en Chile," *Agencia Mexicana de Noticias*, June 2, 2009.
[23] "People Profile: Marco Antonio Enríquez-Ominami, Chile," *Latin News Daily*, May 12, 2009.
[24] "Chile's Enríquez-Ominami Surges Past Frei," *Latin News Daily*, June 3, 2009.
[25] Monte Reel, "Chile's Student Activists: A Course in Democracy," *Washington Post*, November 25, 2006.
[26] Andrea Arango, "The Failings of Chile's Education System: Institutionalized Inequality and a Preference for the Affluent," *Council on Hemispheric Affairs*, July 30, 2008.
[27] Central Intelligence Agency, "World Factbook," September 2008.
[28] "Bachelet Makes Gesture to Chile's Indigenous Groups," *Latin News Weekly Report*, September 25, 2008.
[29] "Chile: Bachelet Reacts to Challenge By Radical Activists," *Latin News Security & Strategic Review*, January 2008; Benjamin Witte, "Chile Dusts Off Pinochet-Era Terror Law," *Latin America Data Base NotiSur*, March 13, 2009.
[30] "Chile Cracks Down on Violent Mapuche Militants," *Latin News Daily*, April 22, 2009.
[31] Jack Epstein, "Augusto Pinochet: 1915-2006/Chilean Leader's Regime Left Thousands of 'Disappeared'," *San Francisco Chronicle*, December 11, 2006.
[32] "Negociaría Estado Chileno Con Bancos Que Ocultaron Dinero de Pinochet," *Agencia Mexicana de Noticias*, March 15, 2009.
[33] Helen Hughes & Jack Chang, "Ex-Chilean Intelligence Chief Gets 2 Life Sentences," *Miami Herald*, July 1, 2008.

[34] "Condenan a General Chileno por Crímenes de 'Caravana de la Muerte'," *Agencia Mexicana de Noticias*, October 15, 2008.
[35] "Chile Arrests 2 in Murder of Singer Victor Jara," *EFE News Service*, May 26, 2009.
[36] "Familiares de Víctimas de Pinochet Mantienen Viva Demanda de Justicicia," *Agencia Mexicana de Noticias*, September 5, 2008.
[37] "Chile: Medium-Term Electricity Supply Looks Secure," *Oxford Analytica*, April 23, 2009.
[38] Oscar Landerretche, "Chile's Choices: Maintaining Growth and Securing Supply," in *Energy and Development in South America: Conflict and Cooperation*, eds. Cynthia J. Arnson et al., 27-34, (Washington, D.C.: Woodrow Wilson International Center for Scholars, 2008).
[39] "Chile: Medium-Term Electricity Supply Looks Secure," *Oxford Analytica*, April 23, 2009.
[40] "Chile: Country Report," *Economist Intelligence Unit*, May 2009.
[41] "Ministro Chileno: Presupuesto Fiscal Sólido Pese a Baja Cobre," *Dow Jones Newswires*, October 22, 2008.
[42] "Country Report: Chile," *Economist Intelligence Unit*, March 2009.
[43] "Chile: GDP May Contract for First Time in Decade," *Oxford Analytica*, May 18, 2009; "Chile: Finance outlook," *Economist Intelligence Unit*, June 1, 2009.
[44] "Chile's Economy: Stimulating," *The Economist*, February 19, 2009; "Chile: Finance outlook," *Economist Intelligence Unit*, June 1, 2009.
[45] "Chile: Finance Outlook," *Economist Intelligence Unit*, June 1, 2009.
[46] For more information on the FTAA, see: CRS Report RS20864, *A Free Trade Area of the Americas: Major Policy Issues and Status of Negotiations*, by J. F. Hornbeck.
[47] Eva Vergara, "EEUU Vuelve a Escuchar a Latinoamérica, Dice Biden en Chile," *Associated Press*, March 28, 2009.
[48] This is the equivalent of $1.6 billion in constant 2006 dollars; U.S. Overseas Loans and Grants (Greenbook) 2006.
[49] U.S. Department of State "FY2010 Congressional Budget Justification for Foreign Operations," May 29, 2009.
[50] For more information on the U.S.-Chile Free Trade Agreement, see: CRS Report RL31144, *The U.S.-Chile Free Trade Agreement: Economic and Trade Policy Issues*, by J. F. Hornbeck.
[51] U.S. Department of Commerce statistics, as presented by *Global Trade Atlas*, 2009.
[52] Enzo Di Nocera García & Ricardo Benavente Cresta, "Chile: Responding to a Regional Crisis," in *Capacity Building for Peacekeeping: The Case of Haiti*, eds. John T. Fishel & Andrés Sáenz, 66-90 (Dulles, VA: Potomac Books, 2007)
[53] Juan Forero, "Friends of Venezuela Are There to Help," *New York Times*, January 31, 2003.
[54] U.S. Department of State Bureau for International Narcotics and Law Enforcement Affairs, "2009 International Narcotics Control Strategy Report (INCSR)," February 27, 2009.
[55] U.S. Department of State Office to Monitor and Combat Trafficking in Persons, "Trafficking in Persons Report," June 2008.

In: U.S. Involvement in Political, Economic and Social … ISBN: 978-1-61209-781-7
Editor: Allen P. Lowell

Chapter 9

U.S.-MEXICO ECONOMIC RELATIONS: TRENDS, ISSUES, AND IMPLICATIONS

M. Angeles Villarreal

ABSTRACT

Mexico has a population of about 110 million people making it the most populous Spanish- speaking country in the world and the third most populous country in the Western Hemisphere. Based on a gross domestic product (GDP) of $1.0 trillion in 2008 (about 7% of U.S. GDP), Mexico has a free market economy with a strong export sector. Economic conditions in Mexico are important to the United States because of the proximity of Mexico to the United States, the close trade and investment interactions, and other social and political issues that are affected by the economic relationship between the two countries.

The United States and Mexico have strong economic ties. An important feature of the relationship is the North American Free Trade Agreement (NAFTA), which has been in effect since 1994. In terms of total trade, Mexico is the United States' third largest trading partner, while the United States ranks first among Mexico's trading partners. In U.S. imports, Mexico ranks third among U.S. trading partners, after China and Canada, while in exports Mexico ranks second, after Canada. The United States is the largest source of foreign direct investment (FDI) in Mexico. These links are critical to many U.S. industries and border communities.

In 2008, about 11% of total U.S. merchandise exports were destined for Mexico and 10% of U.S. merchandise imports came from Mexico. In the same year U.S. exports to Mexico increased almost 10%, while imports from Mexico increased about 3%. For Mexico, the United States is a much more significant trading partner. About 82% of Mexico's exports go to the United States and 50% of Mexico's imports come from the United States. FDI forms another part of the economic relationship between the United States and Mexico. The United States is the largest source of FDI in Mexico. U.S. FDI in Mexico totaled $91.7 billion in 2007. The overall effect of NAFTA on the U.S. economy has been relatively small, primarily because two-way trade with Mexico amounts to less than three percent of U.S. GDP. Major trade issues between Mexico and the United States have involved the access of Mexican trucks to the United States; the access of

Mexican sugar and tuna to the U.S. market; and the access of U.S. sweeteners to the Mexican market.

Over the last decade, the economic relationship between the United States and Mexico has strengthened significantly. The two countries continue to cooperate on issues of mutual concern. On March 23, 2005, the leaders of the United States, Canada, and Mexico met to discuss issues related to North American trade, immigration and defense. After the meeting, the three leaders announced the Security and Prosperity Partnership of North America (SPP), an initiative that is intended to increase cooperation and information sharing in an effort to increase and enhance prosperity in the United States, Canada, and Mexico. In April 2008, the North American leaders held a summit to discuss how they might further advance the goals of the SPP. The three leaders decided that their respective ministers should continue to renew and focus their work in the five SPP priority areas.

INTRODUCTION

Mexico has a population of approximately 110 million people making it the most populous Spanish-speaking country in the world and the third most populous country in the Western Hemisphere (after the United States and Brazil). The bilateral economic relationship with Mexico is among the most important for the United States because of Mexico's proximity and because of the large amount of trade and investment interactions. The most significant feature of the relationship is the North American Free Trade Agreement (NAFTA), through which the United States, Mexico, and Canada form the world's largest free trade area, with about one-third the world's total gross domestic product (GDP).

The United States and Mexico share common interests and are closely tied in areas not directly related to trade and investment. The two countries share a 2,000 mile border and have extensive interconnections through the Gulf of Mexico. There are links through migration and tourism, environment and health concerns, and family and cultural relationships [1]. The economic relationship with Mexico is important to U.S. national interests and to the U.S. Congress for many reasons. As the United States considers free trade initiatives with other Latin American countries, the effects of NAFTA may provide policymakers some indication of how these initiatives might affect conditions in the overall U.S. economy. The 111th Congress will likely maintain an active interest in Mexico on issues related to counternarcotics, migration, trade, and border issues. Comprehensive immigration reform was debated early in the 110th Congress, but the issue was put aside following a failed cloture motion in the Senate on the Comprehensive Immigration Reform Act of 2007 (S. 1348). Immigration reform efforts could be considered once again in the 111th Congress.

This report provides an overview of U.S.-Mexico economic trends, background information on the Mexican economy, the effects of NAFTA on the U.S.-Mexico economic relationship, and major trade issues between the United States and Mexico.

U.S.-MEXICO ECONOMIC TRENDS

The United States and Mexico have strong economic ties. The United States is, by far, Mexico's most important partner in trade and investment, while Mexico is the United States third largest trade partner after China and Canada. Many economists have focused much attention on the ongoing transformation of Mexico into a manufacturing-for-export nation since the late 1980s and the importance of exports to its economy. Exports represent 31% of Mexico's GDP, up from 10% twenty years ago. After oil and gas, most of Mexico's exports are manufactured goods. Over 80% of Mexico's exports are headed to the United States. Mexico's reliance on the United States as a trade partner appears to be diminishing, although slightly. Between 2004 and 2007, the U.S. share of Mexico's total imports decreased from 56% to 50%, while the share of total Mexican exports going to the United States decreased from 89% to 82%. Although Mexican exports to the United States are steadily increasing, Mexico's share of the U.S. market has lost ground since 2002. In 2003, China surpassed Mexico as a supplier of U.S. imports, and Mexico now ranks third, after China and Canada, as a source of U.S. imports. Because over 80% of Mexico's exports are destined for the United States, any change in U.S. demand can have strong economic consequences in Mexican industrial sectors.

The immigration issue has received much attention by political leaders in recent years and it is one that can be linked to the economic situation in Mexico, although it has social and political aspects as well. In March 2008, there were approximately 12 million unauthorized immigrants living in the United States, with 59% from Mexico [2]. Economic conditions in Mexico and other countries, such as poverty and unemployment, are a major factor related to the migration issue. These workers often send money to their families in Mexico to help provide food and shelter.

Worker remittances to Mexico increased from $13.4 billion in 2003 to $24billion in 2007. While Mexico receives the largest amount of remittances in Latin America, remittances comprise a comparatively small share of Mexican national income, accounting for about 3% of Mexico's gross domestic product (GDP) in 2007. The rate of remittance growth slowed to just 1% in 2007, far less than the average annual increase of 19% from 2003 through 2006 [3].

U.S.-Mexico Merchandise Trade

Mexico ranks second among U.S. export markets and is the United States' third largest trading partner in terms of total trade. In 2008, about 11% of total U.S. merchandise exports were destined for Mexico and 10% of U.S. merchandise imports came from Mexico. In the same year U.S. exports to Mexico increased 10.2% while imports from Mexico increased by 7.6%. For Mexico, the United States is a much more significant trading partner. About 82% of Mexico's exports go to the United States and 50% of Mexico's imports come from the United States. Mexico's second largest trading partner is China, accounting for approximately 6% of Mexico's exports and imports [4]. U.S. merchandise trade with Mexico has grown considerably over the last ten years (see Figure 1). Although some of the increase in trade could be attributable to NAFTA, there are other variables that affect trade, such as exchange rates and economic conditions. Mexico's currency crisis of 1995 limited the purchasing power of the Mexican people in the following years and also made products from Mexico less expensive for the U.S. market. Economic factors such as these played a role in the increasing U.S. trade deficit with Mexico which went from a $1.4 billion surplus in 1994 to a $84.8 billion deficit in 2008. U.S. imports from Mexico increased from $85.0 billion in 1997 to

$216.3 billion in 2008, while U.S. exports to Mexico increased from $68.4 billion in 1997 to $131.5 billion in 2007 (see Table 2).

Table 1. Key Economic Indicators for Mexico and the United States
Click here and type the subtitle, or delete this paragraph

	Mexico		United States	
	1998	2008[a]	1998	2008[a]
Population (millions)	97	110	276	304
Nominal GDP ($US billions) [b]	456	1,035	8,747	14,265
GDP, PPP c Basis ($US billions)	917	1,530	8,747	14,265
Per Capita GDP ($US)	4,681	9,410	31,679	46,950
Per Capita GDP in $PPPs	9,426	13,920	31,679	46,950
Total Merchandise Exports (US$ billions)	118	292	682	1,300
Exports as % of GDP [d]	28%	31%	11%	13%
Total Merchandise Imports (US$ billions)	125	309	912	2,100
Imports as % of GDP [d]	30%	33%	13%	18%
Public Debt/GDP	35%	18%	n.a.	

Source: Compiled by CRS based on data from Economist Intelligence Unit (EIU) on-line database.
Notes: Click here and type the notes, or delete this paragraph
[a]. Some figures for 2008 are estimates.
[b]. Nominal GDP is calculated by EIU based on figures from World Bank and World Development Indicators.
[c]. PPP refers to purchasing power parity, which reflects the purchasing power of foreign currencies in U.S.dollars.
[d]. Exports and Imports as % of GDP derived by EIU.

Several studies between 2003 and 2004 on the effects of NAFTA found that trade deficits were largely driven by macroeconomic trends, and, in the case of U.S.-Mexico trade, caused by the respective business cycles in Mexico and the United States [5]. Strong U.S. growth in the 1990s combined with Mexico's deep recession in 1995 were the main factors cited for the large deficits. None of the studies attributed the peso crisis to NAFTA, but to structural misalignments in the Mexican economy combined with political events [6] The leading U.S. import item from Mexico in 2007 was oil and gas, which amounted to $37.93 billion, or 17.5% of total U.S. imports from Mexico (see Table 2). The next leading import items were motor vehicles ($22.02 billion or 10.1% of total); motor vehicle parts ($20.58 or 9.51% of total); audio and video equipment ($17.84 billion or 8.2% of total); and communications equipment ($12.99 billion or 6.0% of total). The leading U.S. export item to Mexico in 2008 was motor vehicle parts, which amounted to $10.06 billion, or 7.6% of total exports to Mexico (see Table 3).

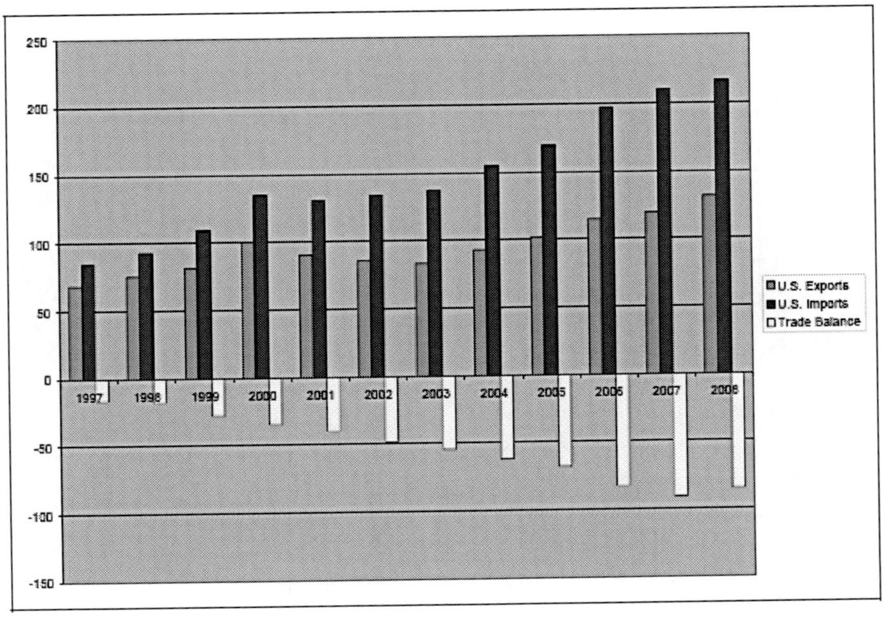

Source: United States International Trade Commission, Interactive Tariff and Trade Data Web. Compiled by CRS.

Figure 1. U.S. Merchandise Trade with Mexico.

The next leading export items were petroleum and coal products ($9.63 billion or 7.3% of total); basic chemicals ($7.16 billion or 5.4% of total); resin, synthetic rubber and products ($5.95 billion or 4.5% of total); and oilseeds and grains ($5.94 billion or 4.5% of total). The U.S. industry with the highest volume of trade (imports and exports) with Mexico is the automotive industry.

Mexico-U.S. Bilateral Foreign Direct Investment Foreign direct investment (FDI) forms another part of the economic relationship between the United States and Mexico. FDI consists of investments in real estate, manufacturing plants, and retail facilities, in which the foreign investor owns 10% or more of the entity. The United States is the largest source of FDI in Mexico. U.S. FDI on a historical cost basis in Mexico increased from $17 billion in 1994 to $91.7 billion in 2007, nearly a 400% increase (see Table 4).

Mexican FDI in the United States is much lower than U.S. investment in Mexico, with levels of Mexican FDI fluctuating over the last ten years. In 2005, Mexican FDI in the United States totaled $8.7 billion, representing an increase of 440% since 1994, as shown in Table 4.

The sharp rise in U.S. investment in Mexico since NAFTA implementation is also a result of the liberalization of Mexico's restrictions on foreign investment in the late 1980s and the early 1990s. Prior to the mid-1980s, Mexico had a very protective policy that restricted foreign investment and controlled the exchange rate to encourage domestic growth, affecting the entire industrial sector. Mexico's trade liberalization measures and economic reform in the late 1980s represented a sharp shift in policy and helped bring in a steady increase of FDI flows into Mexico. NAFTA provisions on foreign investment helped to lock in the reforms and increase investor confidence.

Table 2. U.S. Imports from Mexico: 2002-2008 (US$ in billions)

Leading Items (NAIC 4-digit)	2002	2003	2004	2005	2006	2007	2008	% Change 2007 -2008
Oil and Gas	10.70	13.67	17.23	22.48	29.38	30.27	37.93	25.3%
Motor Vehicles	20.74	19.03	18.77	18.36	23.24	23.08	22.02	-4.6%
Motor Vehicle Parts	15.14	15.99	17.82	19.33	20.81	22.65	20.58	-9.2%
Audio/Video Equipment	7.45	6.91	8.18	9.87	13.89	17.06	17.84	4.5%
Communications Equipment	5.70	5.98	7.45	7.34	8.73	13.06	12.99	-0.6%
Other	74.39	75.62	85.51	91.84	101.01	104.04	104.97	3.9%
Total	134.12	137.20	154.96	169.22	197.06	210.16	216.33	2.9%

Source: Compiled by CRS using USITC Interactive Tariff and Trade DataWeb at http://dataweb.usitc.gov: NAIC4-digit level.
Note: Nominal U.S. dollars.

Table 3. U.S. Exports to Mexico: 2002-2008 (U.S. $ in millions)

Leading Items (NAIC 4-digit)	2002	2003	2004	2005	2006	2007	2008	% Change 2007 -2008
Motor Vehicle Parts	8.14	7.11	7.55	7.39	8.60	9.40	10.06	
Petroleum and Coal Products	2.36	2.31	2.78	4.73	4.98	5.66	9.63	
Basic Chemicals	2.85	3.35	4.43	5.01	5.74	6.50	7.16	
Resin, Synthetic Rubber & Related Products	2.62	2.94	3.57	4.51	5.37	5.43	5.95	
Oilseeds and Grains	2.46	2.61	2.58	2.52	3.05	3.97	5.94	
Other	67.65	64.79	72.11	77.51	86.82	88.42	92.77	
Total	86.08	83.11	93.02	101.67	114.56	119.38	131.51	

Source: Compiled by CRS using USITC Interactive Tariff and Trade DataWeb at http://dataweb.usitc.gov: NAIC4-digit level.
Note: Nominal U.S. dollars.

Table 4. U.S. - Mexican Foreign Direct Investment Positions: 1994-2007 Historical Cost Basis (U.S. $ in millions)

Year	Mexican FDI in the U.S.	U.S. FDI in Mexico
1994	2,069	16,968
1995	1,850	16,873
1996	1,641	19,351
1997	3,100	24,050
1998	2,055	26,657
1999	1,999	37,151
2000	7,462	39,352
2001	6,645	52,544
2002	7,483	55,724
2003	6,680	61,526
2004	8,167	63,502
2005	8,653	71,423
2006	6,075	84,699
2007	4	63

Source: U.S. Department of Commerce, Bureau of Economic Analysis.

Under NAFTA, Mexico gave U.S. and Canadian investors' nondiscriminatory treatment of their investments in Mexico as well as investor protection. NAFTA may have encouraged U.S. FDI in Mexico by increasing investor confidence, but much of the growth may have occurred anyway because Mexico likely would have continued to liberalize its foreign investment laws with or without NAFTA.

Nearly half of total FDI investment in Mexico is in the manufacturing industry of which the maquiladora industry forms a major part. (See "Mexico's Export-Oriented Assembly Plants.") Mexico's maquiladora industry is important to the economic relationship of the United States and Mexico in several ways. In Mexico, the industry has helped attract investment from countries such as the United States that have a relatively large amount of capital. Therefore, Mexico is able to attract some of the foreign direct investment it was seeking when it liberalized trade and investment barriers. For the United States, the industry is important because U.S. companies are able to locate their labor-intensive operations in Mexico and lower their labor costs in the overall production process. Many economists believe that maquiladoras are an important part of U.S. corporate strategy in achieving competitively priced goods in the world marketplace [7]. Other analysts are concerned that the industry has caused U.S. companies to move their manufacturing facilities to Mexico at the expense of U.S. workers.

Mexico's Export-Oriented Assembly Plants [8]

Mexico's export-oriented assembly plants are closely linked to U.S.-Mexico trade in various labor-intensive industries such as auto parts and electronic goods. These export-oriented plants generate a large amount of trade with the United States and a majority of the plants have U.S. parent companies. Foreign-owned assembly plants, commonly called maquiladoras, account for a substantial share of Mexico's imports and about half of its exports. The largest maquiladora operation, Delphi Automotive Systems, headquartered in the United States, had 51 plants with 66,000 employees in Mexico in 2006 [9]. Most maquiladora plants are located along the U.S. - Mexico border. The Mexican metropolitan areas with the highest maquiladora activity as of December 2006 (the latest year for which maquiladora statistics are available) were the Mexican border cities of Tijuana, Baja California, 568 maquiladoras with 164,900 employees, and Cd. Juárez, Chihuahua, 279 maquiladoras with 283,300 employees [10]. Recent changes in Mexican regulations on export-oriented industries merged the maquiladora industry and Mexican domestic assembly-for-export plants into one program called the maquiladora Manufacturing Industry and Export Services (IMMEX).

Private industry groups have stated that these operations help U.S. companies remain competitive in the world marketplace by producing goods at competitive prices. In addition, the proximity of Mexico to the United States allows production to have a high degree of U.S. content in the final product, which could help sustain jobs in the United States. Critics of these types of operations argue that they have a negative effect on the economy because they take jobs from the United States and help depress the wages of low-skilled U.S. workers.

After NAFTA, Mexico's regulations governing the maquiladora industry changed significantly. Beginning in 2001, the North American rules of origin determined the duty-free status for a given import and replace the previous special tariff provisions that applied only to maquiladora operations. The initial program ceased to exist and the same trade rules applied to all assembly operations in Mexico and not just those in the maquiladora program [11]. NAFTA rules for the maquiladora industry were implemented in two phases, with the first phase covering the period 1994-2000, and the second phase starting in 2001. During the initial phase, NAFTA regulations continued to allow the maquiladora industry to import products duty-free into Mexico, regardless of the country of origin of the products. This phase also allowed maquiladora operations to increase maquiladora sales into the domestic market. Phase II made a significant change to the industry in that the new North American rules of origin determined duty-free status for U.S. and Canadian products exported to Mexico for maquiladoras. The elimination of duty-free imports by maquiladoras from non-NAFTA countries under NAFTA caused some initial uncertainty for the companies with maquiladora operations. Maquiladoras that were importing from third countries, such as Japan or China, would have to pay applicable tariffs on those goods under the new rules.

Mexico had another program for export-oriented assembly plants called the Program for Temporary Imports to Promote Exports (PITEX) that was established in 1990 to allow qualifying domestic producers to compete with maquiladoras. PITEX plants are usually in areas located in central and southern Mexico while maquiladoras are more common in states along the U.S.- Mexico border. In recent years, the differences in the customs status of maquiladoras and PITEX plants diminished and the Mexican government decided to merge the two export-oriented programs. In 2007, the Mexican government announced a new set of regulations on export- oriented industries. These new rules merge the maquiladora industry and PITEX plants into the Maquiladora Manufacturing Industry and Export Services, or IMMEX. In 2008, maquiladora industry data will be included in Mexican manufacturing reports, without a distinction for maquiladora plants [12]. Prior to NAFTA, a maquiladora was limited to selling up to 50% of the previous year's export production to the domestic market. By 2000, maquiladoras were allowed to sell up to 85% of the previous year's export production to the Mexican market. Most maquiladoras, however, continue to export the majority of their production to the U.S. market.

The maquiladora industry expanded rapidly in the 1990s. The number of plants grew from 1,920 at the end of 1990 to 3,590 in 2000. After 2000, the number of maquiladoras fell to 2,860 in 2003. Since 2004, the number of plants has stayed at approximately the same levels, totaling 2,819 in 2007 [13] Some observers believe that the correlation in maquiladora growth after 1993 is directly due to NAFTA, but in reality it is a combination of factors that has contributed to growth in this sector. Trade liberalization, wages, and economic conditions, both in the United States and Mexico, have all contributed to the growth of Mexican export-oriented assembly plants. Although some provisions in NAFTA may have encouraged maquiladora growth in certain sectors, maquiladora activity is more influenced by the strength of the U.S. economy and relative wages in Mexico. Maquiladora operations usually increase during periods of economic expansion in the United States. A drop in Mexican wages may also be an incentive for U.S. companies to shift production to Mexico.

Between 1993 and 1996, relative wages in Mexico fell considerably due to the peso devaluation. Since 1997, however, Mexican labor costs have risen, and some manufacturers have closed their Mexican plants and shifted production to other low-wage countries. In 2001, maquiladora employment levels fell for the first time since 1982. Between 2000 and 2004, maquiladora employment levels fell from 1.30 million workers to 1.12 million workers. Approximately 176,000 jobs were lost and 780 plants were shut down nationwide during this time. Employment rose to about 1.23 million in 2006 [14].

Worker Remittances to Mexico

Remittances from workers abroad play a strong role in the Mexican economy and form an important aspect of the U.S.-Mexico economic relationship [15]. Worker remittances account for about 3% of Mexico's GDP and are the second-largest source of foreign currency inflows behind oil exports. Mexico was one of the top three recipients of remittances worldwide in 2007. After high levels of growth rates since 2002, the rate of growth of remittances to Mexico has dropped markedly in the past two years. In 2004, Mexico received a record $16.6 billion in remittances, representing a 24% increase over 2003 [16]. Remittances from the United States to Mexico reached a peak of $6.2 billion in mid-2006 and have been decreasing since. In 2007, remittances grew by only 1%, after years of high growth. In January 2008, remittances to Mexico were down nearly 6%, the biggest drop in 13 years [17]. The decline in the level of remittances is due to a combination of factors. The slowdown in the U.S. economy, the weakening job market in the construction sector, tighter border controls, and increased anti-immigration sentiment in the United States may all be factors in the reduced number of seasonal migrants in the United States and their ability to send remittances to Mexico [18].

Worker remittance flows to Mexico have an important impact on the Mexican economy, in some regions more than others. Some studies on remittance flows to Mexico report that in southern Mexican states, remittances mostly or completely cover general consumption and/or housing. One study estimates that 80% of the money received by households goes for food, clothing, health care, and other household expenses. Another study estimates that remittances in Mexico are responsible for about 27%, and up to 40% in some cases, of the capital invested in microenterprises throughout urban Mexico.19 The economic impact of remittance flows is concentrated in the poorer states of Mexico. The government has sponsored programs to channel the funds directly to infrastructure and investment rather than consumption [20].

Security and Prosperity Partnership of North America

The Security and Prosperity Partnership of North America (SPP) is a trilateral initiative, launched in March 2005, that is intended to increase cooperation and information sharing in an effort to increase and enhance prosperity in the United States, Canada, and Mexico. The SPP is a government initiative that was endorsed by the leaders of the three countries, but it is not a signed agreement or treaty and, therefore, contains no legally binding commitments or obligations. It can, at best, be characterized as an endeavor by the three countries to facilitate communication and cooperation across several key policy areas of mutual interest. Although the SPP builds upon the existing trade and economic relationship of the three countries, it is not a free trade agreement and is distinct from the existing North American Free Trade Agreement (NAFTA). Some key issues for Congress regarding the SPP concern possible implications related to national sovereignty, transportation corridors, cargo security, and border security. These issues are discussed in various sections of the report.

Since 2005, the SPP working groups have made annual recommendations to the North American leaders on how to accomplish the goals of the SPP. In 2008, the working groups agreed to continue to advance the agenda of the SPP by identifying and focusing on a set of high priority initiatives. They decided to: 1) increase the competitiveness of North American businesses and economies through more compatible regulations; 2) make borders smarter and more secure by coordinating long-term infrastructure plans, enhancing services, and reducing bottlenecks and congestion at major border crossings; 3) strengthen energy security and protect the environment by developing a framework for harmonization of energy efficiency standards and sharing technical information; 4) improve access to safe food, and health and consumer products by increasing cooperation and information sharing on the safety of food and products; and 5) improve North American response to emergencies by updating bilateral agreements to enable government authorities from the three countries help each other more quickly and efficiently during times of crisis [21].

Goals of the SPP in the area of prosperity are to increase cooperation and sharing of information in order to improve productivity, reduce the costs of trade, and enhance the quality of life. Leaders from the three countries have highlighted the need to enhance North American competitiveness through compatible regulations and standards that would help the three countries protect health, safety and the environment, as well as to facilitate trade in goods and services across their borders. In the 2008 joint statement, the leaders highlighted the need for the three countries to implement compatible fuel efficiency regimes and high safety standards to protect human health and the environment, and to reduce the costs of producing cars and trucks for the North American market. They also emphasized their efforts to advance intellectual property rights protection in North America through the Intellectual Property Action Strategy.

The SPP is not a form of economic integration, and goes only as far as leading to some measure of regulatory harmonization among the United States, Canada, and Mexico. The SPP working groups are not contemplating further market integration in North America. Such a move would require a government approval process within each of the three countries. In the United States, such an agreement would require the approval of the U.S. Congress.

Some observers state that the SPP is an important step forward in the relationship of the United States with Mexico, and also Canada, in view of the distancing that occurred after the terrorist attacks of September 11, 2001 [22]. However, other analysts believe that the SPP and any subsequent trade-facilitating measures may fall short of any grander vision of further economic integration [23]. Critics of the SPP contend that it may ultimately lead to a so-called "NAFTA Superhighway" that would link the United States, Canada, and Mexico with a 'super-corridor' [24]. However, if the United States were to potentially consider the formation of a customs union or common market with its North American neighbors, it would require approval by the U.S. Congress.

The Mexican Economy

Mexico has a free market economy with a strong export sector, but this has not always been the case. The transformation of Mexico into an export-based economy began in the late 1980s when the government started to liberalize its trade policy and adopt economic reform measures. One of the more distinctive aspects of the Mexican economy is its strong ties to the economic cycle of the United States, making it very sensitive to economic developments in the United States. The state of the Mexican economy is important to the United States because of the close trade and investment ties between the two countries, and because of other social and political issues that could be affected by economic conditions, particularly those related to immigration.

Economic Reform and the 1995 Currency Crisis

In the late 1980s and early into the 1990s, the Mexican government implemented a series of measures to restructure the economy that included steps toward trade liberalization. For many years, Mexico had protectionist trade policies to encourage industrial growth in the domestic economy. The 1980s were marked by inflation and a declining standard of living. Repercussions of the 1982 debt crisis in which the Mexican government was unable to meet its foreign debt obligations were a primary cause of the economic challenges the country faced in the early to mid-1980's. Much of the government's effort in addressing the challenges was placed on privatizing state industries and moving toward trade liberalization. Efforts included privatization of sea ports, railroads, telecommunications, electricity, natural gas distribution and airports. The negotiation and implementation of NAFTA played a major role in Mexico's changing economic policy in the early 1990s.

Mexico's economic reforms initially attracted a large amount of private foreign investment, but by 1993 the inflow of foreign capital began to slow down. The combination of macroeconomic policies at the time, which led to an overvalued exchange rate and domestic political uncertainty helped drive down the flow of capital into the country. The decrease in capital inflows and the low levels of international reserves held by the Mexican government led to a peso devaluation in March 1994. Later that year, foreign exchange reserves continued to fall, domestic government debt increased, and the Mexican central bank had limited dollar reserves to support the current peso rate.

By the end of 1994, Mexico faced a currency crisis, putting pressure on the government to abandon its previous fixed exchange rate policy and adopt a floating exchange rate regime. As a result, Mexico's currency plunged by around 50% within six months, sending the country into a deep recession [25]. Several factors influenced the decision to float the peso: overspending in the economy had generated a significant current account deficit; the Mexican government had accumulated large levels of debt with insufficient reserves; and the banking system was facing a crisis due to overexposure [26]. Mexico's finance minister at the time, Guillermo Ortiz, stated later that Mexico had "no choice" but to float the peso because the government had run out of reserves [27]. In the aftermath of the 1994 devaluation, Mexican President Ernesto Zedillo took several steps to restructure the economy and lessen the impact of the currency crisis among the more disadvantaged sectors of the economy. The goal was to create conditions for economic activity so that the economy could adjust in the shortest time possible. The United States and the IMF assisted the Mexican government by putting together an emergency financial support package of up to $50 billion, with most of the money coming from the U.S. Treasury. The Zedillo Administration wanted to demonstrate its commitment to fulfill all its financial obligations without a default on its debt by adopting tight monetary and fiscal policies to reduce inflation and absorb some of the costs of the banking sector crisis. The austerity plan included an increase in the value-added tax, budget cuts, increases in electricity and gasoline prices to decrease demand and government subsidies, and tighter monetary policy [28].

Following the lead of former President Ernesto Zedillo, former President Vicente Fox continued efforts to liberalize trade, privatize government enterprises, and deregulate the economy. Through tighter monetary and fiscal policies, the Fox Administration was able to decrease the fiscal deficit, control inflation, and help economic growth. The peso steadily depreciated through the end of the 1990s, which led to greater exports and helped the country's exporting industries. However, the peso devaluation also resulted in a decline in real income, hurting the poorest segments of the population and also the newly emerging middle class. NAFTA and the change in the Mexican economy to an export-based economy helped to soften the impact of the currency devaluation. After a real decline in GDP of 6.22% in 1995, the Mexican economy managed to grow 5%-6% in each of the three years to 1998. The combination of a stronger peso and the slowdown in the U.S. economy in 2001, which worsened after the September 11 terrorist attacks, hit Mexico's economy hard. Real GDP growth dropped from 6.2% in 2000 to -0.16% in 2001. Improving economic conditions in the United States helped Mexico's economy improve as well. Real GDP growth in 2004 was 4.37%, up from 1.41% in 2003 and 0.81% in 2002 (see Figure 2). In 2006, real GDP growth was 4.8%, decreasing to 3.3% in 2007 and 1.4% in 2008.

Current Economic Conditions

The global economic crisis is having a significant effect on the Mexican economy. Real GDP growth in Mexico in 2008 was 1.4%, down from 3.3% in 2007. The economy is forecast to contract by 2.6% in 2009 [29]. The expected decline in the Mexican economy in 2009 may be the sharpest decline since the 1995 currency crisis. The decline in U.S. demand for imports from Mexico resulting from the U.S. economic slowdown will have an impact on the Mexican economy because of its dependence on the United States as an export market. Job losses in Mexico have increased in recent months, with possibilities of further job losses in export-oriented assembly plants as they cut capacity due to the downturn in demand [30]. After weakening by an estimated 5% in 2004 and 13% in 2003, the Mexican peso strengthened in 2005 and 2006.

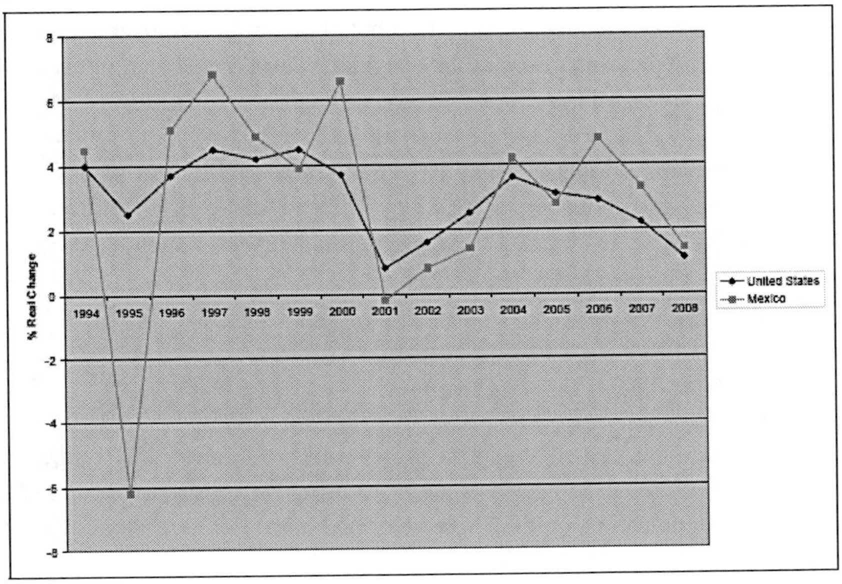

Source: Economist Intelligence Unit.

Figure 2. GDP Growth Rates for the United States and Mexico.

The peso remained relatively stable in 2007, but weakened again in 2008. The peso is expected to weaken further in 2009 due to low oil prices, the downturn in U.S. demand, and heightened risk aversion [31]. President Calderón of Mexico has taken a number of measures to attempt to cushion the Mexican economy from the fallout of the global economic crisis and the onset of recession in the United States. Mexico's dependence on exports and on the economic cycle in the United States is reflected in the economic cycles of the two countries depicted in Figure 2.

Poverty is one of the more serious and pressing economic problems facing Mexico. According to a 2004 World Bank Study, [32] the Mexican government had made progress in its poverty reduction efforts, but poverty continues to be a basic challenge for the country's development. The authors of the study note that poverty is often associated with social exclusion, especially of indigenous groups of people who comprise 20% of those who live in extreme poverty [33].

In 2002, over half of the population lived in poverty. According to World Bank estimates, the percentage of people living in extreme poverty, or on less than $1 per day, fell from 24.2% of the population in 2000, to 20.3% in 2002, and 18% in 2005. Those living in moderate poverty, or on about $10 a day, fell from 53.7% in 2000 to 51.7% of the population in 2002 and 45% in 2005. Mexico's continuing problem of poverty is especially widespread in rural areas and remains at the Latin American average [34].

Former President Fox considered the problem of poverty one of Mexico's principal challenges and stated that the highest priority of his administration was to combat poverty [35]. Mexico's main program to reduce the effects of poverty is the Oportunidades program (formerly known as Progresa). The program began under former President Zedillo and expanded under former President Fox to benefit five million families throughout Mexico. The program seeks to not only alleviate the immediate effects of poverty through cash and in-kind transfers, but to break the cycle of poverty by improving nutrition and health standards among poor families and increasing educational attainment. This program provides cash transfers to families in poverty who demonstrate that they regularly attend medical appointments and can certify that children are attending school. The government provides educational cash transfers to participating families. The program also provides nutrition support to pregnant and nursing woman and malnourished children. Monthly benefits are a minimum of $15 with a cap of about $150. The majority of households receiving Oportunidades benefits are in Mexico's six poorest states: Chiapas, Mexico State, Puebla, Veracruz, Oaxaca, and Guerrero [36].

Mexico's Regional Free Trade Agreements

Since the early 1990s, Mexico has had a growing commitment to trade liberalization and its trade policy is among the most open in the world. Mexico has pursued free trade agreements (FTAs) with other countries as a way to bring benefits to the economy and also to reduce its economic dependence on the United States. By early 2006, Mexico had entered into a total of 12 FTAs involving 42 countries.

The Mexican government has negotiated bilateral or multilateral trade agreements with most countries in the Western Hemisphere including the United States and Canada, Chile, Bolivia, Costa Rica, Nicaragua, Uruguay, Colombia, Guatemala, El Salvador, and Honduras [37].

Mexico has ventured out of the hemisphere in negotiating FTAs, and, in July 2000, entered into agreements with Israel and the European Union. Mexico became the first Latin American country to have preferred access to these two markets. Mexico has also completed an FTA with the European Free Trade Association (EFTA) of Iceland, Liechtenstein, Norway, and Switzerland. The Mexican government has continued to look for potential free trade partners, and expanded its outreach to Asia in 2000 by entering into negotiations with Singapore, Korea and Japan [38]. In 2004, Japan and Mexico signed an Economic Partnership Agreement. It was the first comprehensive trade agreement that Japan signed with any country [39]. Mexico's negotiations on FTAs with Korea and Singapore are stalled.

In addition to the bilateral and multilateral free trade agreements, Mexico is a member of the WTO, [40] the Asia-Pacific Economic Cooperation forum, and the OECD [41]. In September 2003, Mexico hosted the WTO Ministerial Meeting in Cancun.

NAFTA and the U.S.-Mexico Economic Relationship

The North American Free Trade Agreement (NAFTA) has been in effect since January 1994. There are numerous indications that NAFTA has achieved many of the intended trade and economic benefits as well as incurred adjustment costs. This has been in keeping with what most economists maintain, that trade liberalization promotes overall economic growth among trading partners, but that there are significant adjustment costs. Most of the trade effects in the United States related to NAFTA are due to changes in U.S. trade and investment patterns with Mexico. At the time of NAFTA implementation, the U.S.-Canada Free Trade Agreement already had been in effect for five years, and some industries in the United States and Canada were already highly integrated. Mexico, on the other hand, had followed an aggressive import-substitution policy for many years prior to NAFTA in which it had sought to develop certain domestic industries through trade protection. One example is the Mexican automotive industry which had been regulated by a series of five decrees issued by the Mexican government between 1962 and 1989. The decrees established import tariffs as high as 25% on automotive goods and had high restrictions on foreign auto production in Mexico. Under NAFTA, Mexico agreed to eliminate these restrictive trade policies. Not all changes in trade and investment patterns between the United States and Mexico since 1994 can be attributed to NAFTA because trade was also affected by other unrelated economic factors such as economic growth in the United States and Mexico, and currency fluctuations. Also, trade-related job gains and losses since NAFTA may have accelerated trends that were ongoing prior to NAFTA and may not be totally attributable to the trade agreement. Overall, Mexico has experienced a slight shift in the composition of trade with the United States since the late 1980s from oil to non-oil exports. In 1987, crude oil and natural gas comprised 17% of Mexico's exports to the United States. The percentage of oil and natural gas exports had declined to 10.6% in 2004, but increased to 14.4% in 2007 due to higher oil prices.

Effects on the U.S. Economy

The overall effect of NAFTA on the U.S. economy has been relatively small, primarily because two-way trade with Mexico amounts to less than three percent of U.S. GDP. Thus, any changes in trade patterns with Mexico would not be expected to be significant in relation to the overall U.S. economy. In some sectors, however, trade-related effects could be more significant, especially in those industries that were more exposed to the removal of tariff and non-tariff trade barriers, such as the textile and apparel, and automotive industries.

Since NAFTA, the automotive, textile, and apparel industries have experienced some of the more noteworthy changes in trading patterns, which may also have affected U.S. employment in these industries. U.S. trade with Mexico has increased considerably more than U.S. trade with other countries, and Mexico has become a more significant trading partner with the United States since NAFTA implementation.

In the automotive industry, the industry comprising the most U.S. trade with Mexico, NAFTA provisions consisted of a phased elimination of tariffs, the gradual removal of many non-tariff barriers to trade including rules of origin provisions, enhanced protection of intellectual property rights, less restrictive government procurement practices, and the elimination of performance requirements on investors from other NAFTA countries. These provisions may have accelerated the on-going trade patterns between the United States and Mexico. Because the United States and Canada were already highly integrated, most of the trade impacts on the U.S. automotive industry relate to trade liberalization with Mexico. Prior to NAFTA Mexico had a series of government decrees protecting the domestic auto sector by reserving the domestic automobile market for domestically produced parts and vehicles.

NAFTA established the removal of Mexico's restrictive trade and investment policies and the elimination of U.S. tariffs on autos and auto parts. By 2006, the automotive industry has had the highest dollar increase ($41 billion) in total U.S. trade with Mexico since NAFTA passage.

The main NAFTA provisions related to textiles and apparel consisted of eliminating tariffs and quotas for goods coming from Mexico and eliminating Mexican tariffs on U.S. textile and apparel products. To benefit from the free trade provision, goods were required to meet the rules of origin provision which assured that apparel products that were traded among the three NAFTA partners were made of yarn and fabric made within the free trade area. The strict rules of origin provisions were meant to ensure that U.S. textiles producers would continue to supply U.S. apparel companies that moved to Mexico. Without a rule of origin provision, apparel companies would have been able to import low-cost fabrics from countries such as China and export the final product to the United States under the free trade provision [42].

While some U.S. industries may have benefitted from increased demand for U.S. products in Mexico, creating new jobs, other industries have experienced job losses. Data on the effects of trade liberalization with Mexico are limited and the effect on specific sectors of the U.S. economy is difficult to quantify. Trade-related job gains and losses since NAFTA may have accelerated trends that were ongoing prior to NAFTA and may not be totally attributable to the trade agreement [43]. Quantifying these effects is challenging because of the other economic factors that influence trade and employment levels. The devaluation of the Mexican peso in 1995 resulted in lower Mexican wages, which likely provided an incentive for U.S. companies to move to lower their production costs. Trade-related employment effects following NAFTA could have also resulted from the lowering of trade barriers, and from the economic conditions in Mexico and the United States influencing investment decisions and the demand for goods.

Effects on the Mexican Economy

While a number of studies have found that NAFTA has brought economic and social benefits to the Mexican economy as a whole, the benefits have not been evenly distributed throughout the country. Most studies after NAFTA have found that the effects on the Mexican economy tended to be modest at most [44]. While there have been periods of positive growth and negative growth in Mexico after the agreement was implemented, much of the increase in trade began in the late 1980s when the country began trade liberalization measures. Though its net economic effects may have been positive, NAFTA itself has not been enough to lower income disparities within Mexico, or between Mexico and the United States or Canada.

A 2005 World Bank study assessing some of the economic impacts from NAFTA on Mexico concluded that NAFTA helped Mexico get closer to the levels of development in the United States and Canada. The study states that NAFTA helped Mexican manufacturers to adopt to U.S. technological innovations more quickly and likely had positive impacts on the number and quality of jobs. Another finding was that since NAFTA went into effect, the overall macroeconomic volatility, or wide variations in the GDP growth rate, has declined in Mexico. Business cycles in Mexico, the United States, and Canada have had higher levels of synchronicity since NAFTA, and NAFTA has reinforced the high sensitivity of Mexican economic sectors to economic developments in the United States [45].

Several economists have noted that it is likely that NAFTA contributed to Mexico's economic recovery directly and indirectly after the 1995 currency crisis. Mexico responded to the crisis by implementing a strong economic adjustment program but also by fully adhering to its NAFTA obligations to liberalize trade with the United States and Canada. NAFTA may have supported the resolve of the Mexican government to continue with the course of market-based economic reforms, resulting in increasing investor confidence in Mexico. The World Bank study estimates that FDI in Mexico would have been approximately 40% lower without NAFTA [46].

One of the main arguments in favor of NAFTA at the time it was being proposed by policymakers was that the agreement would improve economic conditions in Mexico and narrow the income gap between Mexico and the United States. Studies that have addressed the issue of economic convergence [47] have noted that economic convergence in North America might not materialize under free trade as long as "fundamental differences" in initial conditions persist over time. One study argues that NAFTA is not enough to help narrow the disparities in economic conditions between Mexico and the United States and that Mexico needs to invest more in education; innovation and infrastructure; and in the quality of national institutions. The study states that income convergence between a Latin American country and the United States is limited by the wide differences in the quality of domestic institutions, in the innovation dynamics of domestic firms, and in the skills of the labor force [48]. Another study also notes that the ability of Mexico to improve economic conditions depends on its capacity to improve its national institutions, adding that Mexican institutions did not improve significantly more than those of other Latin American countries during the post-NAFTA period [49].

Mexican wages rose steadily from the early 1980s until the mid-1990s, when the currency crisis hit. After a drop in average real wages in 1996 of 15.5%, real wages increased steadily until 2000, when the average rate of growth was 11.8%. Since then the average rate of growth has only varied slightly (see Figure 2). Mexico's trade liberalization measures may have affected the ratio between skilled and non-skilled workers in Mexico. In 1988, the real average wage of skilled workers in Mexico's manufacturing industry was 2.25 times larger than that of non-skilled workers. This ratio increased until 1996, when it was about 2.9, but then remained stable until 2000 [50]. The World Bank study found that NAFTA brought economic and social benefits to the Mexican economy, but that the agreement in itself was not sufficient to ensure a narrowing of the wage gap between Mexico and the United States. The study states that NAFTA had a positive effect on wages and employment in some Mexican states, but that the wage differential within the country increased as a result of trade liberalization [51].

Major Issues in U.S.-Mexico Trade Relations

Major trade disputes between Mexico and the United States involve the access of Mexican trucks to the United States; the access of Mexican sugar and tuna to the U.S. market; and the access of U.S. sweeteners to the Mexican market [52].

Trucking

A major U.S.-Mexico trade issue relates to the implementation of NAFTA trucking provisions. Under NAFTA, Mexican commercial trucks were to have been given full access to four U.S. border states in 1995 and full access throughout the United States in 2000. Citing safety concerns, however, the United States refused implementation of NAFTA's trucking provisions and the Mexican government objected. A NAFTA dispute resolution panel supported Mexico's position in February 2001. President Bush indicated a willingness to implement the provision, but the U.S. Congress required additional safety provisions in the FY2002 Department of Transportation Appropriations Act (P.L. 107-87). On November 27, 2002, with safety inspectors and procedures in place, the Administration announced that it would begin the process that will open U.S. highways to Mexican truckers and buses, but environmental and labor groups went to court in early December to block the action. On January 16, 2003, the U.S. Court of Appeals for the Ninth Circuit ruled that full environmental impact statements were required before Mexican trucks would be allowed to operate on U.S. highways, but the U.S. Supreme Court reversed that decision on June 7, 2004.

Since the ruling, the U.S. and Mexican Administrations worked on resolving the trucking issues, and the two countries engaged in talks regarding a number of safety and operational issues that needed to be resolved before Mexican commercial trucks were granted authority to operate in the United States. In February 2007, the Bush Administration announced a pilot project to grant Mexican trucks from 100 transportation companies full access to U.S. highways. The Administration announced a delay in the program in April 2007, likely in response to critics who contended that Mexican trucks do not meet U.S. standards. The Iraq War Supplemental (P.L. 110- 28), enacted May 25, 2007, mandated that any pilot program to give Mexican trucks access beyond the border region could not begin until U.S. trucks had similar access to Mexico. In addition, the DOT needed to meet certain reporting and public notice requirements before any pilot program could begin. The DOT's Inspector General needed to prepare a report to Congress to verify that the DOT had established mechanisms to ensure that Mexican truck comply with U.S. federal motor carrier safety laws. The report also needed to verify that Mexican trucks meet the safety provisions of P.L. 107-87, mentioned above.

By September 2007, the Department of Transportation launched the one-year pilot program to allow approved Mexican carriers beyond the 25-mile commercial zone, with a similar program allowing U.S. trucks to travel beyond Mexico's commercial zone. As of early January 2008, 57 trucks from 10 Mexican companies had received permission to operate in the United States and 41 trucks from 4 U.S. companies received permission to operate in Mexico. Department of Transportation data reportedly shows that U.S. carriers have made twice as many trips to Mexico as Mexican carriers have to the United States from the time the program was launched until early January 2008.

In the FY2008 Consolidated Appropriations Act (P.L. 110-161), signed into law in December 2007, Congress included a provision prohibiting the use of FY2008 funding for the establishment of a pilot program. The Department of Transportation determined that it could continue with the pilot program because it had already been established. In February 2008, a coalition of unions and environmental groups filed suit in the 9th Circuit Court of Appeals to end the pilot program, but a decision is still pending [53].

In March 2008, the DOT issued an interim report on the cross-border trucking demonstration project to the Senate Committee on Commerce, Science, and Transportation. The report made three key observations: 1) The Federal Motor Carrier Safety Administration (FMCSA) plans to check every participating truck each time it crosses the border to ensure that it meets safety standards; 2) There is less participation in the project than was expected; and 3) The FMCSA has implemented methods to assess possible adverse safety impacts of the project and to enforce and monitor safety guidelines [54].

In early August 2008, the Department of Transportation announced that it would be extending the pilot program for an additional two years. On September 9, 2008, the House approved (by a vote of 396 to 128) H.R. 6630, a bill that would prohibit the Department of Transportation from granting Mexican trucks access to U.S. highways beyond the border and commercial zone. The bill would also prohibit the Department of Transportation from renewing such a program unless expressly authorized by Congress. No action was taken by the Senate on the measure.

In the recently enacted FY2009 Omnibus Appropriations Act (P.L. 111-8), the U.S. Congress terminated a pilot program begun in September 2007 that allowed Mexican-registered trucks to operate beyond the 25-mile border commercial zone inside the United States. In response to the abrupt end of the pilot program, the Mexican government announced that it would retaliate by increasing duties on 90 U.S. products with an import value of $2.4 billion. The tariffs, effective as of March 19, 2009, range from 10% to 45% and cover a range of products that include fruit, vegetables, home appliances, consumer products, and paper [55]. During Secretary of State Hillary Clinton's recent trip to Mexico, she pledged to resolve the dispute over Mexican-registered trucks. "We are working to resolve it," she said and added that she anticipated Congress would be responsive to the Administration's plans [56].

Other Trade Issues

The United States and Mexico resolved a long-standing trade dispute in 2006 involving sugar and high fructose corn syrup. Mexico argued that the sugar side letter negotiated under NAFTA entitled it to ship net sugar surplus to the United States duty-free under NAFTA, while the United States argued that the sugar side letter limited Mexican shipments of sugar. Mexico also complained that imports of high fructose corn syrup (HFCS) sweeteners from the United States constituted dumping, and it imposed anti-dumping duties for some time, until NAFTA and WTO dispute resolution panels upheld U.S. claims that the Mexican government colluded with the Mexican sugar and sweetener industries to restrict HFCS imports from the United States.

In late 2001, the Mexican Congress imposed a 20% tax on soft drinks made with corn syrup sweeteners to aid the ailing domestic cane sugar industry, and subsequently extended the tax annually despite U.S. objections. In 2004, the United States Trade Representative (USTR) initiated WTO dispute settlement proceedings against Mexico's HFCS tax, and following interim decisions, the WTO panel issued a final decision on October 7, 2005, essentially supporting the U.S. position. Mexico appealed this decision, and in March 2006, the WTO Appellate Body upheld its October 2005 ruling. In July 2006, the United States and

Mexico agreed that Mexico would eliminate its tax on soft drinks made with corn sweeteners no later than January 31, 2007. The tax was repealed, effective January 1, 2007.

The United States and Mexico reached a sweetener agreement in August 2006. Under the agreement, Mexico can export 500,000 metric tons of sugar duty-free to the United States from October 1, 2006, to December 31, 2007. The United States can export the same amount of HFCS duty-free to Mexico during that time. NAFTA provides for the free trade of sweeteners beginning January 1, 2008. The House and Senate sugar caucuses expressed objections to the agreement, questioning the Bush Administration's determination that Mexico is a net-surplus sugar producer to allow Mexican sugar duty-free access to the U.S. market [57].

On tuna issues, the Clinton Administration lifted the embargo on Mexican tuna in April 2000 under relaxed standards for a dolphin-safe label in accordance with internationally agreed procedures, and U.S. legislation passed in 1997 that encouraged the unharmed release of dolphins from nets. However, a federal judge in San Francisco ruled that the standards of the law had not been met, and the Federal Appeals Court in San Francisco sustained the ruling in July 2001. Under the Bush Administration, the Commerce Department ruled on December 31, 2002, that the dolphin-safe label may be applied if qualified observers certify that no dolphins were killed or seriously injured in the netting process, but Earth Island Institute and other environmental groups filed suit to block the modification. On April 10, 2003, the U.S. District Court for the Northern District of California enjoined the Commerce Department from modifying the standards for the dolphin-safe label. On August 9, 2004, the federal district court ruled against the Bush Administration's modification of the dolphin-safe standards and reinstated the original standards in the 1990 Dolphin Protection Consumer Information Act. That decision was appealed to the U.S. Ninth Circuit Court of Appeals, which ruled against the Administration in April 2007, finding that the Department of Commerce did not base its determination on scientific studies of the effects of Mexican tuna fishing on dolphins. In late October 2008, Mexico initiated World Trade Organization dispute proceedings against the United States, maintaining that U.S. requirements for Mexican tuna exporters prevents them from using the U.S. "dolphin-safe" label for its products [58].

On other issues, in early October 2002, the U.S.-Mexico working group on agriculture dealt with major agricultural issues, including Mexico's anti-dumping decisions on apples, rice, swine, and beef, and safeguard actions on potatoes. In January 2003, the countries agreed to permit Mexican safeguard measures against U.S. imports of chicken legs and thighs, and in July 2003, these safeguard measures were extended until 2008, with tariffs declining each year. In September 2006, Mexico revoked anti-dumping duties imposed on U.S. rice imports in 2002 following rulings by the WTO and WTO Appellate Body in 2005, which found that the duties were contrary to WTO rules. Mexico banned beef imports from the United States in December 2003 following the discovery of one cow infected with mad cow disease in Washington State. Mexico resumed importation of boneless beef in early March 2004, and bone-in beef in February 2006, in response to improved beef cattle screening.

POLICY ISSUES

The United States economic relationship with Mexico has strengthened significantly over the last decade and is of mutual importance. Up to this point, the discussion in the report has focused on the background and surrounding issues of the economic relationship, which leads to the issue of policy considerations. First, there is the question of whether to further economic integration with Mexico in view of the increasing trends in regional trade agreements throughout the world. The close economic relationship between the United States and Mexico that was strengthened by NAFTA is likely to continue but there may be challenges in coming years as the influence of China and other low-wage countries increases. According to a recent study on economic integration in North America, a major shift is under way in trade patterns among NAFTA partners with exports among NAFTA economies growing more slowly than their exports with the rest of the world, reversing the previous 10-year trend. The report finds that lower-cost suppliers, primarily China and India, are displacing North American imports and could weaken North American integration. The report states that furthering continental integration would require "renewed efforts at resolving long-standing trade disputes, new liberalization initiatives, or greater policy harmonization in areas such as border security, labor mobility, or corporate taxation" [59].

If the United States continues to deepen economic integration with Mexico, one area that may need more attention is the issue of the difference in income levels between the two countries. The economic relationship with Mexico is unique because of Mexico's proximity to the United States, but also because of the wide differences in levels of economic development between the two countries. Mexico is the first developing country with which the United States entered into a free trade agreement. In Mexico, NAFTA has had an uneven effect in different parts of the country and it has not been a solution to the problem of poverty and unemployment. Mexico's problem with poverty cannot be attributed directly to NAFTA because it was in existence prior to the agreement. At the time of NAFTA there was hope that Mexico's economy would grow sufficiently to create jobs in urban areas and help alleviate poverty in rural areas. However, the economy did not expand as expected and the problem of poverty continues.

Another issue is whether trade agreements are enough, or are the appropriate policy instrument, to resolve income disparities among trading partners or even within a developing country. The World Bank study on the effects of NAFTA on Mexico concludes that NAFTA has helped to improve economic conditions in Mexico but it has not been enough to narrow the economic disparities with the United States. The authors of the study state, among other things, that Mexico needs to invest more in education, infrastructure, and institutional strengthening to benefit more fully from freer trade [60]. A possible consideration for policymakers is whether to help Mexico improve the quality of education and strengthen its national institutions through foreign aid programs or other mechanisms.

The economic hardship in certain sectors and regions of Mexico has been a major reason behind unauthorized Mexican migration to the United States. Mexican President Felipe Calderón made his first official visit to the United States as President-elect in early November 2006, after first visiting Canada and several Latin American countries. During his visit, Calderón criticized the recent authorization of fencing along the U.S.-Mexico border and noted that it complicated U.S.-Mexico relations. He asserted that job-creation and increased investment in Mexico would be more effective in reducing illegal migration from Mexico than a border fence. Calderón signaled a shift in Mexican foreign policy when he noted that while immigration is an important issue in the bilateral relationship, it is not the only issue, as trade and economic development are also important.

Under the Fox Administration, Mexico voiced concern about alleged abuses suffered by Mexican workers in the United States and for the loss of life and hardships suffered by Mexican migrants as they use increasingly dangerous methods to cross into the United States. The Fox Administration held the view that the migrants are "undocumented workers" and that because the U.S. market attracts and provides employment for the migrants, it bears some responsibility. During his administration, former Mexican President Vicente Fox pressed proposals for legalizing undocumented Mexican workers in the United States through amnesty or guest worker arrangements as a way of protecting their human rights. In 2004, President Bush proposed an overhaul of the U.S. immigration system to permit the matching of willing foreign workers with willing U.S. employers when no U.S. documented workers could be found to fill the jobs.

The U.S. Senate began consideration of comprehensive immigration reform in May 2007. Mexico had long lobbied for immigration reform in the United States and cautiously watched the debate in 2007 on this measure. Legal immigration reform has stalled in the 110th Congress. A bipartisan compromise proposal for comprehensive immigration reform negotiated with the Bush Administration was introduced in the Senate on May 21, 2007, as S.Amdt. 1150 to S. 1348. A modified version of that compromise (S. 1639) came to the Senate floor the week of June 26, 2007, but a key cloture vote did not pass [61]. It is unclear whether the 110th Congress will again tackle comprehensive immigration reform. It may, however, consider legislation on selected immigration reform issues, such as foreign workers. Additional border security measures may also be considered.

REFERENCES

[1] See CRS Report RL32724, *Mexico-U.S. Relations: Issues for Congress*, by Mark P. Sullivan and June S. Beittel.

[2] Pew Hispanic Center, *Trends in Unauthorized Immigration: Undocumented Inflow Now Trails Legal Inflow,* October 2, 2008.

[3] CRS Report RL32724, *Mexico-U.S. Relations: Issues for Congress*, p. 7.

[4] Data compiled by CRS using Global Trade Atlas database.

[5] See CRS Report RS21737, *NAFTA at Ten: Lessons from Recent Studies*, by J. F. Hornbeck.

[6]

[7] Federal Reserve Bank of Dallas, "The Binational Importance of the Maquiladora Industry," *Southwest Economy,* Issue 6, November/December 1999.

[8] Mexico's export-oriented industries began with the maquiladora program established in the 1960s by the Mexican government, which allowed foreign-owned businesses to set up assembly plants in Mexico to produce for export. Maquiladoras could import intermediate materials duty-free with the condition that 20% of the final product be exported. The percentage of sales allowed to the domestic market increased over time as Mexico liberalized its trade regime. U.S. tariff treatment of maquiladora imports

played a significant role in the industry. Under HTS provisions 9802.00.60 and 9802.00.80, the portion of an imported good that was of U.S.-origin entered the United States duty- free. Duties were assessed only on the value added abroad. After NAFTA, North American rules of origin determine duty-free status. Recent changes in Mexican regulations on export-oriented industries merged the maquiladora industry and Mexican domestic assembly-for-export plants into one program called the maquiladora Manufacturing Industry and Export Services (IMMEX).

[9] Data from Mexico's *Instituto Nacional de Estadística Geografía e Informática* (INEGI), provided by Global Insight, Inc, at the LIX Maquiladora Industry Outlook Meeting on June 8, 2007 in El Paso, Texas.

[10] Ibid.

[11] Vargas, Lucinda, "NAFTA, the U.S. Economy, and Maquiladoras," *El Paso Business Frontier,* 2001.

[12] Federal Reserve Bank of Dallas, *Southwest Economy*, Issue 3, "Spotlight: Maquiladora Data, Mexican Reform Clouds View of Key Industry," May/June 2007.

[13] Based on data from INEGI.

[14] Ibid.

[15] For information on remittances to Latin America see CRS Report RL31659, *Foreign Remittances to Latin America*, by Walter W. Eubanks and Pauline Smale.

[16] EIU ViewsWire, "Mexico Economy: Remittances Home Hit a Record US$16.6 Billion in 2004," February 9, 2005.

[17] *The Dallas Morning News,* "Remittances to Mexico See Biggest Drop in 13 Years," March 7, 2008.

[18] The World Bank, *Remittance Trends 2007,* by Dilip Ratha, Sanket Mohapatra, K.M. Vijayalakshmi, and Zhimei Xu, November 29, 2007.

[19] The Federal Reserve Bank of Dallas report "Workers' Remittances to Mexico," (2004) evaluated the economic impact of worker remittances to Mexico and cites a number of reports by the World Bank and the Mexican government.

[20] Ibid, p. 4.

[21] Joint statement by President Bush, President Calderon, Prime Minister Harper, April 22, 2008.

[22] "U.S., Mexico, Canada Agree to Increase Cooperation," *The Washington Post,* March 24, 2005, p. A4.

[23] "Neighbors Who Are not Always Friends: Bush's Summit with Mexican and Canadian Leaders Will Probably Take Small Steps Toward Bolder Integration," *The Christian Science Monitor,* March 23, 2005, p. 2.

[24] See for example, Corsi, Jerome R., *The Plan to Replace the Dollar with the 'Amero '*, May 22, 2006; Corsi, Jerome, *I-69: Yet Another NAFTA Superhighway*, September 12, 2006; or Schlafly, Phyllis, *The NAFTA Superhighway*, August 23, 2006.

[25] EIU, "Mexico Finance: The Peso Crisis, Ten Years On," January 3, 2005.

[26] Banco de Mexico, "Mexico's Monetary Policy Framework Under a Floating Exchange Rate Regime," by Agustín G. Carstens y Alejandro M. Werner, May 1999.

[27] EIU, "Mexico Economy: Mexico Begins to See Benefits of Free-Floating Peso," December 20, 2004.

[28] Joachim Zietz, "Why Did the Peso Collapse? Implications for American Trade," *Global Commerce*, by , Volume 1, No. 1, Summer 1995.

[29] EIU, *Country Report: Mexico,* March 2009.
[30] Ibid.
[31] EIU, *Country Report: Mexico,* March 2009.
[32] The World Bank Group, *Mexico Makes Progress and Faces Challenges in Poverty Reduction Efforts,* June 2004.
[33] The World Bank Group Press Release, "Mexico Makes Progress and Faces Challenges in Poverty Reduction Efforts," July 2004.
[34] Ibid.
[35] Associated Press, "Poverty Level Down, But Still Big Challenge for Mexico," July 28, 2004.
[36] Santiago Levy, *Progress Against Poverty*, Brookings Institution, 2006.
[37] Organization of American States, Foreign Trade Information System (SICE), see http://www.sice.oas.org.
[38] The Asahi Shimbun, "Mexico: Loving Free Trade Ever Since NAFTA," March 2002. See http://www.facilitycity.com.
[39] *The Asahi Shimbun,* "Japan: Free Trade with Mexico," *The Asahi Shimbun,* March 12, 2004.
[40] The WTO allows member countries to form regional trade agreements, but under strict rules. The position of the WTO is that regional trade agreements can often support the WTO's multilateral trading system by allowing groups of countries to negotiate rules and commitments that go beyond what was possible at the time under the WTO. The WTO has a committee on regional trade agreements that examines regional groups and assesses whether they are consistent with WTO rules. See The World Trade Organization, "Understanding the WTO: Cross-Cutting and New Issues, Regionalism: Friends or Rivals?" http://www.wto.org.
[41] U.S. Commercial Service, *Country Commercial Guide: Mexico,* August 13, 2004, p. 6.
[42] For more information on textile and apparel trade, see CRS Report RL31723, *Textile and Apparel Trade Issues*, by Bernard A. Gelb.
[43] CRS Report 98-783, *NAFTA: Estimates of Job Effects and Industry Trade Trends After 5 1/2 Years*, by Mary Jane Bolle.
[44] For more information, see CRS Report RS21737, *NAFTA at Ten: Lessons from Recent Studies*, by J. F. Hornbeck.
[45] The World Bank, *Lessons from NAFTA for Latin America and the Caribbean,* by Daniel Lederman, William F. Maloney, and Luis Servén, 2005. (Hereinafter *Lessons from NAFTA,* 2005).
[46] Ibid.
[47] Economic convergence can be broadly defined as a narrowing of the disparities in the economic levels and the manufacturing performances of particular countries or their regions. The goal of the theory of economic convergence is to research and analyze the factors influencing the rates of economic growth and real per capita income in countries.
[48] *Lessons from NAFTA*, 2005.
[49] *Economia*, "NAFTA and Convergence in North America: High Expectations, Big Events, Little Time," by William Easterly, Norbert Fiess, and Daniel Lederman, Fall 2003.

[50] Esquivel, Gerardo, and José Antonio Rodríguez-López, “Technology, trade, and wage inequality in Mexico before and after NAFTA,” *Journal of Development Economics*, 2003.

[51] *Lessons from NAFTA*, 2005.

[52] See CRS Report RL32724, *Mexico-U.S. Relations: Issues for Congress*, by Mark P. Sullivan and June S. Beittel.

[53] “9th Circuit Considers Injunction to Halt Mexican Truck Pilot Program,” *International Trade Daily*, February 13, 2008; Rosalind McLymont, “Long Haul Across the Border,” *Shipping Digest*, January 7, 2008; and “Hoffa Blasts Bush Administration’s Indifference to NAFTA Harm,” *PR Newswire*, March 10, 2008.

[54] Department of Transportation. “Cross-Border Trucking Demonstration Project,” March 11, 2008.

[55] *International Trade Reporter,* “Key GOP House Members Urge obama to Develop New Mexico Truck Program,” March 26, 2009.

[56] Arshad Mohammed, "WRAPUP 2-U.S. to blame for much of Mexican drug violence," *Reuters News*, March 25, 2009.

[57] “Bush Administration Defends Sugar Deal to Congress,” *Inside U.S. Trade*, November 3, 2006; “Grassley, U.S. Industry Welcome Agreement with Mexico on Sugar, HFCS,” *International Trade Reporter*, August 3, 2006; and, “U.S., Mexico Reach Agreement on WTO Soft Drink Dispute Compliance Deadline,” *International Trade Reporter*, July 13, 2006.

[58] *International Trade Reporter,* “Mexico Initiates WTO Dispute Proceeding Against U.S. ‘Dolphin-Safe’ Label for Tuna,” October 30, 2008.

[59] ITR, “North American Integration Slipping Due to China’s Strong Growth, Report Says,” Volume 22, Number 8, February 24, 2005.

[60] The World Bank, *Lessons from NAFTA for Latin America and the Caribbean,* by Daniel Lederman, William F. Maloney, and Luis Servén, 2005.

[61] For more details, see CRS Report RL32235, *U.S. Immigration Policy on Permanent Admissions,* by Ruth Ellen Wasem.

INDEX

A

D

E

F

G

H

I

J

K

L

M

N

O

S

T

U

V

W

Y

Z